Sustaining China's Economic Growth in the Twenty-First Century

Economic growth in China has been exceptionally strong in recent decades, but the country still faces enormous economic problems, including huge poverty, uneven regional development, the problems associated with strengthening capital formation, and modernising – and making more productive – the very large former state sector. This book presents the work of a wide range of leading economists of China, all members of the prestigious Chinese Economics Association, who propose new research findings and new thinking on a wide range of issues connected with the problem of sustaining China's economic growth.

Shujie Yao is Professor and Chair of Economics at the Middlesex University Business School. He was previously research fellow of the University of Oxford and Professor of Development Economics at the University of Portsmouth. He has worked as an economic consultant in many African and Asian countries for the World Bank and other development agencies. His current research interests include economic growth, income inequality and poverty reduction.

Xiaming Liu is Senior Lecturer of International Business at the University of Aston Business School. His main research interests include economic development, technological change and foreign direct investment. He has published extensively in these areas of research. He is managing editor of the *Journal of Chinese Economics and Business Studies*.

Routledge studies on the Chinese economy

Series editors

Peter Nolan
University of Cambridge

Dong Fureng
Beijing University

The aim of this series is to publish original, high-quality, research-level work by both new and established scholars in the West and the East, on all aspects of the Chinese economy, including studies of business and economic history.

1 The Growth of Market Relations in Post-reform Rural China
A micro-analysis of peasants, migrants and peasant entrepreneurs
Hiroshi Sato

2 The Chinese Coal Industry: An Economic History
Elspeth Thomson

3 Sustaining China's Economic Growth in the Twenty-First Century
Edited by Shujie Yao and Xiaming Liu

Sustaining China's Economic Growth in the Twenty-First Century

Edited by Shujie Yao and Xiaming Liu

Routledge
Taylor & Francis Group
LONDON AND NEW YORK

First published 2003 by RoutledgeCurzon
This edition published 2013 by Routledge
Simultaneously published in the USA and Canada by Routledge
2 Park Square, Milton Park, Abingdon, Oxfordshire OX14 4RN
711 Third Avenue, New York, NY 10017

Routledge is an imprint of the Taylor & Francis Group, an informa business

First issued in paperback 2018

Typeset in Times by Wearset Ltd, Boldon, Tyne and Wear

British Library Cataloguing in Publication Data
A catalogue record for this book is available from the British Library

Library of Congress Cataloging in Publication Data
Sustaining China's economic growth in the twenty-first century/edited by Shujie Yao & Xiaming Liu.
p. cm. – (RoutledgeCurzon studies on the Chinese economy; 3)
Includes bibliographical references and index.
1. China–Economic policy–2000– 2. China–Economic policy–1976–2000. 3. China–Economic conditions–2000– 4. China–Economic conditions–1976–2000– I. Yao, Shujie. II. Liu, Xiaming, 1954. III. Series.
HC427.95 .S87 2003
338.951′009′0511–dc21

2002031697

ISBN 978-0-415-29726-4 (hbk)
ISBN 978-1-138-37112-5 (pbk)

Contents

Figures

Figures

Tables

Contributors

Dr Ajit Bhalla is a former Fellow of Sidney Sussex College, Cambridge. He has held research and academic positions at the Universities of Yale, Oxford and Manchester. He has published extensively on the Indian and Chinese economies. His major recent publications include *Uneven Development in the Third World: A Study of China and India* (Macmillan, 1992, 1995); *Poverty and Exclusion in a Global World* (Macmillan, 1999) and *Market Government Failures? An Asian Perspective* (Palgrave, 2001).

Ms Yang Chen is a PhD student within the China Centre, University College of Northampton, writing her thesis on the question of property rights within China in transition. Originally from Wuhan, she gained a first class honours degree in economics from Nankai University, Tianjin, before gaining employment as a lecturer at Huazhong University of Science and Technology, Wuhan. In 1998, she came to the UK and studied successfully for an MBA (football industry) degree at the University of Liverpool before joining University College of Northampton in 2000.

Mr Haico Ebbers is associate professor of Nyenrode University, China Europe International Business School (Shanghai).

Professor Simon Gao is professor of accounting and finance in the School of Accounting and Economics at Napier University, Edinburgh. He received his PhD in accounting and finance from Erasmus University Rotterdam, The Netherlands. He is a guest professor at Southwestern University of Finance and Economics, China. He has previously taught at Glasgow Caledonian University (UK), Staffordshire University (UK), The University of Central Lancashire (UK), and Shaanxi Institute of Technology (China). He has authored *International Leasing: Financial and Accounting Applications* (University of Central Lancashire Publications, 1994), *International Leasing: Strategy and Decision* (Ashgate Publishing, 1999), and co-edited *Perspectives on Accounting and Finance in China* (with John Blake; Routledge, 1995). He has written over 30 articles on leasing in Eastern Europe, leasing accounting, Chinese accounting, social and environmental accounting, and public-sector risk management. His research interests include social and environmental accounting, risk management in the public sector, international accounting, and life insurance demand in China.

Mr Shanyou Guo is a doctoral research student in the School of Accounting and Economics at Napier University, Edinburgh. He has a degree from Yangzhou Teachers College (China) and taught in China for over 10 years. His current research interests include Chinese accounting history, Feng Shui, and China's financial market and dividend policy.

Mr Qihai Huang is a research fellow at Manchester Metropolitan University Business School and a PhD candidate at the Management Research Centre of Bristol University. His research interests include: social capital theory, the private sector in China, SMEs, entrepreneurship, industrial clusters, and innovation.

Dr Aying Liu is a senior lecturer at the Middlesex University Business School. His research interests include forestry economics, environmental economics and development. He has published many papers in various economics journals, including *Regional Studies*, *Journal of Agricultural Economics*, *Environmental and Resource Economics*, *Journal of Policy Modelling* and *Economic System Research*.

Dr Xiaming Liu is a senior lecturer in international business at Aston Business School, Aston University, Birmingham. He is the research convenor of the Strategic Management Group, head of the Aston Centre for Asian Business and Management, and managing editor of the *Journal of Chinese Economics and Business Studies*. He has published a number of academic papers in various journals, including *Applied Economics*, *International Business Review*, *Journal of Applied Econometrics*, *Journal of International Business Studies*, *Regional Studies* and *Welwirtschaftliches Archiv*. He is co-author (with Yingqi Wei) of *Foreign Direct Investment in China: Determinants and Impact* (Edward Elgar, 2001).

Ms Xiaohui Liu is a senior lecturer in international business in the Department of Marketing, Strategy & International Business, Luton Business School, University of Luton. She received her PhD degree in economics at Birmingham University. Her main research interests are international trade, foreign direct investment and economic growth, with applications to China and other East Asian economies. She has published several books in Chinese as well as journal articles in both English and Chinese. Her recent work includes relationships between economic growth, foreign direct investment and trade in *Applied*

Economics, and the relationship between financial development and economic growth in *Studies in Economics and Finance.*

Dr Seamus McErlean is a lecturer in the Department of Agricultural and Food Economics at Queen's University of Belfast, and holds the post of senior agricultural economist in the Department of Agriculture and Rural Development for Northern Ireland. He obtained a BSc degree in Economics in 1988 and was awarded a PhD in agricultural economics in 1996 at the Queen's University of Belfast. His research interests lie mainly in the areas of agricultural price and policy analysis. He has published in *China Economic Review*, *Journal of Agricultural Economics*, *Agribusiness* and *Farm Management and British Food Journal.*

Mr Shufang Qiu is an independent economic consultant, affiliated to Jesus College, Cambridge University, UK.

Dr Richard Sanders is a Reader in political economy at the University College of Northampton and Director of the China Centre. A graduate in economics from Cambridge University, he has postgraduate degrees from London University and South Bank University, London. His PhD research entailed an investigation into Chinese ecological agriculture as a form of sustainable development in the Chinese countryside. His postdoctoral research has involved work on green food and organic agriculture in China and he has recently published work on the links between organic agriculture and property rights. He is the author of *Prospects for Sustainable Development in the Chinese Countryside: the Political-economy of Chinese Ecological Agriculture* (Ashgate, 2000).

Dr Xiaobai Shen is a lecturer in international business, specifically Chinese business, in the School of Management at the University of Edinburgh. Prior to that she worked as a consultant for Chinese-related business in Edinburgh and as a research fellow in IMD – the International Institute for Management Development – in Lausanne, Switzerland. Her research covers a range of areas from technology development strategies for developing countries to enterprise development, joint ventures and cross-cultural management. She is author of *The Chinese Road to High Technology* (1999) and editor of *Casebook on General Management in Asia Pacific* (1999, with Dominique Turpin).

Mr Chengang Wang is currently a Ph.D. student at Aston Business School, Aston University. His Ph.D. topic is 'Openness and Economic Growth' and his main research interests focus on international economics, especially in the areas of international trade, international investment, economic growth and knowledge spillovers, and Chinese economy. His recent work includes studying causal links between foreign direct investment and trade in China in *China Economic Review.*

Dr Ping Wang is a lecturer in economics at Middlesex University Business School. Her research interests cover analysis of stock market prices and returns, the validity of purchasing power parity and business cycle volatility and growth. She has published widely in such journals as *Weltwirtschaftliches Archiv, Empirical Economics, Bulletin of Economic Research, European Journal of Finance* and *Scottish Journal of Political Economy.*

Mr Chee Kong Wong is research fellow of the East Asian Institute at the National University of Singapore.

Professor John Wong is professor and research director of the East Asian Institute at the National University of Singapore. He was formerly Director of the Institute of East Asian Political Economy (1990–1996). His publications include *Land Reform in the People's Republic of China* (1973), *ASEAN Economies in Perspective* (1979), *The Political Economy of China's Changing Relations with Southeast Asia* (1986), *Understanding China's Socialist Market Economy* (1993), *China's Rural Entrepreneurs – Ten Case Studies* (1995), and (with Nah Seok Ling) *China's Emerging New Economy: Growth of the Internet and Electronic Commerce* (2001), as well as numerous papers on the economic development of China, ASEAN and Asian NIEs. Recent books he has edited include: (with Wang Gungwu) *China's Political Economy* (1998), *Hong Kong in China: Challenges of Transition* (1999), *China: Two Decades of Reform and Change* (1999), and (with Zheng Yongnian) *The Nanxun Legacy and China's Development in the Post-Deng Era* (2001).

Professor Wing Thye Woo is professor of economics in the University of California, Davis, USA. He has published many books and journal articles in the fields of economics and development.

Dr Ziping Wu is a lecturer at Queen's University of Belfast. He obtained his PhD at Queen's in 1995 and received the Robert O'Conner Prize for Natural and Resource Economics the same year. Previously he was an economist in the State Planning Commission in China between 1985–1991. His main research interests include Chinese and European Agricultural Policy and Statistical Systems.

Professor Shujie Yao is professor and chair of economics at the Middlesex University Business School, London. He obtained his master and doctoral degrees from the University of Manchester. He was a former research fellow in the Institute of Economics and the International Development Centre at the University of Oxford. He was then lecturer and professor of economics in the University of Portsmouth. He has published over 40 journal articles and three books. His papers have been published in many economic journals, including *Journal of Political Economy, Economic Development and Cultural Change, Journal of*

Comparative Economics, *Journal of Agricultural Economics*, *Journal of Development Studies*, *Regional Studies*, *Applied Economics*, *Environmental and Resource Economics*, and *Journal of Environmental Management*. He has worked for the World Bank, the Food and Agricultural Organisation of the United Nations, the Asian Development Bank, the Department for International Development (UK) and the European Union as economic consultant in many African and Asian countries since 1990. He was formerly president of the Chinese Economic Association (UK) in 1997–1998.

Ms Jane Zhang is a senior lecturer of accounting and finance at the University of Sunderland, UK. She is currently doing her PhD in social audit in secondary health care at Glasgow Caledonian University, UK. She has a degree in medicine from Huashan Medical School, China, and a MSc in risk and financial services from Glasgow Caledonian University. She has published a number of articles in the area of social auditing, in addition to several conference presentations of her working papers. Her current research interests are social auditing in the UK National Health Services and long-term care social insurance.

Ms Jianhong Zhang is a PhD candidate in the Faculty of Economics, Groningen University, The Netherlands.

Dr Zongyi Zhang is professor and dean of the School of Management, University of Chongqing, China. He obtained his PhD degree from the University of Portsmouth, UK. He has published many books and articles in both Chinese and English. Some of his recent papers are published in *Journal of Comparative Economics*, *Journal of Development Studies*, *Economics of Planning*, *China Economic Review* and *Applied Economics Letters*.

Preface

Although China has experienced over 20 years of rapid economic growth, it faces many new challenges to its future development in the twenty-first century. For example, although China has been open to, and integrated with, the global economy, it has only just joined the World Trade Organisation (WTO) and has a long way to go before becoming a truly global economic superpower. In addition, although the living standards of people have been vastly improved, it still has a sizeable number of people living in absolute poverty. Hence, how to sustain China's economic growth and how to eradicate poverty are the main issues of concern for its future development policies.

This volume includes a selection of chapters presented to the 12th Chinese Economic Association CEA (UK), annual conference in 2000. The chapters cover a wide range of issues concerning how to sustain China's economic growth and social development in the twenty-first century after WTO accession. The book is divided into three parts. Part I deals with the general issues of economic reforms and policies. Part II is devoted to the problems related to the economic sectors, including industry, agriculture and the financial markets, and Part III deals with issues related to openness and social problems.

CEA (UK) was established in 1988 by overseas Chinese students and scholars living in the UK. It has now become the leading academic organisation in the UK for research into the Chinese economy. This volume is part of its efforts to disseminate research results of its members, both within the UK and elsewhere. It is the second edited volume of conference chapters. It does not attempt to be comprehensive in its coverage, nor does it aim to provide a coherent perspective on the transition process. Instead, it presents a selection of chapters representing important theoretical and empirical contributions to our understanding of China's reform experience, the policies adopted and their impacts.

The board of directors and the editors of this volume encourage research students and scholars to contribute to our academic activities and publications in books and our newly launched in-house journal, the *Journal of Chinese Economics and Business Studies*, published by Taylor & Francis (Routledge).

Acknowledgements

The chapters included in this book are selected from the 12th Chinese Economic Association (UK) Annual Conference held at Middlesex University Business School in London, in 2000. The conference was generously sponsored by the following institutions and organisations: the Department for International Development, the Education Section of the Chinese Embassy, ESRC, Virgin Atlantic and the University of Middlesex, Bank of China and Ford Foundation. The editors of this book are grateful for the generous financial support from these organisations. The editors are also indebted to the CEA advisors, the board of directors and all CEA members for their support of, and participation in, the CEA conferences and other academic activities. They are particularly grateful to Professor Peter Nolan and Mr Peter Sowden for their encouragement to publish this collection. The editors are also indebted to Dr Richard Sanders, Professor Anthony Cluniess-Ross, Dr Martin Dedman and Dr Paul Walker for their editorial assistance.

Abbreviations

ABC	Agricultural Bank of China
ADF	Adjusted Dickey–Fuller
ASEAN	Association of South-east Asian Nations
CAS	Chinese Academy of Sciences
CASS	Chinese Academy of Social Sciences
CCP	Chinese Communist Party
CCTV	Chinese Central Television
CDMA	Code division multiple access
CNC	China Netcom Corporation
CSE	China Stock Exchange
CSRC	China Securities Regulatory Commission
DRC	Development Research Centre
EA	East Asia
EAE	East Asian Economy
ECM	Error correction mechanism
ECT	Error correction term
EIU	Economic Intelligence Unit
EMH	Efficient market hypothesis
EU	European Union
FDI	Foreign direct investment
FFW	Food-for-work
FIE	Foreign-invested enterprise
FMP	Free market price
GDP	Gross domestic product
GITIC	Guangdong International Trust and Investment Company
GNP	Gross national product
GSM	Global System for Mobile
IAJV	Iranian–American Joint Venture
IF	Iranian firm
IIT	Inter-industry trade
IPO	Initial public offering
LTC	Long-term care
MBFT	Ministry of Broadcast, Film and Television

MEI	Ministry of Electronic Industry
MEP	Ministry of Electrical Power
MFN	Most favoured nation
MII	Ministry of Information Industry
MNC	Multinational corporation
MNE	Multinational enterprise
MOA	Ministry of Agriculture
MOFTEC	Ministry of Foreign Trade and Economic Cooperation
MOR	Ministry of Railways
MPT	Ministry of Post and Telecommunications
NBS	National Bureau of Statistics
NBFL	Non-bank financial institutions
NDE	Newly developed economy
NGO	Non-governmental organisation
NIE	Newly industrialised economy
NP	Negotiated price
NPC	National People's Congress
NPL	Non-performing loan
OECD	Organisation for Economic Cooperation and Development
OLI	Ownership, location and internalisation
OLOE	Other local-owned enterprise
PADO	Poverty Alleviation Development Office
PAF	Poverty Alleviation Fund
PBC	People's Bank of China
PLA	People's Liberation Army
PPP	Purchasing power parity
QP	Quota price
RCC	Rural credit cooperative
R&D	Research and development
RMB	Renminbi
SARFT	State Administration Radio Film and Television
SHBI	Shanghai B-share Index
SHSE	Shanghai Stock Exchange
SGMA	State Grain Marketing Agency
SOAC	Speed of adjustment coefficient
SOE	State-owned enterprise
SPC	State Planning Committee
SRC	State Economic System Reform Committee
SSB	State Statistical Bureau (see NBS)
SRRC	State Radio Regulatory Committee
SZBI	Shenzhen B-share Index
SZSE	Shenzhen Stock Exchange
TACS	Total Access Communications system
TFP	Total factor productivity
TIC	Trust and investment companies

TVE	Township and village enterprise
UNFD	United Nations Foreign Department
VAR	Vector autoregression
WAP	Wireless application protocol
WTO	World Trade Organisation
2G	Second generation
3G	Third generation

Introduction

Shujie Yao and Xiaming Liu

China formally started its strategy of economic reform and opening up to the outside world in 1978 in order to achieve the objective of modernisation. On the domestic front, local experiments in the household responsibility system (HRS) in the agricultural sector were extended across the nation, and town and village enterprises (TVEs) were rapidly expanded. The success in economic reforms in the agricultural sector provided a strong impetus for reforms in the price system, state-owned enterprises, and banking and finance. On the external economic front, China formulated the Joint Venture Law in 1979, permitting foreign direct investment (FDI) for the first time since 1949, and the foreign trade and exchange rate systems were liberalised. In response to the progress in economic reforms and opening-up in the past two decades or so, the Chinese economy has achieved a spectacular annual growth rate of over 8 per cent, and China is now among the top trading countries and a major host for FDI inflows in the world. The entry into the World Trade Organisation (WTO) makes it necessary for China gradually to establish an economic regime with economic mechanisms that are more harmonised to those of the advanced market economies, and this will promote further reforms and opening-up, and will accelerate economic growth.

How should economic reforms and opening-up be further enhanced so that high economic growth could be maintained? The theme of the 12th Chinese Economic Association (UK) Annual Conference, held in London in 2000, was 'Sustaining China's Economic Growth in the Twenty-First Century', and a number of chapters presented at the conference addressed this theme in various contexts. Some of these chapters have been revised following a double blind refereeing process and selected for publication in this collection. Clearly, this book does not intend to provide a comprehensive coverage of China's reforms and opening-up, and we believe that no single book can fulfil this task. Rather, it is aimed at bringing together the theoretical and empirical contributions made by the authors, who are from various academic institutions in the UK, the USA, the Netherlands and Singapore but who share strong interests in Chinese economic development.

This book is organised into three parts. Part I deals with general economic development issues; Part II covers industry, agriculture and the financial market; and Part III is about openness and social issues. An overview of the chapters is provided as follows.

General economic development issues

Part I consists of three chapters. In the first chapter, Wing Thye Woo begins with an explanation of why the growth between 1996 and 1999 was below the average annual growth rate achieved in the last two decades. Contrary to the dominant explanation outside China, he argues that the structural flaws in China's economy were not the direct cause for the slowdown in 1996–1999. Rather, the 1996–1997 slowdown was the result of the austerity programme introduced in mid-1993, and the 1998–1999 slowdown was largely caused by the fall in exports due to the Asian economic crisis.

As part of the reflation programme, the Chinese government made large-scale infrastructure investments from 1998 onwards. While helping to lift aggregate demand to maintain full capacity usage and alleviate production bottlenecks to ease inflationary pressures, the investments were regarded by Woo as only a temporary measure to deal with external shocks. Furthermore, the larger credit growth in the second half of 1998 was achieved only after implicit assurances were given to state bank managers that they would not be held responsible if the ratio of non-performing loans (NPLs) in total loans were to increase. The long-term answer to the NPL problem is to change both the supply and demand side of the credit market, and the most fundamental changes include the transformation of state banks and state-owned enterprises (SOEs) into shareholding corporations in order to make profit-maximisation their primary objectives, the establishment of a modern legal framework to promote transparency and reduce transaction costs, and the creation of a prudential regulatory body to reduce excessive risk-taking by banks.

Woo argues that restructuring SOEs could worsen short-term growth while improving long-term growth prospects, but restructuring state-owned banks could improve both short- and long-term growth. A clear commitment to a restructuring strategy based on promoting the convergence of China's economic institutions to the institutional norms of modern market economies improves the short-term trade-off between growth and inflation. China's accession into the WTO facilitates this convergence, and offers China the only chance to achieve sustained high growth.

While Woo focuses on the relationship between economic reforms and short and long term growth in China, John Wong – in Chapter 2 – discusses the implications of China's dynamic growth for the East Asian region. Wong argues that China's growth since 1978 has interacted with many high-growth East Asian economies positively to each other's advantage. On the one hand, China has been able to harness the region's trade and investment opportunities to facilitate its own economic growth. Simultaneously, China's growing economic integration with the region also provides new opportunities to enhance the region's overall growth potential.

However, China's hyper economic growth has also created competitive pressures for other East Asian economies, especially the ASEAN economies, which are also competing for inward FDI with China and competing head-on with China's manufactured exports in the developed markets. For instance, China's export of apparel, footwear and household products to the US showed a large jump compared with ASEAN's merely moderate increase in recent years. China has a much larger pool of both skilled and unskilled labour than ASEAN. China has a large domestic market for all sorts of products – high or low tech – to take advantage of economies of scale. As a result, China is able to enjoy its natural cost advantage compared with ASEAN.

Wong indicates that China is a rare continental-sized economy with such great diversity that it can contain the evolution of comparative advantage within its own boarders. China's basic comparative advantage vis-à-vis other developing Asia-Pacific economies becomes even more pronounced after China's accession to the WTO. As is already happening, the more developed coastal regions of China are transferring their decreasing comparative advantage in labour-intensive products to Central and Western China, which is currently the focus of China's future development efforts. Thus, China can continue for years to flood the world market with low-cost manufactured items even when many parts of China have achieved middle-income status. In the longer run, the East Asian economies should benefit from increased access to China's market. However, at the current stage of development, China and ASEAN tend to be more competitive than complementary, as they share a great deal of similarity in the structures and destinations of their exports.

The final chapter of Part I is on the linkage between economic growth and the knowledge building process. In this chapter, Xiaobai Shen argues that a nation's economic growth is closely linked to how well the system can generate incentives for its development objectives and how many people are engaged in learning to achieve these objectives. China's economic growth over the past two decades rested upon the success of economic reform in opening up people's mindset, through creating a variety of incentives and establishing multiple channels for people to gain access to technical, social and economic knowledge of the wider world.

To sustain economic growth in the twenty-first century, China has to work out its own way to build up a sophisticated civil society that allows the individual and the nation to develop hand in hand. Chinese government policies should help people gain access to global information and knowledge; create incentives to encourage development of knowledge and thoughts; and formulate institutional infrastructures that support ever-wider participation by people from different social groups in the management of their community, and in the social, economic and political development of the nation.

Industry, agriculture and financial markets

Part II consists of five chapters discussing various specific issues in the development and evolution of China's industry, agriculture and financial market. Given that China has already emerged as the world's second largest telecommunications market after the United States, John Wong and Chee Kong Wong discuss in Chapter 4 the reasons for the fast growth of China's telecommunication industry and assess the impact of WTO accession on its further development.

The phenomenal growth of the telecommunications industry in the 1990s was due to rapid economic expansion, market liberalisation, competition, and technological progress, particularly in the wireless and internet sectors. The WTO accession has forced the industry to be more open to competition, both domestically and internationally. Thus, China faces two dilemmas. First, how will China safeguard its national security whilst opening up and allowing free access to information? Second, how will China guarantee its commitment of universal services to all parts of the country while promoting market orientation of the industry? Wong and Wong suggest that China should ensure the dominant position of its domestic firms and that the government should intervene to ensure universal services and narrow the economic disparity between the eastern and western regions and between the urban and rural areas.

To sustain growth of the Chinese economy in the twenty-first century, China faces several important challenges: there exist a large number of indebted SOEs, the growth rate of TVEs has been declining, and FDI has been falling in recent years due to the Asian financial crisis. While further reforms and opening up are necessary to vitalise SOEs and TVEs and attract more FDI, Qihai Huang indicates in Chapter 5 that the domestic private sector has already become the main engine of economic growth in China. Between 1989 and 1998, the average growth rates of total registered capital and employment in domestic private enterprises were greater than foreign-owned enterprises and substantially higher than SOEs and TVEs in particular.

Ironically, the private sector survived and developed under an adverse environment as the promotion of this sector conflicted with the ideology of socialism. Huang feels that the formal recognition of the country's emerging private sector by a constitutional amendment in 1999 represented the Chinese government's recognition of the long-term importance of the sector. The acknowledgement of private ownership and property rights strengthens the confidence of private entrepreneurs, helps attract investment in private enterprises, and opens the door for the transformation of SOEs. Huang is very optimistic about the further development and impact of the private sector in China. He concludes that this sector, which had demonstrated its vigour under the discriminated policy and environment, would definitely grow faster and contribute more to sustaining the growth of the Chinese economy.

In Chapter 6, Yang Chen and Richard Sanders discuss the extent to which publicly listed companies have improved efficiency as a result of adopting stock mechanisms and corporate governance. Using an institutional approach Chen and Sanders feel that the main objective of the establishment of the Chinese stock market was apparently to 'support the further rudimentary reform of SOEs by clarifying their ownership and property rights'. According to the existing institutional arrangement, the assignment of valued rights in the Chinese stock exchange was allocated by traditional norms of behaviour through the extant administrative hierarchy rather than being defined and enforced through the legal structure. Therefore, the stock market lacked the formal legal constraints of duty and liability. Under this arrangement, organisations engaged in stock market practices were less concerned with economic performance than survival in emerging, unstable and uncertain institutional practices. Companies that were transformed superficially into publicly listed companies remained tied to the old corporate governance mechanisms – i.e. they remained in the hands of the 'mother group company' and the bureaucratic network to which this company belonged. State agents within the institutional framework had dual identifications – governing bodies as well as economic actors.

Chen and Sanders argue that if the stock market process within the extant rules ineluctably promotes corruption and stimulates speculative behaviour, it will not lead to a balanced and well-functioning market. Thus, the challenge to Chinese decision-makers is how, through further institutional innovation, to make ownership and property rights – no matter whether state-owned or private by nature – function efficiently under the pressure of intertwined social, political and economic forces. This demands a more sophisticated structure of government based on clearer laws, stronger institutions and greater public accountability.

Turning to Chapter 7, Ziping Wu and Seamus McErlean examine the efficiency of Chinese grain markets. Between 1978 and 1985, China liberalised and commercialised the Chinese marketing system by allowing free trading of grain between non-government economic agents, the increasing use of negotiated purchases, and replacing the government quota procurement by the contract purchase system. During 1992–1994, the government further diminished central planning in the grain sector by reducing subsidised 'rationed sales' in urban areas and increasing the rationed sale price to a level consistent with government purchase prices, and eventually replacing rationed sales by free market trade. Did these two periods of reforms improve grain market efficiency as was intended? In this study, market efficiency means that the same information should be reflected in the quota price, the negotiated price and the free market price in each of the wheat, corn, early rice and late rice markets, and that a long run equilibrium should exist between the prices. Based on cointegration analysis, they conclude that the Chinese grain market became more integrated and more efficient following the reforms of 1992–1994. Thus, the reforms were regarded as being successful. Of course, further reforms are still needed to improve grain market efficiency.

The remaining two chapters of Part II deal with the Chinese stock market. Chapter 8 by Ping Wang and Aying Liu assesses the volatility and its spillover effects on the market. Using univariate and multivariate GARCH models, Wang and Liu find that the GARCH mechanism was at work in all the major Chinese stock indices – Shanghai A-shares, Shanghai B-shares, Shenzhen A-shares and Shenzhen B-shares. The return and volatility trade-off effect was strong for Shanghai and Shenzhen B-shares and was very week for Shanghai and Shenzhen A-shares. Bidirectional spillover effects are identified between the same types of shares, but unidirectional spillover effects were detected from B shares to A-shares. Wang and Liu argue that these results were plausible for the following reasons: A-shares were more insulated from the outside world than B shares; and the Shanghai and Shenzhen markets were running in parallel for A-shares and B-shares.

Openness and social issues

As mentioned earlier, opening up is part of the strategy formed by the Chinese government in 1978 to modernise its economy. International trade and FDI are the two main channels for economic integration and have played an important role in promoting economic growth in China. Four chapters in this part address issues related to China's opening up to the outside world. Haico Ebbers and Jianhong Zhang in Chapter 9 examine the Chinese–EU trade relation between 1990 and 1998, a period of increasing regional economic interdependence in both the EU and Asia. They raise five interesting research questions. (1) Whether trade between China and the EU was in line with what would be expected in terms of volume? (2) Did individual countries within the EU show a similar pattern with respect to their bilateral trade with China? (3) Were Chinese exports mainly concentrated on primary products while EU exports were concentrated on manufacturing? (4) Were China's terms of trade deteriorating? (5) Were there any visible comparative advantages of EU manufacturing exports to China?

By applying such criteria as the trade intensity index, geographical and commodity composition, terms of trade, intra-industry trade index and comparative advantage index to measure trade activities between EU and China, their authors' answers to the above questions are as follows. (1) The bilateral trade between EU and China was less than what would be expected in terms of economic power. (2) While Germany, France, Finland and Sweden increased their bilateral trade with China to a greater extent than their shares in world exports, the Netherlands, Italy and the United Kingdom failed to do so. (3) Both Chinese and EU exports were concentrated on manufacturing at the one-digit level. However, an examination at the six-digit level reveals that Chinese exports were dominated by labour-intensive products. (4) The terms of trade for China actually improved. (5) Finally, China demonstrated the revealed comparative advantage in manufactured goods and miscellaneous manufactured articles while the EU's advantage was in beverages and tobacco, and machines and transport equipment. Ebbers and Zhang argue that a small number of sectors having high revealed comparative advantage are a sign of a relatively developed pattern in which intra-industry trade is an important characteristic. Based on their analysis, there is much room for further development of China–EU trade.

Another important element of openness is FDI. Two chapters in Part III are concerned with this. In Chapter 10, Xiaming Liu compares labour productivity of foreign invested, state-owned and other local-owned enterprises in Chinese industry. The study shows that foreign invested enterprises (FIEs), which enjoy greater capital intensity, higher labour quality and possess other specific advantages, have significantly higher value-added per worker than state-owned enterprises (SOEs) and other local-owned enterprises (OLOEs). Scale economies are exploited in FIEs but not in SOEs and OLOEs. Xiaming Liu also indicates that OLOEs are not significantly more productive than SOEs unless capital intensity and labour quality are both controlled for. The overall results suggest the importance of foreign presence, domestic investment in physical and human capital and further economic reforms for efficiency improvements in the whole industrial sector.

Using the same data set, Xiaohui Liu in Chapter 11 examines the impact of FDI on total factor productivity (TFP), instead of labour productivity. It is found that FDI is a significant determinant of TFP in Chinese industries. FDI inflows are not merely a source of capital, but a conduit of technology transfer. In addition, average domestic R&D and firm size are important in enhancing TFP. Human capital intensity helps to improve TFP only when interactions between this variable and R&D are taken into account, implying that the higher the level of R&D, the more productive human capital will become. One important policy implication is that Chinese industries need to attract high-quality, technologically intensive FDI and to provide incentives for multinational enterprises to upgrade production at their sites in China. Xiaohui Liu feels that China's accession to WTO will create great opportunities for further FDI inflows and therefore promote further improvement of TFP.

Unlike Chapters 9–11 where either trade or FDI is the focus, Shujie Yao and Zongyi Zhang, in Chapter 12, examine the relationship between three factors of openness and GDP. In their development model, economic growth is regarded as the core. Output is determined by physical inputs (physical capital and labour), the internal production environment (human capital, transportation, institutions, and the like), and the external environment or openness (FDI, export and foreign exchange mechanism). In this model, the real exchange rate is treated as an exogenous variable. Their authors' empirical results suggest that the exchange rate had a significant and sizeable effect on the three endogenous variables: FDI, export and GDP. The gradual devaluation of the RMB towards its real equilibrium exchange rate with the US dollar was one of the most important determinants of China's success in attracting FDI, promoting export, and stimulating economic growth. FDI inflows and exports stimulate GDP growth, which in turn provides a solid basis for attracting more FDI and export push. Such interactions formed a virtual circle of openness, growth, more openness and more growth. China's open policy was successful in the past, and will continue to help China achieve sustainable growth in the future.

During the process of reforms and economic growth, various social issues have emerged. The remaining two chapters of this part aim to address two of these issues: the care of the ageing population and the alleviation of poverty. Increased life expectancy leading to rapid population ageing and the family planning policy of 'one couple with one child' has brought about widespread concerns with China's affordability of long-term care (LTC) in the twenty-first century. This is a great challenge to the Chinese authorities in reforming their social welfare system in the next decade. Jane Zhang, Simon Gao and Shanyou Guo, in Chapter 13, argue that the provision of LTC finance is vital to sustaining China's long-term economic development because the ageing population will have a significant impact on the Chinese economy and social welfare. By comparing various options they feel that LTC social insurance, contributed by individuals through levying LTC tax on savings income, by enterprises through business tax and by the state through the re-allocation of social welfare funds, is the practicable measure available to China in pooling resources to finance LTC for the elderly in the new century.

Although economic growth rates have been very impressive since China's adoption of economic reforms and opening up to the outside world, a large number of people in China still remain absolutely poor. Bhalla and Qiu assess, in Chapter 14, the impact of three main micro interventions for poverty reduction in Guizhou Province: namely, the food-for-work programme, the micro-credit programme and the rural labour mobility programme. The food-for-work programme (*Yigong-daizhen*) involves the building of agricultural infrastructure and the improvement of land productivity. The government supplies equipment and materials whereas the local people supply free labour up to 15 days per year if they benefit from these projects directly. Any additional labour input is rewarded by wage payment in cash, which varies from county to county and project to project. However, the programme does not directly benefit the poorest segments of the population, as projects target the village communities instead of rural individuals or households.

Under the micro-credit programme, funds were channelled directly to households. Although interest rates were very low, loan repayments in Guizhou were low because of transport difficulties, especially in remote mountainous areas, and the relative inefficiency of the Agricultural Bank in collecting repayments. Government intervention in labour mobility involves three aspects: population migration programmes, induced labour mobility through public projects and employment promotion programmes. While one cannot argue against the movement of people from low to high productivity areas, Bhalla and Qiu suggest that the social costs of dislocation of rural people need to be taken into account in designing and implementing the labour mobility programme for poverty alleviation. Illiterate and semi-literate migrants, women and older people are particularly vulnerable to poor working conditions and low incomes and employment security in urban areas. To reduce the social costs, the government needs to provide better labour market information, training schemes for rural migrants, a monitoring system to ensure safety and good living conditions.

While addressing different aspects of China's economic development process, the theme of most chapters in this volume is clearly the sustainable growth of the Chinese economy. Theoretical discussions and empirical studies are provided, followed by various policy suggestions for sustaining economic growth. Examples include: reforming state banks and state-owned enterprises, upgrading industrial bases in the coastal areas and transferring their decreasing comparative advantages in labour-intensive products to the inner areas in order to maintain international competitiveness, building an advanced civil society to allow the individual and the nation to develop together, narrowing the economic disparity between the coastal and inland areas, promoting the growth of the private sector, further reforms to improve grain market efficiency, making ownership and property rights function efficiently, promoting trade and FDI, providing long-term care for the elderly, and reducing poverty. Some authors have also assessed the impact of WTO membership on the Chinese economy. Taken together, this book should contribute to the theoretical and empirical literature on China and other transition economies, and be of interest to academics, business people as well as policy makers.

Part I

General economic issues

1 China

Confronting restructuring and stability

Wing Thye Woo

Introduction

China has been the world's star performer in economic growth for the last two decades. China registered an average annual growth rate of 9.7 percent in the 1978–1999 period. However, the growth rates for 1996–1999 were not only below the average of the period, they also declined monotonically from 9.6 percent in 1996 to 7.1 percent in 1999. Naturally, many questions and concerns have arisen about this four-year deviation from the average. How much of the deviation was due to trend slowdown, how much to the internal economic cycle, and how much to the external shock from the Asian financial crisis? Furthermore, what could be done to offset the decline, and what are the long-term implications of these countermeasures?

In the public pronouncements of Chinese officials, the usual explanation for the slowdown has been a drop in consumption and the stagnation of exports caused by the Asian financial crisis. Large-scale infrastructure investment programs were started in 1998 and 1999, and a third round of infrastructure spending is planned for 2000. The rationale is straightforward: infrastructure investment lifts aggregate demand to maintain full capacity usage, and alleviates production bottlenecks to ease inflationary pressures.

The above diagnosis and cure have been rejected by a number of economists. In the opinion of Thomas Rawski (1999):

> This diagnosis is mistaken and the policy misconstrued. Weakness in the economy, which pre-dates the Asian crisis of 1997/98 runs much deeper than China's leaders appear to believe. The difficulties are structural rather than cyclical. Short-term pump-priming exacerbates structural problems and undercuts long-term reform objectives.

Nicholas Lardy (1998a), while not offering an explanation for the slowdown, also deemed China's reflation program to be a mistake:

> China's leadership has made its short-term growth objective its highest priority. Longer-term structural reform of state-owned banks and enterprises is being postponed. Ironically, even if the program

increases the rate of growth, ultimately, the costs of postponed reforms will be even greater, meaning it likely will fail to alleviate social unrest.

We agree with some elements in each of the above analyses but we differ in emphasis, and, sometimes also, in conclusions. To anticipate the analysis in this chapter, we argue that:

a the structural flaws in China's economy in 1995, if left uncorrected, would surely cause growth to slow down in the future, say within a decade, but these structural flaws were not responsible for the significant slowdown in 1996–1999;
b the slowdown in 1996–1997 was largely the result of the austerity program that Zhu Rongji had implemented since mid-1993, simultaneously to wring inflationary pressures out of the economy and to restructure the economy;
c the further slowdown in 1998–1999 reflected the export decline caused by the Asian financial crisis; and
d the reflation program of 1998–1999 did not represent a wavering of commitment to restructuring; its emphasis on infrastructure investment (as opposed to a generalized increase in investment) was a sensible response to a temporary external shock.

Thomas Rawski and Nicholas Lardy are correct that radical restructuring of the state enterprise sector and the state bank system is absolutely crucial to avoiding a drastic drop in the trend growth rate in the future. The maintenance of the 1996 status of the state enterprises and state banks is not a viable option in the long run because the economy will simply not be able to support the growing burden from these two sectors.

The Chinese view that under-consumption (high saving) has made macroeconomic management more difficult is correct, a point that we will develop later, but we do not see larger state spending, even if it is in infrastructure, to be the optimum policy response. The correct response is restructuring not stabilization; there should be financial restructuring to create financial institutions that would quickly channel the additional saving to investments with the highest rates of return.

Our general view is that the short-run costs of economic restructuring may have been overstated. Restructuring state-owned enterprises (SOEs) could worsen short-term growth while improving long-term growth prospects; but restructuring state-owned banks could improve both short-term and long-term growth. Financial restructuring is a win–win reform activity because it will eliminate the liquidity trap that now exists in credit creation, and neutralize the short-run deflationary effects of higher saving. Finally, the macroeconomic record suggests the interesting possibility that a clear commitment to a restructuring strategy based on promoting the convergence of China's economic institutions to the norms of modern market economies improves the short-term trade-off between growth and inflation.

This chapter is organized as follows. The next section presents the case for economic restructuring, while the section after analyzes the macroeconomic record. The post-1997 reflation package is then evaluated, and then we consider the susceptibility of China to the type of financial crisis that hit Asia in 1997–1998. The following section examines the issue of underconsumption and the need for financial restructuring, especially in the rural sector, if China's high growth is to be prolonged. The issue of enterprise structuring is then discussed, and the final section contains brief concluding remarks.

The restructuring imperative

The successful completion of the bilateral US–China negotiations in November 1999 over the conditions of China's entry into the World Trade Organization (WTO) marks a watershed on many fronts for China. First and foremost, China's admission into the WTO marks an important improvement in the economic security of China. Trade and foreign investment have constituted an important engine of growth since 1978. The requirement for annual renewal by the US Congress of China's normal trading relationship with the United States made China's economic growth vulnerable to the vagaries of American domestic politics. Through WTO membership, this engine of growth could no longer be unilaterally shut off by the United States without the action being a major violation of international law.

WTO membership also marks a watershed in China's public recognition of the primary source of its impressive growth in the last two decades. The WTO is an international economic organization that specifies and enforces broadly similar economic policy regimes on its membership. China's willingness to join such an institution reflects more than a desire to protect itself from potential blackmail by the United States; it also reflects China's realization that the active ingredient in Deng Xiaoping's recipe for conjuring up growth was the convergence of China's economic institutions to the economic institutions of modern capitalist economies, particularly of the East Asian capitalist economies.

In the early stages of China's reform, when most of the intelligentsia did not know the full extent of the economic achievements of their capitalist neighbors, and when most of the top leaders were ideologically committed to Stalinist-style communism, it was important for the survival of the reformist faction of that time that the changes to China's economic institutions were comfortingly gradual, conveniently located in areas far from Beijing, and cloaked in the chauvinistic rhetoric of experimentation to discover new institutional forms that are optimal for China's socialist system and particular economic circumstances. After 20 years of evolution in economic institutions, of rotation in political leadership, and of tectonic change in the political fortune of the communist parties in Eastern Europe and the former Soviet Union, the only organized opposition today to the continued convergence of China's economic institutions to international forms comes form a small group of sentimental Stalinists such as Deng Liqun.[1] The social and political landscape in China has changed so much that the political leadership now incurs only minimal ideological liability when they introduce more capitalist incentives (e.g. differentiated pay, leveraged buy-outs, stock options for managers) and capitalist tools (e.g. joint-stock company, bankruptcy law, unemployment insurance). The leadership is hence confident that its explicit embrace of capitalist institutions under WTO auspices would be seen by the general Chinese public (and the Chinese elite) as a step forward in the reform process rather than as a surrender of China's sovereignty in economic experimentation.[2]

It must be emphasized that WTO membership will involve considerable costs to China. China has agreed to reduce its industrial tariffs from an average of 24.6 percent to 9.4 percent by 2005, and its agricultural tariffs from an average of 31.5 percent to 14.5 percent by 2004. China has also agreed to liberalize trade in many services, including telecommunications, insurance and banking. Compliance with WTO rules will create substantial dislocation in China, albeit for the sake of a better future. China is a natural food-importer and a natural factory-oriented society given its low land–man ratio. The agricultural sector employs over 332 million people, which is over two-thirds of the rural labor force. The bulk of China's state-owned sector survived only because of various forms of subsidies and import barriers. Both these sets of instruments contravene WTO regulations, and this sector employs over 40 percent of the urban labor force. The agricultural sector and the state sector together employed 60 percent of the total labor force in 1998. Conservatively, a fifth of China's workers may have to change jobs, and this could be a politically destabilizing process if not handled adeptly, and if external shocks were to slow economic growth.

The trade-off between stability and restructuring that is so starkly brought to the forefront by China's admission into WTO is not a new trade-off. China's WTO membership has really accentuated an existing dilemma and not introduced a new one. The government has always realized that the soft budget constraint of the inefficient state-owned enterprise (SOE) sector is a constant threat to price stability, and the diversion of resources to keep this sector afloat is a drag on economic growth. But serious restructuring of SOEs means much more than facing higher urban unemployment; it also means confronting the politically powerful industrial–military complex and the industrial–bureaucratic complex. Economic rents now pose a bigger obstacle to restructuring than ideological sentimentality, and, unlike the latter, it is not something that the mere passing of time will resolve.

Luckily for China, the job of restructuring had been made easier because China's economic structure could allow growth to occur without restructuring. This is because China, in 1978, was still an undeveloped economy dominated by self-subsistence peasant agriculture, unlike the urbanized Central European and Russian economies in 1989, which had an overabundance of heavy industries. This meant that the introduction of market forces caused economic development in China, but economic restructuring in Poland and Russia, which translated, respectively, into output growth and output decline.[3]

The movement of Chinese labor from low-productivity agriculture to higher-productivity industry, and from the poor inland provinces to the richer coastal provinces, produced an average annual growth rate of 10 percent in the 1978–1995 period. The Chinese state sector certainly did not wither away in this period; it employed 18.6 percent of the workforce in 1978 and 18.0 percent in 1995; there were 38 million more state workers in 1995 than in 1978.[4] There was reallocation of labor from agriculture to industry but not reallocation of labor from state to non-state enterprises. China, in 1978, was hence very different from Russia in 1991, as extensive growth was still possible in China whereas it had run its course in Russia.[5]

Since China was in the fortunate situation of being able to postpone most of the pain of restructuring, it was quite understandable that China did so. The result is that, after two decades of "reform and opening," the job of economic restructuring is far from done. Among the many daunting tasks left are:

- a government sector that is still too large (despite a recent cut in the size of the central bureaucracy), too intrusive, and susceptible to corruption;
- a state-owned enterprise (SOE) system that has proved itself resistant to numerous efforts to increase its efficiency and profitability;
- a state-dominated financial system where the banks lack the ability to assess the economic merits of proposed projects, and, worse, have shied away from lending to non-state enterprises, the most dynamic component of the economy; and
- an inadequate institutional infrastructure to allow the smooth running of a market economy; for example, an efficient commercial court system, speedy bankruptcy procedures, independent mechanisms to mediate labor conflict, uniform accounting standards, and social safety nets are really not yet in place.

It was only after the ascent of Zhu Rongji to the prime ministership in early 1998 that a decisive program of restructuring was implemented. The size of the central government was cut by a third, and the process of privatizing many small and medium enterprises was accelerated. Twenty million workers left the payroll of state-owned units in 1998 compared with two million in 1997. This represented an 18 percent reduction in state employment in one year![6]

Now that China is entering the WTO, it can no longer postpone the required restructuring of the inefficient components of its economy. However, the restructuring job was made more difficult in the last two and a half years because of negative external shocks. The Asian financial crisis caused Chinese exports to East and South-east Asia to decline tremendously, and Chinese exports to North America and Western Europe to face increased competition from the Asian countries whose currencies had fallen in value against the Renminbi (RMB). Inward foreign direct investments amounted to $40 billion in 1999, down from $45 million in 1998. The result was a GDP growth rate of 7.8 percent in 1998 and 7.1 percent in 1999, despite the government's vigorous attempts to reflate the economy since mid-1998.

The macroeconomic situation

Figure 1.1 summarizes the growth and inflation record since 1978 when China embarked on the first steps toward a market economy. There have

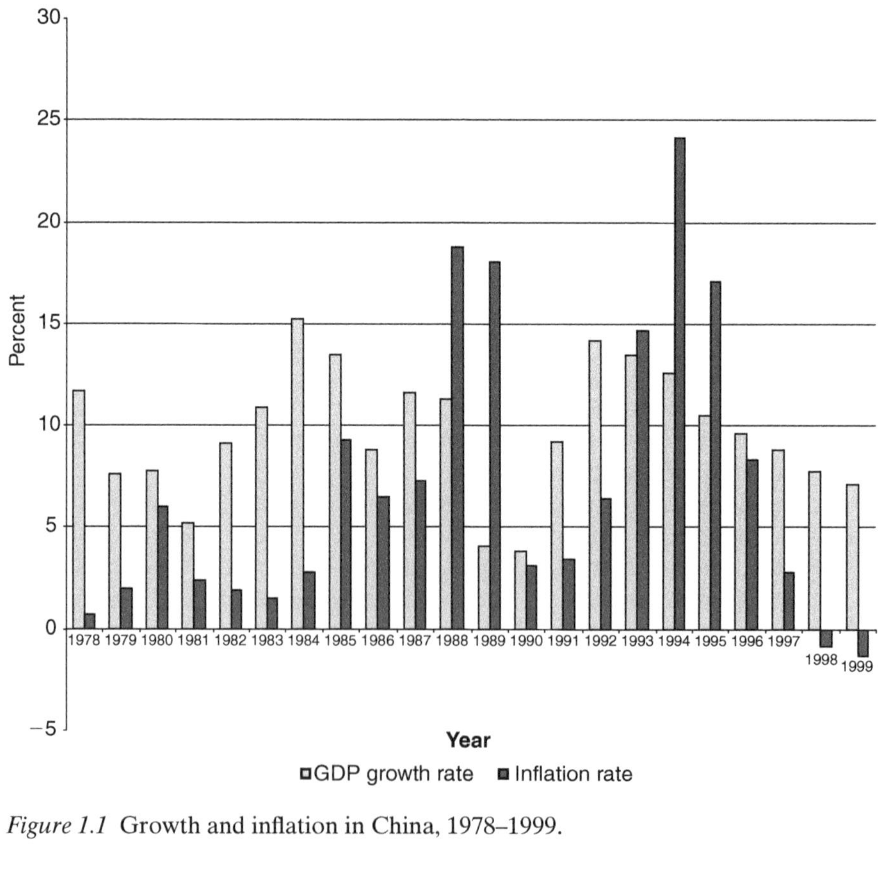

Figure 1.1 Growth and inflation in China, 1978–1999.

been two episodes of high inflation, 1988–1989 and 1993–1995, in both of which the inflation rate exceeded 10 percent. It is interesting that the output costs of wringing out inflation were very different from one episode to the other. The drop in inflation from 18.8 percent in 1988 to 3.1 percent in 1990 was accompanied by a 7 percentage point drop in the growth rate; whereas the drop in inflation from 24.1 percent in 1994 to 2.8 percent in 1997 saw less than a 4 percentage point drop in the growth rate.

What accounted for the drastically more favorable trade-off between growth and inflation in the second episode? In statistical analysis not reported here, we found that the differences in the inflation and growth performance across the two episodes could not be systemically linked to differences in the credit polices that started and then ended the two high inflations. My hypothesis for the different trade-offs in these two episodes is that consumers' confidence and investors' confidence about China's future were very different between the two stabilization programs. The 1989–1990 stabilization occurred amid widespread doubt about whether the convergence toward a market economy would continue, if it were not indeed reversed. Following the unfortunate Tiananmen tragedy in June 1989, economic policymaking returned to the hands of the central planners, and numerous announcements were made about reining in capitalist tendencies. The implementation of the 1994–1997 stabilization, in contrast, occurred after the 14th Party Congress in 1992 had pledged to build "a socialist market economy with Chinese characteristics." This denial of a universal norm for socialism was correctly read as renewed commitment by the Communist Party towards convergence to a market economy.

Our hypothesis is that this difference in anticipation about the future direction of China's economic policy meant that what was done in the two cases had very different effects on the behavior of consumers and investors. The heightened confidence in a prosperous future was responsible, in large part, for why fixed capital formation contributed over 2 percentage points to GDP growth in 1996–1997 compared with the negative 1.7 percentage points in 1989–1990; and why consumption spending contributed an average 4.5 percentage points to growth in 1996–1997 versus 1 percentage point in 1989–1990 (Table 1.1).

Since inflation in 1996 was down to 8.3 percent from 24.2 percent in 1994, and the 1996 growth rate of 9.5 percent almost equaled the average 10 percent growth rate of the 1978–1995 period, one could say that the Chinese stabilization program that started in mid-1993 achieved a soft-landing in 1996. Some observers have used this reasoning to describe the continuation of tight macroeconomic policies until early 1998 as a case of "macroeconomic policy overkill." While the precipitous plunge in money (M1) growth from an inflationary 43 percent in 1993 to 20 percent in 1996 was desirable, the further drop to 10 percent in 1998:2Q was an overkill, as shown by the fall in the level of retail prices since October 1997.[7]

I do not dispute the macroeconomic consequences of the tight

Table 1.1 Sources of aggregate demand in the reform period 1978–1998 (%)

	Annual GDP growth	*Rural HHC*	*Urban HHC*	*GOVC*	*Fixed capital formation*	*Change in inventory*	*Net Net x*	*Total HHC*
1979–1998	9.8	2.4	2.3	1.2	3.3	0.3	0.2	4.7
1988	11.3	3.1	4.1	0.4	3.2	1.7	−1.2	7.2
1989	4.1	0.7	1.3	1.1	−4.0	5.2	−0.1	2.0
1990	3.8	−0.8	0.7	0.4	0.5	−1.0	4.0	−0.1
1991	9.2	0.9	2.2	2.2	4.7	−1.3	0.4	3.2
1992	14.2	2.5	4.0	2.1	8.8	−1.6	−1.7	6.5
1993	13.5	0.5	2.9	1.3	10.5	1.5	−3.3	3.4
1994	12.6	2.1	2.7	1.4	3.0	−0.1	3.5	4.7
1995	10.5	2.9	3.4	−0.2	2.2	1.6	0.5	6.3
1996	9.6	3.7	1.9	1.2	2.7	−0.4	0.6	5.5
1997	8.8	1.3	2.2	1.2	2.4	−0.4	2.0	3.6
1998	7.8	0.6	2.7	1.2	4.5	−1.4	0.3	3.3

Notes
HHC = household consumption, GOVC = government consumption.

monetary policies and the tight controls over investment spending before mid-1998, but I note that these restrictive policies had succeeded in forcing considerable restructuring in the inefficient state-owned enterprise (SOE) sector. Because most loss-making SOEs did not receive their accustomed allotments of credit to continue production (a large portion of which went straight into inventory), the default outcome was that many were taken over by new owners who reorganized the firms and changed the output mix.[8] The point is that a temporary slowdown in growth is certainly necessary in order to force resources to move to a new growth path that would lead to a more competitive economy in the future. We have to recognize in the so-called "macroeconomic policy overkill" the audacity of the top Chinese leadership, which has chosen dislocating reforms that would produce sustained dynamic growth in the future over Brezhnev-style maintenance of the comfortable status quo that ensures a dismal future.

The "macroeconomic policy overkill" from 1997:1Q to 1998:2Q, in short, reflected a deliberate decision to accept growth rates that were lower than the 10 percent average growth rate of the 1978–1995 period in order to ensure an acceptable rate of economic restructuring and to moderate the boom–bust cycles of the previous two decades. The implicit growth range that policymakers appear to think is compatible with achieving the restructuring and stabilization objectives seems to be about 7.0 percent to 8.0 percent. When the Asian financial crisis hit in 1998, causing China's exports to fall, and hence rendering growth lower than intended, it was only natural that the government undertook stimulation of domestic demand to reflate the economy.

Responding to the post-1997 deflation

The government responded to the onset of price deflation in 1997:4Q by cutting the average lending rate from 10.1 percent to 8.6 percent. However, the anticipated surge in credit expansion did not occur. This is largely because of the newfound reluctance of the state commercial banks to extend more credit to traditional clients, the SOEs – especially the loss-making SOEs – a "liquidity trap" phenomenon that we will discuss later.

By early 1998, in the wake of the collapse of several important Pacific Asian economies, Chinese policymakers recognized that stronger reflation was required to offset the coming collapse in external demand. Furthermore, the SOE reform program announced at the 15th Party Congress in September 1997 was beginning to bite, and firms would soon begin to shed excess workers. Consequently, stronger reflation was also desirable in order to induce the establishment of new urban enterprises to soak up the newly released SOE workers.

The reflation program sought to boost aggregate demand by trying to:

a increase investment by approving quicker the backlog of investment applications;
b increase government spending;
c loosen monetary policy; and
d stimulate private spending through housing reform.

Faster approval of investment applications

The State Planning Commission was literally put on an overtime schedule in early 1998 to accelerate the approval of investment projects. "Increased economic openness" was a fortuitous byproduct of this measure. Approval was given to a number of large foreign projects that had been held up for several years because of concern either about the possible domination of these particular lines of business by foreign firms or about the possible competition that such foreign firms might provide to domestic firms of national strategic importance.

One unexpected check on approval acceleration as a reflation tool was that many local governments had not bothered to turn in local investment plans for 1998 because of the across-the-board rejection of local investment plans since the start of the serious implementation of the stabilization program in 1994. The greatest obstacle to the effectiveness of investment approval as an economic stimulus is that approval does not necessarily translate into realization. The translation of approval of investment into realization of investment is usually low in times of declining aggregate demand. Hence, not surprisingly, many foreign and domestic firms postponed the actual investment until sustained economic recovery seemed imminent. Partly because of the low aggregate demand in China and abroad, but mostly because of the panic in international credit markets, actual FDI was US$40 billion in 1999, 10 percent down from US$45 billion in 1998, despite the "increased economic openness" noted above.[9]

Expansionary fiscal policy

In July 1998, the government announced the issuance of RMB 100 billion in bonds to finance *new* infrastructure investment by the central and local governments. It seems that these bonds were purchased mainly by state banks. This announcement was quickly followed by new spending plans on telecommunications, railways and roads. As the economy continued to slow steadily throughout 1999, a new fiscal stimulus package of RMB 60 billion was implemented in August 1999. In March 2000, the government announced that it would soon issue RMB 100 billion of bonds to finance additional infrastructure investment, especially in the interior provinces.[10]

A natural question raised by the recent expansionary fiscal policy is whether the level of public debt in China is still at a level that would not be too heavy a burden in the future. The issue is what should be counted as "public debt" when so much of the economy is still state owned. If public debt is defined to be the stock of government bonds that has been issued to finance budget deficits (and which is held by both domestic and foreign agents), then the public debt–GDP ratio was 7.3 percent of GDP in 1996 and 8.1 percent in 1997.

It has been argued, however, that since the government is the guarantor of the state banks, the non-performing loans (NPLs) of the state banks ought to be counted as public debt. Estimates of the extent of non-performing loans range from 20 percent to 50 percent of total bank loans.[11] If we take the NPL ratio to be 33 percent, then the broader definition of public debt would put the "broader public debt"–GDP ratio at 37.0 percent of GDP in 1996 and 41.1 percent in 1997.

What about the debt of SOEs and other state institutions (for example, the regional trusts and investment companies, TICs)? The government could be construed as being responsible for these bad debts just as it was construed as being responsible for the bad debts held by the banks. Since the bulk of the *domestic* borrowing of SOEs and state institutions is from the state banks, the inclusion of non-performing loans of the state banks in the broader definition of public debt has already taken into account the bad debts of SOEs and state institutions that are owed to domestic agents.

Foreign debts of SOEs and other state institutions may deserve different treatment from their domestic debts because of the government's great concern about China's continued access to international financial markets at favorable interest rates. In order to arrive at the "broadest" definition of public debt, we take into account all the bad debts that SOEs and other state institutions could potentially owe to foreigners. We constructed the "maximum" public debt as the sum of the broader public debt plus the entire foreign debt of SOEs and public institutions. The "maximum public debt"–GDP ratio was 50.1 percent of GDP in 1996 and 55.1 percent in 1997.[12]

Is a debt–GDP ratio of 55.1 percent too low or too high? Compared with the Italian, Swedish and US situations, where central government debt (after deducting intragovernmental debt) to GDP ratios were, respectively, 117.6 percent in 1995, 70.8 percent in 1995, and 50.5 percent in 1996, it might appear that there is still substantial room for the Chinese government to increase its borrowing to finance its expansionary fiscal policy without causing serious debt problems in the future. However, such a conclusion would be overly optimistic. This is because China raises much less state revenue (as a share of GDP) than these other countries, and hence has a much lower capacity to service its public debt. The revenue–GDP ratio was 11 percent for China in 1995, 30 percent for Italy in 1995, 38 percent for Sweden in 1995, and 21 percent for the US in 1996. The point is that, until China increases its tax collection, there is a real trade-off between restructuring the state financial sector and increasing infrastructure investment to stimulate the economy. In addition, it is important to note that increasing tax collection is as much a political challenge as it is an administrative challenge.

Easier monetary policy

The People's Bank of China has cut interest rates several times since price deflation became obvious. For example, the bank lending rate has been reduced steadily from 10.1 percent in September 1997 to 5.9 percent in September 1999. Furthermore, the bank reserve ratio has been lowered twice: from 13 percent to 8 percent in March 1998 and then to 6 percent in November 1999. However, the money (M1) growth rate continued its downward course from 25 percent in 1997:3Q and 1997:3Q to 13 percent in 1998:1Q, and then to 10 percent in 1998:2Q, prompting some Chinese economists to be like their Japanese colleagues in postulating the existence of liquidity traps.

This reluctance by banks to extend credit has its origin in the determined efforts of Zhu Rongji to improve the balance sheets of the state banks and to promote restructuring in the SOE sector since he took over as economic czar in mid-1993. By the end of 1997, the twin facts that Zhu Rongji would be promoted to become the Prime Minister in 1998 and that he had peremptorily dismissed bank managers when the proportion of NPLs in their banks had gone up instilled a new sense of prudent lending in the entire state-bank system. Until the typical bank manager faced personally severe consequences from an increase in the ratio of NPLs, he had not had to respond to the knowledge that the demand for credit by bankrupt SOEs was always high because they really did not expect to repay any of their debts. The loss-making SOEs were engaging in the gamble of the desperate and new loans offered the only chance of a lucky investment that would pull them out of their seemingly hopeless financial straits. This new behavior by bank managers is the reason why, despite additional reductions in interest rates and the required reserve ratios by the central bank, money growth continued to drop in line with the decline in GDP growth.

This slowdown in loans to the SOEs has unfortunately not been replaced by an increase in loans to non-state enterprises, the primary engine of growth in China's economy. The state banks are reluctant to lend to the non-state enterprises, partly because the latter's non-standard accounting makes risk assessment difficult, but more importantly because a banker knows that – while a NPL to an SOE is financially undesirable – a NPL to a private enterprise is more than that – it is also politically undesirable. The banker feared that the NPL to a private firm could result in his being accused afterward of working with capitalists to embezzle the state. Thus, we have the present situation where the loans that state banks are most willing to make are infrastructure loans guaranteed by the central government.

It was only after the central bank implicitly assured the banks in mid-1998 that new NPLs incurred in support of SOEs that were producing saleable goods would be overlooked that money growth increased to 14 percent in 1998:3Q. But then caution reasserted itself as bank managers were rightly skeptical about the credibility of the government's implied assurance that the new NPLs would not count against them in the future. The result was that money growth, after the 14 percent spurt in 1998:3Q, declined steadily to 11.3 percent in 1999:3Q.

Hence, the practical short-run solution to this "liquidity trap" is for the government to undertake *new* infrastructure spending financed by the state banks (and ultimately by new reserves from the central bank). However, a larger sustained increase in credit is possible only if the state commercial banks will use the new deposits (new reserves) to extend new loans, i.e. only if banks act according to the standard "money multiplier" process. As the banks' willingness to lend depends now on finding truly economically viable projects, the government has sought to create new safe lending opportunities for the banks by announcing housing reforms, including privatization of the housing stock. The hope is that the banks will then expand mortgage lending on the basis that the household debt will be fully (and, presumably, also safely) backed by a marketable asset, and hence boost aggregate demand.

Housing reform as a short-run stimulus

The majority of the urban population has, until very recently, lived in virtually free housing supplied by their employers.[13] In early 1998, the government announced that SOEs and other state institutions would stop providing free housing after 1 July and that the housing stock would be privatized.[14] To compensate for the loss of free housing, and to encourage their workers to buy the houses that they are presently staying in, many local governments are giving subsidized mortgages to civil servants. By the end of 2000, government workers had purchased 60 percent of the public housing stock.[15] The marketization of housing is now in full swing, marking another significant milestone on the way to a market economy. The marketization of housing will enhance labor mobility and free the SOEs to focus on production and distribution of goods.

The *China Macroeconomic Analysis* (1998:3Q issue) estimated that, with a functioning mortgage system in place, the marketization of housing would increase the annual demand for housing by 20 to 30 percent. Since housing investment is presently about 4.3 percent of GDP, the housing reform would increase GDP growth by 1 percentage point.[16]

However, in our assessment, the short-run result of the housing reform was a decrease in aggregate demand, even though the new steady-state level of housing demand under the market regime is higher than the old steady-state level of housing demand under the entitlement regime. First, the demand for new residential construction by SOEs stopped abruptly on 1 July 1998 and, because it takes time for private agencies to appear to intermediate between the builders and the millions of disparate buyers, the immediate impact was more likely to have been a drop in housing demand than an increase.

Second, the mortgage system is not yet in place. The banks need time to build up their expertise in mortgage lending, and the certification/registration system of house ownership is usually not standardized province-wide. More importantly, at the moment, only the richest 5 to 10 percent of the urban population can qualify for mortgage loans; and these well-to-do folk are likely to have already acquired most of the housing that they want.

Results of the reflation package

The reflation package has worked much better than expected by most observers. When the negative effects of the Asian financial crisis started hitting in early 1998, and slowing China's GDP growth, most observers steadily revised their forecasts of 1998 growth downward. For example, the Economist Intelligence Unit's (EIU) *Country Report on China* predicted a 1998 growth rate of 7.3 percent in the 1998:1Q issue, 6.7 percent in the 1998:2Q issue, and then 6.1 percent in the 1998:3Q issue. The credit spurt and investment splurge in the last half of 1998 disappointed all these forecasts by lifting GDP growth to 7.6 percent in 1998:3Q and 9.6 percent in 1998:4Q, to produce an annual growth rate of 7.8 percent for 1998. The decomposition of aggregate demand in Table 1.1 shows that fixed capital formation added 4.5 percent points to the 1998 growth rate.

However, given the widespread expectation that the Asian financial crisis would be a long-lasting crisis, and the skepticism that China would be able to undertake sustained fiscal stimulus, the EIU continued to predict low growth rates for 1999, despite the falsification of its gloomy forecasts for 1998. The 1999:3Q issue predicted a 1999 growth rate of 6.7 percent. The actual 1999 growth rate turned out to be 7.1 percent, partly due to the additional fiscal and monetary stimulus in the last quarter, and partly to the rapid recovery of exports in response to the end of the Asian financial crisis.

It must be mentioned that a number of observers believe that the official growth numbers are wrong and that actual growth in 1998 was between 3 and 5 percent. The basis of this skepticism is the low usage of electricity, the low volume of goods being transported, and the continued fall in the level of retail prices. The well-known Chinese economist, Mao Yushi, was quoted as saying that: "The GDP figure is still dubious... There must be some local government trying to please the central government by reporting inflated statistics."[17] There is credibility in Mao Yushi's statements because Premier Zhu had criticized provincial leaders in early December for each reporting a provincial growth rate greater than 10 percent in the first half of 1998 when the national growth rate was only 7.2 percent.[18]

The 1999 growth rate of 7.1 percent, low as it is, also deserves skepticism for the same reasons. First, only two provinces, Shanxi and Sichuan, have reported growth rates below 7.1 percent. Second, the sum of all individually reported provincial GDP figures exceeded the official national GDP by 7 percent.[19]

In Woo (1998), we found that the annual GDP growth rate in the 1985–1993 period could have been overstated, on average, by as much as 2 percentage points; and, after taking various factors into account, we suggested a downward correction of about 1 percentage point. The overstatement is less serious, however, when the inflation rate is low. In the light of our work, the negative inflation and the skepticism expressed in the two preceding paragraphs, we think that the actual GDP growth rate could plausibly be about 7 percent in 1998 and around 6.5 percent in 1999.

Table 1.2 compares exports in each quarter to its level in the same quarter of the previous year. It shows that the negative effects from the Asian financial crisis reached their peak in the period from 1998:3Q to 1999:2Q. With the recovery of the Asian crisis economies in 1999, China's

Table 1.2 Export earnings (fob, in US$ million)

	Q1	*Q2*	*Q3*	*Q4*	*Year total*
1996	28,249	35,803	39,979	47,166	151,197
1997	35,585	45,360	48,173	53,759	182,877
1998	40,072	46,488	47,190	49,839	183,589
1999	37,290	45,727	54,201	na	na

exports leaped to $54 billion in 1999:3Q. Since the Asian crisis countries are expected to continue their economic expansion in 2000, China now has more room to undertake continued restructuring.

Susceptibility of China to a financial crisis

The Asian financial crisis was typified by (a) a collapse of the exchange rate because of heavy capital outflow, and (b) a collapse of the domestic financial system causing a shortage of working capital that, in turn, caused output to collapse. So how vulnerable is China to a meltdown scenario of this type?

A dramatic speculative attack on the RMB can be ruled out simply because the RMB is not convertible for capital account transactions in financial assets. It is difficult for a person to borrow RMB from a Chinese bank to buy US dollars in order to speculate against the exchange rate, because the purchase of US dollars requires documentation to prove that the transaction is trade-related.

Capital outflow by foreign private agents has not occurred because most of the foreign private investments in China are foreign direct investments, and there is very little short-term foreign debt. At the end of 1999, short-term foreign debt was less than 20 percent of the total foreign debt of US$168 billion. The fact that China also had US$155 billion in foreign-exchange reserves made defense of the exchange rate feasible even if all short-term foreign debts had been recalled.

Furthermore, foreign participation in the Chinese stock markets is limited to transaction in B-shares. Only foreigners can own B-shares, and B-shares are denominated in US dollars and transacted using US dollars. In short, an abrupt withdrawal by foreigners from the Chinese stock markets can affect the value of the yuan-dominated A-shares (that only Chinese can own) only if their withdrawal would cause Chinese speculators to revise downward their expectations of future Chinese growth.

Of course, capital flight can occur through channels such as over-invoicing of imports and under-invoicing of exports. A successful speculative attack on the RMB via large and pervasive mis-invoicing is theoretically possible, but difficult to prove because the paper trail would point to trade imbalance rather than portfolio adjustment as the cause of the exchange-rate collapse. An exchange-rate collapse from mis-invoicing of trade requires that the government be rigidly committed to current-account convertibility, but this is not credible. Any government, such as China's, that has in place a comprehensive administrative system that processes every import application to buy foreign exchange (in order to prevent capital movements) can be easily tempted to defend the exchange rate by delaying approvals of import applications. Therefore, imports could be compressed to a significant degree whenever a trade deficit threatened to materialize.

We turn now to the issue of whether China's banking system would collapse spectacularly, as in the countries experiencing the Asian financial crisis. To a first approximation, when the won, baht and rupiah went into free fall, many Korean, Thai and Indonesian banks were rendered insolvent through a combination of the following channels: the sudden increase in the value (measured in domestic currency) of their foreign liabilities; the default on bank loans by domestic corporations bankrupted by the soaring of their external debts; and the default on bank loans by exporters who could not get short-term credit from their foreign suppliers of inputs. Many of the Korean, Thai and Indonesian banks were already financially fragile before their collapse because of undercapitalization, and because of considerable NPLs that had been hidden by accounting gimmicks. The exchange rate shock pushed these fragile banks over.

Much alarm has been raised in recent months about the amount of NPLs in China's banking system, with the estimate for NPLs ranging from 20 to 50 percent of total bank loans. It has even been raised as a serious possibility several times, that a run by depositors is almost inevitable, causing a banking collapse that would trigger a general output decline.

We find the likelihood of either a bank run or a collapse of the banking system to be minimal. Admittedly, there have been bank runs in China since 1978, e.g. in 1988. But these bank runs were motivated by anticipations of high inflation caused by the imminent lifting of price controls, and not by anticipations of bank failures. Whenever the government began indexing interest payments to the inflation rate, the bank runs reversed themselves. In the present time of falling prices, inflation-induced bank runs will not occur.

It is true that there is no depositor insurance in China, but this in itself is unlikely to cause a bank run induced by fear over the large amount of NPLs. This is because all but one of the banks are state-owned and the government has repeatedly pledged to honor all deposits in the state banks. This pledge is credible because the government is in a position to make good its promise. As pointed out earlier, the government can easily borrow to cover the NPLs; and, assuming an NPL ratio of 33 percent, the borrowing would raise the public debt–GDP ratio to just 40 percent. Alternatively, the government could always raise taxes to cover the NPLs.

Even if a bank run does occur, there need not be a collapse in bank credit because the central bank could just issue currency to the state banks to meet the withdrawals. This expansion of high power money cannot be easily translated into a loss of foreign reserves because capital controls are in place. This expansion of high power money will also not have much impact on inflation because this is mainly a shift out of bank deposits into cash, and not a shift into goods.

Simply put, even if the state banks are truly insolvent as has been alleged, and even if the insolvency does induce bank runs, a collapse in bank credit does not have to follow. It is well within the technical ability of the government to accommodate the bank runs, and it is also well within the financial ability of the government to recapitalize the state banks. Furthermore, these two government actions would not cause much damage (if any) to the economy, such as lower growth and higher inflation.

While China can prevent NPLs of the state banks from maiming the payments system and crippling production, we recognize that NPLs have imposed real costs on the economy. With NPLs accounting for a third of total bank loans (our estimate), bank loans accounting for about a fifth of fixed investments since 1985, and fixed investments at about 35 percent of GDP, it is implied that about 2.3 percent of GDP has been wasted annually in the last decade. Moreover, since most of the bank loans are extended to SOEs with little going to the more efficient non-state sector, the performing loans are not in investments with the highest rates of return. In short, the productive capacity of the economy could be higher than it is.

Of course, we also recognize that the NPL problem might be even worse at the non-bank financial institutions (NBFIs) such as the regional trust and investment companies (TICs).[20] However, because NBFIs constitute only a small part of the national credit system, their failure is not capable of bringing down the payments system. The biggest dangers from the collapse of NBFIs are social instability (especially when the base of NBFIs is small depositors), and reduction in foreign credit.

In the 1998 closure of the financial arm of the Guangdong International Trust and Investment Company (GITIC), the central government assumed responsibility for all properly-registered foreign debt. Since trade-related credit with a maturity of less than three months and foreign debts of GITIC's branch in Hong Kong did not require official registration, it is likely that a very substantial amount of GITIC's foreign debt will not be assumed by the Chinese government. In October 1999, GITIC's liquidation committee reported that, after rejecting illegal contingent guarantees issued by GITIC, the total liabilities had been reduced from US$4.7 billion to the range of US$1.7 billion to US$2.7 billion. The value of recoverable assets was put at US$0.9 billion.[21]

As discussed earlier, this assumption of all the properly-registered debt of state institutions and SOEs would raise the public debt–GDP ratio to 55 percent – still a very low level when compared with the public debt–GDP ratios of most Western European countries. As a general principle, the government's decision to let NBFIs fail is important to reducing the moral hazard problem inherent in supervision of the financial sector. Both domestic depositors and foreign creditors have to be encouraged to assess and mange risks better.

As things stood at the beginning of 2000, it looks unlikely that China will soon succumb to a financial crisis marked by bank runs, capital flight, a severe shortage of working capital, and a deep recession.

The importance of financial intermediation for stabilization and growth

Part A of Table 1.3 shows, that total household consumption has declined steadily as a proportion of GDP. It dropped from an average of 52 percent in 1979–1983 to 46 percent in 1994–1998. However, this fall in consumption is not seen in all sectors. While rural consumption fell from 33 percent of GDP in 1979–1983 to 23 percent in 1994–1998, urban consumption rose from 19 percent to 23 percent. But since the share of population living in urban areas has increased from 20 percent in 1979–1983 to 30 percent in 1994–1998, it is not surprising that urban consumption has risen relative to GDP, while rural consumption has fallen. The important analytical issue is whether urban consumption did increase relative to GDP, once the demographic shift has been controlled for.

Part B of Table 1.3 presents a decomposition of the change in rural and urban consumption behavior after taking the rural–urban movements into account. The decomposition follows from:

$$(C_i/\text{GDP}) = [L_i/L] \times [(C_i/L_i)/(\text{GDP}/L)] \qquad (1.1)$$

where C_i = consumption in sector i
L_i = population in sector i
L = total population

The decomposition in equation (1.1) can be described as:

(consumption in sector i as share of GDP) = (share of population living in sector i) × (normalized per capita consumption in sector i)

Taking differences, equation (1.1) becomes:

$$\begin{aligned}\Delta(C_i/\text{GDP}) = {} & [(C_i/L_i/(\text{GDP}/L)] \times \Delta[L_i/L] \\ & + [L_i/L] \times \Delta[(C_i/L_i)/(\text{GDP}/L)] \\ & + [\Delta(L_i/L)] \times [\Delta\{(C_i/L_i)/(\text{GDP}/L)\}]\end{aligned}$$

The decomposition in equation (1.2) can be described as:

Percentage point change in (consumption in sector i as share of GDP) = Percentage point contribution from the shift in the share of population in sector i
+ Percentage point contribution from the shift in normalized consumption in sector i
+ Percentage point contribution from interaction of the two shifts

We note that the normalized per capita consumption in sector i can, in turn, be decomposed into:

Table 1.3 Consumption shifts in the reform period 1978–1998 (%)

Part A. Expenditure as % of GDP

Periods	*Rural HHC*	*Urban HHC*	*GOVC*	*Capital formation*	*Inventory change*	*Net export*	*Total HHC*	*Rural population share*
1978	30.3	18.5	13.3	29.8	8.4	−0.3	48.8	82.1
1988	30.4	21.5	11.7	31.4	5.9	−1.0	51.9	74.2
1998	22.1	24.1	11.9	35.3	2.8	3.8	46.2	69.6
1979–1983	32.6	19.0	14.4	27.6	6.1	0.4	51.6	79.7
1984–1988	31.9	19.5	13.1	30.7	6.3	−1.5	51.4	75.5
1989–1993	26.5	22.2	12.9	30.0	7.7	0.7	48.7	73.0
1994–1998	22.8	23.3	11.9	34.8	4.7	2.6	46.1	70.5

Part B. Decomposing the change in consumption–GDP ratio

	Total change in consumption /GDP ratio	*Of the change in consumption/GDP ratio*		
		Rural/urban shift	*Consumption shift*	*Interaction effects*
		For the rural sector		
Change 1978–1998	−8.2	−4.6	−4.2	0.6
Change period 1–period 4	−9.7	−3.8	−6.7	0.8
		For the urban sector		
Change 1978–1998	5.6	12.9	−4.3	−3.0
Change period 1–period 4	4.2	8.7	−3.0	−1.4

Notes
HHC = household consumption, period 1 = 1979–1983, period 4 = 1994–1998.

$$[(C_i/L_i)/(\text{GDP}/L)] = (C_i/Y_i) \times [(Y_i/L_i)/(\text{GDP}/L)]$$
$$(C_i/Y_i) = \text{average propensity to consume in sector } i$$
$$[(Y_i/L_i)/(\text{GDP}/L)] = [(\text{per capita income in sector } i)/(\text{per capita GDP})]$$
$$= \text{normalized per capita income in sector } i$$

We now have a natural definition of chronic under-consumption; it can be seen as a secularly declining average propensity to consume.

Since per capita income in China's urban sector has risen faster than per capita GDP over the entire reform period, normalized consumption in the urban sector would increase if average propensity to consume in the urban sector had remained unchanged. A drop in normalized consumption in the urban sector could only mean that the average propensity to consume among urban residents has decreased, i.e. that there is chronic under-consumption in the urban sector.

A drop in normalized consumption in the rural sector is more ambiguous. It would be consistent with both a drop or a rise in the average propensity to consume of rural dwellers because growth in per capita income in rural areas has lagged behind growth in per capita GDP.

Part B of Table 1.3 shows that there is unambiguous chronic under-consumption in urban China, and that this is also likely to be the case in rural China. There has been a downward shift of 3 percentage points in the normalized consumption of urban residents between Period 1 (1979–1983) to Period 4 (1994–1998), and a downward shift of 6.7 percent points in the normalized consumption of rural residents. This much bigger downward shift in rural normalized consumption suggests that the rural average propensity to consume has also fallen.

Keynes pointed out in his paradox of thrift that an increase in the saving rate could, in the short run, depress aggregate demand, and cause the economy to produce below capacity. Only if financial markets were informationally perfect would the increased saving be translated instantaneously into investments, and the level of aggregate demand be maintained. The paradox of thrift is based on coordination failure between savers and investors, and the minimization of its occurrence requires highly sophisticated financial intermediation. In a centrally planned economy, the paradox of thrift would not exist because the planner controls both the amount of saving and the amount of investment; but then, for well-known reasons, a large portion of the saving would be wasted on value-subtracting projects.

China's marginally reformed financial system contains the worst aspects of the preceding two financial systems: the coordination failure of the market financial system, and the allocation irrationality of the command financial system. China's high saving rate is actually also partly a reflection of this serious problem in financial intermediation. The steady liberalization of the economy has increased the number and range of profitable investment opportunities. However, because of the refusal of the state banks to lend to private entrepreneurs to enable them to reap these high rates of return, the private entrepreneurs have to engage in self-financing, and this requires high saving to accumulate the required threshold amount of capital.[22] In short, the convergence of financial intermediation in China to the level of financial sophistication in the United States would lower China's saving rate as well as ensure the full employment of saving and allocate it to the most profitable projects.

Most of the attention on China's financial sector has focused on its urban banks. This neglect of rural financial intermediation is most unfortunate because rural enterprises (popularly known as township and village enterprises, TVEs) have constituted the main engine of China's economic growth since 1984.[23] It has been clear since the 15th Party Congress in September 1997 that China has decided to reduce sharply the importance of state-owned enterprises (SOEs) by accelerating the diversity of ownership forms. The amendment of the constitution in March 1999 to accord private ownership the same legal status as state ownership is a logical development from the 1997 policy decision. Implicitly, TVEs are expected to become an even more important engine of growth in the future.

In Woo (1999), we argued that this expectation of continued high TVE growth may be unrealistic however, given recent investment trends. TVE investment in the 1990s has declined relative to both GDP and total fixed investment, in a period in which total investment went from 30 percent of GDP in 1987 to 33 percent in 1997 (see Table 1.4).

So far, the TVEs have increased their output share not only without getting any of the investment share released by the shrinking SOE sector but with a decreased investment share, from 29 percent in 1987 to 23 percent in 1997. This is unlikely to be a sustainable situation. It is hard to see how the TVEs could move up the value-added chain in production without significant capital investments in the near future. Consequently, if China's capital markets continue not to allocate sufficient investment funds to the most dynamic sector of the economy, China's high growth rate is probably not going to continue in the medium run.

The Agricultural Bank of China (ABC) was established in 1955 to provide financial services to the rural sector, and to channel funds for grain-procurement purchases. Small-scale collectively-owned rural credit cooperatives (RCCs, *Nongcun Xindai Hezuoshe*) were started in the early

Table 1.4 Investment and output by ownership forms

	Fixed investment as % of GDP		*Share of fixed investment, %*		*Share of industrial output, %*	
	1987	*1997*	*1987*	*1997*	*1987*	*1997*
All ownership forms	30.4	33.4	100.0	100.0	100.0	100.0
SOEs	19.2	17.5	63.1	52.5	59.7	25.5
TVEs	8.9	7.7	29.1	23.0	32.5	47.6

1950s, under the supervision of ABC, to be the primary financial institutions serving the rural areas. RCCs operate an extensive network of branches, savings deposit offices, and credit stations in market towns and remote areas. The number of RCC units rose from 389,726 in 1981 to 421,582 in 1984, and then fell steadily to 365,492 in 1995.[24] We want to highlight this decline in the number of RCC units after 1984 because this decline means a decrease in the effort to mobilize rural saving, and a decrease in the access of the rural community to investment financing.

In our opinion, the primary reason for the drop in TVE investment (as a share of GDP and as a share of total domestic investments) is that TVEs suffer from two big disadvantages in investment financing. The first disadvantage is that the still heavily-regulated financial system is directing too much of the investment funds to the SOE sector, thus starving the TVEs sector of investment funds. The second major disadvantage of the TVEs in raising capital is that, because of political discrimination against private ownership, many TVEs generally have vague, collective forms of property rights that cannot attract market-driven investment funds.

The deregulation of financial intermediation will allow the appearance of new small-scale local financial institutions that will mobilize local savings to finance local TVE investments. Our expectation is based on the impressive growth of folk finance (*minjian rongzhi*) since 1978 despite the absence of legal recognition and legal protection. According to Liu (1992), folk finance was the source of the development of TVEs in Wenzhou city in Zhejiang Province:

> Ninety-five per cent of the total capital needed by the local private sector has been supplied by "underground" private financial organizations, such as money clubs, specialized financial households and money shops. . .[25]

It cannot be overemphasized that financial deregulation has to be accompanied by the introduction of adequate banking supervision and of prudential standards that comply with international norms. The rash of banking crises in Eastern Europe in the early 1990s and in East and Southeast Asia recently should serve as warnings of financial deregulation in the absence of adequate improvement in the government's ability to monitor the activities of the financial institutions.

Besides deregulating rural financial intermediation, it is also important that the property rights of rural enterprises are clearly defined, protected legally and freely tradable, like the property rights of shareholding firms. The present trend of restructuring TVEs into shareholding cooperatives by dividing their assets among the workers (sometimes among the original inhabitants of the community) is a natural convergence to an enterprise form which, international experiences have shown, assures investors that managers will have the incentive to maximize profits in a prudent manner.

The many disappointments of state enterprise reform

When China started its SOE reform two decades ago, it followed the principles of market socialism to motivate the SOE manager to maximize profits. The state entered into a profit-sharing arrangement with the firm, and gave increasing operational autonomy to the manager. The official conclusion is that the decentralization of decision-making to the firms has failed to improve their performance.

> The current problems of SOEs are: excessive investments in fixed assets with very low return rates, resulting in the sinking of large amounts of capital; and a low sales-to-production ratio, giving rise to mounting inventories. The end result is that the state has to inject an increasing amount of working capital through the banking sector into the state enterprises.
>
> (Vice-Premier Zhu Rongji, 1996)[26]

> The situation as regards the economic efficiency of [state] enterprises has remained very grim ... And the prominent feature is the great increase in the volume and size of losses.
>
> (Vice-Premier Wu Bangguo, 1996)[27]

There has been a steady increase in SOE losses since additional decision-making powers were given to SOE managers in 1985.[28] The three most commonly cited reasons for this development are: the emergence of competition from the non-state enterprises, the failure of the SOEs to improve their efficiency, and embezzlement by SOE personnel.

The competition explanation is perhaps the weakest explanation because the profit rates of SOEs in the sectors of industry that experienced little entry by non-SOEs showed the same dramatic drop as the profit rates of SOEs in sectors with heavy penetration by non-SOEs. Fan and Woo (1996) compared the SOE profit rate and the proportion of output sold by SOEs in different sectors of industry in 1989 and 1992. In four of the five cases where the degree of SOE domination was unchanged, the profit rates were lower in 1992, e.g. the profit rate of the tobacco industry dropped 82 percentage points, and that of petroleum refining dropped 13 percentage points. The 1992 profit rates were lower in six of the seven cases where the degree of SOE domination had declined by less than 5 percentage points.

The failure-to-improve explanation has generated a heated debate in the academic literature. There is a wide range of total-factor-productivity (TFP) estimates, going from large negative to large positive, and the variety could be due to a whole array of factors, such as the possibility of Potemkin data sets, the functional form, the estimation method and the choice of price deflators.[29] Our reading of the evidence is that any improvement in TFP was minor, and, most likely, temporary.

The attribution of China's SOE losses to embezzlement of profits and asset-stripping by employees (managers and workers) is reminiscent of the relentless escalation of SOE losses during the decentralizing reforms in pre-1990 Eastern Europe. With the end of the central plan and the devolution of financial decision-making power to the SOEs, the key source of information to the industrial bureaus regarding the SOEs were reports submitted by the SOEs themselves. This reduction in the monitoring ability of the state in a situation of continued soft-budget constraint meant that there was little incentive for state-enterprise managers to resist wage demands because the future promotion of these managers to larger SOEs was determined in part by the increases in workers' welfare during their tenure. The reduction in the state's monitoring ability combined with the steady reduction in discrimination against the private sector also made it easier for the managers to transfer state assets to themselves.[30]

Besides creating a fiscal crisis for the state, the "disappearing profits" at the SOEs have also contributed to social instability. The increasing public outrage over the inequity of the informal privatization of the SOE sector is well captured in a recent book by He Qinglian who wrote that the SOE reform has amounted to:

> a process in which power-holders and their hangers-on plundered public wealth. The primary target of their plunder was state property that had been accumulated from forty years of the people's sweat, and their primary means of plunder was political power.[31]

There can be little doubt that the Chinese leadership recognizes the increasingly serious economic and political problems created by the agency problem innate in the decentralizing reforms of market socialism. This is why the debate between the conservative reformers and the liberal reformers has progressed from whether privatization is necessary to the question of the optimal form and amount of privatization. The emerging consensus is that all but the thousand largest SOEs and the defense-related SOEs are to be corporatized, with part of their shares sold to employees and the general public. The preferred privatization method for small and medium-sized SOEs has been employee (insider) privatization. Even for the larger SOEs that are to be corporatized, the state need not be the biggest shareholder.

The thousand largest SOEs will be given preferential financing to develop into business groups (such as the Japanese *zaibatsus* and the Korean *chaebols*) that allegedly will enjoy enormous economies of scale. The truth is more prosaic. Given the coexistence of conservative and liberal reformers, any SOE reform package needs to contain a component that appeases each group. The upshot is dual-track SOE reform: state-sponsored conglomerates for the conservative reformers, and publicly-traded joint-stock companies for the liberal reformers. However, in the light of the 1997–1998 external debt crisis in South Korea caused by imprudent borrowing by the *chaebols*, one should question the wisdom of creating such large state business groups.

We must emphasize that the key to SOE reform is not privatization per se, but a transparent, legal privatization process that society at large can accept, at the minimum, as tolerably equitable. Because an adequate privatization program must compensate the retired and laid-off workers, permit takeover by core investors, and respect the rights of minority shareholders, it is important that legal reforms be carried out simultaneously. Without a transparent, equitable privatization process (overseen by an adequate legal framework), China is likely to repeat the mistakes of the Russian privatization program implemented by Premier Chernomyrdin. Just as the creation of the new *kleptoklatura* in Russia robbed the Yeltsin government of its political legitimacy, a similar occurrence in urban China could be socially explosive.

Concluding remarks

We want to highlight one possible negative long-run result from the present reflation package. There is strong evidence that the larger credit growth in the third and fourth quarters of 1998 was achieved only after implicit assurances were given to bank managers that they would not be held responsible if the NPL ratio was to increase. A temporary deviation from the firm policy of cleaning up the balance sheets of the state banks may be defensible in the midst of the Asian financial crisis, but a prolonged deviation would undermine the credibility of the commitment to reform the state banks and mean a return to the traditional socialist boom–bust cycle.

The long-term answer to the NPL problem goes beyond punishing bank managers who experienced increases in the NPL ratio. It lies in changing both the supply-side and the demand-side of the credit market. Many changes are required on both sides of the credit market, and the most fundamental changes include the transformation of the state banks and the SOEs into shareholding corporations to make profit-maximization their primary objective, the establishment of a modern legal framework to promote transparency and reduce transaction costs, and the creation of a prudential regulatory body to reduce excessive risk-taking by banks.

The above complex institutional changes that are necessary in order to address the NPL problem, illustrate that most of China's economic problems cannot be individually addressed, and that success depends on systemic reform. This brings us to the basic point that while President Jiang and Premier Zhu deserve much credit for their competent handling of the current macroeconomic problems so far, their position in Chinese history will depend more on their success in addressing the many and varied long-term development challenges facing China. These challenges include the slowdown in agricultural productivity growth, the decline in job creation in the rural enterprise sector, the acceleration of losses by state-owned enterprises (SOEs), the relentless growth in non-performing loans (NPLs) at the state banks, the inability of the legal system to meet the demands of an increasingly sophisticated economy, and the inadequacy of social safety nets to cope with the temporary dislocations that are characteristic of a fast-growing economy. The ability of China to maintain its international competitiveness after the Asian financial crisis is over is conditional upon the resolution of the above problems.

China's accession to the WTO reveals first a recognition by the top leaders that convergence of China's economic institutions to the institutional norms of modern market economies offers China the only chance to achieve sustained high growth, and second, more importantly, a commitment by the top leaders to make sure that convergence will occur.

Notes

1 For recent warnings from this faction against perceived suicide by the Communist Party, see "Elder warns on economic change," *South China Morning Post* 13 January 2000, and "Leftists make late bid to slow reforms," *South China Morning Post* 10 February 2000.

2 This de facto public recognition by the government that the *deus ex machina* of China's impressive growth since 1978 is the convergence of its economic institutions to those of market economies will unfortunately not end the academic debate on this issue. Many China specialists have waxed eloquently about how China's experimentation has created economic institutions that are optimally suited for transition economies in general; see Sachs and Woo (2000) for a survey of this debate.

3 This argument is developed in Sachs and Woo (1994).

4 The 18.0 percent for 1995 is calculated from the *China Statistical Yearbook* 1996 because the total workforce data from 1990 onward were revised upward in the *China Statistical Yearbook* of the succeeding years by increasing the size of the rural workforce. The revised data are inconsistent across time, the growth in labor force between 1989 and 1990 is now 15.5 percent (!), while the old data show an increase of 2.5 percent. Using the revised data, the SOEs employed 17 percent of the total labor force.

5 Easterley and Fischer (1994) showed that extensive growth came to a quicker end in Russia than would it in capitalist market economies because the elasticity of substitution between capital and labor in Russia was much lower.

6 This is such a large shift that it raises the discomforting thought that some of the shift may be a mere change in employment classification without change in work conditions; an issue that we cannot go into here.

7 Except in August and September 1998 when the heavy flooding disrupted supplies in several heavily-populated parts of the country.

8 In many cases, the new owners were employees of the firms.

9 "Foreign capital off the rails," *South China Morning Post* 16 February 2000.

10 "Zhu pledges to keep cash flowing," *South China Morning Post* 6 March 2000.

11 This range reflects our selection of credible estimates (e.g. a missed interest payment does not necessarily mean that the loan is bad), so this range does not encompass all estimates that have been reported in the press. For example, Bloomburg News has reported that some analysts believed bad loans to be 70 percent of total loans, *New York Times*, "China hopes to sell bad loans at discount," 5 January 1999.

12 The terms "broader public debt" and "maximum public debt" are from Fan

(1998), he differs from my calculations in that he assumes a NPL ratio of 25 percent.

13 Of course, housing and other subsidies are in fact largely paid for by the employees themselves; this is why their take-home pay is so low.

14 The practical method of privatizing the housing stock is to offer the houses to the existing tenants at prices that approximate the present discounted value of the stream of low rent payments. By giving the existing tenants the right of first refusal, this method makes explicit whatever existing inequality there is in housing allocation. This method does not create new inequalities.

15 "Civil servants own 60% of public housing," *The Straits Times* 24 February 2000.

16 The Minister of Construction has claimed that the housing reform contributed 1.5 to 2 percentage points to the 1999 growth rate; see "Civil servants own 60% of public housing," *The Straits Times* 24 February 2000. The construction of housing might have contributed this amount, but the relevant question is whether the housing reform had actually increased the amount of construction without housing. We doubt this claim for the reasons given in the paragraphs below.

17 "China just misses 8 percent growth rate," *South China Morning Post* 30 December 1998, updated at 2:43 pm.

18 "China admits to cooking the books: editorial," Agence France Presse, 23 December 1998, 4:31 pm.

19 "Beijing has $546b chasm in key data," *South China Morning Post* 29 February 2000.

20 According to the *Far Eastern Economic Review* ("Tic fever: China's shaky trust and investment houses start to fall," 22 October 1998), "most of the country's 243 Tics are on the rocks." Lardy (1998b) reported the claim that 50 percent of the assets of the non-bank financial sector was not performing.

21 "Illegal Gitic deals delay payout," *South China Morning Post* 23 October 1999.

22 A formal model and testing of this argument is in Liu and Woo (1994).

23 The industrial output alone from rural enterprises accounted for about 31 percent of the increase in GDP between 1984 and 1993; calculated from Woo (1998).

24 The number of RCC units is the number of RCCs plus the number of branches, saving deposit offices and credit stations.

25 The competition from the new rural financial institutions is likely to force the ABC–RCC system is improve its operations. This expectation is again based on Wenzhou's experience:

> In order to compete with [the new folk finance institutions]. . . , as early as 1980 a local collective credit union, without informing the superior authority, abandoned for the first time the fixed interest rate and adopted a floating interest rate which fluctuated in accordance with market demand but remained within the upper limit set by the state. Despite the dubious legality of the floating interest rate, the local state bank branches and all the credit unions in Wenzhou had already adopted it before the central state officially ratified it in 1984.
>
> Liu (1992).

26 *"Guo you qiye sheng hua gaige ke burong huan,"* (No time shall be lost in further reforming state owned enterprises), speech at the Fourth Meeting of the Eighth People's Congress, *People's Daily, Overseas Edition* 11 March 1996.

27 "Losses of state-owned industries pose problems for China's leaders," *The Washington Post* 3 November 1996.

28 Recent evidence suggests that past reports on SOE losses (e.g. two-third of SOEs make zero or negative profits) may be understated. A national audit of 100 SOEs in 1999 found that 81 falsified their books, and 69 reported profits

that did not exist; and an audit of the Industrial and Commercial Bank of China and the China Construction Bank found that accounting abuses involving RMB400 billion, of which RMB200 billion was overstatement of assets. ("China: finance ministry reveals widespread accounting fraud," *Financial Times* 24 December 1999). In January 2000, auditors in Hebei caught 67 SOEs covering up losses of RMB 600 million ("Beijing moving to improve quality of statistics," *South China Morning Post* 29 February 2000).

29 For a review of the empirical findings, see Huang *et al.* (1999).

30 It is hence not surprising that of the 327 cases of embezzlement, bribery and misuse of public funds that were tried in Beijing in 1999, "76 percent took place in SOEs" ("Judicial attention to SOEs pledged," *China Daily* 19 February 2000).

31 The translated quote is from Liu and Link (1998, p. 19).

Bibliography

Easterley, W. and Fischer, S. (1994) "The Soviet economic decline: historical and republican data," Working Paper No. 4735, National Bureau of Economic Research, May.

Fan, G. (1998) "Fiscal stimulus and debt-financing: potential and constraints," manuscript, September.

Fan, G. and Woo, W.T. (1996) "State enterprise reform as a source of macroeconomic instability," *Asian Economic Journal*, November, 207–224.

Huang, Y., Woo, W.T. and Duncan, R. (1999) "Understanding the decline of the state sector in China," *MOCT-MOST: Economic Policy in Transitional Economies*, 9(1).

Lardy, N. (1998a) "China chooses growth today, reckoning tomorrow," *Asian Wall Street Journal*, 30 September.

Lardy, N. (1998b) "Financial reform: fast track or back track," *Global Emerging Markets*, Credit Lyonnais Securities Asia, November.

Liu, Y.-L. (1992) "Reform from below: the private economy and local politics in the rural industrialization of Wenzhou," *China Quarterly*, 130 (June), 293–316.

Liu, B. and Link, P. (1998) "China: the great backward?" *The New York Review of Books*, 8 October.

Liu, L.-Y. and Woo, W.T. (1994) "Saving behavior under imperfect financial markets and the current account consequences," *Economic Journal*, May, 512–527.

Rawski, T. (1999) "China's move to market: how far? What next," manuscript, 25 October.

Sachs, J. and Woo, W.T. (1994) "Structural factors in the economic reforms of China, Eastern Europe, and the former Soviet Union," *Economic Policy*, April.

Sachs, J. and Woo, W.T. (2002) "Understanding China's economic performance," (with Jeffrey Sachs) *Journal of Economic Reform*, forthcoming.

Woo, W.T. (1998) "Zhongguo Quan Yaosu Shengchan Lu: Laizi Nongye Bumen Laodongli Zai Pei Zhi de Shouyao Zuoyong" ("Total factor productivity growth in China: the primacy of reallocation of labor from agriculture"). In *Jingji Yanjiu*, 3, 31–39.

Woo, W.T. (1999) "Some observations on the ownership and regional aspects in financing the growth of China's rural enterprises," translated into French as "La croissance des entreprises rurales selon les regions et la propriete". In *Revue d'Economie du Developpement*, June.

2 China's economic reform and development

The impact on the Asia-Pacific region

John Wong

Introduction

The Chinese economy has experienced spectacular growth since it started economic reform and the open-door policy in 1978. Real growth of gross domestic product (GDP) during 1979–1999 was at an annual rate of 9.7 per cent. In 1978, China's total GDP was only US$44 billion or just 70 per cent of that of South Korea's. By mid-2000 China's total nominal GNP had reached US$1 trillion, which was two and a half times that of South Korea's and ranked the world's seventh largest. In terms of purchasing power parity (PPP), the Chinese economy in 1999 became the world's second largest after the USA, although one needs, of course, to be aware of the problem of overstating China's real GDP by the PPP measure (World Bank, 2000–2001).

According to the World Bank, it took Britain about 58 years to double its per capita income (from 1780–1838), 34 years for Japan (1885–1919) and 11 years for South Korea (1966–1977) but only 9 years for China (1978–1987) and another 9 years for it to double again (1987–1996) (World Bank, 1997). If the World Bank could also report on Guangdong province, it would find Guangdong's growth performance even more impressive. With a total population of 72 million (larger than France, which has only 59 million), Guangdong increased its per capita GDP 32 times from 1978 to 1999 (Statistical Bureau of Guangdong, 2000). This, amongst other things, suggests that latecomers, once having successfully taken off, can achieve faster economic growth and take a shorter time span to double their per capita income as they take advantage of the backlog of technological progress and surplus capital created by the forerunners.

China's economic performance in the past two decades has indeed been breathtaking. Viewed in the overall East Asian context, China's hyper-growth is not really exceptional. Nor is it unprecedented. However, on account of its vast size and diversity, China's dynamic growth has far-reaching implications for the East Asian region.

The East Asian (EA) region is commonly defined to comprise Japan, China, the four Newly Industrialized Economies (NIEs) of South Korea,

Table 2.1 Performance indicators of East Asian economies

	Population (Mn)	*GNP per capita (US$)*	*PPP estimates of GNP per capita (US$)*	*Growth of GDP (%)*							*Annual export growth (%)*	*Mfg exports as % of total exports*	*Exports as % of GDP*	*Gross domestic savings as as % of GDP*	*Gross domestic investment as % of GDP*		
	1999	*1999*	*1999*	*1960–1970*	*1970–1980*	*1980–1990*	*1990–1998*	*1998*[a]	*1999*[a]	*2000*[b]	*1990–1998*	*1997*	*1999*	*1990–1997*	*1999*	*1990–1997*	*1999*
Japan	127	32,230	24,041	10.9	5.0	4.0	1.3	−2.5	0.8	2.3	3.9	95	11	34	30	30	29
China	1,250	780	3,291	5.2	5.8	10.2	11.1	7.8	7.1	8.0	14.9	85	22	43	42	39	40
NIEs																	
South Korea	47	8,490	14,637	8.6	9.5	9.4	6.2	−5.8	10.0	9.2	15.7	87	42	36	34	37	27
Taiwan	22	13,248	n.a.	9.2	9.7	7.1	n.a.	4.6	5.6	4.1	2.4	96	42	26	26	23	24*
Hong Kong	7	23,520	22,939	10.0	9.3	6.9	4.4	−5.1	2.1	6.8	9.5	93	132	32	30	31	25
Singapore	3	29,610	27,024	8.8	8.5	6.4	8.0	0.3	5.6	11	13.3	84	n.a.	48	52	36	33
ASEAN-4																	
Indonesia	207	580	2,439	3.9	7.6	6.1	5.8	−13.2	0.1	5.1	8.6	42	54	33	24	33	14
Malaysia	23	3,400	7,963	6.5	7.8	5.3	7.7	−7.5	5.4	6.5	13.2	76	124	38	45	39	32
Philippines	77	1,020	3,815	5.1	6.3	1.0	3.3	−0.5	3.2	3.6	11.0	85	56	17	16	22	21
Thailand	62	1,960	5,599	8.4	7.2	7.6	7.4	−10.4	5.0	2.6	11.1	71	57	34	32	39	21

Sources: World Bank, *World Development Report 2000/2001* (Washington DC: Oxford University Press); Statistics Department, Taiwan Ministry of Economic Affairs, http://www.moea.gov.tw; 'Bottomline', *Asiaweek*, 23 March 2001 and 30 March–6 April 2001; and 'Prices & Trends', *Far Eastern Economic Review*, 13 April 2000.

Notes
a denotes data obtained from *Far Eastern Economic Review*.
b denotes statistics from *Asiaweek*.
*denotes figure extracted from *Asian Development Outlook 2000*.
n.a. denotes not available.

Taiwan, Hong Kong and Singapore, and the four Association of Southeast Asian Nations (ASEAN) of Indonesia, Malaysia, the Philippines, and Thailand – the original ASEAN members. Situated on the western rim of the Pacific, all these East Asian economies (EAEs) have displayed a strong capacity for dynamic growth, with many having experienced high growth for a sustained period – until 1997 when they were hit, to varying degrees, by the regional financial crisis. In fact, several of the EAEs had, one after another, broken the past world growth records, so much so that the World Bank, in its well-known study, referred to the high growth phenomenon of East Asia as the 'East Asian Miracle' (Table 2.1; World Bank, 1994).

Japan was the first non-Western country to become industrialized. Its high growth started back in the 1950s after it had achieved its post-war recovery, and the growth momentum carried over to the 1960s. Japan's economic growth engine was initially based on the export of labour-intensive manufactured products, but it was soon forced by rising wages and increasing costs to shed its comparative advantage for labour-intensive manufacturing in favour of the four NIEs, which started their industrial take-off in the 1960s. These four NIEs, once dubbed 'Asia's Four Little Dragons', constituted the most dynamic component of the EA region, and their near double-digit rate growth was sustained for three decades, from the 1960s to the 1980s. By the late 1970s and early 1980s, high costs and high wages had also caught up with these NIEs, which had to restructure their economies towards more capital-intensive and higher value-added activities and to pass their comparative advantage in labour-intensive products to the latecomers of China and the four ASEAN economies. Some Japanese scholars like to depict this pattern of development as the 'flying geese' model (Akamatzu, 1962).

Japan today is a world-class economic superpower, second only to the United States. In 1999, Japan's nominal per capita income, at US$32,000, was 40 times that of China's and 20 times that of the ASEAN-four's. However, the income gaps between Japan and the four NIEs have been closing up, as the NIEs have graduated to become 'NDEs' or 'newly developed economies'. South Korea, with the lowest per capita income of the four NIEs, is already a member of the OECD. For political reasons, Singapore has chosen not to join the OECD, even though Singapore's per capita income in 1999 ranked the world's ninth highest – just below the United States.

More significantly, the ASEAN-four (which were originally resource-based economies, depending heavily on the export of natural resources and primary commodities for growth) have all become industrialized, in the sense that their overall economic growth is now primarily fuelled by the growth of their manufacturing sector, particularly manufactured exports (Wong, 1979). The same is true for China. When it started the open-door policy 20 years ago, half of China's exports were still made up of primary products, compared with only 16 per cent today. Suffice it to say that, as a result of their sustained economic growth, the EAEs have also been rapidly industrialized.

An important feature of these EAEs is their growing economic interdependence. The EAEs, despite their inherent political, social and economic divergences, can actually integrate economically quite well as a regional grouping. This is essentially the underlying meaning of the 'flying geese' principle. Thus, Japan is obviously the natural economic leader of the group and has, in fact, been the prime source of capital and technology for other EAEs. The resource-based ASEAN-four complement well the manufacturing-based NIEs while both are complementary to the more developed Japanese economy. Then the huge potential of China, with its vast resource base and diverse needs, offers additional opportunities for all.

Not surprisingly, the EA region has already developed a significant degree of economic interdependence as manifested in its fairly high level of intra-regional trade. As shown in Table 2.2, the EA region in 1999, despite still recovering from the Asian financial crisis, absorbed 47 per cent of China's total exports, 47 per cent of the average of the NIEs', 48 per cent of the average of the ASEAN-four's, although only 36 per cent of Japan's – which is still unusually high for Japan as a global economic power.

Apart from intra-regional trade, intra-regional foreign direct investment (FDI) flows have increasingly operated as a strong integrating force for the EA region, especially since a great deal of regional FDI is trade-related in nature. The EAEs are essentially open and outward-looking in terms of being heavily dependent on foreign trade and foreign investment for their economic growth. In particular, China and ASEAN have devised various incentive schemes to vie for FDI, which is generally treated not just as an additional source of capital supply but, more importantly, as a means of technology transfer and export market development.

Initially, Western capital, particularly from the United States, dominated the FDI scene of EA. Then came Japanese capital as a second wave, especially after the late 1970s. Today, the cumulative stock of Japanese FDI has surpassed that of American investments. Since the late 1980s, the EA region has witnessed a new but no less significant development associated with the steady growth of FDI flows from the NIEs to ASEAN and China. The NIEs, particularly Taiwan, Hong Kong and Singapore, having transformed themselves from capital-shortage into capital surplus economies, became a new source of FDI flow into the ASEAN and China to form the third wave. Table 2.3, on the intra-regional FDI flows in East Asia, serves to show how the EAEs have invested a lot in one another.

This is particularly the case for China which, in recent years, has become the most favoured destination of all developing economies for FDI. As can be seen from Table 2.4, the EA region, especially Hong

Table 2.2 Intra-regional trade in East Asia, 1999

	Total exports (US$ million)	*To industrialized countries (%)*				*China (%)*	*NIEs (%)*	*ASEAN-4 (%)*	*East Asia (%)*	*East Asia less Japan (%)*
		Total	*USA*	*Japan*	*EU*					
China	194,931	57.0	21.5	16.6	16.0	–	27.3	3.2	47.1	30.5
Japan	419,207	53.7	31.1	–	18.7	5.6	21.6	8.6	35.8	35.8
NIEs										
S. Korea	143,647	50.5	20.6	11.0	15.8	9.5	14.1	7.7	42.3	31.3
Taiwan	121,590	n.a.	25.4	9.8	15.7	2.1	26.7	7.3	45.9	36.1
Hong Kong	173,793	49.4	23.9	5.4	16.9	33.4	6.4	3.2	48.4	43
Singapore	114,730	45.6	19.2	7.4	15.5	3.4	15.7	23.4*	49.9	42.5
ASEAN-4										
Indonesia	57,282	55.7	16.1	20.0	15.3	4.8	23.4	5.7	53.9	33.9
Malaysia	84,550	53.0	21.9	11.6	16.0	2.7	28.5	6.3	49.1	37.5
Philippines	35,474	63.6	29.6	13.1	19.3	1.6	23.8	6.9	45.4	32.3
Thailand	61,797	57.5	21.5	14.5	17.8	3.6	19.0	7.3	44.4	29.9

Notes

East Asia region here comprises Japan, China, the four NIEs and ASEAN-4.

*Figure for Indonesia is not available.

n.a. denotes not available.

Sources: IMF, *Direction of Trade Statistics Yearbook 2000*; Statistics Department, Taiwan Ministry of Economic Affairs, http://www.moea.gov.tw.

Table 2.3 Foreign direct investment by countries (US$ millions)

Japan's FDI outflow	*1987*	*1988*	*1989*	*1990*	*1991*	*1992*	*1993*	*1994*	*1995*	*1996*	*1997*	*1998*
China	1,226 (3.7%)	296	438	349	579	1,070 (3.1%)	1,691	2,565	3,834	2,628 (5.2%)	2,266	1,267 (2.6%)
ASEAN-5												
Indonesia	545 (1.6%)	586	631	1,105	1,193	1,676 (4.9%)	813	1,759	1,596	2,414 (4.8%)	2,514	1,285 (2.7%)
Malaysia	163 (0.5%)	387	673	725	880	704 (2.1%)	800	742	573	572 (1.1%)	791	614 (1.3%)
Philippines	72 (0.2%)	134	202	258	203	160 (0.5%)	207	668	718	559 (1.1%)	524	427 (0.9%)
Singapore	494 (1.5%)	747	1,902	840	613	670 (2.0%)	644	1,054	1,152	1,115 (2.2%)	1,824	760 (1.6%)
Thailand	250 (0.7%)	859	1,276	1,154	807	657 (1.9%)	578	719	1,224	1,403 (2.8%)	1,867	1,637 (3.4%)
Korea's FDI outflow												
China	n.a.	n.a.	6	16	42	141 (11.6%)	264	632	824	836 (19.7%)	633	630 (16.2%)
ASEAN-5												
Indonesia	126 (30.7%)	20	75	164	170	164 (13.5%)	59	68	200	154 (3.6%)	178	75 (1.9%)
Malaysia	1 (0.2%)	1	3	18	–	24 (2.0%)	24	20	114	44 (1.0%)	17	21 (0.5%)
Philippines	n.a.	1	3	32	48	20 (1.6%)	14	45	57	49 (1.2%)	31	65 (1.7%)
Singapore	n.a.	n.a.	n.a.	3	5	13 (1.1%)	4	4	22	55 (1.3%)	11	128 (3.3%)
Thailand	n.a.	10	9	13	32	26 (2.1%)	37	27	22	24 (0.6%)	186	93 (2.4%)
Taiwan's FDI outflow												
China	n.a.	n.a.	n.a.	n.a.	174	247 (n.a.)	3,168	962	1,093	1,229 (n.a.)	4,334	2,035 (n.a.)
ASEAN-5												
Indonesia	1 (0.9%)	2	0.3	62	160	40 (4.5%)	26	21	32	83 (3.8%)	56	20 (0.6%)
Malaysia	6 (5.7%)	3	159	185	442	156 (17.6%)	65	101	67	94 (4.3%)	85	20 (0.6%)
Philippines	3 (2.6%)	36	66	124	1	1 (0.1%)	7	10	36	74 (3.4%)	127	39 (1.2%)
Singapore	1 (1.3%)	6	5	48	13	9 (1%)	69	101	32	165 (7.6%)	230	158 (4.8%)
Thailand	5 (5.2%)	12	52	149	86	83 (9.4%)	109	57	51	71 (3.3%)	57	131 (4.0%)

Notes

n.a. denotes not available.

Statistics for Japan's FDI outflow to ASEAN-5 from fiscal year 1995 onwards were released in yen and hence, have been converted to US dollars at average inter-bank rates.

1998 figures for Japan's and Korea's FDI outflows are estimated data.

FDI figures for Taiwan actually refer to approved outward investment.

Figures in parentheses refer to FDI outflow as a proportion of total FDI outflow of source country.

Sources: OECD, *International Direct Investment Statistics Yearbook 1999* (Paris: OECD Publications); Japan External Trade Organization (JETRO), *Japanese Outward FDI Declines While Inward FDI Increases*, http://www.jetro.go.jp/; and Investment Commission, Taiwan's Ministry of Economic Affairs, http://www.moea.gov.tw/.

Table 2.4 Foreign direct investment in China (US$ million)

	1992		*1993*		*1994*		*1996*		*1997*		*1998*		*1999*		*2000*	
	Actual amount invested	%	*Actual amount invested*	%	*Actual amount invested*	%	*Actual amount invested*	%	*Actual amount invested*	%	*Actual amount invested*	%	*Actual amount invested*	%	*Actual amount invested*	%
Total	11,292	100.0	27,771	100.0	33,946	100.0	42,135.0	100.0	45,257	100.0	45,463	100.0	40,319	100.0	40,715	100.0
Asia Pacific	9,900	87.7	23,333	84.0	28,267.0	83.2	32,714.0	77.6	30,389	67.1	26,626	58.6	23,210	57.4	22,202	54.5
Hong Kong	7,706.0	68.2	17,445.0	62.8	19,823.0	58.4	20,852.0	49.5	20,632	45.6	18,508	40.7	16,363	40.6	15,500	38.1
Taiwan	1,053.0	9.3	3139.0	11.3	3,391.0	10.0	3,482.0	8.3	3,289	7.3	2,915	6.4	2,599	6.4	2,296	5.6
Japan	748.0	6.6	1361.0	4.9	2,086.0	6.0	3,692.0	8.8	4,326	9.6	3,400	7.5	2,973	7.3	2,916	7.2
South Korea	120.0	1.1	382.0	1.4	726.0	2.0	1,504.0	3.6	2,142	4.7	1,803	4.0	1,275	3.1	1,490	3.7
ASEAN	271.6	2.4	1,005.9	3.6	22,40.6	6.6	3,184.3	7.6	3,418	7.6	4,197	9.2	3,274	8.2	2,837	7.0
Indonesia	20.2	0.18	65.8	0.2	115.7	0.3	93.6	0.2	80	0.2	69	0.2	129	0.3	147	0.4
Malaysia	24.7	0.22	91.4	0.3	509.4	1.5	460.0	1.1	382	0.8	340	0.7	238	0.6	203	0.5
Philippines	16.6	0.15	122.5	0.4	201.0	0.6	55.5	0.1	156	0.3	179	0.3	117	0.3	111	0.3
Singapore	125.9	1.1	491.8	1.8	1,179.6	3.5	2,247.0	5.0	2,606.	5.8	3,404	7.5	2,642	6.6	2,172	5.3
Thailand	84.3	0.75	234.4	0.8	234.9	0.7	328.2	0.8	194	0.4	205	0.5	148	0.4	204	0.5
USA	519.0	4.6	2,068.0	7.4	2,491.0	7.0	3,444.0	8.2	3,239	7.2	3,898	8.6	4,216	10.5	4,384	10.8
Others	873.0	7.7	2,370.0	8.5	3,188.0	9.0	5,977.	14.2	8,192	18.1	10,729	23.6	9,619	23.9	10,218	25.1

Sources: *Statistical Yearbook of China (1992–2000)*; and *China Monthly Statistics*.

Kong, Taiwan, Japan, Singapore and South Korea, accounted for an overwhelming share of FDI inflow to China. In other words, Japan and the NIEs have been able to capture most of the benefits arising from China's open-door policy. However, such regional predominance has been declining in recent years, as China has made efforts to attract more FDI from North America and the EU. By 2000, the East Asian share of FDI in China declined to 55 per cent, down from 88 per cent in 1992.

Suffice it to say that China's economic growth fits in very well with East Asian growth. In fact, China's dynamic economic growth since 1978 has interacted with many high-growth EAEs positively, to each other's advantage. China has been able to harness the region's trade and investment opportunities to facilitate its own economic growth. Simultaneously, China's growing economic integration with the region has provided new opportunities to enhance the region's overall growth potential.

Common growth-inducing characteristics

Why have the EAEs been able to sustain dynamic growth for such a long period? Development economists can easily explain this within the neoclassical framework. On the supply side, rapid economic growth in the EAEs, especially in their early phases of industrialization, was the outcome of the rising labour force and increasing productivity. Growth of labour productivity is associated with the shift of labour from low-productivity agriculture to high-productivity manufacturing. This has happened in Japan, South Korea, Taiwan and China.

Viewed from the demand side, the high growth of the EAEs stemmed from their high levels of domestic investment, which were generally matched by the equally high levels of domestic savings. As shown in Table 2.1, the EAEs, particularly China and the NIEs, have earmarked a high proportion of their GDP for domestic investment, which is generally matched by their high levels of domestic savings. High savings and high investment in the EA region have allowed what may be called the 'virtuous circle of growth': high savings, high investment, high export growth, high GDP growth and then high savings again. This is the simplest explanation of the arithmetic of the region's high economic growth.

To create wealth, capital must be combined with labour in terms of both quantity and quality. But continuing high economic growth cannot be sustained just by dumping more and more capital on a growing labour force. More crucial to the process of sustained economic growth is the condition of technological progress resulting from the acquisition of knowledge. Such is the 'endogenous growth theory', which emphasizes improvements in productivity and investment in human capital.

Paul Krugman has argued that East Asian growth has been based exclusively on the accumulation of capital per worker rather than on increases in output per worker, i.e. on productivity growth. In that light, the East Asian growth model could be viewed as fundamentally flawed in that growth has taken place without improvements in 'total factor productivity' (TFP) – the amount of measured overall growth that cannot be explained by such factors as capital or labour – and is thus in danger of collapse, as in the former Soviet Union (Krugman, 1994). His observation has since stirred up a lively debate among economists and commentators. Several researchers have argued that Krugman has exaggerated the TFP problem of East Asia and that many EAEs have in fact experienced TFP growth (Young, 1995; Boswell *et al.*, 1995).

Productivity or technological progress is admittedly a nebulous concept, difficult to measure empirically or quantify. It is well known that, in East Asia, particularly Japan and the NIEs, the accumulation of human capital has been highly successful, much like its accumulation of physical capital. The best proxy to indicate successful human resource development of the EAEs is to examine their achievements in education. It is clear that many EAEs have made remarkable progress in education and human resource development. This, coupled with the EAEs' acclaimed entrepreneurship, must have made a positive impact on their TFP.

In the case of China, for instance, the high growth during the last 20 years has, indeed, been accompanied by substantial productivity gains. In accounting for China's 9.4 per cent growth of 1978–1995, the World Bank has identified 8.8 per cent (elasticity: 0.4) for physical capital growth, 2.7 per cent (elasticity: 0.3) for human capital growth measured by years of education per worker, and 2.4 per cent (elasticity: 0.3) for labour force increases, leaving the unexplained share of growth at 46 per cent. This means that of China's 9.4 per cent GDP growth, 4.3 per cent is the unexplained residual, which is unusually large compared with South Korea and Japan for the appropriate periods. A substantial part of the residual portion could be the growth in TFP, which was generated from economic reform and the open-door policy (World Bank, 1997). In other words, China's high growth for the past two decades has, indeed, been sustained by a productivity boom.

High savings and high investment alone would not have generated such sustained high growth for China. Operating under socialist planning before 1978, China also had relatively high savings and high investment because of controlled consumption. But China's average annual growth during 1952–1978 was only 5.7 per cent, which was achieved with gross inefficiency coupled with a great deal of fluctuation. After 1978, with the introduction of economic reform and the open-door policy, China's economy started to take off by chalking up consistently near-double digit rates of growth. Economic reform, by introducing market forces to economic decision making, had brought about greater allocative efficiency. The open-door policy, by reintegrating China into the global economy, had also exposed China to greater external competitive pressures, hence higher TFP (Hu and Khan, 1997).

This brings to the fore the importance of export orientation in East Asian economic development. All EAEs share the salient common feature of operating an export-oriented development strategy, as reflected in their generally high export–GDP ratios and high export growth, as shown in Table 2.1. This is not only the case for Singapore and Hong Kong on account of their entrepôt trade role in the region, but also for South Korea and the ASEAN-four. As a result of following the export-oriented strategy, the EAEs have been able to reap the gains from trade and specialization and to attract more FDI. It has also enabled them to capture a rising share of the world market for their manufactured exports.

Specifically for China, as a result of the open door policy, China's exports grew at the hefty annual rate of 18 per cent from US$13.7 billion in 1979 to US$249 billion in 2000. China is now the world's ninth largest exporting country. China's success in attracting FDI has been even more impressive. From 1988 to 2000, total actual FDI inflow amounted to US$339 billion, making China the second-largest recipient of international capital in the world after the United States. In all, more than 200 of the world's largest global multinationals have invested in China (NBS, 2000).

All the EAEs have, in varying degrees, exploited the export-oriented development strategy for their economic growth. But China has been particularly successful, even though it is a late convert to this strategy.

China's competitive pressures for ASEAN

China, in sharing many of the common growth-inducing characteristics of the EAEs, has fitted in well with the dynamic EA region. However, China's 'hyper economic growth' has also created competitive pressures for other EA economies, particularly the ASEAN economies, which are also vying for FDI with China as well as competing head-on with China's manufactured exports in the developed country markets (Loungani, 2000).

How far has China's dynamic export drive been achieved at the expense of the other EA exporters? Since all the EAEs have derived an important source of economic growth by pushing their manufactured exports relentlessly in the US market, an analysis of the EAEs' shares in the US market would reveal, in a broad way, China's competitive pressures on the other EAEs. Figure 2.1 shows the steady rise of China's market share in the US since 1989, particularly after the Renminbi devaluation in 1994, while the share for the NIEs' exports in the US market has sharply declined in the same period.

This implies that China's export drive to the US market has produced a general displacement effect for the NIEs. It also means, however, that the NIEs have been relinquishing their comparative advantage in labour-intensive products to China. In fact, a substantial part of China's exports (48 per cent in 2000) came from the foreign-invested enterprises, particularly those from Taiwan and Hong Kong: parts of China's manufactured

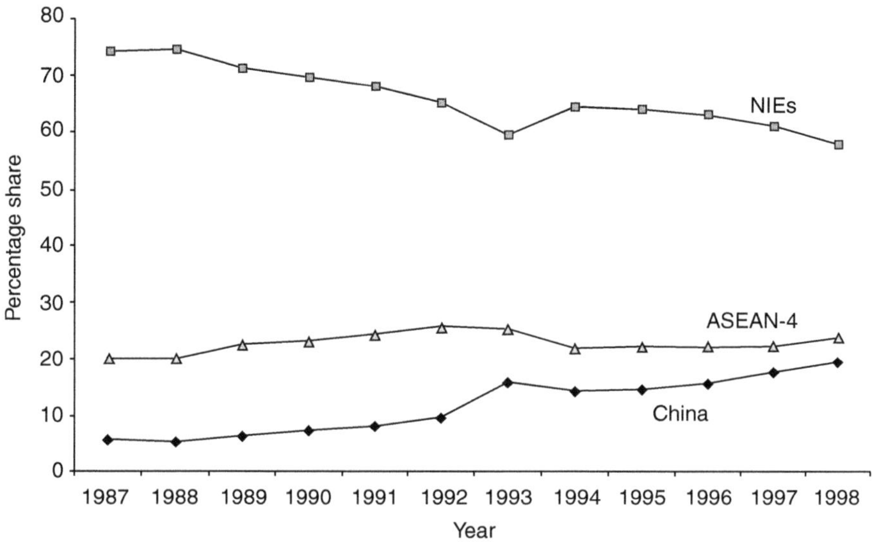

Figure 2.1 China and ASEAN-4 increased their market share in the US market, 1987–1998.

Source: IMF, *Direction of Trade Statistics 1991 and 1999.*

exports actually *belong* to the NIEs. In this sense, the economic rise of China has really not been a threat to those NIEs that are complementary to the Chinese economy. China's economic growth, apart from providing trade and investment opportunities for the NIEs, has also facilitated their industrial restructuring.

For ASEAN, however, it is a different story. At the macro level, the share of the ASEAN-4 in the US market has also increased over the years, suggesting that China's expansion has not been at the expense of the ASEAN economies. But a more detailed analysis in Figure 2.2, by focusing on China's dominant export items of apparel, footwear and household products, brings out China's big jump in the US market vis-à-vis ASEAN's moderate gains, especially after the latter's sharp currency devaluation in recent years. This indicates that China does pose strong competitive pressures for the ASEAN economies in respect of their labour-intensive manufactured exports.

What has made China different from ASEAN is the fact that China has a far larger pool of both skilled as well as non-skilled labour. Furthermore, China has a large domestic market for all sorts of products – high-tech and low-tech – to allow the advantages of economies of scale to be enjoyed. With lower costs generated as a result of high volume production, China is thus able to enjoy its natural cost advantage compared with ASEAN and other smaller developing countries.

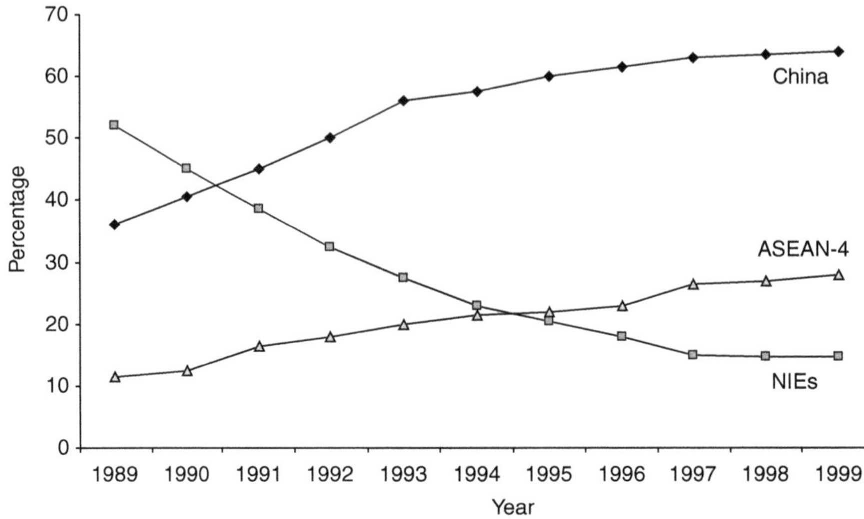

Figure 2.2 China's gain in the US market has been concentrated in apparel, footwear and household products, 1989–1999.

Source: IMF, Direction of Trade Statistics; and US Department of Commerce.

In future, Sino-ASEAN export competition in such non-traditional items as electrical and electronics products will grow even more intense. As illustrated in Figure 2.3, although the electrical and electronic exports of the ASEAN-4 and the NIEs combined are significantly higher than China's, China is rapidly taking on these Asian competitors, as evident in its increasing share of the US market for these products over the years. In 1990, for instance, China's share of the US electronics market was only around 2 per cent. This share increased to 9.7 per cent by 2000, comparable with 8.4 per cent for Taiwan and 9.8 per cent for South Korea and higher than the ASEAN-4 countries – 9.2 per cent for Malaysia, 1.02 per cent for Indonesia, 3.0 per cent for the Philippines, and 4.5 per cent for Thailand. China is set to overtake both the NIEs (which are relocating their production bases to China) and the ASEAN-4 whose export competitiveness will be fast eroded by China's growing strength in these non-traditional items (*Far Eastern Economic Review*, 2001).

The WTO effect

China's basic comparative advantage vis-à-vis other developing Asia-Pacific economies will become even more pronounced after China's accession to the WTO. For ASEAN, China's WTO membership is supposed to bring about both opportunities and challenges. In the longer run, ASEAN economies should benefit from increased access to China's markets. At

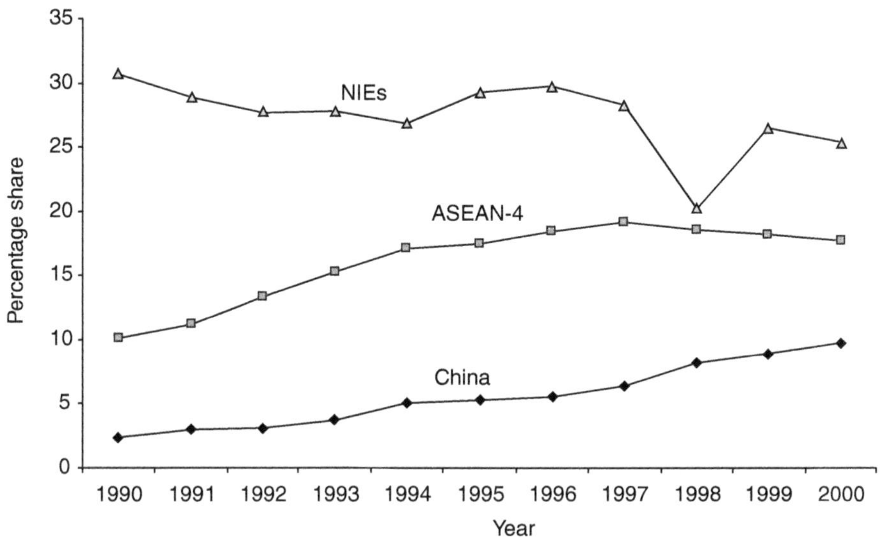

Figure 2.3 East Asian electrical and electronics exports to the US market (%).
Source: US Census Bureau, US Department of Commerce.

their present phase of development, however, China and ASEAN tend to be more competitive than complementary to each other as far as manufactured exports and FDI are concerned. Both China and ASEAN share a great deal of similarity in their export structures and both are economically oriented towards the industrial countries of the West and Japan.

For Japan and other smaller NIEs, as discussed earlier, the shifting comparative advantage forced them to relocate their labour-intensive manufactures to neighbouring economies with lower costs. But China is a rare continental-sized economy with such great diversity that it can contain the evolution of comparative advantage within its own borders. As is already happening, the more developed coastal regions of China are transferring their declining comparative advantage in labour-intensive products to central and western China, currently the focus of China's future development efforts. This means that China can continue for years to flood the world market with low-cost manufactured items even when many parts of China have achieved middle-income status.

Lest anyone should forget this, China actually started to industrialize in the 1950s – China's famous 'Liberation' trucks were rolling out from the Changchun No. 1 Auto Plant back in July 1956 – well ahead of ASEAN and even the NIEs. Consequently, China's industrial base is far larger and longer established than that of any country in ASEAN. Currently, most of China's electronics and high-tech exports are spearheaded by foreign invested enterprises. An increasing share is expected to come from

China's own domestic firms once they have completed their restructuring and upgrading after China's WTO entry.

In 1999, China produced 43 million colour TV sets, 13 million washing machines and 12 million refrigerators (NBS, 2000). Chinese factories must have already acquired the right technology and the right cost structures (i.e. economies of scale) to produce these consumer durables efficiently and cheaply in order to out-compete others (Liu, 2001). After China's accession to WTO, ASEAN will certainly have an economically resurgent China to reckon with, one that is dualistic in nature, capable of producing both low value-added as well as technology- and capital-intensive goods for the world market.

Bibliography

Akamatzu, K. (1962) 'A historical pattern of economic growth in developing countries', *Developing Economics*, 1 (March/August).

Bosworth, B., Collins, S. and Chen, Y.-C. (1995) 'Accounting for differences in economic growth', *Brookings Discussion Papers in International Economics*, 115.

Hu, Z. and Khan, M. (1997) 'Why is China growing so fast', *International Monetary Fun, Economics Issues* No. 8.

Far Eastern Economic Review (2001) 29 March.

Krugman, P. (1994) 'The myth of Asia's miracle', *Foreign Affairs* (November/December).

Liu, G. (2001) 'China's WTO access and the impact on its large manufacturing enterprises', *East Asian Institute Contemporary China Series*, No. 30.

Loungani, P. (2000) 'Comrades competitors? Trade links between China and other East Asian economies', *Finance and Development*, June.

National Bureau of Statistics (NBS, 2000) *China's Statistical Yearbook* Statistical Press (Beijing: Statistical Press).

Statistical Bureau of Guangdong (2000) *Guangdong Statistical Yearbook 2000*.

Wong, J. (1979) *ASEAN Economies in Perspective: A Comparative Study of Indonesia, Malaysia, the Philippines, Singapore and Thailand* (London: Macmillan Press).

World Bank (1994) *The East Asian Miracle* (New York: Oxford University Press).

World Bank (2000–2001) *World Development Report*, various issues (Oxford: Oxford University Press).

World Bank (1997) *China 2020: Development Challenges in the New Century*.

Young, A. (1995) 'The tyranny of numbers: confronting the statistical realities of the East Asian growth experience', *Quarterly Journal of Economics*, 110 (3).

3 China's economic growth and the development of popular understanding and knowledge

Xiaobai Shen

Introduction

This chapter seeks to address the prospects for China's economic development in the twenty-first century, and whether recent progress can be sustained and how it may best be pursued. At the end of the last millennium, many people were predicting that the twenty-first century would be the century of Asia. Many Chinese might well hope that the twenty-first century would be the century of China. However, at the turn of the millennium, things are far from certain. China and her neighbouring economies are grappling with deep structural problems. A variety of sceptical and critical commentaries have emerged, particularly from Western analysts. To assess these conflicting claims it is crucial to produce a comprehensive assessment, underpinned by research and sound evidence.

Most Western scholars agree that China has made some progress, but that big problems remain (Pye, 1999). For example to take the case of political systems, many comment that China's political institutions and constitution have not changed very much but have remained with their main features largely as they were in the 1950s (Burns, 1999; *WenHui Bao*, 1999). In contrast, even the most sceptical Western scholars acknowledge the enormous achievements in economic development in China over the past 50 years, and particularly in the last two decades, and rank the emergence of 'the new China' as among the most important economic developments of the twentieth century (Dernberger, 1999).

Given the challenges China is facing, there is a virtual consensus that problems in both economics and politics are massive. In the economics arena, most notable is the current decline in the rate of growth of the economy. This has resulted from constraints in those very factors that underpinned the rapid growth rates in the early period of China's economic reform. It is associated with the stagnation of domestic demand, the challenges of increasing competition in the export market, shrinking foreign direct investment, unimpressive progress in the transformation of state-owned enterprises, high pressure over financing loss-making state sectors and the insolvency of the banking system.

In the social and political sphere, problems faced by China today may well pose threats to social stability: pressing demands for completion of the social security system, heightened dissatisfaction amongst Chinese people with rampant corruption, smuggling, and tax evasion, the widening gap between the poor and the rich. Worrisome indications include increasing organised crime, mass protests, and an emerging trend of cynicism amongst people in affluent regions.[1] Economic and social reform in the institutional framework is far from completed: the market system has not been fully established; and newly established legislative mechanisms lack effective institutional means and human resources to enforce the law.

While the Chinese government is facing domestic pressure affecting the very stability of society, economic and political pressures from international communities are also increasing in response to the Chinese government's tightened measures against political dissidents and religious groups and also with further trade demands in relation to China's changed status in the World Trade Organisation (WTO). Therefore, the most serious question is whether or not the leaders of the Chinese government can sustain their purpose under pressure from all these fronts and, associated with this, whether the Chinese people will continue to give their support.

Given these factors, even optimistic Western scholars could only comment that: 'Things are never as black or white, as good or as bad, as Westerners tend to expect them to be... The Chinese have a great tradition of muddling through' (Pye, 1999). However, we must ask, how can China muddle through? What paths are possible? Which are best?

This chapter argues that existing approaches used by scholars from different fields are often based on narrow analyses, for example drawing upon a single academic discipline. In particular, we find a separation between programmes of economic reform and discussions of the political system. Equally, analysis and policy prescriptions are often overgeneralised: addressing the country as a whole and usually focused at the macro-level upon economic or social structures. Such analysis seems largely divorced from an understanding of the local operation of organisations, communities and individuals. These segmented views cannot provide a complete picture needed to provide a comprehensive explanation or effective interventions. For example, one of the themes of this chapter concerns the importance of knowledge development and, in particular, the development of the knowledge base, the broader culture and public perceptions. The latter two, for example, are often overlooked and underestimated by economics-based approaches. Many of the prevailing views about China can thus be challenged.

At the start of a new era in which a nation's competitiveness is increasingly knowledge-based, the role of knowledge development in the economic and social development of a nation has become a central focus of many scholars from different fields. Drawing upon recent debates by the

World Bank on knowledge for development and research in the field of technology studies and organisational learning, this chapter suggests that new perspectives are emerging for developing countries such as China to gain competitiveness in global markets. Using notions from technology studies and organisational learning, this chapter discusses some key issues for knowledge development–national strategies for learning and knowledge build-up; knowledge development and supportive institutional infrastructures; and incentives and mass participation. Finally, this chapter focuses on the opportunities for China to develop popular understanding and knowledge in order to speed up and sustain its development in future.

New prospects – knowledge for development

The beginning of a new millennium provokes some reassessments of our civilisation. In particular, some questions arise that may challenge the dominant global paradigm of Western industrialism. The Western pattern of development – the industrial market system – which may have provided material wealth and opportunities to the people of the advanced industrial countries, is a destructive force as well as a stimulus to creative dynamism. Today, as we are increasingly forced to recognise, it has resulted in widespread environmental degradation, man-made climatic change, accumulating toxic wastes, receding forests, diminishing topsoil, expanding deserts and a depleting ozone layer (Clark and Clegg, 1998).[2]

The challenges facing today's world are how to deal with an under-resourced, overpopulated and globally interconnected planet and our realisation that unlimited material progress through economic growth is unsustainable. Clark and Clegg (1998) suggest '*A dematerialisation of the economy* is required, with minimum consumption of energy and primary materials.' Others from different standpoints point to a profound shift in the key forces underlying the dynamics of development of the economic system. Scholars in the management field stress that, in this new era, business is becoming knowledge-based. Developing better information systems is a part of this challenge, while the utilisation of state-of-art knowledge is the critical ingredient for commercial viability. Researchers from technology and innovation studies addressing the interaction between technology and social development point to the critical role of knowledge in innovation – and, in particular, embodied knowledge and expertise. This work distinguishes the roles of local and external knowledge and addresses the contribution of institutional structures and contexts for knowledge exchange and creation (Williams *et al.*, 1998).

The recent advances in China's economy have rested largely upon its success in taking over production processes from the West – particularly in relation to low value-added and mass produced goods in sectors such as toys and textiles. These exploit China's resource of cheap labour. However, the preceding considerations all point to the need to shift from an energy–material–consumption based economy to a 'knowledge economy' and the crucial role of knowledge for development. A recent World Bank debate concludes that there is a growing consensus that the future prosperity and progress of all countries will depend on how people and governments access, interpret, use and create knowledge and information (World Bank, 1999). We shall further argue that a new sophisticated, modern civil society is needed to create collaborative cultures, supportive infrastructures and sensitive evaluation systems. Given these, learning and innovation become key objectives for developing countries, and need to be backed up by the development of thinking and understanding amongst the wider population about relevant social, economic and political issues and knowledge of technology development and its relation with the natural world and rational choices for living our lives.

Therefore, we see new prospects arising in this new era for a developing country such as China, which has the largest population in the world – an enormous potential human resource for knowledge development. However, to take this opportunity, China has to face a number of major challenges:

- formulating strategies for gaining access to global information,
- encouraging mass participation in learning and innovation,
- establishing supportive institutional infrastructures,
- creating incentives for learning and knowledge and thought development.

National strategies for learning and innovation

As noted above, better information systems are a crucial part of a knowledge-based economy. The advent of new information technologies that permit rapid and inexpensive worldwide dissemination of information presents considerable opportunities for developing countries but, by the same token, the barriers are retained for those with limited access to these technologies. In addition, developing countries have poorer institutions to gather and disseminate the information needed for business transactions and other social-development uses.

To overcome these weaknesses, the World Bank report suggests that governments have to play a key role in formulating national strategies. Government policies need to foster the acquisition of knowledge; enhance a country's learning capacities; improve the effectiveness of communications and reduce costs; and strike a balance between tapping global knowledge from abroad and creating local knowledge at home (World Bank, 1999).

> Developing countries should explore all the means available for acquiring knowledge from abroad and creating it locally. They should:

- Find new and better ways of producing goods and services through trade – ever more important as the structure of trade shifts from commodities and simple manufactured goods to increasingly knowledge intensive products
- Work with foreign direct investors that are leaders in innovation, spurring domestic producers to try to match best practice and to tap potential knowledge spillovers.
- Get assess to new proprietary technical knowledge through technology licensing.
- Stimulate domestic innovation and get access to global knowledge through establishing laws and institutions for the protection of intellectual property rights.
- Attract back home talented people who have studied or worked abroad, and
- Promote domestic R&D to make it more responsive to the market.

(World Bank, 1999)

The above points are all important. But the approach of the World Bank does not provide the practical means to help developing countries work out appropriate strategies that are valid for the countries' particular stages of development and contexts. This is because knowledge- and capability-building processes are path dependent and operate cumulatively under the constraints of time, existing knowledge frames, contingencies of economic environment and history, and the resources and channels available for learning. A developing country with limited resources and a large population can neither afford nor achieve all-round changes nor seek to put everything in place in every respect overnight. This mandates in favour of a processual and evolutionary approach that emphasises the role of government in monitoring progress and adjusting policies and practical measures in response to emerging demands.

There are many different kinds of knowledge, e.g. scientific and technical knowledge, management knowledge, knowledge about life and the links with nature. Knowledge can also be categorised into different types, e.g. formal and informal knowledge, public knowledge, external knowledge, indigenous knowledge (Williams *et al.*, 1998). Knowledge is not the same as information. Knowledge embodies the insights, beliefs, expertise and capacities of those who have it. Knowledge can be built up through learning, a process of seeking, evaluating, and interpreting information. Knowledge, once learned, is no longer the same as it was in its original state. Some knowledge (knowledge absorptive capability) is needed in order to evaluate and exploit external knowledge sources. Indigenous knowledge is the basis for further learning.[3]

Many researchers point to a fundamental issue regarding the role of 'indigenous knowledge' and indigenous capabilities in learning, adapting, generating and acting on knowledge (Panos Institute, 1998). A focus on local and indigenous knowledge has two main implications. First, recognition of the role of indigenous knowledge in economic development necessitates paying attention to a wider range of actors – not just management and technical experts – who are an integral part of the economic process within that society. Second such an approach rejects the resort to standardised formulaic policy/strategy 'recipes' and calls instead for a learning perspective, stressing the active involvement of a range of local players, and addressing their particular contexts and contingencies. The policy focus shifts to the social, economic and political factors and institutional structures that are key to such learning. Such perspectives are especially crucial for developing countries, where the roles of indigenous knowledge and capabilities are largely ignored and undervalued and where the main focus is upon a political, managerial, technological and scientific elite. The importance of mass participation in interpreting, evaluating information and decision-making in economic and social life is often neglected. Given this, developing countries ought not only to focus on global knowledge but also to explore indigenous and popular knowledges.

Here, we shall borrow some notions from organisational learning, to see the link between individuals' learning and the learning activities of a whole organisation, in order to achieve synergies within the broader socio-economic framework. The notion of organisational learning has gained widespread recognition since Senge's book, *The Fifth Discipline,* hit the bookstores in 1992, although the concept has been around for several decades (Argyris and Schon, 1978).[4]

To conclude, strategies must integrate the other two key issues we will discuss below: learning activities and the supportive institutional infrastructure; and people's inspirations for learning and development of knowledge and thought.

Knowledge development and supportive institutional infrastructures

Studies of organisational learning show that learning can take many forms. It may involve accelerating learning curves through the institutionalisation of personal knowledge into widespread organisational knowledge, for example through Quality Circles. It may involve introducing behavioural change through trial and error, where actions are checked against their outcomes in order to make subsequent adjustments to the actions so as to improve quality or reduce cycle-time, through continuous improvement (Gherardi, 1997).

Many scholars agree in their emphasis on the role of environmental adaptation, the distinctiveness of organisational learning, and the identification of culture, strategy, structure and the environment as the major sources of innovation that create and reinforce learning (Clark and Clegg,

1998). Organisational learning is the result of learning by individuals, but must be institutionally embedded in the procedures of an organisation (otherwise the learning will remain at the individual level). This requires a culture that is conducive to it.

Levinthal and March (1993) distinguish two ways in which organisations can strive for advantage: *exploitative* or *exploratory* learning. They argue that there has to be a strategy for linking exploratory learning to exploitative learning: the survival of any organisation depends upon it being sufficiently exploitative to ensure current viability and sufficiently exploratory to ensure future viability. Too much exploitation threatens organisational survival by creating a competency trap, where increasingly obsolescent capabilities continue to be elaborated. Too much exploration insufficiently linked to exploitation leads to too many undeveloped ideas and too little distinctive competence.

It is possible to resort to portable, commodified, exogenously developed knowledge. We have to make sure that reliance on such knowledge does not cut us off from sources of exploratory learning. The socio-technical conditions that give rise to exploratory learning are unique and highly contingent upon the features of the social-technical systems that have produced them. Certain systems of education and training, and education/training/work articulation, will offer greater opportunities for exploratory creativity to develop.[5]

The implications of these developments are substantial for those organisations that can achieve exploratory and portable exploitative gains. They are even more substantial for the national system of governance within whose administrative frameworks such exploratory breakthrough may occur. Thus, state strategies for development need to take into account the promotion of both exploratory and exploitative learning and, moreover, strike the balance between them.

In relation to the development of an economy we must look beyond learning at the level of the organisation. An important contribution here has come from evolutionary economists and their concept of 'the learning economy' (Lundvall, 1988, 1992). This stresses the inefficiency of market signals as a source of feedback about product and service innovation, the consequent importance of knowledge exchange between supplier and user (with their respective strengths in understanding technological possibilities and customer requirements and business contexts) and the variety of channels for learning that make up the national system for innovation (e.g. between public sector research and technology supply). The learning economy concept raises issues of crucial concern for this chapter – particularly in relation to the development of industrial goods. When we come to consider consumer rather than industrial goods, there is an important shift in the social setting from the relatively direct forms of supplier–use engagement with intermediate products to the primarily indirect linkages between suppliers and final consumers – particularly in relation to mass-produced commodified consumer goods. Consider the difficulties for individual consumers in getting their voices heard in such a context. In relation, for example, to product quality, this draws attention to a variety of institutions: organisations representing consumer interest, access by consumers to the legal system for redress, the effectiveness of the media in raising issues about product reliability, product information legislation and standards, levels of technical understanding across the general population, the system of industrial and product regulation and its enforcement. Compared with the more advanced economies, developing countries and emerging markets are much more likely to lack such an institutional framework. This is crucially a social and political as well as an economic framework. It is about the effective operation of these institutions and broader accountability, the openness of public debate, freedom of speech and democracy.

The importance of mass participation and incentives

Much of the writing on learning and the knowledge economy operates within a rationalistic model that makes rather simplistic sets of presumptions about the organisation and its members – for example, that all members of the organisation are equally committed to the top management goals. However, a large body of research shows that organisations are highly complex entities and their various members, individually or collectively, may experience different incentives and pressures and perceive different ways of pursuing their interests.

Hodgetts *et al.* (1994) assume that organisation members are responsible, thinking adults who inherently want to do their best. Regardless of whether this assumption is true or false, we agree that human resources are too valuable to waste, and that there is no monopoly on creativity – creative talents and skills may be widely distributed at all levels of an organisation or a society. This may depend on the engagement of organisation members. People will raise important problems and concerns if they feel the organisation or the society will respond appropriately and their voice can be heard. Life and work are more interesting when people feel they are taking part. People take pride in training others and contributing to the development of their organisations, communities or society. Creativity will be encouraged when artificial barriers and political taboos are removed and incentives for participation are generated.

Based on earlier studies on building up technological capabilities in China (Shen, 1999), we argue that a nation's economic growth has always been linked to how well the state mechanism and policies can generate incentives for moving its development toward objectives and how effectively people are engaged in achieving these objectives. China's success in generating productive capability for high technology products has depended not just upon access to new technological knowledge but also, crucially, on recognition of the importance of product quality issues.

Improvements here have rested not only on the skill of the engineers and managers in charge of the production process. Rather, they require more widespread understanding amongst the people participating in the production process and, moreover, across the supply chain of suppliers and customers. Shen's study highlighted the low expectations in relation to quality under the old socialist system amongst producers and consumers. Without pressing demands from customers for sophisticated and high-quality products, there is no need for sophisticated and high-standard producers and designers.

Shen's study showed that building up the technological capabilities of an organisation and a nation requires mass participation. However, the importance of wide participation and of people's inspiration are frequently overlooked.

The past 20 years of economic reforms in China have brought dramatic changes: 200 million people were lifted out of poverty, and the country was caught up in a spirited enjoyment of consumerism, as families became the proud owners of washing machines, television sets, bicycles and, for some, cars. China constitutes the world's largest population of cellular-phone users. The number of Internet users has now reached 10 million, which is doubling every six months – the fastest growth in Asia. By some calculations, China will have the second largest population of web surfers in the world, after the US, by 2005 (McCarthy, 2000). These developments have to be attributed to the fact that the economic reforms greatly liberated people's thinking and their desires to pursue economic gain. 'Getting rich is glorious' (Deng)! This has freed the long-suppressed instincts of the Chinese people who had desired a better material life. 'Smashing the iron rice bowl' – a series of administrative reform measures – allowed organisations to explore a variety of material incentives. People across the country, from rural to urban, from grass-roots labour to high-rank intellectual elite, from civilians to military, became highly motivated. This led to an unprecedented and immense release of energy and contributed to the liberation of social productivity. At the same time, the government policy of opening China up to the world established multiple channels for people to gain access to technical, social and economic knowledge of the world, which began to mobilise the whole populace in a learning process.

These considerations draw our attention to the profound changes in organisations and the broader social setting in different historical contexts in China.

Changing contexts and incentives I – the first 50 years of the PRC

The key role of people's participation and inspiration in economic development can also be noted in the first 30 years of the new People's Republic of China's construction. An article in China News Digest's online publication *Hua Xia Wen Zhai Supplement zk9911b*, 2.11.1999, entitled '50 years, 30 years and 20 years (*Wushi Nian, Sanshi Nian he Ershi Nian*)' reminds us of China's achievement in industrialisation in the first 30 years of the People's Republic – developments that took Great Britain 100 years (De Qiang, 1999). According to these data, for 'major agriculture and industrial products', the growth rate in the first 30 years was higher than in the subsequent 20 years. He argues that the Chinese masses did not enjoy much improvement in living standards because the state kept most of the surplus back for further investment. Other statistics also show a record of impressive economic growth – from 1952 to 1975, China's gross domestic product (GDP) grew at an average annual rate of 6.7 per cent and the secondary sector (industry) increased its share of GDP from 20.9 per cent to 45.7 per cent. Even during the most difficult phases of the Cultural Revolution economic growth did not altogether stop (Xu *et al.*, 1982).

We can see, during that period of time, that although material incentives were largely restricted, people's motivation was extremely high for 'a new society' in which, as Mao proposed, the people are the masters, while the officials are servants; there is no exploitation by capitalists and landlords; and equal rights are promoted between women and men, rural and urban dwellers, intellectuals and labourers. Such an ideal society appealed not only to the Chinese, but also to a large number of people in the rest of the world. Despite criticism and condemnation of political movements, such as the Great Leap Forward and the Cultural Revolution, we have to acknowledge the achievements of a highly motivated populace and, associated with this, their hardwork, creativity and participation, which greatly contributed to the success of the nation in reducing illiteracy, eliminating common diseases, freeing up social productivity, and the construction of a new independent country that was very different from the one it replaced. The economic statistics that indicate the lowest point of economic growth, in 1976, confirm the cynicism that gradually developed in the Cultural Revolution. People's respect for politics, the government and socialist ideology fell to the lowest point in the late-Cultural Revolution.

Changing contexts and incentives II – China's strengths and weaknesses today

Now everyone in China would admit that China is not *Di Da Wu Bo* (a huge land with abundant resources) as the Chinese official propaganda machine used to claim, and instead it has limited resources except for one – the potential human resource of having one fifth of the world's population. Perhaps, at some time, Mao's dream 'the more people, the more aspiration and the more productivity' (*ren duo, reqi gao, ganjing da*), which led to the disastrous consequences of the Great Leap Forward and population explosion, will become true in the era of the knowledge-based economy.

China is an extremely large country. Its size and population alone give it a special position in the world economy and politics. The huge market makes it an extremely attractive arena for many businesses across the world. The sheer size of Chinese markets opens up particular opportunities (which may not be available for smaller developing economies). Of course, Chinese consumers have, for years, been forced to accept poor quality products – with the result that, today, many prefer foreign goods, which they see as assuring good design and high quality. However, customers are not necessarily passive. They can play an active role by selecting what goods they want and even participating in the design of products that can best meet their needs. The case of Genetically Modified foodstuffs in the West today shows clearly that customers' decisions can force large companies to alter their products and shift their strategies of technology development. The environment-consciousness of a market can eventually drive companies to develop more environment-friendly products.

The question remains as to whether China can take advantage of this situation and turn its huge population into a strength. Different strategies and conducts may lead to different outcomes. For example we could draw a dichotomy between two competing strategies.

Strategy 1. Mimicry, whereby China follows Western markets. If Chinese producers and consumers follow the trends of those in the industrialised countries, China will always be a step behind. Regardless of how quick learners they are, Chinese companies will have little chance to overtake, or even catch up, the established competitors in the industrialised world, who are already leaders in the market and who know the market better. Moreover, this fails to take advantage of the base of indigenous knowledge and culture within China – resources that are neglected or even seen as obstacles.

Strategy 2. Development of indigenous markets. In contrast to the above, if Chinese customers are encouraged to make independent decisions with sophisticated choices about what products they want, empowered with institutional networks. The sheer size of the Chinese markets may well drive the direction of the global technology development and design of products, in which case the position of global competitors may be reversed. Moreover, such a strategy builds upon Chinese culture – and Chinese companies may have a better chance to prevail in competition because of their knowledge about local Chinese markets.[6]

However, realities are never as simple as this dichotomy would indicate. Although innovation studies have pointed out the important role of the market, in reality, even in developed countries, the power of customers has not been fully established. In the process of technology development, customers often play passive roles, particularly in relation to mass market commodified products. In this sense, to foster sophisticated customers and empower them to play an active and forceful role is a new challenge for all countries.

To foster such a critical and demanding market, customers need a sophisticated attitude to technology, possessing basic technological knowledge, and access to up-to-date technological information and some kinds of links with those who develop the technology. In the West, technology suppliers are developing more sophisticated knowledge bases about customers and novel kinds of structures to link consumers and to provide feedback. These include not just market research, but techniques more suited to evolving product markets, such as consumer panels, alpha and beta testing of new products etc. However, the institutions and incentives that would allow consumers to become active and participate in decisions about technology development are weak or wholly lacking in China.

Today, a growing number of voices are calling for a 'knowledge economy' in China and highlighting its importance: 'in today's human society, a nation's prospects and fate depend on this. To some extent, this is the critical historical moment, the last opportunity for the Chinese nation' (Yang, 2000). Yang also points to the importance of the development of philosophy, humanities and social sciences, as well as the development of natural sciences and technologies. He suggests that these are a key to understanding why industrial economies were first established in the West.

> The growth of knowledge economy requires a set of basic social conditions bearing individual liberalisation, and man with capacity of independence, free mindset, autonomy.... Without such individuals as evolving units of a society, a knowledge economy is impossible.... High technologies depend on innovation, innovation will not take place without a creative mindset. Peoples' mindset of a nation must surpass the orientation of static, linear, plane, propositional and superstitious, in order to create new knowledge.... Lessons have been drawn from the Chinese history: forbidden zones of thoughts and ideological boundaries have confined Chinese people's creativity, and the development of whole nation.
>
> (Yang, 2000)

A supportive environment and institutional infrastructures are needed, we have argued, to encourage the development of thought and knowledge. However, that is something China has lacked. China is still a relatively poor country with a large number of under-educated peasants and limited educational facilities; and also a long-standing tradition of segregation of intellectuals and labourers, which has set barriers limiting the involvement of the majority of people in the process of knowledge development. Moreover, China lacks an established democratic system and culture that could facilitate the development of knowledge and thought.

However, China also has opportunities provided by the new era of world development; its domestic circumstances; people's intensive experiences of 'socialism' and 'capitalism' in the past 50 years, and its size.

Numerous issues need to be discussed, carefully studied and subject to experiment, as history offers no simple guide or clear pathway allowing China even to muddle through. For example, how can China push forward the reforms and democracy without tipping over the balance of stability? This will depend upon establishing effective dialogue between the government and the people.

One important question is whether to introduce a western-style democratic system based upon multiparty elections. The experience of the developing and former socialist countries that have adopted the Western system provides important cautionary lessons – particularly the pitiful condition of Russia, and even the difficulties in East Germany, which still lags far behind, despite all the help its has received from a prosperous West Germany. The so-called newly democratised Russia was highly praised by the West. However, as we know, Russia's reforms were a catastrophe. Democracy has not been installed by merely introducing multiparty elections. As Alexander Solzhenitsyn recently noted,

> (The) state Duma is not a collection of people's representatives.... Now, a couple of guys who get together in their kitchen and found a party can take part in the Duma elections. Half the deputies enter the Duma with that sort of party list, and they dominate the other half – the people who were really directly elected.... Millions of Russian are blocked by a wall of administrative and bureaucratic arbitrariness. They have no one to complain to; no court protects their rights.
>
> (The *Guardian*, 18 March 2000, p. 1)

It is evident that adopting the western political system can guarantee neither a nation's democratisation nor its economic and social development. It has been suggested that simply adopting a political system from other countries will not work for China, given the historical experience of the failure of liberal democracy as a political system in China (Lindau and Cheek, 1998). For example, since the late nineteenth century, market liberalisation emphatically did not coincide with, or promote, democratisation. In the late Qing period, reforms that sought to revive the failing dynasty through market liberalisation and state support of industrialisation did not bring democracy. In the Republic since 1911, whether under Sun Yat-sen (Sun Yixian) or under Chang Kai-shek (Jiang Jieshi), although the government stressed its liberal democratic trappings in order to curry favour with the United States, these efforts did not work either.

The Western democratic political system itself has been evolving over time, and has progressed and flourished well, hand in hand with the development of western philosophy, humanities and social sciences and people's thought. However, it would be a guaranteed failure if today China sought simply to mirror such a system. What China needs is a political system that matches the state of the development of its people's thought, is compatible with current internal and external circumstances and, moreover, which can further evolve over time.

The Chinese will have to engage with, and overcome, the weaknesses inherited from their culture. For example, its traditions never set much store upon the rule of law, relying instead on a mix of moral ideals and extensive interpersonal obligations. Chinese individualism is based on a pragmatic scepticism towards one another, rather than an understanding of the individual's responsibilities and rights in society. Chinese collectivism provides strict social boundaries, which, on the one hand, operate as a constraint, preventing individuals from independent and autonomous expression, and, on the other, act as a safety net, protecting individuals who follow the majority path from blame when things go wrong. These characteristics can turn individuals into angels; but also devils in certain circumstances. Mao's ultimate failure in the Cultural Revolution was a case in point. Although Mao was a most effective leader who successfully motivated the Chinese people to go down the road and shape themselves to be communist 'new men', the process was equally rooted in China's history and contemporary political structure. His formula of combining mass participation with proletarian dictatorship ignored the very weakness of individual rights and responsibilities in China. Eventually, a highly motivated populace was driven to the extreme where almost everyone was a victim as well as a tormentor. This turned a mass participative cultural and political movement into a great atrocity in Chinese history.

Despite these weaknesses, the recent historical experiences of different paths of development provide the Chinese with great potential to face the new challenge – to build up a modern civil society. The recent history of humiliation by foreign invasion in the centuries before revolution makes the Chinese fully aware of the importance of stability and a strong State. Fifty years of intense experiences of different models of 'socialist' and 'capitalist' development provide tools for the Chinese to compare the advantages and disadvantages of different social and economic systems. Socialism has provided the Chinese with strong sense of 'equality' and 'social fairness'.[7] The current openness of China to the Western world has brought in many influences from Western civilisation. Moreover, modern information technology has provided the Chinese with adequate means of communication, allowing the rapid and easy exchange of information between individuals and organisations.

Conclusions

We see growing recognition in China of the need to move towards a knowledge-based economy in the face of global competition and other (e.g. environmental) factors. In this new era, new challenges and opportunities arise for a developing country, such as China, to leap forward by focusing on the knowledge development of the nation.

Although 'the knowledge economy' sounds like a buzzword, we can see that the role of knowledge in the economic and social development of a nation has become a central focus of many scholars from different fields. The physical means and institutional framework provided by a country for its people to gain access to global knowledge are crucial factors. Because knowledge development is a complex process, we need to distinguish different types of knowledge and to study effective ways of building up different kinds of knowledge through learning. Different kinds of learning have different outcomes. For example, exploitative and exploratory learning are both necessary for individuals, organisations and a country. Distinguishing these two can help us understand what institutional framework and incentives are needed for promoting these two learning processes and how to balance them.

Previous studies of technology development suggest that mass participation in, and incentives for, learning are key. Retrospective examination of 50 years of economic growth in People's Republic of China confirms the important link between economic growth and mass participation in learning and the development of people's knowledge.

Concerning the prospects for China to embark on a knowledge-oriented development path, we see many weaknesses that are rooted in Chinese history and tradition as well as in the current social and political system. In the history of Chinese civilisation, humanism has never been well established, with the result that Chinese collectivism lacks a rationale based on understanding the individual's responsibilities and rights within the society. Associated with this, the social and political systems in Chinese history have never been able to establish a sophisticated mechanism, which on the one hand protects individual rights and allows independent and autonomous expression, while on the other it protects public interests from intrusion by any aggressive individual activities.

As to overcoming these very weaknesses, the preceding discussion allows us to conclude that 'all-out Westernisation' will not work in China. At best, the outcome would be China merely following the West, always a step behind; at worst, it could lead to tipping the balance of the stability of society. China has to work out its own way to build up a sophisticated civil society, which allows the individual and the nation to develop hand in hand. Chinese government policies should help people gain access to global information and knowledge; create incentives to encourage development of knowledge and thought; and formulate institutional infrastructures that support ever-wider participation by people from different social groups in the management of their community, and in the social, economic and political development of the nation.

This discussion points to one potential strength of China – the Chinese people. However, it requires the Chinese government and its populace to take the initiative in order to transform the sheer size of the population into enormous human resources. The government has a major role to play in helping people gain access to global knowledge, and at the same time, in vigorously promoting learning and the development of thought and knowledge. Knowledge development is a complex process of learning and building up capacity, and both global-knowledge and indigenous-knowledge development are necessary and valuable. Because indigenous knowledge has often been undervalued in developing countries, it needs particular attention in a developing country such as China. Balancing exploitative and exploratory learning and individual and organisational learning also needs attention. Because learning at individual, organisational, and national level may need different features in terms of the broader socio-economic and institutional context, different strategies are needed that can lead to better outcomes at different levels.

To summarise, economic development relies on scientific and technological development, innovation and creativity. To the extent that the thinking and creativity of the entire nation is liberated, it will create enormous energy to lift social productivity and to contribute to the economy.

The Chinese believe in the importance of 'timing' and 'conditions'. Now the time and conditions are right: new perspectives are looming for a developing country such as China in the era of the knowledge economy; pressures from external and internal socio-economic and political environment require both the Chinese government and the Chinese people to react.

The government's controversial and changing attitudes toward political reform and its retreat from tolerating free expression and calls for political reform clearly shows the dilemma it has been facing – between social stability and political reform, which are both in acute demand. The party's pragmatic balancing of market and central planning is legitimated through imprecise and contradictory formulations such as 'a Socialist market economy with Chinese characteristics'. As a result, the Party lacks an articulate 'ideology' that can pull the nation together with a clear collective sense of direction, and the government lacks alternative means for dealing with unstable outcomes arising from economic reforms and popular political activities. However, the Chinese government has rather limited room to manoeuvre. There is little alternative to pushing forward the reforms that will democratise the society, in order to grab the opportunity provided by the new era of world development. Clearly, even top leaders know that political repression will not work in the long run and that further reforms are necessary.

Chinese intellectuals have taken some initiatives. Since China has already made headway in providing a basic economic livelihood (Goldman, 1999), the people's search for non-material satisfactions has become salient. Amongst intellectuals, there is a resurgence of the discourses about liberalism which were introduced in the early decades of the twentieth century. Some point out that one could not act as a 'citizen' unless one also had political and civil rights. Re-evaluation of, and gaining deeper insight into, the Cultural Revolution has brought together scholars in China and overseas. Their attempts at an in-depth study of the causes, phenomenon and consequences of the Cultural Revolution provoke further re-thinking of the legitimacy of Chinese values and the views of the neo-conservatives who insisted that civil and political rights were alien to China.

At the same time, advocates of the 'knowledge economy', many of whom are highly placed intellectuals, have called for liberating people's thought for the sake of China's competitiveness in the face of new trends and challenges in world development.

Most importantly, Chinese people want stability and want economic growth; they want peaceful unification with Taiwan and to solve the problem with Tibet. The Chinese people want national self-esteem, they want to be respected by the rest of the world. The way to achieve these things is to free their mindset, engage in learning and knowledge development, and participate in the process of building a modern civil society. However, the difficulties are immense and the road toward a fully modern nation-state may well be long.

Notes

1 Not to mention problems for the Chinese national project such as Taiwan, Tibet, the separatist movement in the west and conflicts between different ethnic groups.

2 Although an increasing number of peoples and organisations in the world have recognised the problems caused by current patterns of unsustainable economic growth, many others still cling to outdated world views and established production and consumption patterns. Whereas many in industrialised countries are beginning to take environmental problems seriously as their material standard of living improves, in developing and underdeveloped countries environmental issues are mainly a matter of concern amongst scholars, the social elite, and better-off segments of the population, as the bulk of the population is still struggling to survive and maintain their basic living conditions. With its size and speed of industrialisation, China is potentially one of the largest sources of pollution. If China, with one fifth of the world's population. follows the path of the West, and every Chinese household possesses just one car, the pollution from vehicle exhaust emissions will make a substantial contribution to global warming. The Chinese government has committed itself to combat environmental problems; however, this will requires people's support – and in turn requires greater public understanding of the nature and importance of environmental problems.

3 Equally, exogenous knowledge can become endogenised and provide the basis for further local learning; local learning can blur the boundaries between endogenous and exogenous knowledge (Shen, 1999).

4 Senge (1992), using cybernetic terms, distinguished 'single-loop' or 'double-loop' learning. Single-loop learning feeds back on to the present competencies and routines of knowledge and their application in order to improve an existing function. Double-loop learning only occurs when the new acquisition of knowledge has gone through elaboration, development and diffusion throughout the organisation, which transforms the existing competencies. To achieve this

requires activities at individual level; activities that are not just sensitive to the social and organisational conditioning of thought.

5 The typical schooling system of rote learning, characteristic of much of East Asia, is hardly conducive to exploratory forms of innovation. Throughout East Asia this is a matter of considerable policy concern.

6 It has been suggested that Japanese competitive success, particularly in areas such as consumer electronics, rests to no small degree on the indigenous market comprising enthusiastic but demanding consumers.

7 Another comparison that it may be instructive to make is between progress in the past half century by China and India, countries that were arguably at comparable developmental states after the end of the colonial period. India installed the Western political system on independence in August 1997. The average expectancy of the Chinese male is 69, and Chinese woman 71 years, whereas the average expectancy of Indian people is 62 years. Since 1960, the average lifespan of Chinese people has increased by 20 years. China's adult literacy rate has reached 81 per cent, while India's rate is only 52 per cent. India's GDP per head was $320 in 1994, while China was $530 (De Qiang, 1999).

Bibliography

Anon. (2000) 'Lun Zhishi Jingji (Comments on Knowledge Economy)', *People's Daily Overseas Edition*, 17 February.

Argyris, C. and Schon, D. (1978) *Organisational Learning* (Reading MA: Addison-Wesley).

Burns, J.P. (1999) 'The People's Republic of China at 50: national political reform', *China Quarterly*, 159, June.

Clark, T. and Clegg, S. (1998) *Changing Paradigms: The Transformation of Management Knowledge for the 21st Century* (London: Harper Collins).

Clegg, S.R. and Hardy C. (eds) (1996) *Studying Organisation – Theory & Method* (London: Thousand Oaks, and New Delhi: Sage Publications).

De Qiang (1999) 'Wushi Nian, Sanshi Nian he Ershi Nian (50 years, 30 years and 20 years)', CND online magazine, *Huaxia Wenzhai Suplement, zk9911b*, www.cnd.org.

Dernberger, R.F. (1999) 'The People's Republic of China at 50: the economy', *China Quarterly*, 159, June.

Deluges, G. and Weiermair, K. (eds) (1981) *Management Under Differing Value Systems – Political, Social and Economic Perspectives in a Changing World* (Berlin and New York: Walter de Gruyter).

Gamer, R.E. (1999) *Understanding Contemporary China* (London and Colorado: Lynne Rienner).

Gherardi, S. (1997) 'Organisational learning'. In A. Sorge and M. Warner (eds), *International Encyclopaedia of Business and Management: the Handbook of Organisational Behaviour* (London: International Thomson Business Press).

Goldman, M. (1999) Politically-engaged intellectuals in the 1990s', *China Quarterly*, 159, June.

Hodgetts, R.M., Luthans, F. and Lee, S.M. (1994) 'New paradigm organisations: from total quality to learning to world-class', *Organisation Dynamics*, 22(3), 5–19.

Levinthal, D.A. and March, G. (1993) 'The myopia of learning', *Strategic Management Journal*, 14, 95–112.

Li, Z. (1987) *Zhongguo Xiandai Sixiangshi Lun* (*A Review of Chinese Contemporary History of Thoughts*) (Beijing: East Publishing House).
Lindau, J.D. and Cheek, T. (eds) (1998) *Market Economics and Political Change – Comparing China and Mexico* (Maryland and Oxford: Rowaman & Littlefield).
Lundvall, B.-A. (1988) 'Innovation as an interactive process: from user–producer interaction to the national system of innovation'. In G. Dosi *et al.* (eds), *Technical Change and Economic Theory* (London: Pinter).
Lundvall, B.-A. (1992) *National Systems of Innovation: Towards a System of Innovation and Interactive Learning* (London: Pinter).
McCarthy, T. (2000) 'China's internet gold rush', *Time*, 155(8).
Panos Institute (1998) 'Information, knowledge and development', A series of Panos perspective papers, online documents at http://www.worldbank.org/, 10.1998.
Pye, L.W. (1999) An overview of 50 years of the People's Republic of China: some progress, but big problems remain', *China Quarterly*, 159, June.
Senge, P.M. (1992) *The Fifth Discipline* (London: Century Business, New York: Doubleday).
Shen, X. (1999) *The Chinese Road to High Technology: a Study of Telecommunications Switching Technology in the Economic Transition* (Basingstoke and London: Macmillan, and New York: St. Martin's Press).
Solzhenitsyn, A. (2000) 'Russia's darkest night of the soul' (interview), *The Guardian,* 18 March 1–2.
Svensson, M. (1996) *The Chinese Conception of Human Rights – the Debate on Human Rights in China, 1989–1949* (Sweden: Studentlitteratur's printing office, Lund University).
Wenhui Bao (1999) Hong Kong, 16 January.
Williams, R., Faulkner, W. and Fleck, J. (eds) (1998) *Exploring Expertise* (London: Macmillan).
World Bank (1999) 'Knowledge for development', *World Development Report* 1998/99 (Washington, DC World Bank).
Xu, D. *et al.* (1982) *China's Search for Economic Growth: The Chinese Economy Since 1949* (Beijing: New World Press).
Yang, Z. (2000) *Exposition of Knowledge Economy* (Lun Zhishi Jingji), *People's Daily Overseas Edition*, 17 February.

Part II

Industry, agriculture and the financial market

4 China's telecommunications industry

Poised to grow after WTO

John Wong and Chee Kong Wong

Introduction

China has emerged as the world's second largest telecommunications market after the United States as a result of phenomenal growth in the 1990s brought about by reform, deregulation and development of communications technology. Restructuring of the industry saw the break-up of the dominant operator, China Telecom, and the entry of new telecoms players, thereby opening up the telecommunications market to competition. WTO accession has further put strong competitive pressures on domestic telecoms corporations. To ensure growth in the age of information technology, China must pay greater attention to expansion of the wireless network. Ultimately, in opening up the telecoms industry, China faces two dilemmas. First, will the country's security be compromised as it allows freer access to information? Second, will greater emphasis on market orientation hinder the development of an integrated nationwide telecoms network and undercut the country's objective of providing universal service to all parts of the country?

Explosive growth in the 1990s

China is now the world's second largest telecommunications market after the United States, in terms of network capacity and number of subscribers. By the end of 2001, China has installed almost 200 million lines, with 179 million fixed-line phone subscribers (*China Economic News*, 2002). It has also emerged as the world's largest mobile phone market, with mobile phone subscriptions at 145 million in 2001, after having topped the US in July that year (MII website, 25 January 2002). The penetration rate (total number of fixed-line and mobile telephones per 100 persons) now stands at about 25 per cent while teledensity (number of main telephone lines per 100 residents) has reached 15 per cent (Table 4.1).

China has targeted itself to be the world's largest telecommunications market in terms of network capacity in five years. According to Wu Jichuan, China's Minister of Information Industry (MII), the industry will grow at 20 per cent per year over the next five years to achieve a

Table 4.1 Penetration rate and teledensity in China, 1985–2001

Year	*Penetration rate*	*Teledensity*
1985	0.60	
1986	0.67	
1987	0.75	
1988	0.86	
1989	0.98	
1990	1.11	
1991	1.29	
1992	1.61	
1993	2.20	
1994	3.20	
1995	4.66	3.36
1996	6.33	4.49
1997	8.11	5.68
1998	10.53	7.00
1999	13.00	8.64
2000	17.96	12.00
2001	25.00	15.42

Sources: *China Statistical Yearbook* and *Yearbook of China Transportation and Communications*, various issues. The 2000 and 2001 figures for penetration rate are calculated based on the number of fixed line and mobile phone subscribers per 100 persons in China's total population.

penetration rate of 40 per cent, with total telecommunications subscribers (fixed line and mobile) surpassing 500 million by 2005 (*China Daily*, 17 February 2001). By then, the number of mobile phone users is expected to hit 300 million (*South China Morning Post*, 28 March 2001).

The build-up of the telecoms infrastructure in China since the mid-1990s has simply been astonishing. Switchboard capacity doubled from 50 million lines in 1994 to 100 million in 1997 (Table 4.2). The number of fixed-line phone subscribers climbed from 11 million in 1992 to 55 million in 1996, and then shot up to above 100 million in 1999 – a tenfold jump in seven years (Table 4.3 and Figure 4.1).

Since the mid-1990s, China's telecoms growth has also been driven by the expansion of mobile telephony. There were only 1.6 million mobile subscribers in 1994, but this increased to 6.9 million in 1996, passed the 20 million mark in 1998 and surpassed 85 million in 2000 (Table 4.4), an eighty-fold increase over a short span of six years! Symbolic of changes in this sector is the country's mobile phone code growing to 11 digits by July 1999. Such an increase amplifies the code capacity from 50 million to about 500 million, which should meet the country's demand by 2010 (*China Daily*, 22 July 1999).

Driven by the worldwide drive towards deregulation and technological progress, the telecommunications markets in Asia, especially Japan and the NIEs (Taiwan, Hong Kong, Singapore and South Korea), have indeed experienced dramatic growth during the 1980s (*Far Eastern Economic*

Table 4.2 Local switchboard capacity in China, 1985–2001

Year	*Local switchboard capacity*	
	Million lines	*% change*
1985	6.134	
1986	6.724	9.62
1987	7.739	15.10
1988	8.872	14.64
1989	10.347	16.63
1990	12.318	19.05
1991	14.922	21.14
1992	19.151	28.34
1993	30.408	58.78
1994	49.262	62.00
1995	72.036	46.23
1996	92.912	28.98
1997	112.692	21.29
1998	138.237	22.67
1999	153.461	11.01
2000	179.000	16.64
2001	199.764	11.60

Sources: *China Statistical Yearbook* and *Yearbook of China Transportation and Communications*, various issues. For 2000 and 2001 figures, see Ministry of Information Industry website, http://www.mii.gov.cn/.

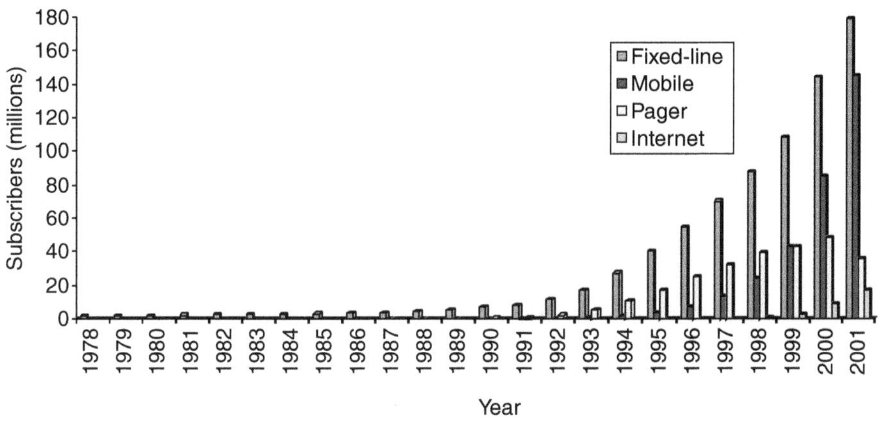

Figure 4.1 China's telecommunications services subscribers (millions), 1978–2001.

Review, 1990). Similar factors have been responsible for the phenomenal growth of the Chinese telecoms industry in the 1990s. For China, its rapid economic expansion, which in turn has stimulated demand for telecoms services and the opening up of the market for greater competition, has provided an additional impetus for its telecoms growth.

The rapid growth of the telecoms industry has also spurred the rise of

Table 4.3 Number of fixed-line phone subscribers in China, 1978–2001

Year	*Fixed-line phone subscribers*	
	No. of subscribers (million)	*% change*
1978	1.925	
1979	2.033	5.61
1980	2.141	5.31
1981	2.221	3.74
1982	2.343	5.49
1983	2.508	7.04
1984	2.775	10.65
1985	3.120	12.43
1986	3.504	12.31
1987	3.907	11.50
1988	4.727	20.99
1989	5.680	20.16
1990	6.850	20.60
1991	8.451	23.37
1992	11.469	35.71
1993	17.332	51.12
1994	27.295	57.48
1995	40.706	49.13
1996	54.947	34.99
1997	70.310	27.96
1998	87.421	24.34
1999	108.716	24.36
2000	144.000	32.46
2001	179.034	24.33

Sources: *China Statistical Yearbook* and *Yearbook of China Transportation and Communications*, various issues. For 2000 and 2001 figures, see Ministry of Information Industry website, http://www.mii.gov.cn/.

the high-tech sector, in at least two ways. First, China's Internet sector has exploded (Table 4.5), with telecoms service providers such as China Mobile and China Unicom offering Internet services such as WAP (Wireless Application Protocol) networks. Second, the convergence of the telecoms industry with the IT industry has, in turn, resulted in greater demand for high-tech products and services in the country.

Reform and corporatization

In the 1980s, faced with a 'shortage economy', China focused primarily on industrial growth. The telecoms sector was regarded as 'seriously backward', with huge supply and demand gaps constraining economic growth. To remove such bottlenecks, the development of the industry was heavily supported (*Yearbook of China Transportation and Communications*, 1996). Up to 1994, the Ministry of Post & Telecommunications (MPT) was the sole regulatory and operating power over the public telecoms network

Table 4.4 Number of mobile phone subscribers in China, 1988–2001

Year	*Mobile phone subscribers*	
	No. of subscribers (million)	*% change*
1988	0.0032	
1989	0.0098	206.25
1990	0.0183	86.73
1991	0.0475	159.56
1992	0.177	272.63
1993	0.639	261.01
1994	1.568	145.38
1995	3.629	131.44
1996	6.853	88.84
1997	13.233	93.10
1998	23.863	80.33
1999	43.300	81.45
2000	85.260	96.91
2001	144.812	69.85

Sources: *China Statistical Yearbook* and *Yearbook of China Transportation and Communications*, various issues. For 2000 and 2001 figures, see Ministry of Information Industry website, http://www.mii.gov.cn/.

Table 4.5 Number of Internet subscribers in China, 1995–2001

Year	*Internet subscribers*	
	No. of subscribers (million)	*% change*
1995	0.0072	
1996	0.0357	394.27
1997	0.1602	349.22
1998	0.6768	322.58
1999	3.0145	345.44
2000	9.1300	202.87
2001	17.364	90.19

Sources: *China Statistical Yearbook* and *Yearbook of China Transportation and Communications*, various issues. For 2000 and 2001 figures, see Ministry of Information Industry website, http://www.mii.gov.cn/.

in China. The network expansion and development goals were then based on China's periodic five-year plans rather than on consumer demand.

During this period, the telecoms market was initially supply-constrained due to low teledensity and inadequate infrastructure (Lu, 2000). Subsequent demand-driven growth was primarily induced by investments in the telecoms infrastructure aimed at accumulating capacity. The industry invested only 5 billion yuan in 1990 and 35 billion in 1993, in contrast to the more than 100 billion in 1997 and 200 billion in 2000 (Figure 4.2). China Telecom (formerly known as the Directorate General of Telecom

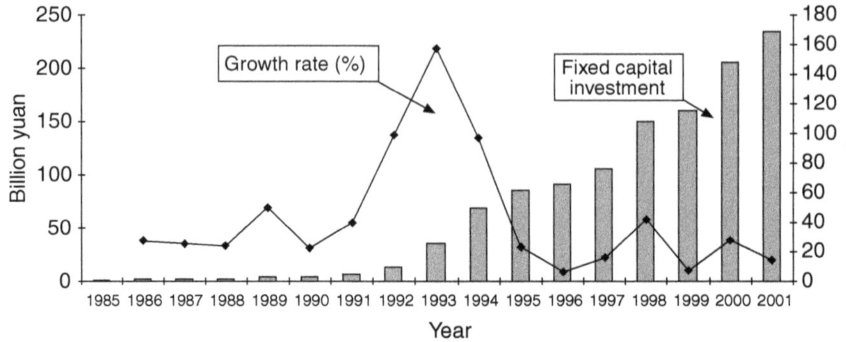

Figure 4.2 Fixed capital investment in China's telecommunications sector, 1985–2001.

within the MPT) was the monopoly operator, a position it held for more than four decades. Even after the 1994 entry of China Unicom, which was only able to capture less than 5 per cent market share, China's telecoms industry was still not open to serious competition.

In the meantime, however, pressures were mounting. As market reform took shape after the late 1980s, the MPT was under increasing pressure to open up for greater competition (Harwit, 1998). Prior to the deregulation of the mid-1990s, there were several specialized networks maintained by different ministries or government bureaux (Mueller and Tan, 1997). These included the People's Liberation Army (PLA), State Radio Regulatory Committee (SRRC), Ministry of Broadcast, Film and Television (MBFT), Ministry of Electronic Industry (MEI), Ministry of Railways (MOR), Ministry of Electric Power (MEP), China Academy of Science (CAS) and State Education Commission (SEC). Tensions between the ministries eventually prompted the government to reorganize the Chinese telecoms market in the mid-1990s. Understandably, these government bureaux were reluctant to give up control over their own telecoms networks, even though the central authorities were keen to bring their various networks (e.g. the PLA, the aerospace industry and provincial interest groups) under MPT control (*Far Eastern Economic Review*, 7 March 1991).

For instance, the MEI's interests gradually came into direct conflict with those of MPT, as the MEI was in charge of the electronics industry and responsible for the manufacturing of electronic systems and equipment, including telecoms equipment. In 1992, the MEI, MEP and MOR jointly proposed to the State Council the establishment of China United Telecommunications Corporation (Unicom/Lian Tong). The birth of China Unicom was thus a result of high-level 'lobbying' by a political coalition formed by the MEI, the MEP and the MOR (He, 1994).

The need to end the fragmentation in the country's telecoms industry received added urgency with worldwide deregulation and rapid technological progress. In line with state-owned enterprises (SOE) reform, the telecoms industry had to be run like a market-oriented modern corporation. The structure of China's telecoms market thus began to undergo some changes in 1994, with the establishment of new corporations – namely, China Unicom and Jitong Communication Corporation – to compete with the dominant operator, China Telecom.

Jitong, formally registered in June 1993, was organized under the MEI and more than 20 other shareholders, comprising state-owned enterprises and research institutes in Beijing, Guangzhou, Shanghai and Shenzhen. Its primary functions were to set up joint ventures with overseas companies in communications research and product development, the building of local trunk radio, paging and cellular networks, and the running of public data and value-added network services in China (Ure, 1994). Structural change, designed to free local telecoms operators from provincial and central regulators, was also supposed to put competitive pressures on the monopolistic China Telecom, strengthen China Unicom's infrastructure and induce more foreign investment to the sector (*China Economic Review*, 1999).

It was against this background that China's telecoms industry began the process of corporatization in the mid-1990s. To meet the challenge of competition, China's local telecoms enterprises modernized their management in line with the practices spelt out in the Company Law of the country. In April 1995, China Telecom became a legal entity after having formally registered with the State Administration of Industry and Trade (Liang *et al.*, 1998). China Telecom has since become an autonomous enterprise with an accounting and personnel system independent from the MPT.

China's telecoms sector underwent further restructuring after 1999, mainly with the break-up of China Telecom to form four separate companies (China Telecom Group, China Mobile Telecom Group Corp, China Paging Telecom Group Corp and China Satellite Telecom Group Corp) serving different functions, namely, fixed-line, mobile, paging and satellite operations respectively. In May 2000, the telecoms industry saw another round of revamping with the MII's arrangement for China Mobile (Group) Corp to acquire the 43 per cent stake in China Telecom (Hong Kong) (CTHK) from the parent company, China Telecom (Group) Corp, thus becoming the 100 per cent owner of CTHK. The revamp also saw China Telecom's name changed to China Mobile (HK) Corp (*South China Morning Post*, 15 May 2000).

Including China Unicom, there were then five large self-supporting and independently operating entities competing in China's telecoms market. The paging sector of China Telecom, with the help of government intervention, has already merged with China Unicom, strengthening the latter carrier, which also now has the approval to expand in mobile and internet telephony (*Beijing Review*, 21 June 1999). The entry of a sixth operator, China Netcom Corporation (CNC), in April 1999, as well as China's newest and seventh telecom operator, China Railway Telecom (or China

Railcom, which started operations on 1 March 2001), further opened up China's telecoms market to competition.

China Netcom (CNC), which has Jiang Mianheng, the son of Chinese President Jiang Zemin, on its board, was set up by the Shanghai Municipal Government, the Chinese Academy of Sciences, State Administration for Radio, Film and Television (SARFT) and the Ministry of Railways (MOR). It was created to provide high-speed voice and data service in 15 cities, and can connect with 70 countries (*South China Morning Post*, 15 December, 1999). China Railcom was set up by the Ministry of Railways, with the MOR holding 51 per cent of its equity, and 13 local railway companies holding the rest, to compete with China Telecom in the fixed-line business. It will provide domestic long-distance calls, fax and telegram services, network leasing and Internet connections and content.

As part of an effort to deepen economic reform, China has intensified its campaign against monopoly, the foci of which are the telecoms, power, railway and aviation sectors. In preparation for foreign competition following China's accession to the WTO, the telecoms industry headed for further restructuring, with plans to break up or merge the telecoms players into four major operators, namely China Telecom, China Netcom, China Unicom and China Mobile, each having licences to provide integrated telecoms services (*Business China*, 5 November 2001).

The plan for restructuring China Telecom was mulled over in May 2001 when three suggestions were proposed. The first was to split China Telecom into two regional companies, to be based in north and south China respectively. The second was to split it into three companies along product lines. The third plan, considered least likely, called for transferring ownership of the phone network to a new state company while China Telecom would still remain as an operator (*Asian Wall Street Journal*, 22 May 2001). However, such plans were later denied by the MII (*Mingbao*, 24 May 2001). Only one plan has been revealed, that is, the State Council's announcement in December 2001 to split China Telecom formally along geographical lines, as mentioned above.

According to the approved plan, announced by MII Minister Wu Jichuan, the northern firm will merge unlisted carriers China Netcom and Jitong Communications into the renamed China Netcom Group. It will run China Telecom's networks in the ten provinces, municipalities and autonomous regions north of the Yellow River, i.e. Hebei, Shanxi, Inner Mongolia, Liaoning, Jilin, Heilongjiang, Henan and Shandong, as well as the cities of Beijing and Tianjin. The southern firm, on the other hand, will remain as China Telecom and operate the telecoms networks in the remaining 21 provinces and autonomous regions located south of the Yellow River and in the north-west region (*People's Daily*, 17 October 2001).

To ensure universal access to services, both firms will be allowed to build local telephone networks and offer local fixed-line phone services in each other's regions on the condition that access to their respective local networks be fair and mutually beneficial. In addition, the new China Telecom will be allowed to use 70 per cent of the original parent's network capacity, with the remainder allocated to the new China Netcom, thus preserving new China Telecom's near-monopoly on fixed-line services.

The break-up plan has sparked debates over whether it would bring in greater competition to the telecoms sector. Even though the aim of breaking up China Telecom is to inject more competition into the telecoms sector, some have argued that the merger of China Netcom and Jitong will lead to Netcom becoming a new monopolistic telecoms operator. Such a move would be in contradiction to the reform campaign against monopoly. The break-up of China Telecom would further weaken the dominant operator's competitiveness and lead to the possible danger of it being squeezed out by foreign telecoms giants. However, Zhang Xin from the Chinese Academy of Social Sciences (CASS) agreed that allowing the north and south telecoms companies to offer services in each other's network will prevent the emergence of a new monopolistic situation (EIU, 2000).

Zhou Qiren, a telecoms specialist from Beijing University, has offered an alternative view. He questions whether the split of China Telecom will really introduce competition, arguing, furthermore, that any reckless move to split the giant operator will incur huge costs if real competition cannot be realized. He suggests that the state should instead give preferential policies to encourage more operators to enter the industry and challenge the market's 'big brother'.

As a sign of enhancing competitiveness and transparency of the telecoms industry in preparation for eventual WTO entry, the State Council has set up a new cabinet-level body, known as the State Council Information Management Committee, to be headed by Premier Zhu Rongji, with MII Minister Wu Jichuan as one of the members. The task of this commission would be to halt the ministerial in-fighting – between the MII and its rivals such as the SARFT, the Ministry of Foreign Trade and Economic Cooperation (MOFTEC) and the MOR – the consequence of which is the slowing pace of telecoms reform.

China Telecom currently has 80 per cent of China's total network capacity. By 2000, China had a total telecoms revenue of 307.4 billion yuan, of which China Telecom earned 170.9 billion (55.6 per cent), China Mobile 111.6 billion (36.3 per cent), and China Unicom 24.5 billion (8.0 per cent) (*China Daily*, 23 March 2000). This could change with competition from China Railcom in the fixed line business and the further break-up of the dominant operator. Planning to offer fixed-line phone services for 10 per cent less than what China Telecom is offering, China Railcom is also expected to capture more than a quarter of China Telecom's fixed-line market share within two years (*Asiaweek*, 2001).

Corporatization has also allowed China's major telecoms players, although still essentially state-owned enterprises, to raise capital from more diverse sources. The first is the raising of equity funds through public listing.

Accordingly, China Unicom launched an IPO (initial public offering) in June 2000 to raise US$5 billion – the biggest ever by a mainland company – on the Hong Kong and New York stock exchanges. China Unicom also procured loans of 10 billion and 1.6 billion yuan from the China Development Bank and the Bank of China, respectively, in March 2000 to finance its construction of mobile and digital communication networks.

In February 2001, China Netcom became the first Chinese telecoms operator to make direct use of foreign capital when it signed a US$325 million equity deal – equivalent to 12 per cent of its total assets – with Rupert Murdoch's News Corps and Goldman Sachs. Such funding is crucial to Netcom's plan to launch its broadband network in 17 cities throughout the country. China Unicom and China Mobile (Hong Kong) have also planned to raise funds through floating their A shares on the domestic stock markets (MII website, 5 April 2001).

Technology spurs further growth

Communications technologies, especially wireless technology and the Internet, have also played a crucial role in the explosive growth of China's telecommunications industry. This is evident from the rapid expansion of the mobile and paging sectors since the beginning of the 1990s. First, the revolution in information and communications technologies has improved telecoms service efficiency by lowering the costs of transmission through a more diverse media (World Bank, 1998–1999). Second, the advantages in cost-effectiveness in new wireless technologies provide opportunities for developing countries, including China, to benefit from 'leap-frogging' the developed countries by switching to digitized networks.

The expansion of the cellular network in China has featured prominently in the telecoms industry, especially after 1996. The number of mobile phone subscribers has consistently increased by 80–90 per cent annually. The sharp increase has been made possible by China's booming economy and more intensified competition in the telecoms market as a result of industrial restructuring. Mobile telephony has captured attention for two main reasons. First, compared with fixed-line networks, cellular networks are less costly and time-consuming to install. Second, it represents the forefront of communications technology. The surge in demand can be attributed to the convenience that comes with the portability of hand-phones.

China began its utilization of cellular technology with the analogue TACS (Total Access Communications System) in 1987. In 1995, China Telecom, as well as the newly-established China Unicom, switched to the European GSM (Global System for Mobile) due to higher demand for more sophisticated services (*T&P Economy*, 2001). As a measure of bringing in more advanced technology, China Telecom Great Wall, a joint venture between MII and the PLA, experimented with the US-standard CDMA (Code Division Multiple Access) in 1998. This was followed by

China Unicom's plan to construct a nationwide CDMA network to rival China Telecom's (now China Mobile's) GSM system which presently dominates the mainland mobile phone market.

MII policies on mobile telephony are favourable towards China Unicom's CDMA expansion plans. China Unicom is the country's first mainland company to be approved for a CDMA network, and has planned to issue A-shares on the domestic stock market to raise funds for the construction of its CDMA network (*Asian Wall Street Journal*, 1 May 2001). Furthermore, under the MII arrangement, China Unicom is also allowed to operate the GSM system, whereas its primary rival, China Mobile, will only operate the TACS and GSM systems. However, the acquisition of 2 per cent of its assets in September 2000 by Vodafone, which has one of the world's leading 3G (third generation) technologies, could help China Mobile benefit from such a deal in competition with China Unicom's CDMA network.

In May 2001, China Unicom signed CDMA contracts worth 12.1 billion yuan with ten suppliers to build its mobile network. The ten suppliers comprise both foreign firms – Lucent Technologies, Motorola, Nortel, Ericsson and Bell – and domestic firms – Shenzhen Zhongxin Telecom, Datang Telecom Technology, Jinpeng Group, Oriental Communication and Huawei Technologies. Having completed the construction of its CDMA network at the end of October 2001, China Unicom launched its first trial CDMA operation in January 2002 (*The Nikkei Weekly*, 3 September 2001). The mobile carrier has further targeted the capturing of about a quarter of China's mobile market by 2003, which is projected to hit 200 million subscribers by then, i.e. China is expected to have a total CDMA capacity of 50 million within three years. Chinese President Jiang Zemin himself was reported to be supportive of the CDMA at the Fortune Global Forum 2001 held in Hong Kong (*China On-line News*, 15 August 2000). Premier Zhu Rongji has also sought greater participation by South Korean firms in China's CDMA business.

The wireless network is suitable for remote and rural areas and it also speeds up development as cable laying is minimized. The mobile network has also been hailed as the solution for telecoms access in China's Western region and rural areas, where the teledensity and penetration rate are among the lowest in the country (Tables 4.6 and 4.7). For this reason, and as a precaution against obsolescence of the 2G (second generation) technology after 2003, China is also experimenting with home-grown technology such as the 3G Standard TD-SCDMA, jointly developed by MII and Siemens (of Germany), to compete with two other types of 3G technology – the European wideband CDMA (W-CDMA) and the US's CDMA 2000 (Wu, 2001). The development of home-grown 3G was also seen as a way to reduce Chinese dependence on costly foreign technology. Furthermore, China will have its own patent rights over intellectual property on home-grown wireless technology.

The fact that mobile subscription has grown two or three times faster

Table 4.6 China's fixed line penetration rate by region, 1999

Area	*Population (millions)*	*Fixed-line subscribers (millions)*	*Fixed-line penetration (%)*
National	1,259.1	108.66	8.63
Municipalities			
Shanghai	14.74	4.76	32.29
Beijing	12.57	3.76	29.91
Tianjin	9.59	2.04	21.27
Provinces			
Guangdong	72.70	11.37	15.64
Zhejiang	44.75	6.66	14.88
Liaoning	41.71	5.79	13.88
Fujian	33.16	4.36	13.15
Jiangsu	72.13	9.03	12.52
Jilin	26.58	2.98	11.21
Heilongjiang	37.92	4.03	10.63
Ningxia	5.43	0.48	8.84
Xinjiang	17.74	1.48	8.34
Shandong	88.83	6.98	7.86
Hubei	59.38	4.46	7.51
Hebei	66.14	4.87	7.36
Hainan	7.62	0.53	6.96
Henan	93.87	6.39	6.81
Inner Mongolia	23.62	1.55	6.56
Chongqing	30.75	1.98	6.44
Shaanxi	36.18	2.32	6.41
Hunan	65.32	4.10	6.28
Shanxi	32.04	1.95	6.09
Jiangxi	42.31	2.55	6.03
Qinghai	5.10	0.28	5.49
Yunnan	41.92	2.30	5.49
Anhui	62.37	3.42	5.48
Gansu	25.43	1.18	4.64
Sichuan	85.50	3.82	4.47
Guangxi	47.13	2.10	4.46
Tibet	2.56	0.08	3.13
Guizhou	37.10	1.08	2.91

Sources: *China Statistical Yearbook 2000*, Beijing and *Yearbook of China Transportation and Communications 2000*, Beijing.

than that of fixed-line testifies to its popularity (Figure 4.3). In 1990, mobile subscription was only 0.3 per cent of the total fixed-line subscribers. In 1994, when the number of mobile phone users hit one million, the ratio was 5.7 per cent. It further increased to 18.8 per cent when mobile subscription exceeded 10 million in 1997, and by 2000, it had already made up more than half of the fixed-line subscribers – at about 59 per cent.

The development of the Internet and mobile telephony has moved the

Table 4.7 China's mobile penetration rate by region, 1999

Area	*Population (millions)*	*Mobile phone subscribers (millions)*	*Mobile penetration (%)*
National	1,259.1	43.30	3.44
Municipalities			
Beijing	12.57	1.85	14.72
Shanghai	14.74	2.04	13.84
Tianjin	9.59	0.70	7.30
Provinces			
Guangdong	72.70	n.a.	9.57
Fujian	33.16	n.a.	8.53
Zhejiang	44.75	n.a.	7.76
Liaoning	41.71	2.52	6.04
Heilongjiang	37.92	1.64	4.32
Jilin	26.58	1.09	4.10
Hainan	7.62	n.a.	4.04
Jiangsu	72.13	n.a.	4.03
Shandong	88.83	2.49	2.80
Chongqing	30.75	0.81	2.63
Inner Mongolia	23.62	0.53	2.24
Hebei	66.14	1.46	2.21
Shanxi	32.04	0.67	2.09
Sichuan	85.50	1.74	2.04
Ningxia	5.43	0.11	2.03
Xinjiang	17.74	0.35	1.97
Henan	93.87	n.a.	1.95
Shaanxi	36.18	0.69	1.91
Hunan	65.32	1.25	1.91
Jiangxi	42.31	0.77	1.82
Hubei	59.38	1.08	1.82
Yunnan	41.92	0.76	1.81
Guangxi	47.13	0.77	1.63
Anhui	62.37	1.01	1.62
Qinghai	5.10	0.07	1.37
Tibet	2.56	0.03	1.17
Gansu	25.43	0.29	1.14
Guizhou	37.10	0.01	0.46

Sources: *China Statistical Yearbook 2000*, Beijing and *Yearbook of China Transportation and Communications 2000*, Beijing.

telecoms industry, both in developed and developing countries towards a general trend – convergence of computing and telephony (Figure 4.4). Such convergence has significantly altered the traditional notion of telecoms as a natural monopoly, as sharper segmentation and hence increased competition is made possible with greater computing power and innovations. China has since recognized that the future of its telecoms industry hinges on the pace of its 'informatization' progress (*Xinbao,* 10 December

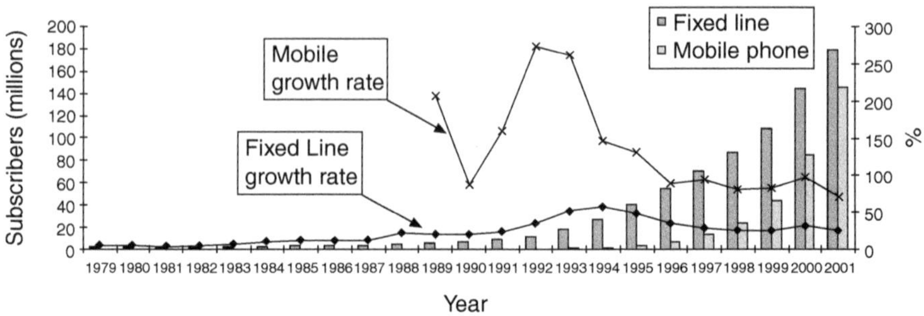

Figure 4.3 Growth of fixed-line and mobile subscribers in China, 1979–2001.

Sources: *China Yearbook of Transportation and Communications*, various issues, Beijing; For 2000 and 2001 figures, see Ministry of Information Industry website, http://www.mii.gov.cn/.

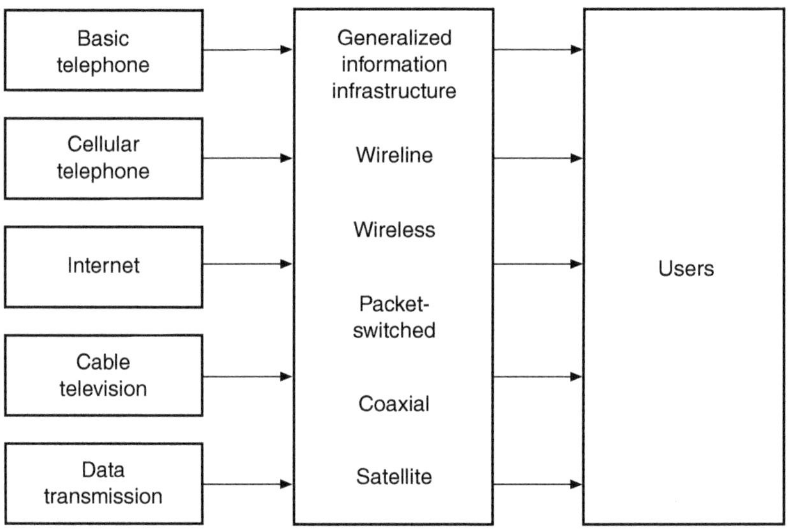

Figure 4.4 Convergence in the telecommunications industry.

Source: World Bank, *World Development Report 1998/99: Knowledge for Development*, p. 58.

1999). In the Tenth Five-Year Plan (2001–2005), China has set 'informatization' as a major task for all industries and has earmarked eight key areas for heavy investment, namely, optical communications, monitors, data storage, integrated circuits, digital TV, switching networks, mobile communications and CDMA technologies.

Preparing for WTO

According to MII, China's telecoms industry now adopts a 'breaking up the monopoly and bringing in competition' (*pochu longduan, yinru jingzheng*) development strategy. To prepare for global competition, it relies on the market to improve its services and accelerate technological innovation. Underlying China's commitment to open its telecoms market is the issue of further deregulation and a strengthening of the regulatory framework demanded by its accession to WTO.

A real test of its commitment to open its telecoms sector has been shown in the emerging regulatory framework. In September 2000, the State Council promulgated the 'Telecommunications Regulations of the People's Republic of China'. Aimed at standardizing the regulatory framework of the telecoms sector, the new ruling unified all existing regulations relating to telecoms licences, interconnection of telecoms networks, tariffs and private/foreign participation, and so on. The promulgation of 'Telecom Regulations' demonstrated the MII's recognition of the need to set up rules of competition to promote open competition and faster technological advancement. It was also a major step towards increasing transparency in the telecoms industry. According to MII Minister Wu Jichuan, developing an effective legal framework for telecoms and Internet businesses is one of the country's top priorities for the next five years.

China also made it clear that no new regulations allowing foreign investment in the telecoms sector would be introduced until its official entry into the WTO. However, there were indications of China becoming more active in preparing for foreign participation in its telecoms market. In December 2000, for example, US telecoms giant AT&T, in a joint venture with Shanghai Telecom and Shanghai Information Investment, became the first foreign telecoms carrier to offer telecoms services in China. This marked a great step forward for foreign firms, barred from telecoms network investment in China since 1993, to return to the country. Further openings for private investors appeared to be on the cards when Orient Group, a mainland private firm, became the first non-state firm to enter the Chinese telecoms market, after its listed associate, Jinzhou Port, bought 14.7 per cent of Jitong's equity in April 2001.

The Sino–US WTO accord of November 1999 paved the way for foreign investors to take controlling stakes in the mainland's telecoms sector and also opened the door for investments in the Internet sector (Table 4.8). Earlier, in April 1999, Premier Zhu Rongji offered up to 49 per cent foreign ownership of all services and 51 per cent foreign ownership for value-added and paging services within four years. The November deal was a slight step backward, but nonetheless, foreign firms were allowed to hold 49 per cent in Sino-foreign ventures after Beijing's accession into WTO, rising to 50 per cent after two years. China also signed the Sino-European Union accord in May 2000, which further opened up the mobile phone market by allowing foreign ownership of 25 per cent upon accession, 35 per cent after one year, and 49 per cent after three years. According to Minister Wu Jichuan, the Sino–US WTO agreement provided an impetus to the ongoing reform of the telecoms industry: 'Without

Table 4.8 China's terms of WTO agreement with the US

Sector	*Maximum % of foreign ownership allowed*	*Geographical limitations*
Value-added and paging services		
Upon accession	30	Beijing, Shanghai and Guangzhou
2001	49	In Beijing, Shanghai, Guangzhou and 14 other cities – Chengdu, Chongqing, Dalian, Fuzhou, Hangzhou, Nanjing, Ningbo, Qingdao, Shenyang, Shenzhen, Xiamen, Xian, Taiyuan and Wuhan
2002	50	Nationwide
Mobile services		
2001	25	Beijing, Shanghai and Guangzhou
2003	35	Beijing, Shanghai, Guangzhou and the 14 cities
2005	49	Nationwide
Fixed line services		
2003	25	Beijing, Shanghai and Guangzhou
2005	35	Beijing, Shanghai, Guangzhou and the 14 cities
2006	49	Nationwide
Internet content providers (ICP)		
Upon accession	30	Beijing, Shanghai and Guangzhou
2001	49	Beijing, Shanghai, Guangzhou and the 14 cities
2002	50	Nationwide
Internet service providers (ISP)		
2003	25	Beijing, Shanghai and Guangzhou
2005	35	Beijing, Shanghai, Guangzhou and the 14 cities
2006	49	Nationwide

Source: The Economist Intelligence Unit, 'WTO means more open sector', *Telecoms & Wireless Asia* (14 January 2000), London.

entry into the WTO, the reforms would still be cruising along its set course. The Sino–US agreement has made the issue more urgent.'

Indeed, why has the issue of China's WTO accession taken on such urgency? In an era of globalization, China will benefit from its WTO membership in several ways. First, membership will further promote institutional reform of telecoms corporations to render them more market-oriented. Second, the pressure expected from a potentially fierce competitive domestic market will spur Chinese firms to improve their operational efficiency and hence their competitive edge. Third, WTO membership will induce more foreign investment and advanced technology to China, thereby hastening the industry's overall development.

Furthermore, with WTO accession, China becomes a member of the Basic Telecommunications Agreement. In fact, by signing up to the WTO, China effectively agrees to the principles as outlined in the WTO Basic Telecommunications Agreement of 1997, which stipulates that China must implement regulations that will deter anti-competitive practices. This includes separating the roles of the telecoms regulator from the dominant operator, thus paving the way for the establishment of interconnection rights and a new telecoms law.

Potential problems after WTO

In opening up the telecoms industry as a preparation for China's accession to the WTO, the government progressively reduced state control over the industry and subjected it to greater market forces. China, now officially in the WTO, will inevitably face two dilemmas.

First, how will China safeguard its national security whilst opening up and allowing free access to information? Of particular concern is the extent to which the MII will be able to exert control over the sector after WTO entry. On the one hand, the country has to grasp every opportunity to utilize the latest foreign communications technology to speed up the construction of an information infrastructure, such as the installation of a satellite broadband network, for national economic development. On the other hand, too much opening up and freer access to information in the country may compromise, to a certain degree, its national security. To address this, China needs to ensure the dominant position of its domestic firms after WTO accession, through controlling stakes in these firms as well as setting upper limits for foreign investors. A new law, which took effect on 1 January 2002, requires foreign firms to operate with a Chinese partner while vesting the majority control of their mainland operations with Chinese companies.

Under the Sino–US agreement, geographical and ownership limitations continue on foreign investment in telecoms services. Indeed, Table 4.8 shows the sequence in which China has agreed to open up its telecoms sector. Upon accession to the WTO, a maximum 30 per cent of foreign ownership is allowed in value-added services in the cities of Beijing, Shanghai and Guangzhou and 25 per cent and 49 per cent, respectively, in the mobile service and value-added service sectors after one year. China will not allow a 49 per cent ownership in mobile services until 2005, and in the fixed line and ISP service sectors, foreign investors are only allowed to have a 49 per cent ownership by 2006.

These restrictive ownership rules make it most likely that competition will begin first in the value-added service and mobile service sectors. Foreign telecoms operators will invest mainly in the mobile market in more developed areas before having access to broadband data and 3G wireless areas. In the short run (over the next five or six years), Chinese carriers that operate value-added services, such as China Netcom, and those that operate mobile services, such as China Unicom and China Mobile, will face more intensive competition from the foreign players. Enterprises that operate the fixed-line service, such as China Telecom and China Railcom, will be unlikely to experience much competition from foreign telecoms companies.

Second, how will China guarantee its commitment of universal service to all parts of the country while promoting market orientation of the industry (Gao, 1999)? China's telecoms industry, as a key national infrastructure, is opening up amidst relatively low teledensity (Yang, 1999). For instance, China's teledensity is still relatively low compared with developed and some developing countries in the Asia-Pacific region – 7 per cent in 1998 compared with Japan's 50 per cent, Singapore's 56 per cent and Malaysia's 20 per cent (ITU, 2000).

Some are concerned whether China's telecoms industry should become a fully profit-oriented industry at such an early stage. Government intervention would still be necessary to ensure universal service and to narrow the economic disparity between the more developed eastern seaboard and the less developed western regions, as well as the gap between the urban and rural areas (Li and Shi, 1999). Rendering the telecommunications industry more profit-oriented and operationally efficient to meet the challenges arising from WTO membership, whilst boosting the industry's international competitiveness, would certainly reduce its incentive to invest in poor and backward regions. This would clearly be inimical to the government's cherished goal of developing an integrated nationwide telecommunications network providing universal service.

Bibliography

Asian Wall Street Journal, various newspaper articles (Hong Kong).

Asiaweek (30 March 2001) 'Networking for a New China' (Hong Kong).

Asiaweek (1 December 2000) 'Who will win China's phone wars?' (Hong Kong).

Beijing Review (1 November 2001) 'Removing monopoly: next reform focus' (Beijing).

Beijing Review (21 February 2000) 'WTO entry to promote telecom reform' (Beijing).

Beijing Review (21 June 1999) 'Opening a line to more foreign investment' (Beijing).

Beijing Review (14–20 June 1993) 'No overseas firms will manage telecom' (Beijing).

Chen, Q. (1999) (in Chinese) 'The impact of China's entry into WTO on the telecom industry and its strategies', *P&T Economy*, 48(3), 13–15.

China Daily, various newspaper articles, Hong Kong.

China Economic News (14 January 2002) 'Impact of WTO membership on the telecommunication industry' (Beijing).

China Economic News (22 January 2001) 'Telecommunications regulations of the People's Republic of China' (Beijing).

China Economic News (25 December 2000) 'China to be world's largest mobile communication market' (Beijing).

China Economic Review (July 1999) 'Reforms on hold' (London).

China Economic Review (June 1998) 'Cellular bridges the gap' (London).

China's Foreign Trade (January 2001) 'Foreign telecoms intend to unite to play in China' (Beijing).

China Online News, http://www.chinaonline.com.

Economist Intelligence Unit (5 November 2001) 'Missing the point', *Business China* (London: EIU).

Economist Intelligence Unit (14 January 2000) 'WTO means more open sector', *Telecoms & Wireless Asia* (London: EIU).

Far Eastern Economic Review (29 March 2001) 'Next-generation frustration' (Hong Kong).

Far Eastern Economic Review (19 October 2000) 'Stepping stone' (Hong Kong).

Far Eastern Economic Review (7 March 1991) 'Asia's poorer countries in technology leap' (Hong Kong).

Far Eastern Economic Review (2 August 1990) 'Revolutionary changes reshape Asia's telecommunications' (Hong Kong).

Gao, Y.(1999) (in Chinese) 'China's opening up of the telecom sector will have to address six major problems', *P&T Economy*, 48(3), 11–14.

Harwit, E. (1998) 'China's telecommunications industry: development patterns and policies', *Pacific Affairs*, 71(2), 175–193.

He, F.C. (1994) 'Lian Tong: a quantum leap in the reform of China's telecommunications', *Telecommunications Policy*, 18(3), 206–210.

International Telecommunications Union, *World Telecommunication Development Report 2000* (Geneva: ITU).

Laws of the People's Republic of China (*Civil Commercial Laws*), Falu chubanshe (Beijing).

Li, S. and Shi, L. (1999) (in Chinese) 'Telecom reform: retaining the roots', *P&T Economy*, 48(3), 18–20.

Liang, X., Zhang, X. and Yang, X. (1998) 'The development of telecommunications in China', *IEEE Communications Magazine*, November, 54–58.

Lu, D. (2000) 'Beefing up for competition: China's telecom industry on the eve of WTO entry', *EAI Working Paper No. 63*, East Asian Institute, National University of Singapore.

Mingbao, various newspaper articles (Hong Kong).

Ministry of Information Industry website, http://www.mii.gov.cn/.

Mueller, M. and Tan, Z. (1997) *China in the Information Age: Telecommunications and the Dilemmas of Reform* (Washington, DC: The Center for Strategic and International Studies).

Organisation for Economic Co-operation and Development (July 1999) *Implications of the WTO Agreement on Basic Telecommunications* (Paris: OECD).

South China Morning Post, various newspaper articles (Hong Kong).

Ure, J. (1994) 'Telecommunications, with Chinese characteristics', *Telecommunications Policy*, 18(3), 182–194.

World Bank, *World Development Report 1998/99: Knowledge for Development*.

Wu, C. (2001) (in Chinese) 'A discussion of essential problems with telecom reform and development', *Youdian Jingji* (P&T Economy), 54(1), 8–10.

Xinbao, various newspaper articles (Hong Kong).

Yang, P. (1999) (in Chinese) 'The strategic choices of our telecom industry under conditions of market opening', *Youdian Jingji* (P&T Economy) 48(3), 2–7.

Yearbook of China Transportation and Communications, various years (Beijing: Yearbook House of China Transportation and Communications).

5 Private enterprise

The engine for sustaining growth in the Chinese economy?[1]

Qihai Huang

Introduction

By the end of 2000, the United States' economy had grown to US$10 trillion, the first in the world to do so, while China's gross domestic product (GDP) exceeded US$1 trillion for the first time (*China Information News*, 1 January 2001). Andy Xie, a Hong Kong-based economist with Morgan Stanley Dean Witter, commented that China's economy is next in line, 'We believe that China will be the next economy to reach US$10 trillion in today's dollar terms. It will probably take place within two decades and could happen in 15 years (Chinaonline, 6 February 2001).

Such confidence is based on the precondition that the growth of the Chinese economy is sustained. It is well recognised that China's economy has grown rapidly in the past two decades, but whether this state-of-affairs can be sustained is questionable, given the challenges posed by the indebtedness of state-owned enterprises (SOEs), declining growth rates and increasing problems in township and village enterprises (TVEs) and falling foreign direct investment (FDI).

Although the reform of the SOEs has been the main objective of the Chinese government and a range of policy measures has been introduced to that effect, the reforms so far do not seem to have achieved the objective of transforming the SOEs into efficient economic entities. The SOEs have not only performed badly in terms of productive efficiency but have also been a burden on the economy. The government has had to subsidise the loss-making SOEs (Woo *et al.*, 1994), and the subsidies have become a drag on the efficient allocation of funds that the state could direct to, or invest in, more productive firms (Warner, 1995). Even in the publicly listed companies, where the proportion of state shares increases, labour productivity tends to decline (Xu and Wang, 1999). This is because the measures introduced in SOEs, including incentive mechanisms, did not elicit sufficiently efficient behaviour (Caulet *et al.*, 1999).

Many believe that foreign direct investment (FDI) and township and village enterprises (TVEs) have been the main driving forces for China's fast growth in the past (e.g. Shan *et al.*, 1997; Chen, 1996; and Chen *et al.*,

1995; Walder, 1995; Naughton, 1995). With regard to the former, after China started to open its door during the 1980s, FDI averaged about $2 billion a year. In the 1990s, the figure soared. Firms with foreign investment accounted for more than 40 per cent of China's exports, over 13 per cent of national tax revenues and about 10 per cent of urban employment and contributed 18 per cent of 'China's added value' (*The Economist*, 19 June 1999). However, the high growth rate has been eroded by the Asian financial crisis since 1997. Meanwhile, the other engine driving growth, the TVE sector, has not functioned well in recent years either. Its growth rate is falling and it is beset with increasing problems. In the mid-1990s, TVEs contributed one-third of rural per capita incomes and employed about 130 million workers or about half of China's surplus rural labour. Although they contributed 28 per cent of the nation's GDP in 1998, their growth rate had already begun to fall off dramatically after 1993, from 65 per cent in that year, to about 18 per cent in 1997. Meanwhile, the development of TVEs faces problems, such as declining funds owing to low financial and policy support from local governments, the inability to adapt to a market economy, deficient product mix, out-of-date technology, poor management, lack of talent, especially of college graduates, and the practice of pursuing short-term profit at the expense of sustainable long term development.

With the outbreak of the Asian financial crisis in 1997, the growth of TVE exports plunged from 16.8 per cent to 8 per cent. Even after foreign trade had begun to recover, many countries maintained restrictions on Chinese products, including, for example, those Latin American countries that had erected non-tariff barriers against Chinese textiles.

Nee (1992) argues that the decline of the relative importance of TVEs was to be expected, since they owed their success to the initial reform of the Chinese economy. In addition, though Bowles and Dong (1999) insist that collective enterprises have advantages in terms of worker solidarity and commitment over private enterprises, contributing to productivity levels higher in the former than the latter, they accept that the success of TVEs will inevitably be undermined by the marketisation process. A senior official from the Ministry of Agriculture in charge of China's TVEs has confessed that TVEs lacked the internal force to sustain rapid development given the uncontrolled interference of village and township administrations in their operation (Chinaonline, 31 May 2000).

Under such circumstances, can China sustain its rapid growth in the twenty-first century and reach the growth goal predicted by the optimists? This chapter is not aimed at answering this question directly by joining the debate over the performance and contribution of SOEs, TVEs and FDI as listed above; instead, it examines the dynamism of private enterprise within the Chinese economy, which has largely been neglected by researchers. It is hoped that, on the one hand, this chapter will shed some light on how growth can be sustained in the Chinese economy from the perspective of the new growth engine and, on the other, that it will attract more researchers to pay attention to the sector. In the following sections, this chapter will examine policy developments with regard to the private sector of the economy in China and the growth and contribution of private enterprises to this sector. In order to demonstrate its dynamics, comparisons with other sectors will be presented.

The re-emergence of the private economy and the recognition of private enterprise

According to Kraus (1991), at the beginning of the 1950s, after the founding of the People's Republic of China, there were 7.24 million independent private craftsmen, merchants and industrialists in the cities and towns, with about 40 million employees engaged in private business activities. The private sector produced more than half of China's industrial output. Thereafter, however, the Chinese Communist Party (CCP) set about systematically eliminating private business (through so-called nationalisation), as small-scale production and businesses were increasingly limited and finally annihilated. By the end of 1956, only 160,000 small-scale businesses remained and the numbers continued to decline. Although there was a brief flurry of individual business activity following the failure of the Great Leap Forward, individual business was attacked by the Cultural Revolution as the 'rat-tail of capitalism'. Not until the late 1970s did the private business sector re-emerge. By 1978, China's industry was concentrated in urban areas and was mostly owned by the state, with its output accounting for 90 per cent of the total – the remainder coming from collective enterprises. The private sector at that time comprised only about 150,000 individual peddlers, craft-people and repairers.

In 1978, 72 per cent of the overall 43.5 million industrial workforce worked in the state sector and 91.8 per cent of the industrial sector's RMB 242.37 billion was in fixed assets belonging to the state. Despite a high average annual growth rate of 14 per cent for industrial output over nearly three decades, China's industry suffered from low efficiency, using obsolete technologies to produce unwanted products at high costs. The average productivity of capital had declined substantially: in 1957, RMB 100 worth of capital produced RMB 139.3 worth of industrial output, the same amount produced only RMB 95.5 in 1977. Some recent studies have found evidence of stagnating total factor productivity (Chang and Wang, 1994). Byrd (1992) argues that the necessity for economic reform was recognised because of the pervasive inefficiency in SOEs and the need to shift from Soviet-style extensive growth to intensive growth based on improved resource allocation. It is argued that the re-emergence of the private economy was based on the need to revive the economy on the one hand and the necessity of dealing with the threat of mass unemployment on the other.

In rural areas, with the introduction of the household responsibility system, peasants started to diversify their economic activities, market their products and invest in non-agricultural businesses. However, townships and villages lacked the resources to develop collective industry to employ the surplus labour released from agriculture. The household responsibility system itself was a form of private economy and became the initial stimulus to the development of private enterprise in rural areas.

In urban areas, the ailing SOEs could neither absorb more employees from the growing numbers of unemployed nor meet the demand of consumers for numerous, varied and atomised goods and services. Urban unemployment became a severe problem for the government: many of the 17 million 'educated youth' began to return from the countryside to join a residue of young people who had evaded being sent to the rural areas but who had no jobs. In addition, there were about 3–5 million school leavers each year who needed jobs. By 1982, 7 million people were joining the waiting lists for jobs every year. Thus, the most important motive for the government to allow the development of private business was the need to increase employment opportunities.

However, at the beginning of the re-emergence of the private economy, it was limited to individual enterprise (*getihu*), as the communist party emphasised that only very small, simple businesses would be allowed and that these would be limited by state regulations and their dependence on the socialist public economy. The framework envisaged in this policy still consisted of the traditional hierarchy of state, collective, and individual ownership, with state enterprises viewed as politically and economically superior. The private sector was intended to play a marginal role and to act as a supplement to the state and collective sectors. In line with these ideas, private sector policy at the beginning of the 1980s was aimed at allowing a limited amount of private business to take on some of the small-scale tasks that were difficult for the planning system to perform effectively. Private operators were not issued business licences if their businesses competed with local state or collective firms. In addition, licences were initially restricted to people who did not have other employment prospects. Kraus (1991) finds that the employees in the private sector came from young people looking for jobs, workers who had lost their old jobs, the unemployed and pensioners. The unemployed comprised many different groups, including those who, as a result of work disabilities, had been eliminated from the normal work system, and former convicts, who had no chance of getting work in the state or collective enterprises.

The policy of promoting a limited private sector was confirmed by the State Council's regulations on the urban private economy issued in July 1981. The regulations encouraged and supported 'unemployed youth' to work in fields whose products 'were urgently needed by the masses, but which could not be supplied or could only be supplied to a limited extent by the state or collective sector'. Operators were permitted to engage in small-scale handicrafts, retail commerce, catering, services, repairs, non-mechanised transport and building repairs. The regulations specified that individual enterprises should employ at most two assistants and five apprentices, 'the activity of private business is performed by one person or family. If necessary, one or two helpers may be employed with the approval of the State Administration for Industry and Commerce. Workers with great or unusual technical experience may employ two or three, maximally five, apprentices' (cited in Kraus, 1991, p. 18). Later, in March 1984, the government issued a decree to encourage the extension of individual business in rural areas but, more importantly, it raised the previous employment limit of two helpers or five apprentices to a total of seven persons. But all these changes affirmed the role of the private economy as a 'necessary supplement' to the state and collective sectors, and placed limits on the size and scope of these businesses. By 1982, there were 2.63 million private (or individually-owned) businesses, employing more than 3.2 million people.

Private enterprises expanded production and scale and grew way beyond the employment limits set by the state, but it was not until October 1987 that the breakthrough to full recognition for private enterprises came, when the 13th Party Congress of the Chinese Communist Party formalised the theory of the 'initial stage of socialism'. The theory claimed that economic development was the primary goal of the first phase of socialism and thus capitalistic phenomena such as large private enterprises still had a positive role to play. Private enterprise, i.e. a privately owned enterprise hiring more than seven workers, was acceptable to the state for the first time. In April 1988, the revised Constitution legalised the existence and development of the private sector and promised state protection and support. This was followed by the Provisional Regulations on Private Enterprises issued by the State Council in 1988 and the Rules for Implementation of the Provisional Regulations on Private Enterprises promulgated by the State Administration of Industry and Commerce in 1989. According to the regulation, private enterprise referred to those economic organisations where assets were held in private hands, with more than seven employees and which were run for profit making. The status of private enterprises in the socialist economy was thereby clearly defined, although still perceived as merely a 'necessary complement to the socialist public economy'. By the end of 1988, China had 90,581 private enterprises (*China's Private Economy Yearbook*, 1994). Currently, the Chinese government defines three kinds of ownership as private enterprises. They are sole ownership, partnership and limited liability companies.

The status of the private enterprises was given further recognition in November 1993, when the CCP held the third plenary session of the 14th Central Committee and officially declared that it was aiming for a market economy (for some years the official phrase had been 'commodity economy'), albeit a socialist market economy. The government regarded the private sector as 'an important economic force in developing new productive forces' and an integral part of 'socialism with Chinese characteristics'.

Then, in 1997, came the greatest change in the government attitude to the private sector when the 15th Chinese Communist Party Congress decreed that private enterprise was an important component of the economy and allowed the sales of state-owned enterprises to the private sector. Amendments to the constitution recognising the private sector were finally made in 1999.

Obstacles to the development of private enterprises

The development of private enterprise is a history of a struggle to overcome opposition and obstruction, to survive and grow. Barriers included discrimination by both individuals and government. Since the promotion of the private economy conflicts with the ideology of communism, the growth of the sector was not easy in China.

First, people were hostile to private enterprises. People's attitudes may have derived from the marginal status of the sector itself in the hierarchical ownership structure, where the state comes first, collective second, and the private goes nowhere. The initial composition of private business people from marginal social groups, including former prisoners, was another factor contributing to their low social status. Engaging in the private economy for many young people was perceived as resulting from a failure to go to university or to get a proper job. Kraus (1991) argues that hostility to private enterprises was due not only to traditional social hierarchies and political prejudice but also envy of the wealth of many private business people.

Second, there were restrictions imposed by the government. The size and business scope of an enterprise were controlled by the government. Private businesses were not allowed to compete with collective and state-owned enterprises. In the planned economy, business premises, labour, raw materials, energy, etc, were allocated by the government, and private enterprises, excluded from the plan, often found it difficult to obtain these resources (Kraus, 1991; Wank, 1999). Local government officials often used their control over key inputs as leverage over private enterprises, blocking licences or approvals, cutting off access to credit and adding new restrictions on private enterprises' activities. Moreover, when the government carried out austerity policies, private enterprises were always the target. It was estimated that 15 per cent of private businesses (including individual enterprises) were driven out of business in 1989 alone.

Third, exorbitant levies and sundry taxes become burdens to private enterprises, which were regarded as a source of government revenues rather than explicit taxes (Brown and Rose, 1998). These charges were numerous. For example, there were altogether 20 charges levied on one private restaurant in Chengdu city: industrial and commercial tax, income tax, a city reconstruction charge, an education charge, a city grain fund, a provincial grain fund, a meat fund, management charges, business administration charges, revenue stamp tax, public order charges, sanitation charges, an energy source fund, front-door-cleanliness-guarantees, a clean transportation charge, a trade association membership fee, employees' contract charges and an excessive signpost charge. Only two of the dozens of charges on private shops – the income tax and the industrial and commercial tax – were imposed by the central government. The rest were levied at the discretion of local governments.

Fourth, private enterprises' start-up and capacity for survival and growth were constrained by the lack of capital. In the West, capital becomes manageable when an enterprise has developed to a certain stage, however, in China, capital is not easy to obtain for private enterprises at *any* stage of growth. According to David Mackenzie, chief of mission for the International Finance Corporation's China operation, the major restriction for the development of private enterprises has been lack of efficient funding channels. Liu Yong Hao, vice chairman of the All China Industry and Commerce Federation, who also runs China's largest feed producer, the New Hope Group, confirms that many private enterprises have difficulty in getting funds from banks.[2] The state commercial banks are usually reluctant to lend to private businesses out of concerns about their trustworthiness and repayment capability. Fang Haixing, general manager of the Group Coordination Committee of China Construction Bank, has also admitted that China's banking sector lacks a tier of institutions offering loans for those projects in the private sector which are judged too risky by the commercial banks. He thus suggested that genuinely privately owned banks become a key to the solution, 'Only they can understand the real needs of the private enterprises' (*AFX*, 27 April 1999; *China Daily*, 2 May 1999). Even in one of the major cradles of the private economy, Zhejiang Province, private enterprises have still faced difficulties in obtaining financing. The chairman of a private group corporation said that the lack of a high-tech fund was a big obstacle for private enterprises in their drive to enter the high-tech sector because such a fund for non-state enterprises does not exist anywhere in China (*China Daily*, 20 December 1998).

Walder (1995) points out that state banks and official sources of credit generally offer loans more on the basis of political considerations than economic criteria. Private enterprises lack the legitimacy and necessary political backing to enjoy reliable access to capital and thus must depend on private and informal sources of credits, which are limited and available only at substantially higher interest rates.

Although foreign investors have been interested in private enterprises, it was not until September 1998 that the International Financial Corporation, a World Bank member, became the first foreign investor to provide a loan, of US$6.5 million, to a Chinese private company (*China Reform News*, 11 September 1998). It was also the first time that private enterprises were allowed to attend the China Fair for International Investment and Trade held in September 1999. However, 'although the Ministry of Foreign Trade and Economic Cooperation in charge of the fair has not set down any explicit discriminatory policies against private businesses regarding their cooperation with foreign investors, private companies have received unequal treatment in the actual implementation of foreign investment policy', claimed Maochun He, deputy director of the World Trade Research Department of the Chinese Academy of International Trade and Economic Cooperation (*China Daily*, 11 April 1999).

Another important capital resource is the stock market.[3] In market economies, stock markets work as mechanisms both to allow enterprises to raise capital and to effect a more rational allocation of resources. They channel savings to their most efficient users and put pressure on firms to raise their efficiency. However, according to Bowles and Dong (1999), China's stock markets have another important function, that is, serving SOE reform. In China, bonds and shares have functioned as an instrument in a complex struggle for resources between political, institutional and economic actors. Meanwhile, share issues have, in the event, been less important economically as politically in that they have challenged the ideological and institutional underpinning of a 'socialist' economy – the issue of state ownership. Predictably, most companies listed in the Chinese stock markets are state owned and few are non-public. Bowles and Dong (1999) therefore advocates that more private enterprises should be treated equally without discrimination and be allowed to be listed on Chinese stock markets.

China has yet to enact any laws to help finance the private sector, although according to *China Security News* (23 January 1999), the Financial and Economic Committee of the National People's Congress (NPC) planned to submit a draft private enterprise and investment law to the NPC. Meanwhile the Ministry of Finance has begun to draft measures to require local governments to set aside part of their budgets as financial guarantees for loans extended to the enterprises in the private sector (*China Daily*, 2 May 1999), but the consequences have yet to be seen.[4]

In sum, all these problems reflect the difficult conditions experienced by the private sector. As a strategy to outweigh these disadvantages, private entrepreneurs were forced to operate their businesses under the guise of collective or state enterprises.[5] Not surprisingly, a survey conducted by the State Industry and Commerce Bureau reveals that 80 per cent of TVEs in 1995 were, in fact, private enterprises (*China's Private Economy Yearbook*, 1996). In addition, many private entrepreneurs are forced to cultivate personal connections (*guanxi*) with government officials or state-owned enterprise managers. To maintain such connections, private entrepreneurs have to pay good prices and gifts, and sometimes even commissions and bribes (Wank, 1999, Zhu, 1998; Tao and Zhu, 2001). For some large private enterprises, spending on developing and maintaining these connections was as much as 20–30 per cent of gross income.

The vigour and rapid development of private enterprises

Despite their highly vulnerable social status and the discriminatory environment, private businesses demonstrated vigour and dynamism, not only to survive but also to develop quickly. There was a boom in their development in rural areas in the form of family enterprises. Some families, the so-called specialised households (*zhuanyehu*), were indeed private non-agricultural businesses and extended far beyond the scope previously supposed possible for private economic activity. A survey conducted in 1984 by the Rural Development Research Centre under the State Council found that 0.07 per cent of investigated households had already hired more than seven workers. It was estimated that, by the end of 1988, there were about 500,000 family businesses (*getihu*) that could be counted as private enterprises (Zhang and Liu, 1995, p. 55).

A second source of private enterprise development has been *public* assets. During the transitional period, China has not had an effective legal system, let alone laws preventing public assets from going into private pockets. Covertly or overtly, legally or illegally, public assets have been transformed into private assets by those who control them. In Xiamen, for some private entrepreneurs who were born into cadre families, their enterprises were financed by public funds with help from certain connections (Wank, 1999). Since a state or collective firm is under the auspices of a certain government or governmental department, the end result is that 'the firm director is responsible for any gains, the firm for deficits and the bank for debts', while the government has to be responsible for the whole firm (Xu, 1996). A state-owned firm's manager is more than pleased to take bribes from non-state trade partners in exchange for the enforcement of contracts between the two parties (Tao and Zhu, 2000, 2001). In addition, the dual price system introduced in the early 1980s provided a new way for corrupt officials to milk state property.

Besides the embezzlement of public property, legal leasing of publicly owned enterprises has led to asset accumulation by individuals.[6] Under the reform policy, small and medium sized state-owned and collectively-owned firms, in particular those in the red, were allowed to lease to individuals, since leasing was regarded as an effective measure to separate decision making powers from ownership rights. In some areas, 50 per cent of all the collective firms were leased to individuals (Zhang and Liu, 1995, p. 29). The leasee paid the collective a fixed rent and the residual from the operation went to the individual. With asset accumulation by individuals in this way, the share of collective ownership was gradually reduced and the firm was transferred into solely private hands.

A third source of private enterprise development has been the so-called start-up enterprises. After legal status was granted to private enterprises, in particular after Deng Xiaoping's Southern Tour in 1992, more and more private enterprises were registered. The period from 1992 to 1994 saw the explosive development of private enterprises, not only in terms of the number of private enterprises and employment but also in terms of registered capital and output. People continued to invest their savings – say, from moonlighting or from borrowing money from friends and relatives – to set up their own firms. In 2000, there were 295,300 new private enterprises, which meant an average of 809 new private enterprises every day (*China Business Times*, 30 March 2001).

As has been pointed out previously, private enterprises are the most dynamic component of China's economy. The rapid development of private enterprise is seen not only with respect to the number of firms, registered capital and employment but also with respect to output and their contribution to retail trade and industrial and commercial tax revenues.

The development of private enterprises is reflected in their growing number. Table 5.1 shows the development of private enterprises and compares their development with other forms of ownership. The number of private enterprises was more than 1.2 million in 1998, or 13 times the number in 1989. Between 1989 and 1998, the number of private enterprises grew at an average annual rate of 33.3 per cent, while the growth rates for SOEs, TVEs and FDI were 5.4 per cent, 0.3 per cent and 34.4 per cent respectively. Although the average growth rate of private enterprises was slightly lower than that of FDI, it was much higher than those of SOEs and TVEs. More importantly, while the numbers of SOEs, TVEs and FDI started to decrease since 1996 and 1997, the number of private enterprises was still growing. The trend is better shown in Figure 5.1.

Increasing registered capital is another indicator of the growth of private enterprises. The changes in registered capital for private enterprises and the comparison with other ownerships are demonstrated in Table 5.2. In 1989, the registered capital in private enterprises was RMB 8.4 billion. Ten years later in 1998, it grew more than 85 times to RMB

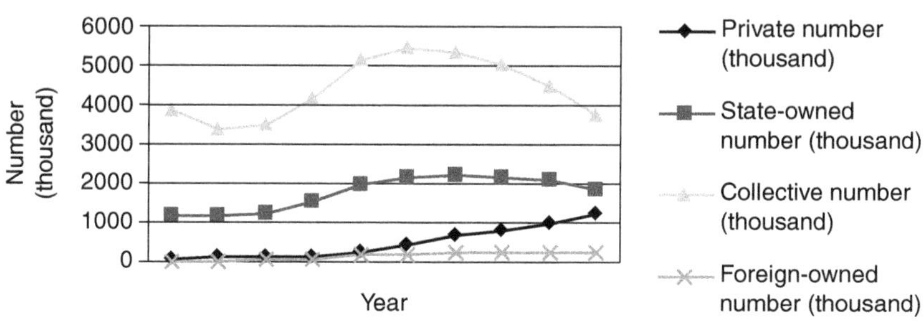

Figure 5.1 Growth of the number of enterprises.

Table 5.1 Development of enterprises by ownership during 1989–1998

Year	*Private*		*State owned*		*Collective*		*Foreign owned*	
	Number (thousand)	*Growth (%)*	*Number (thousand)*	*Growth (%)*	*Number (thousand)*	*Growth (%)*	*Number (thousand)*	*Growth (%)*
1989	90.6		1,146.9		3,829.6		15.9	
1990	98.1	8.35	1,151.5	0.4	3,381.9	−11.7	25.4	59.5
1991	107.8	9.89	1,253.7	8.9	3,480.0	2.9	37.2	46.6
1992	139.6	29.5	1,547.2	23.4	4,159.4	19.5	84.4	126.7
1993	237.9	70.4	1,951.7	26.1	5,156.5	24.0	167.5	98.5
1994	432.2	81.7	2,166.3	11.0	5,456.8	5.8	206.1	23.0
1995	654.5	51.4	2,218.6	2.4	5,337.7	−2.2	233.6	13.3
1996	819.3	25.2	2,163.3	−2.5	5,013.4	−6.1	240.4	2.9
1997	960.7	17.3	2,078.3	−3.9	4,470.5	−10.8	235.7	−2.0
1998	1,200.1	25.0	1,836.3	−11.7	3,736.4	−16.4	227.8	−3.3
Average		33.3		5.4		0.3		34.4

Source: *China Statistical Yearbook*, 1989–1998; Statistical Documents of China Industry and Commerce Management, 1991–1998

Table 5.2 Total registered capital of enterprises by ownership 1989–1998

Year	*Private*		*State owned*		*Collective*		*Foreign owned*	
	Capital (RMB billion)	*Growth (%)*	*Capital (RMB billion)*	*Growth (%)*	*Capital (RMB billion)*	*Growth (%)*	*Capital (US$ billion)*	*Growth (%)*
1989	8.4		1,123.2		565.3		27.6	
1990	9.5	13.1	1,192.5	6.2	544.4	−3.7	33.0	19.8
1991	12.3	29.5	1,368.3	14.8	577.1	6.0	44.7	35.2
1992	22.1	79.7	1,794.8	31.2	824.2	42.9	116.0	159.7
1993	68.1	208.1	2,546.2	41.9	1,322.6	60.5	245.6	111.8
1994	144.8	112.6	2,886.9	13.4	1,576.8	19.2	312.3	27.1
1995	262.2	81.1	3,166.4	9.7	1,623.1	2.9	399.1	27.8
1996	375.2	43.1	3,284.4	3.7	1,726.5	6.4	441.5	10.6
1997	514.0	37.0	3,629.4	10.4	1,624.4	−5.9	459.8	4.1
1998	719.8	40.0	3,488.0	−3.8	1,512.5	−6.9	467.3	1.6
Average growth		64.0		13.0		11.7		36.9

Source: *China Statistical Yearbook*, 1989–1998; Statistical Documents of China Industry and Commerce Management, 1991–1998.

719.8 billion. The average annual growth rate was 64 per cent. During the same period, the average annual growth rates for SOEs, TVEs and FDI were 12.9 per cent, 11.6 per cent and 36.9 per cent respectively. The average annual growth in private enterprises in terms of registered capital was much higher than in other ownerships.

Meanwhile, the average registered capital for a private enterprise increased very fast, demonstrating growing economies of scale. From 1989 to 1998, the average registered capital for a private enterprise grew from RMB 92.7 thousand to RMB 599.3 thousand with an average annual growth rate of 23 per cent, compared with 7.6 per cent for SOEs, 11.9 per cent for TVEs and 1.9 per cent for FDI (see Table 5.3).

Ever-growing employment in private enterprises is also important evidence of the development of private enterprises. In 1998, private enterprises had over 171 million employees, more than ten times the number in 1989. The figure was not significant compared with that of SOEs and TVEs, but it was higher than that of foreign invested firms at 2.9 million in the same year (Table 5.4).

The rapid development of private enterprises is also illustrated by the growth in output and turnover. From Table 5.5 and Figure 5.2 it can be seen that the output and turnover of private enterprises grew rapidly between 1989 and 1998. In 1989, the output value of private enterprises was only RMB 9.7 billion. By 1998, it was RMB 585.3 billion, registering an annual growth rate of 51 per cent in real terms. During the same period, the turnover of private enterprises grew from RMB 3.4 billion to RMB 305.9 billion, with an annual growth rate of 57 per cent in real terms.

The rapid development of private enterprises is also reflected in the growth of industrial and commercial taxes paid by them. Table 5.6 gives the details of the growth in industrial and commercial tax for private enterprises in comparison with other ownerships. Starting from a low base of RMB 0.11 billion contribution to industrial and commercial tax in 1989, private enterprises provided a RMB 9.05 billion in 1997. Although the amount itself was still small, compared with that of SOEs and TVEs, the average annual growth rate of 73.2 per cent is much higher than the other two forms of ownership.

All the above information shows the importance of private enterprises

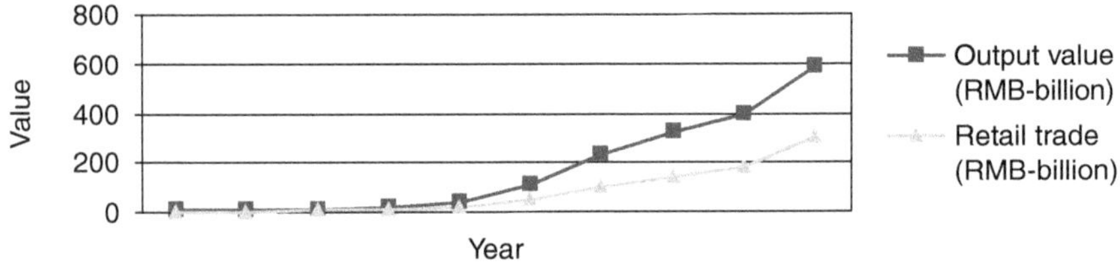

Figure 5.2 Growth in output and turnover for private enterprises.

Table 5.3 Average registered capital for an enterprise by ownership during 1989–1998

Year	*Private*		*State owned*		*Collective*		*Foreign owned*	
	Reg. capital (RMB 1,000)	*Growth (%)*	*Reg. capital (RMB 1,000)*	*Growth (%)*	*Reg. capital (RMB 1,000)*	*Growth (%)*	*Capital (US$ 1,000)*	*Growth (%)*
1989	92.7		979.3		147.6		1,733.1	
1990	96.8	4.4	1,035.6	5.8	161.0	9.1	1,301.4	−24.9
1991	114.1	17.8	1,091.4	5.4	165.8	3.0	1,200.1	−7.8
1992	158.3	38.8	1,160.0	6.3	198.2	19.5	1,374.7	14.6
1993	286.2	80.8	1,304.6	12.5	256.5	29.5	1,466.4	6.7
1994	335.0	17.0	1,332.6	2.2	289.0	12.7	1,515.2	3.3
1995	400.6	19.6	1,427.2	7.1	304.1	5.2	1,708.8	12.8
1996	458.0	14.3	1,518.2	6.4	344.4	13.3	1,836.1	7.5
1997	535.0	16.8	1,744.1	15.0	363.4	5.5	1,951.1	6.3
1998	599.3	12.0	1,899.5	8.9	404.8	11.4	2,051.2	5.1
Average growth		23.0		7.6		11.9		1.9

Source: *China Statistical Yearbook*, 1989–1998; Statistical Documents of China Industry and Commerce Management, 1991–1998.

Table 5.4 Growth in employment by ownership during 1989–1998

Year	*Private (%)*	*State (%)*	*Collective (%)*	*Foreign (%)*	*Total (%)*
1989					
1990	3.7	2.4	1.3	40.4	15.5
1991	8.2	3.1	2.2	150.0	1.4
1992	26.1	2.1	−0.2	33.9	1.2
1993	60.9	0.3	−6.3	30.3	1.3
1994	73.7	2.7	−3.2	−32.3	1.3
1995	47.3	0.4	−4.2	23.6	1.1
1996	22.5	−0.2	−4.2	14.1	1.3
1997	15.3	−1.8	−4.4	9.1	1.1
1998	26.7	−18.0	−31.2	−2.3	0.5
Average	29.7	−0.01	−0.06	22.6	2.6

Source: *China Statistical Yearbook*, 1989–1998; Statistical Documents of China Industry and Commerce Management, 1991–1998

Table 5.5 Growth in output and turnover by ownership during 1989–1998

Year	*Output value (RMB billion)*	*Growth (%)*	*Turnover (RMB billion)*	*Growth (%)*
1989	9.7		3.4	
1990	12.2	23.7	4.3	23.4
1991	14.7	17.6	5.7	29.2
1992	20.5	34.1	9.1	53.3
1993	42.2	92.7	19.0	94.1
1994	114.0	148.4	51.3	145.9
1995	229.5	86.5	100.6	79.0
1996	322.7	34.5	145.9	36.7
1997	392.3	20.8	185.5	24.3
1998	585.3	51.8	305.9	65.7
Average growth		51.9		57.2

Source: Statistical Documents of China Industry and Commerce Management, 1991–1998.

to the Chinese economy. Moreover, the performance of private enterprises has been a catalyst for SOE reform. An important element of SOE reform has been privatisation: by 2001, about 80 per cent of SOEs owned by governments at or below the county levels have been privatised.

Some reasons for the rapid growth of private enterprises

It is ironic that the rapid expansion of private enterprises contrasts sharply with the adverse environment under which they have survived and developed. What are the factors behind the robust growth of private enterprises? Chen (1990) assumes that there are three aspects to the superiority

Table 5.6 Growth in industrial and commercial tax by ownership during 1989–1998

Year	*Private*		*Individual economy*		*State*		*Collective*	
	Tax (RMB billion)	*Growth (%)*	*Tax (RMB billion)*	*Growth (%)*	*Tax (RMB billion)*	*Growth (%)*	*Tax (RMB billion)*	*Growth (%)*
1989	0.11		11.96		127.85		43.13	
1990	0.20	78.6	13.20	10.3	134.92	5.5	42.68	−1.0
1991	0.34	69.0	15.08	14.2	144.70	7.3	44.11	3.3
1992	0.46	34.6	17.66	17.2	155.92	7.8	47.81	8.4
1993	1.05	129.9	31.50	78.2	252.24	61.9	83.71	75.1
1994	1.75	67.5	36.04	14.5	298.10	18.1	81.10	−3.1
1995	3.56	103.1	40.13	11.3	329.48	10.5	96.94	19.5
1996	6.02	69.2	39.78	−0.9	295.93	−10.2	99.60	2.7
1997	9.05	50.2	46.05	15.7	386.49	30.6	105.23	5.7
Average growth		73.2		60.8		14.8		11.8

Source: *China Tax Yearbook*, 1990–1998.

of private enterprises. First, there is a close relationship between the performance of an enterprise and the income of its entrepreneur. Second, the entrepreneur has managerial and administrative talent, with an innovative, risk-taking and pioneering spirit developed in the course of fierce competition. Third, private entrepreneurs have complete autonomy in making decisions.

Nee (1992) finds that private entrepreneurs have the greatest autonomy in business operations, risk taking and innovation, entrepreneurial incentive and profit maximising, compared with factory directors of SOEs and collective firms. For a private enterprise, the firm is responsible for its operation, because no one (no government) will be responsible for its bankruptcy. In contrast, a state or collective firm is under the auspices of a certain government or governmental department.

Prospects for private enterprises

The constitutional amendment, which gave formal recognition to the country's emerging private sector in 1999, is a significant step to setting China's economy on a course of major structural change. In a sense, the amendment was propelled by the sector itself, which has experienced the most dynamic growth in the past two decades. While the SOEs, TVEs and foreign-invested firms have stagnated, domestic private enterprises continue to grow rapidly. Perhaps more importantly, the amendment represents the government's recognition of the long-term importance of fostering private enterprises. President Jiang Zemin announced that the Communist Party would accept private businessmen as members at the 70th anniversary celebration of the party (*Washington Post*, 2 July 2001). This is another policy confirming the increasingly powerful role of private enterprises and private entrepreneurs in determining China's future.

Most importantly, the Chinese government has addressed the enterprise reform in terms of property rights and ownership, which opened the door for the transformation of SOEs. The recognition of private ownership and property rights has strengthened the confidence of private entrepreneurs and helped to attract investment into the private sector. As foreign investment has been eroded by the Asian Financial crisis, the Chinese economy has had to rely on more domestic capital (*China News Digest*, 23 March 1998; *South China Morning Post*, 19 March 1998).

In 1995, the central government formulated a policy of 'changing the ownership' (*gaizhi*) and 'keeping the large ones and letting the smaller ones go' (*zhuada fangxiao*). This policy was aimed at keeping 500 to 1,000 large SOEs under the state's ownership and reforming the smaller SOEs through reorganisations, mergers, acquisitions, leasings and sales. Now, statistics show that, under the effects of the Asian economic crisis, the private sector has become the main engine of Chinese economic growth (*Financial Times*, 20 July 1998). A survey (*People's Daily*, 30 July 1998) shows that 62 per cent of private entrepreneurs are eager to buy SOEs to expand their scale of production and enterprise. Undoubtedly, a certain proportion of SOEs will be bought and, in fact, many have already been bought by private enterprise owners. The output value of this sector is becoming increasingly larger, and the role of this sector is becoming ever more important. The information on how many SOEs have been bought by private enterprises is not available. However, the impact is implied in the following case: the Zhejiang-based China-People's Electric Group, a private company, bought 34 state-owned and collective enterprises as part of its plan to expand its production of electrical appliances (Economist Intelligence Unit, 4 April 2001).

In addition, there will be more space for private enterprises to develop. According to research by the National Bureau of Statistics, SOEs will eventually withdraw from 146 of the 196 industrial sectors, including garments, textiles, food, beverages, daily consumer goods and electronics. A state monopoly will only be retained in 15 sectors, including military industries and electricity. Of the remaining 35 sectors – including coal, iron and other major mineral resources, petrochemicals, aerospace, new materials, computers and electronics, etc – the state will only maintain partial control (*China Securities*, 12 November 2000). This will create many new opportunities for private enterprises.

All levels of government have started to abandon discrimination against the private sector, allowing the private economy to compete fairly and develop together with the state-owned and collective economy. They have also initiated many policies designed to foster the growth of the private economy. According to a senior official from the State Economic and Trade Commission, the government has proposed to take further measures to promote the development of private enterprises. First, the restrictions on market access will be relaxed. Second, the policy of equal treatment will be adopted more widely. The government will create an environment of fair competition for non-state enterprises by treating them equally with regard to registration, taxation, finance, credit loans, government services and international trade. Third, the government will improve its services to non-state enterprises (*China News Service*, 8 December 2000). As a result, local governments will provide favourable policies to improve access to credit and technology, offer tax concessions and other assistance to private enterprises and make private business development a part of their economic plans.

The latest statistics show that private enterprises maintain high growth rates. In 2000, the total sales, revenue and consumer goods retail sales by private enterprises increased 39.7 per cent, 38.3 per cent and 38.7 per cent, respectively, over the previous year. The number of employees in private enterprises reached 24.07 million, including 4.58 million new jobs created, the revision of employment for 1.07 million laid-off workers and the absorption of 1.99 million surplus rural labourers. Meanwhile, the number of private enterprises earning foreign exchange through exports increased sharply by 4,294, or 51.4 per cent, to a total of 12,700. Foreign exchange earned through exports reached RMB 74.1 billion (US$8.95 billion), an increase of RMB 38.1 billion (US$4.60 billion), or 105.92 per cent, over the previous year (*China Business Times*, 30 March 2001).

The reasons for the growth pattern of private enterprises are not sufficiently clear at this point and thus further research is desired. However, the rapid development of the sector and its dynamics are convincing evidence. It is undoubtedly true that the sector will play an increasingly important role in the Chinese economy. As property rights theorists would predict, the recognition of private property rights and the legal status of private enterprises in China will have boosted the growth of the sector. The private sector, which has demonstrated its vigour within a largely hostile policy environment, will definitely grow faster and thereby increasingly contribute to sustained growth of the Chinese economy, provided an environment of equal competition for them remains. As Wang (1999) argues, the main engine of accelerated economic growth has been the improvement in factor allocation among sectors, and so the potential for growth of the non-state sector is thus predictable. Based on a statistical analysis of data on 29 provinces, municipalities and autonomous regions, Chen and Feng (2000) have found that private and semi-private enterprises have led to an increase in economic growth in China.

Notes

1 In this chapter, the private sector is defined as domestic private businesses under the effective control of Chinese citizens. It included 1.2 million private enterprises (*siying qiye*) and 31.2 million individual enterprises (*getihu*) in 1998, providing about 20 per cent of employment and industrial output in China.

2 In June 1999, the Industrial and Commercial Bank, China's biggest lender, reported that 21 per cent of its loans were held by non-state enterprises. However, the majority of this was lent to collective and foreign-invested firms. Individually owned and private enterprises shared only minute 0.5 per cent of the funds. Credit managers at the big four state-run commercial banks are still pressured by the government to lend to SOEs. When they do lend to private firms, it is only for the safest projects (the Economist Intelligence Unit, 21 September 2000).

3 China opened its first bourse in Shanghai in December 1990.

4 According to the *South China Morning Post* (24 July 1999), by May 1999 about 18 provinces and regions had tried the experiment of establishing a credit-guarantee system, but the aim was quoted as 'to help small and medium-sized enterprises solve their financial difficulties', instead of private businesses. In terms of size, most of the private enterprises are small and medium. However, compared with the huge number of the dominant publicly owned enterprises, they are 'small ethnic minorities '. The *People's Daily* (16 June 1999) seemed to try to propagate such cases that supported private businesses. It reported a magic result of financial injection to a private firm: in April 1999, Fuan City set up the first credit-guarantee company in Fujian Province to help private enterprises. In two months, it helped 24 funding-hungry private enterprises to borrow

loans from commercial banks. With loan backing, one private company's monthly output doubled.

5 According to Jia *et al.*'s (1994) survey of 475 private enterprises in a county, there were many preferential policies if a private enterprise could succeed in registering as a collective enterprise.

1 More bank loans. The maximum bank loan a private firm could be granted was 15,000 yuan; while that for a collective firm could be several hundred thousand yuan.

2 Lower interest rates. The highest bank interest rate for private firms was 11.52 per cent; while the interest rate set for collective firms was only 6.6 per cent, and 6.3 per cent if the loan was under a certain amount.

3 Free administration fees. Private enterprises had to pay the Industry and Commerce Bureau 2 per cent of administration fees while collective firms were not charged.

4 Favoured tax. Private firms paid tax at a ten-scale accumulated-value-added system, while collective firms paid at an eight-scale system, which was lower.

Other preferences. Collective firms were exempted from product tax in the first year of business start up and from gain tax in the first two years. The policy did not apply to private firms. Similarly, in Fushan County of Guangdong province, where the private economy was active, the private sector was in an unfavourable position. A private enterprise had to pay 3 per cent of its turnover and another 3 per cent of its gain as tax, while a collective firm only paid a tax of 1 per cent of its turnover.

6 According to Shen *et al.* (1996), there are three types for leasing collective firms: total capital leasing, partial capital leasing and intangible capital leasing. In the last category, a collective firm only 'leases' its intangible capital, such as firm title, business licence, and credit. One collective firm leased its trademark for an annual payment of RMB 10,000.

Bibliography

Bowles, P. and Dong, X. (1999) 'Enterprise ownership, enterprise organisation, and worker attitudes in Chinese rural industry: some new evidence', *Cambridge Journal of Economics*, 23(1).

Brown, J.R. II, and Rose, D.C. (1998) 'On the absence of privately owned, publicly traded corporations in China: the Kirby Puzzle,' *The Journal of Asian Studies*, 57(2), 442–452.

Byrd, W.A. (1992) *Chinese Industrial Firms under Reform* (London: Oxford University Press).

Caulet, J. *et al.* (1999) 'Stakeholder incentives and reforms in China's state owned enterprises: a common-property theory,' *China Economic Review*, 10(2), 99–110.

Chang, C. and Wang, Y. (1994) 'The nature of the township-village enterprise,' *Journal of Comparative Economics*, 19, 434–452.

Chen, C. (1996) 'Regional determinants of direct foreign investment in mainland China,' *Journal of Economic Studies*, 23(3), 18–30.

Chen, B. and Feng, Y. (2000) 'Determinants of economic growth in China: private enterprise, education, and openness,' *China Economic Review*, 11(1), 1–15.

Chen, C., Chang, L. and Zhang, Y. (1995) 'The role of direct foreign investment in China's post-1978 economic development,' *World Development,* 23(24), 691–703.

Chen, R. (1990) 'A preliminary analysis of the "big labour-hiring households".' In P. Nolan, Dong, F. (eds), *Market Force in China* (London: Zed Books).

Economist Intelligence Unit (2000) 'China's economy: Full steam ahead?' http://www.chinaonline.com/issues/econ_news/NewsArchive/secure/2000/November/C000110251.asp.

Jia, T., Liang, C. and Qing, S. (1994) Research on contemporary China's private entrepreneur class,' internal publication, Beijing.

Kraus, W. (1991) *Private Business in China* (Honolulu: University of Hawaii Press).

Naughton, B. (1995) *Growing Out of the Plan: Chinese Economic Reform, 1978–1993* (New York: Oxford University Press).

Nee, V. (1992) 'Organisational dynamics of market transition: hybrid forms, property rights, and mixed economy in China,' *Administrative Science Quarterly*, 37, 1–27.

Shan, J., Tian, G.G. and Sun, F. (1997) 'The FDI-led growth hypothesis: further economic evidence from China, *Economics Division Working Paper*, No. 2, National Centre for Development Studies, The Australian National University.

Shen, J.M., Jiang, K.Y. and Ye, Y. (1996) 'Survey on township and village enterprise leasing system in Wujiang City,' *China Rural Economy*, 10, 61–65.

Tao, Z. and Zhu, T. (2000) 'Agency and self-enforcing contracts,' *Journal of Comparative Economics*, 28, 80–94.

Tao, Z. and Zhu, T. (2001) 'An agency theory of transactions without contract enforcement: the case of China,' *China Economic Review*, 12(1), 1–14.

Walder, A. (1995) 'Local government as industrial firms: an organisational analysis of China's transitional economy,' *American Journal of Sociology*, 101, 263–301.

Wang, X. (1999) 'Sustainability of China's Economic Growth,' *China Conference Papers*, National Centre for Development Studies, The Australian National University.

Wank, D.L. (1999) *Commodifying Communism: Business, Trust, and Politics in a Chinese City* (Cambridge: Cambridge University Press).

Warner, M. (1995) *The Management of Human Resources in Chinese Industry* (London: Macmillan).

Woo, W., Hai, W., Jing, Y. and Fan, G. (1994) 'How successful has Chinese enterprise reform been? Pitfalls in opposite biases and focus,' *Journal of Comparative Economics*, 18, 410–437.

Xu, H. (1996) 'Innovation of township and village enterprise leasing system,' *China Rural Economy*, 10, 66–69.

Xu, X. and Wang, Y. (1999) 'Ownership structure and corporate governance in Chinese stock companies,' *China Economic Review*, 10(1), 75–98.

Zhang, H. and Liu, W. (1995) *China's Private Economy and Entrepreneurs* (Beijing: Zhishi Press).

Zhu, T. (1998) 'A theory of contract and ownership choice in public enterprises under reformed socialism: the case of China's TVEs,' *China Economic Review*, 9(1), 59–71.

6 Institutional constraints on changes in ownership and control within Chinese publicly listed companies

Yang Chen and Richard Sanders

Introduction

There has been remarkable, if uneven, development of China's stock markets in the past 10 years. After years of intense debate, the Shanghai Stock Exchange (SHSE) and the Shenzhen Stock Exchange (SZSE) were officially established in 1990 and 1991 respectively, and in a surge of reform in 1992, the government approved a 'bolder' plan to experiment with the shareholding system in state-owned enterprises (SOEs). By the end of 1996, the number of shareholding companies at, or above, the county level exceeded 8,000, although the shares of most of these companies were non-transferable[1] *market* capitalisation at the end of 1997 reached 1,753 billion yuan, up from 105 billion yuan at the end of 1992 (Ma, 2000, p. 74). Value traded in the market grew from 68 billion yuan in 1992 to 4,600 billion yuan in 2000. From 1991 to 2000, the number of listed companies increased from 14 to 1,160 while the number of individual stock investors exceeded 50 million by the end of 2000.[2]

By December 2000, the SHSE and SZSE had made public offerings totalling 340 billion yuan shares, of which 120 billion yuan were transferable, and listed companies had collected a total of 483.4 billion yuan from the stock market. In just 10 years the two markets provided 150 billion yuan revenue to the government and generated fees of 120 billion yuan. In total, the government collected 770 billion yuan funds from its two stock markets in the 1990s, an amount equal to three times the state fiscal revenue in 1990 and equivalent to 38 times the funds generated by issuing government bonds. Yet the question remains: while the government was obviously a big winner, did the publicly listed companies achieve their desired objectives and did general investors get satisfactory rewards?

Although the stock market has surged in the past 10 years, the merits of this surge are hotly debated. In October 2000, the magazine *'Finance'* delivered a paper that exposed the role of investment funds in speculation and in the manipulation of stocks,[3] while in early 2001 the economist Wu Jinglian[4] initiated a nationwide debate on the Chinese stock market, arguing that the Chinese stock market was both overheated and operated like a casino. Meanwhile, intensive debate and analysis continues unabated concerning the common misfortune of publicly listed companies in China and of the majority of their general investors. Many observers argue that, given the lack of legal, institutional and governance structures necessary to support the stock market, the resource allocation function cannot be expected to improve the economic efficiency of listed companies. They support Wu Jinglian's argument that China's stock market operates merely like a casino for the privileged groups to obtain money – *quanqian*.[5] Public surveys reveal that the majority (about 75 per cent[6]) of citizens support this view although, as general investors, most of the same citizens were victims of the stock market crash after the Spring Festival 2001, allegedly caused by Wu's criticisms.

The recent arguments regarding the development of China's securities markets and its publicly listed companies reflect the intertwined systemic crisis of the Chinese economy in transition. This chapter attempts to identify the relevance of relations between bureaucratic changes, other forms of structural innovation and the efficiency of organisations. In so doing, it aims to answer two important and interlinked questions: first, are the publicly listed companies merely different in organisational form but essentially the same in terms of substantial control? Second, to what extent have publicly listed companies improved their efficiency as a result of adopting stock mechanisms and corporate governance? In answering these questions, this chapter aims to make clear why recent innovations in terms of ownership and property rights have failed to deliver the improvements in corporate efficiency the decision-makers originally hoped for.

China's stock markets: the first ten years

The stock mechanism: beleaguered policy choice

The dominant view with regard to the transition process in China, widely held by observers both within and outside China, is that a market economy requires property rights that are defined with sufficient clarity and enforced with sufficient predictability to encourage individuals and firms to expend effort, plan, invest and bear risks (Oi and Walder, 1999, p. 1). Since the late 1980s, Chinese firms have been adopting a number of economic strategies and practices that resemble the rational bureaucratic systems found in firms in advanced market societies. The aim of these strategies and practices has always been the reform of ownership and property rights. Yet maintaining public ownership as the dominant form of the property rights arrangement was a central concern in the design of China's reform policies, from the 'four cardinal principles' spelled out in 1979 to the blueprint of the 'socialist market economy' presented at the 14th Party Congress in 1992 (Oi and Walder, 1999, p. 2).

Property is considered as a 'bundle of rights' (Demsetz, 1967, p. 104).

Property rights in emerging market economies have long been perceived as 'hybrid', combining features of private and public property (Stark, 1990, pp. 351–392). But corporate reform in China has focused on the reassignment of property rights within a *socialist ideological commitment.* And given that this ideological conformity precludes outright privatisation, just how clear can property rights be defined?

China's reform has been conducted largely by 'trial and error'. Instead of seeking to implement a blueprint for reform, changes in ownership and property rights have continued without strategic research and systematic analysis. Changes in ownership and property rights started in the early 1980s by extending the independence, and enlarging the decision-making powers, of SOEs. This early strategy, with the 'contract responsibility system' (with remuneration linked to output) at its heart, did not bring about the efficiency of SOEs but instead resulted in a weak, stagnating state-owned sector within an otherwise booming economy. It was believed that the existing institutional arrangements were not capable of ensuring the requisite clarity and predictability and the perceived problem was thus to create a system which did so. By the end of 1980s, the dominant view was that the development of a stock mechanism (*gufen zhi*) could be the answer and an effective prescription to save the SOEs.

Those Chinese economists who opted for the establishment of a stock market did not acknowledge or, for some reason, ignored the fact that the fundamental function of western stock markets was to raise funds. Rather than placing high hopes on the resource allocation function of the stock mechanism, the main objective of establishing the Chinese stock market was to 'support the further rudimentary reform of SOEs by clarifying their ownership and property rights'. The economists and decision makers expected to effect a strengthening of the supervision over key agents, specifically the leaders of the SOEs, thereby forcing the SOEs to establish a self-constraint mechanism through the stock market system. They optimistically predicted that all the defects of the SOEs would be eliminated through 'stock mechanism reconstruction' (*gufen zhi gaizao*).

Yet how would property rights be specified and enforced through the stock market? The economic transition of China since 1978 onwards has been widely identified as reform 'growing out of plan' (Walder, 1995, pp. 969–971). Fligstein argues that the reform process is a 'state-building' project of market construction and transformation (Fligstein, 1996, pp. 656–673), in which the state shapes the dynamics and structure of the markets that emerge under its guidance. But could a functioning stock market system, which emerged through a long process of evolution within western capitalism (Chaudhry, 1993, pp. 245–274) be created overnight and enforced in China 'by design' (Murrel, 1992, pp. 79–95, Stark, 1992, pp. 7–54)? And in any event, how closely should economic institutions conform to models provided by western European or North American capitalism? Without seeking to solve these puzzles, China's stock market trials, affectionately referred to as 'groping for stones to cross the river',[7] unfolded in unanticipated directions.

The uneven development of China's stock market in the 1990s: a 'policy-driven market' (zhengce shi)

In the early days of reform, mainstream western economists argued that it would take 25 years for China to establish fully a properly functioning securities market, although they welcomed the adoption of a stock market as a means of encouraging the process of economic transition. In the mid 1980s, the Chinese government sent economists to advanced market economies, including the USA and Japan, to learn techniques of stock market management and, at the end of the decade, economists who had trained in Wall Street returned to China and initiated the *lianban* – The United Office for Research and Design of a Securities Market. This later became the Centre for China's Security Market Research and Design and originated the first formal document with regard to the establishment of a stock market: 'The Tentative Plan for the Creation and Management of China's Stock Market'.[8] Yet owing to ideological constraints, intensive debate among academics and government decision-makers over the creation of a stock market within a socialist context lasted a very long time, even after the establishment of the SHSE and SZSE in the early 1990s.

While the economists attempted to expound and prove the rationality of a stock mechanism within a 'socialist commodity economy', 'bold' trials were implemented in enterprises in southern China in 1990. But the Chinese stock market was out of balance in terms of supply and demand at an early stage. Because of the intense ideological debate around the formation of a stock market, the number of companies allowed to float was very limited. From 1991 to 1992, for example, there was only one new company floated on the SHSE. As a result, the share price continued to increase no matter whether the company was profitable or not. Since the governing bodies of the stock market had evolved from the system of planning, it was inevitable that they would wish to shape the development of the stock market.

The inconsistent, changing policies of the governing body reflected the conflicts raised by the establishment of the stock market in these circumstances. The first important action of the authorities was the Shenzhen government saving the declining SZSE in August 1991. In early 1991, for the purpose of containing the SZSE within the government plan, the Shenzhen government[9] implemented strict control over the fluctuation of stock prices on a daily basis (within 0.5 per cent for an increase, 5 per cent for a decrease), and collected 6 per cent revenue from each exchange. As a result, the SZSE declined continuously from December 1990 to August 1991, and the market value fell by over 800 million yuan. The SZSE was in chaos and, on 2 September the mayor called on government institutions and companies to save it. The government gathered 200 million yuan and put in for the leading share 'SZ Development'. On 7 September, the SZSE stopped declining and increased by 0.88 per cent. By the end of October, the SZSE rose off the bottom.[10]

The watershed came after Deng Xiaoping's comments on the stock market during his southern tour in spring 1992. Deng pointed out: '[you are] allowed to take a see-saw policy, [you should be] determined to have trials; see-saw for one or two years, if [it turns out to be] right, open the stock market; if wrong, close it.'[11]

Before 1992, there were only eight listed companies on the SHSE with transferable shares worth less than 80 million yuan, resulting in a huge gap between the supply of, and demand for, shares on the exchange. After Deng's speech, from 5 February, the Shanghai government gradually loosened its control over share prices (allowing fluctuations within 5 per cent daily) and arranged new companies' flotation. On 21 May, the government lifted all price controls, leading to the first 'blow-out' (*jingpen*) on the SHSE. The SHSE index increased 94 per cent in one day – it climbed from 616 on 20 May to 1,256 on 21 May. By 25 May, the index had reached 1,420. The market advanced far more vigorously than the 'planner' could expect, leaping beyond his control. As a result, in order to meet the unexpectedly large demand, the government responded by first floating seven companies simultaneously and subsequently floating 34 companies within one month. But on 10 August, the SHSE index declined sharply below 1,000 and, on 17 November hit a new low of 393. The SHSE lost 1,000 points within 5 months.[12]

Institutional economists identify that organisations and individuals are as likely to act according to social norms and the mandates of the institutional and cultural environments in which they are embedded, as they are to act according to the nebulous push of the market's invisible hand. But they are not passive recipients of top-down policy – rather, they interpret, adapt, modify and even subvert the formal measures that come from on high. One of the typically Chinese characteristics of economic transition is that it is 'bottom-up', not in the plan of the government, but a spontaneous process within a more relaxed political and economic environment. Furthermore, the 'Great Leap Forward' nature of this spontaneous process is another, somewhat bizarre, typically Chinese aspect of the transition. In the 1980s, there was a chaotic nationwide trade in steel (*dao gangcai*) after the central government relaxed price controls and implemented the 'dual-track price system' over industrial materials. Then, in the 1990s, there came a period of 'stock fantasy' (*gufeng*) after Deng's 'see-saw' speech leading to the initial wealth 'blow-outs' in the SZSE and SHSE.

Stock market reform ran rampant across China from the second half of 1991. Local governments directly or indirectly supported and pushed the transformation of local enterprises. Enterprises employing the stock mechanism and issuing 'inner shares'[13] increased remarkably in a short time. From 1992 to the first half of 1993, more than 200 enterprises were reconstructed and held the title of 'stock mechanism enterprises' in Jiangsu province alone (Wang, 1993). In Hubei province, there were only 23 stock companies in early 1992, yet within one year, the number had reached 133 (Zheng, 1994). By the end of 1992, more than 10 billion yuan in funds were raised by enterprises issuing 'inner shares' in Guangdong province. Indeed, the newly transformed stock companies increased so quickly that the authorities could not keep proper account. By the end of October 1993, approximately 3,800 'stock mechanism enterprises' in a variety of forms were registered across China (Qian, 1997, pp. 215–240).

The soaring stock market in the late 1991 and in the summer 1992 generated a group of millionaires and ignited a fever of enthusiasm towards the stock market. Under such circumstances, it was rare to worry about whether the newly publicly listed companies successfully reconstructed property rights and improved efficiency after flotation. What local government officers and SOE managers were concerned about was not the 'clarification of property rights and the reform of corporate governance' but the success of the flotation itself. It was only after 1993 that the focus of interest concerning the stock market shifted towards the quality of listed companies.

China's stock market evolved at a miraculous pace after 1992, although in the form of 'retreating by two feet but advancing by three feet' (*tui liangbu jing sanbu*) influenced by the changing policies of the authorities. On 12 March 1994, the China Securities Regulatory Commission (CSRC) issued strategic policies such as tax holidays on stock exchange income and the establishment of investment funds, encouraging corporate investors. The market reaction came in August 1994. After the news was announced on 30 July, 'the CSRC and the State Council make decisions to stabilise and develop the stock market', the SHSE increased 33.46 per cent overnight. But the stock market fell into stagnation in November as the result of monetary retrenchment campaigns to restrain inflation during that period.

In May 1995, a three-day 'blow-out' of the stock market occurred. On 18 May, CCTV broadcast that the government was temporarily to stop bond dealing and, as a direct result, between 18 and 22 May, the SHSE index jumped from 723 to 897 and the SZSE index increased from 1043 to 1425. As a result, on 22 May the Security Committee of the State Council declared that, for the sake of the sustainable development of the stock market, the government should control and balance the pace of new flotation. The next day, 23 May, the SHSE and SZSE indexes dropped 16.39 per cent and 16.9 per cent respectively.

Yet, from 1 April to 1 December 1996, the SHSE and SZSE indexes increased 124 per cent and 346 per cent respectively with the expectation of positive effects of the Hong Kong handover in 1997. From October, the CSRC issued relevant policies for the purpose of regulating and cooling down the overheated stock market, e.g. 'Notice on regulating listing companies' illicit behaviour', and 'Regulation of the management of brokers'. On 16 December, the *People's Daily* editorial 'The proper attitude towards the stock market' concluded that the huge increases in the stock market were 'unusual and irrational'. On 19 December, the major media reported the guiding principles mentioned by the General Managers of the SHSE and the SZSE in their interview in Beijing: 'legality, supervision, self-discipline, standardisation'. Within one week, the SHSE and SZSE indexes decreased 31 per cent and 38 per cent respectively, involving the evaporation of 120 billion yuan of paper-value.

The top leaders' attitude towards the stock market fundamentally changed by the time the 15th Plenum of 1997 passed the guiding principles for further reform of the SOEs. The 15th Plenum was a watershed in terms of changes in ownership and property rights. At that meeting, not only outright state ownership but also 'mixed public ownership' (in which the state held the majority of shares within companies with collective, individual and foreign shareholders) was defined as 'public'. This redefinition implied that the stock mechanism would become the principal mode for corporate development in China and the stock market was designated as the correct channel for implementing further reform of the ailing SOEs through leasing, merging and capital reorganisation. By 1997, China's stock market had reached a point from which there was no going back.

Thus, the stock market remained essentially a 'policy-driven market'. The indexes of the SHSE and SZSE, ignited by high technology, particular so-called E-shares,[14] climbed significantly in May 1999. This time, however, the government did not suppress the market, as it had done before, rather the government supported it by positive comments in the *People's Daily*. But the indexes did not fly as high as they were expected to do, indeed they dropped vigorously on 1 July, the day on which the 'Security Law' was implemented.

Institutional analysis

Institutional arrangements of the Chinese stock market

Unable to escape the habits built up within the planned economy, the Chinese government has so far used the financial system to achieve objectives such as rescuing the ailing SOEs, achieving sectoral and regional balances of development and mobilising resources for specific purposes. Instead of changing the way of thinking and exploring governance innovation in order to adapt to the increasing demands made on it to manage an ever more complex and sophisticated economy, policy making simplistically constructed 'the market' through the extant administrative hierarchy.

The most significant control imposed on the primary market is the annual stock issuance plan and the associated cumbersome approval procedures. The process of quota distribution across regions has been highly political in nature, reflected by the fact that different provinces have been given the same quota for several years in a row.

In the primary market, the public offerings have to go through a complicated approval procedure in which the CSRC (Chinese Securities Regulatory Commission), the State Planning Committee (SPC), the State Economic System Reform Commission (SRC), and the People's Bank of China (PBC) jointly determine the annual stock issuance plan, stipulating the total number of new stocks to be listed on the exchanges and the total value of initial public offers.

Since 1993, each province has been given a quota of new listings and the provincial Planning Commission and System Reform Commission selects the candidates. The selection at the provincial level is, in principle, based on industrial bureaux recommendations and the overall balance between industrial sectors. Since 1997, the emphasis of quota allocation has been to support 1,000 key SOEs, 120 large enterprise groups and 100 enterprises experimenting with the modern enterprise system. The final approval for an enterprise's Initial Public Offering (IPO) is made by the CSRC, based on the recommendation of the provincial government, its assessment of the enterprise's financial and management conditions, current government policies, and stock market conditions (Ma, 2000, pp. 73–76).

The provision of markets is an entrepreneurial activity and has a long history in the west. But unlike commodity and stock exchanges in the West, which are normally organised by a group of traders (the members of the exchange) and where transactions within the exchanges are highly regulated by convention (quite different from any government regulations), Chinese stock exchanges are shaped by the state and remain subject to extensive administrative control and intervention. A key question thus presents itself. Does the institutional framework of China's stock market, characterised by strong administrative intervention, provide sustainable support to publicly listed companies to 'clarify property rights' and thereby improve their efficiency, or does it hinder or constrain them in so doing?

Institutional dilemma

The more complex the exchange and the larger its economic scale, the more necessary is it to have complex and credible institutions acting *impartially* as third parties in policing and enforcing agreements (North, 1990).[15] One assumption implied within the design of the institutional framework of Chinese stock markets is that their governing bodies are genuinely *impartial* agents of the state.

Agents, as well as other organisations, are purposive entities. Agency theory analyses the important impact on incentives and the behaviour on agents, defined by the opportunities afforded to them by the institutional structure of society. Bureaucratic agents' behaviour is not static and immutable and analysis of economic change therefore requires an understanding both of officials as economic actors and of the varying incentives, constraints, and resources that shape their opportunities and choices (Qian and Weingast, 1997, pp. 83–92).

A school of scholars[16] identifies the following characteristics of Chinese polity in terms of the country in transition: (i) the *party/state* governance structure has remained dominant, but (ii) there is a conflict between the vertical hierarchy classified by industry and the horizontal local bureaucracy over the control of benefit streams (*tiaokuai feige*), and (iii) – ineluctably derived from (iv) – the central government is comparatively weakened in terms of the essential control over the economy in the face of strong local powers, resulting from the process of decentralisation.

As we have seen above, it has been political agents as purposive entities at central and local level, which have shaped the direction of institutional change of the Chinese stock market. At the central level, in 1992, the CSRC was institutionalised within the extant regime of power rather than as an independent governing body of the stock market. The CSRC was granted a parallel administrative rank and similar powers to other formerly established bureaux, such as the SPC, SRC and the PBC – the arrangement reflecting the balance of power among different interest groups. At local level, the local authorities hold the right of recommendation (of companies for flotation) while the CSRC tightly keeps the final approval in its pocket. However, as stated before, the propensity of the market to 'blow-out' has gone beyond policy control. As a result, central control over the stock market has shrunk and shifted, through preferential quota allocation, towards key SOEs and national champions under direct vertical control of the central government. Constrained within such an institutional framework, stock market outcomes are determined largely by a bargaining process between political agents, rather than resulting from entrepreneurial behaviour. The hybrid 'policy-driven' market discussed above has been the inescapable result of such a linear construction and incorporation of 'the market mechanism' within 'the plan'.

The policy shapers identify and reiterate that the main official objective of establishing the stock exchange has been aimed at 'clarifying ownership and property rights'. Even in ideal circumstances, it is an unachievable target: the existence of perfectly specified property rights is one of the assumptions of the textbook neoclassical economic model; however, it can never be realised in the 'real' world, full of uncertainties and positive transaction costs. In addition, in contemporary China, the circumstances are very far from ideal.

Property can be understood as a benefit (or income) stream (Bromley, 1991, p. 2) and property rights as 'claim(s) to a benefit stream that the state will agree to protect through the assignment of duty to others who may covet, or somehow interfere with, the benefit stream' (Bromley, 1991,

p. 2). North concludes: 'the rights to an asset generating a flow of services are usually easy to assure when the flow can be easily measured. Therefore, when a flow is known and constant, it is easy to assure rights. When the flow of income from an asset can be affected by the exchange parties, assigning property rights becomes more problematic' (North, 1990, pp. 57–58). The institutional arrangements of the Chinese stock exchanges have granted central authorities the rights of distributing quotas for listing, final approval of IPOs etc and local authorities the rights of recommendation. The opportunity for enterprises (no matter what their nature, whether public or private) to float is scarce while the possibility of collective 'blow-out' is irrationally high and irresistibly attractive. Governing bodies are essentially granted control over enterprises' benefit streams, a right provided by the opportunities afforded by the institutional arrangements. The authorities do not act as agents but are directly or indirectly involved in the enterprises as shareholders and stakeholders. Therefore, the property rights of enterprises are obscured and entrepreneurs' control over their assets are weakened, rather than clarified and strengthened, as had been originally hoped.

Therein lies the fundamental dilemma: how does one get agents to behave as impartial third parties in a complex world with growing opportunities for exercising discretion over the use of property and enhanced opportunities for rent-seeking?

'Black curtain' – an inevitable institutional trap?

Some scholars argue that reforms of property rights in publicly owned organisations are driven by the private interest of the parties concerned, thus embodying a process of hidden, if partial, privatisation. Arbitrage has often been a key channel of hidden privatisation within the existing institutional context in China. According to Wu Jinglian, the process of arbitrage involved consumer goods in the late 1970s and early 1980s, shifted to industrial materials in the mid and late 1980s when the 'dual-track price system' was adopted, and subsequently moved to land and capital in the early 1990s, when the markets for real estate and securities were opened up (Wu, 1995).

A major contributing factor to the persistence of the above phenomenon is the efforts by the state to justify it. In the stock markets, all public offerings are assisted by investment banking firms, which are controlled by the government and which have mushroomed at the height of each spell of policy liberalisation since Deng Xiaoping's southern tour in 1992. The call by central leaders to accelerate economic change has often been opportunistically used by state agents as a means of justifying their attempts to expand their own interests (Lin and Zhang, 1999, pp. 211–226). In the second market, brokerage functions are performed, mainly by two types of non-bank financial institutions: securities firms and Trust and Investment

Corporations (TICs) (Ma, 2000, pp. 80–87). Until recently, most securities firms owned by state banks and TICs belonged to local governments or large state enterprises. They have been facilitated by growing inconsistencies and uncertainties in the state's trial-and-error style of reform and intermittent spells of accelerated economic liberalisation that have created more opportunities for expanding and justifying the use of public resource for group gains.

Nee seems to view 'the pursuit of power and plenty by economic actors in society' as the linchpin of economic transitions (Nee, 1996, p. 945) while similar views from Chinese economists consider 'the bureaucrats' corruption as a more efficient way to allocate resources' (He, 1998, p. 86). It is the argument of this chapter, however, that the above views, particularly when applied to the stock market, pose dangers for China and that, on the contrary, more sophisticated governing tools – formal rules, informal constraints and substantial enforcement – are increasingly necessary as the stock market grows. Chinese scholars have emphasised the importance of security regulations over stock exchanges. However, they have failed to realise that laws cannot work by themselves. The law that is not carried out is tantamount to no law. One dilemma lies in the difficulty of defining the powers of the judiciary within the current institutional framework – an institutional framework that has failed to provide incentives for governing bodies to carry out punishments when called upon to do so.

For instance, most securities companies and TICs with SHSC or SZSE memberships have been authorised to serve as brokers as well as dealers on their own accounts. These financial institutions have been established through conversion, creation and adoption within the existing bureaucratic networks (Lin and Zhang, 1999, pp. 211–226).[17] Corporate investors, such as the investment funds, are connected to the governing bodies in control of large amounts of resources and are well positioned to reap huge gains from the practice of insider dealing and to generate significant profits for themselves and their upper authority – the governing bodies of the stock exchanges. At the local level, in order to get approval for the enterprise's Initial Public Offering (IPO), the local authorities convert, create and adopt companies to meet the assessment criteria set by the CRSC. Local government officials are then involved in recommending companies for public offering on the basis of sometimes-speculative financial reports.

Although the publicly listed companies and the financial organisations represent the respective interests of the bureaucratic systems to which they belong, their intertwined political and economic interests lead inevitably to collusion among the financial institutions, the publicly listed companies and their governing bodies. The bulk of the collusive activity takes place in the grey area of law and regulations. Many previous restrictions are lifted and previous rules modified in the name of 'promoting reform and opening economic development'.

As stated before, the assignment of rights in the Chinese stock exchange is allocated by traditional norms of behaviour through the extant administrative hierarchy rather than being defined and enforced through the legal structure. Rights are assigned simply by administrative power, a process that, from the beginning, has lacked the formal legal constraints of duty and liability.

'Bad legislation is worse than no legislation ... if those who violate the law are not punished, laws will become void as soon as they are proclaimed'. Liang Qichao, a Chinese intellectual, wrote these words nearly 100 years ago, just before the Qing dynasty fell and China entered a long period of political turmoil. And today, failure to define the powers of the judiciary and to modernise the country's governance with regard to the stock market question could undermine not only the smooth transition of the economy but also the stability of the country once more.

The neglect of efficiency

Under the circumstances identified above, organisations engaged in these stock market practices are less concerned with economic performance than with survival in emerging, unstable and uncertain institutional practices.

The oft-quoted Chinese argument 'solve the problem of development by developing' has proved to be wrong with regard to publicly listed companies. After flotation, many listed companies have not been able to avoid misfortune and have frequently operated by 'making profits in the first year (after flotation), breaking even in the second, and going into debt in the third.' The companies have been transformed superficially into public listed companies but, in essence, they remain tied to the old corporate governance mechanisms. The governance of the listed companies has not been independent but has remained in the hands of the 'mother group company' and the bureaucratic network to which it belongs.

To some extent, the destructive phenomenon of the public listed company – 'value flotation, avoid institutional change' – is inevitable within the existing institutional arrangements. Companies obviously value flotation through which vested interests are generated and maintained: by contrast, substantial institutional change and good corporate governance would weaken insider control of listed companies and restrict those vested interests.

Furthermore, the majority shareholders of publicly listed companies substantially neglect the rights of general stockholders. Stephen Green mentions the phenomenon of the abuse of minority shareholders in his recent research on the Chinese stock market (Green, 2001, p. 6). No matter what the difference is in the nature of publicly listed companies in terms of ownership, whether it is the state or individuals who hold the majority shares, infringement of the rights of minority shareholders has run rampant within publicly listed companies. This has happened as a result of a series of practices. Before flotation, assets are scraped together and sometimes-speculative financial statements are made. After flotation, the mother company takes funds by 'relevant dealing' with the listed company, e.g. the mother company sells it 'intangible assets' and, in the end, the listed company becomes an 'empty shell'. Of the 841 companies listed at the end of 1998, for example, 467 of them had had their funds used by their majority shareholders (Green, 2001, p. 6).

The patronage between the state agencies and financial organisations, the local government officials and the listed companies makes the supervision and monitoring of the financial organisations and listed companies very difficult. The patronage has led to two surprising features of the Chinese stock market: (i) no IPO has ever failed in the primary market and (ii) no publicly listed companies have ever been delisted. Under these circumstances, the failure of 'corporate governance' within publicly listed companies in China is inevitable. As Stephen Green describes: 'Countless listed companies laugh at the concept of good corporate governance' (Green, 2001, p. 4).

Conclusions

The first conclusion from the development of China's stock markets is that contingencies create opportunities for institutional change. In the 1980s, expediency in central policy-making created a fracture in the rules governing administrative financing, which was subsequently enlarged and perpetuated by opportunistic adaptations by state agents seeking to derive private gains from the public resources under their collective stewardship. Rationalisation and rational action are separate matters. In the institutional perspective, the assumption of rational action is set aside as patterns of decision making and individual (or organisational) choice are empirical questions, not to be simplified as assumptions for the convenience of economic modelling. Chinese stock market designers took it for granted that organisations make decisions only to increase efficiency. This assumption has been proved wrong by the hybrid characteristics of Chinese publicly listed companies.

This chapter argues that changing the nature of Chinese enterprises through flotation seems less and less driven by competition or by the need for efficiency. It is not the drive toward efficiency that guides enterprises' decisions to float on the stock market in the context of China's transforming economy. Rather, the decisions and practices of most publicly listed companies are shaped by a combination of the vested interests of social networks, the political institutions in which they are embedded and the economic uncertainty they experience. Furthermore, their flotation is less a pursuit of efficiency than a superficial mimicry of advanced market societies. Misgovernance of companies, specifically SOEs, and the agency problem remain – and have frequently worsened – after flotation.

Some economists regard the stock market process as a cheap and effective means of transition from socialism to capitalism in China. They criticise state control over the publicly listed companies and argue that it will slow down the transition process, 'allowing parts of the state to have guaranteed control over listed companies undermining corporate governance and encouraging the abuse of minority shareholders' (Green, 2001, p. 7).

These arguments cloud the issue, however. Like managers in Chinese state-owned publicly-listed companies, today's managers in publicly-held corporations in the West also exercise great discretion over the use of assets and maintain considerable on-the-job consumption and other rents. The more interesting question concerns the merging of private companies with state-owned enterprises for the purpose of flotation, adopting the SOE's governance structure after flotation.

The crucial point is that state agents within an institutional framework are, in essence, economic actors. In terms of the substantial control, their behaviour is like that of any other market actor. They live in obscure worlds where it is never clear which actions will have which consequences. They 'construct an account of the world that interprets the murkiness, motivates and determines courses of action, and justifies the action decided upon' (Fligstein, 1996, p. 660). They are no longer passive recipients of top-down policy, as they were expected to be within the administrative hierarchy – rather, they interpret, adapt, modify, and even subvert the formal measures that come from on high. The 'dual identifications' – governing bodies as well as economic actors – of state agents within the Chinese stock market has raised the need for more sophisticated tools of governance than the disciplines of the CCP and its statements of determination and commitment to fight corruption.

The *grey* collusion among those who hold power and capital is deeply rooted in the formal institutional system in China and is widely accepted as a social norm.[18] It would be somewhat naive and too simplistic to suggest that merely reducing the number and size of state shareholdings would contribute enormously to the quality of corporate governance. Institutions define markets. Institutional weakness is getting more pronounced and reflects the importance of institutional development for governing and managing a more complex market by increasingly impersonal means.

If the stock market process within the extant rules ineluctably promotes corruption and stimulates speculative behaviour, it will not lead to a balanced and well-functioning market. Institutional change involves changing the rules. Further empirical studies on institutional innovation should be considered by the decision makers before they implement further 'bolder' policies, such as the outright sell-off of state shareholdings and the opening of the 'second board' in 2001. The challenge to Chinese decision-makers is how to make ownership and property rights, no matter whether state-owned or private by nature, function efficiently under the pressure of intertwined social, political and economic forces. This non-ideological but important task demands a more sophisticated structure of governance based on clearer laws, stronger institutions and greater public accountability.

Notes

1 State Statistical Bureau (1997).
2 *Yangcheng Wanbao*, 15 December 2000.
3 '*Caijing*', 'Finance', October, 2000: paper entitled 'Black curtains in funds – the analysis on the report with regard to the behaviour of investment funds' (*Jijing heimu – guanyu jijing xingwei de yanjiu baogao jiexi*).
4 CCTV finance channel had an interview with Wu Jing Lian in January, 2001.
5 *quanqian: 'quan'*: draw a circle on the ground and occupy, *'qian'*: money.
6 China Central TV and Sina.com surveys, February 2001.
7 Deng XiaoPing's famous saying: '*mozhe shitou guohe*', a key doctrine in China's reform in the past 20 years.
8 '*zhongguo gushi fengyu shinian*' (Ten year review of China stock market), '*caijing shibao*' (Contemporary Finance) 4 December 2000.
9 At the initial stage of SZSE, there was a Stock Price Control department within the Shenzhen municipal governance.
10 '*Zhongguo gushi fengyu shinian liu da guidian*' (Six break points: Chinese stock market 10 years on), in *zhengquan wuxian zhoukan* (*Security Weekly*), 5 December 2000.
11 Deng XiaoPing delivered this speech during his 'south tour' in spring 1992.
12 '*Zhongguo gushi fengyu shinian liu da guidian*', (Six break points: Chinese stock market 10 years on), in *zhengquan wuxian zhoukan* (*Security Weekly*), 5 December 2000.
13 Non-transferable stock issued within the enterprises.
14 The bubble of IT shares in China's stock market following the surge in America and West Europe.
15 Detailed discussion on this view can be seen in North (1990, ch. 8).
16 In the research of Solinger (1994), Lieberthal (1985), You (1998).
17 Lin and Zhang (1999, pp. 211–226): 'conversion' refers to the formation of self-financing spin-off organisations that used to be parts of state agencies, 'creation' involves a partial or full supply of resources by state agencies for the establishment of new backyard profit generators while 'adoption' means the provision of patronage by state agencies to existing public or private enterprises.
18 Some scholars identified the synergy between this phenomenon in contemporary China and that in the *Qing* Dynasty.

Bibliography

Bromley, D.W. (1991) *Environment and Economy-Property Rights & Public Policy* (UK: Blackwell).

Chaudhry, K.A. (1993) 'The myth of the market and the common history of late development,' *Politics and Society*, 21(3) (Sept).

Demsetz, R.H. (1967) *Ownership, Control, and the Firm: The Organisation of Economic Activity* (Oxford: Blackwell).

Fligstein, N. (1996) 'Market as politics: a sociological view of market institutions.' *American Sociological Review*, 61.

Green, S. (2001) 'Something old, something new', *China Review*, Spring.

He, Q.L. (1998) *xiandaihua de xianjin* (*The Catch of Materialisation*) (Beijing: China Today Press).

Lieberthal, K. (1985) *Governing China – From Revolution Through Reform* (New York: W.W. Norton).

Lin, Y.M. and Zhang, Z.X. (1999) 'Backyard profit centres, property rights and economic reform in China'. In J.C. Oi and A.G. Walder (eds), *Property Rights of Economic Reform in China* (Stanford, California: Stanford University Press).

Ma, J. (2000) *The Chinese Economy in the 1990s* (New York: Macmillan),

Murrel, P. (1992) 'Evolutionary and radical approaches to economic reform,' *Economics of Planning*, 25(1).

Nee, V. (1996) 'The emergence of a market society: changing mechanisms of stratification in China.' *American Journal of Sociology*, 101.

North, D.C. (1990) *Institution, Institutional Change and Economic Performance* (Cambridge: University of Cambridge Press).

Oi, J.C. and Walder, A.G. (eds) (1999) 'Property rights in the Chinese economy contours of the process of change'. In *Property Rights of Economic Reform in China* (Stanford, California: Stanford University Press).

Qian, Y.Y. (1997) 'Reforming corporate governance and finance in China'. In M. Aoki and H.-K. Kim (eds), *Corporate Governance in Transitional Economies* (Washington, DC: The World Bank).

Qian, Y.Y. and Weingast, B.R. (1997) 'Federalism as a commitment to preserving market incentives,' *Journal of Economic Perspectives* 11(4).

Solinger, D. (1994) *Chinese Business Under Socialism* (Berkeley: University of California Press).

Stark, D. (1990) 'Privatisation in Hungary: from plan to market or from plan to clan?' *East European Politics and Societies*, 4(3).

Stark, D. (1992) 'Path dependence and privatisation strategies in eastern Europe,' *East European Politics and Societies*, 6(1) (winter).

Streeten, P. (1992) 'Markets and states: against minimalism,' *World Development*, 21(8).

Wang, L.L. (1993) 'lushi wei gufenzhi qiye tigong falu fuwu de diaocha yu fenxi' ('Investigation and analysis on how solicitor provide legal service to stock mechanism enterprises'), *Shenzhen Fazhi Bao* (*Shenzhen Legal News*), 12 October.

Walder, A.G. (1995) 'China's transitional economy: interpreting its significance', *The China Quarterly*, 144 (December).

Wu, J.L. (1995) *China's Economic Reform: Retrospect and Prospect*. The Chinese Economic Reform Workshop, Hong Kong, May.

You, J. (1998) *China's Enterprise Reform – Changing State/society Relations After Mao* (London: Routledge).

Zheng, J.R. (1994) 'gufenzhi muqian buyi quanmian tuikai' ('Too early to implement stock mechanism nationwide'), *Hubei Caijing* (*Hubei Finance and Economics*), August.

7 Chinese grain market efficiency in the post-reform period

Ziping Wu and Seamus McErlean

Introduction

Beginning in 1978, a series of gradual reforms sought to end the dominance of central planning as the system of governance for Chinese grain marketing. More efficient markets were created where freely determined prices played a primary role in resource allocation. By the end of 1985, the reform process had established a dual system of governance that placed freely operating markets alongside that of central planning. Further reforms, which aimed to increase market efficiency and to further diminish central planning in the grain sector, took place between 1992–1994. However, sharp increases in the price of grain during 1994 caused some provinces temporarily to rescind a number of the latter reforms. These retrenchment policies may have stalled or reversed efforts to improve the efficiency of Chinese grain markets (Rozelle *et al.*, 1997).

Despite the significance of the 1992–1994 reforms, little attempt has been made to assess their impact. The objective of this chapter is to test the efficient market hypothesis (EMH) in the Chinese grain market and to assess whether the level of market efficiency has improved following the two periods of reform. The improvement of market efficiency is a stated aim of the Chinese authorities and this study examines how successful these authorities have been in achieving this aim, particularly in the face of the retrenchment policies implemented by the regional authorities in the mid 1990s. The analysis focuses on the wheat, rice and corn markets. These three crops accounted for 85 per cent of total grain production in 2000 and are likely to be fiercely guarded during future WTO negotiations, because of their strategic importance. The markets for these three grain crops are similar in operation and are subject to the same policies, reforms and levels of government intervention.

In the next section, the key reforms of the Chinese grain marketing system are outlined, the motivations behind the reforms are discussed and the problems encountered in the reform process are reviewed. The section after outlines the concept of market efficiency in the context of Chinese grain markets and the methodology for testing the efficient market hypothesis. The results of the analysis are reported and interpreted in the following section, while the final section contains discussion and conclusions.

Reform in the Chinese grain marketing system

Several significant reforms of the Chinese grain market occurred between 1978 and 1985. One of the most significant of these reforms occurred in 1983 when, due to the changing political climate, the free trading of grain between non-government economic agents was permitted. Food processing enterprises in particular were allowed to buy grain directly from farmers in the rural marketplace, subject to the conditions of approval for the quantity of purchase from the authority, and operating after the government agencies (State Grain Marketing Agency – SGMA) had fulfilled their purchasing plans, thus easing for the government the burden of supplying these enterprises. Another key reform was the increasing use of negotiated purchases. Prior to this policy change, government grain requirements (for the system of 'rationed' sales to urban residents) were met almost entirely through the procurement quota system.[1] However, the demand for 'rationed' grain was growing as a result of the expanding urban populations. The prices set by central government for procurement quotas were failing to encourage the additional supplies needed to meet this growing demand and, as such, were not achieving allocative efficiency in the grain market. With reform, the additional supplies required to meet the increasing demand for 'rationed' sales were to be purchased directly from farmers at over-quota prices and negotiated prices (which tended to be significantly higher than quota prices). According to Zhao *et al.* (1988), negotiated purchase transactions were then taking place either on the premises of the local State Grain Marketing Agencies (SMGA) or in the rural free markets, usually towards the end of the day when the market was about to close. Clearly, as a result of negotiated purchases, the government was directly involved in free market grain trading.[2]

The government's aim in permitting free market trade in grain and initiating negotiated purchases was to facilitate the formation of a more Pareto optimal price (determined purely by the interaction of buyers and sellers, and not set by the government), which would guide resource allocation. These reforms sought to improve allocative efficiency in the grain sector. The grain traded through free markets has increased tremendously (Wu, 1995). This increase was partly due to the expansion of trade between individuals and partly due to increasing levels of negotiated purchases by the government.

A further significant reform occurred in 1985, when the quota purchase system was replaced by the contract purchase system. Under the new system, quota purchases and over-quota purchases were merged as 'contract' purchases and the negotiated purchases were retained and expanded. However, the contract purchases were simply a change in name only, because the new system still made use of procurement quotas, which required delivery of quota grain by each farmer at a price set annually by the authorities. In setting this price, the authorities were influenced primarily by their budget constraints and also, but to a lesser extent, by grain production costs and market supply and demand. However, the new national quota was fixed at the reduced amount of 50 million tonnes (only 10 per cent of national production). Significantly, this was less than 50 per cent of the total government grain requirements. The rest of the government grain requirements were to be purchased directly from farmers at negotiated prices (Wu, 1995; Watson, 1997, Wang and Davis, 2000).

Although these early reforms did stimulate additional grain production, other problems arose. In particular, because of their use of negotiated purchases, the government faced substantial increases in the costs of procuring grain. This was a problem because there was no corresponding change in the sales prices of 'rationed sales'. Thus, as Sicular (1995) indicates, high running costs were associated with the reformed grain marketing system and further reform was required.[3]

These further reforms were introduced in 1992–1994 to address the budgetary problems, improve market efficiency, and to further diminish central planning in the Chinese grain sector. To begin with, urban grain reforms reduced 'rationed sales' and increased the 'rationed sales' price to a level consistent with government purchase prices. In addition, a direct payment to urban residents was introduced to compensate for the increase in rationed sales prices. These changes were introduced only after a series of trials in selected areas during the late 1980s. By June 1993, these reforms had been adopted in over 95 per cent of counties (and cities) in China. Indeed, in most regions, the rationed grain sales system was phased out as the rationed grain sales prices approached free market prices. At the same time, the grain retailers in the cities, who had been involved in rationed sales, were encouraged by means of various incentives to involve themselves in free market trade (Rozelle *et al.*, 1997). In an attempt to improve the efficiency of the SGMA, their role and function was altered. The SGMA, although still required to carry out certain policy functions, were converted to commercial trading companies with the potential to earn profits (or losses). The command system operated by central government to allocate procurement quota grain from surplus to deficit regions was replaced with a new system in which regional SGMAs traded amongst themselves in order to achieve reallocation of quota grain from surplus to deficit areas.[4] At the same time, provincial authorities were given control of local contract (procurement quota) purchases.

In addition, in 1994, a further reform directing that the quota purchase price should follow the free market price was announced. In part, this was the recognition that the current system heavily taxed farmers. The central government would still determine a 'recommended' quota price on an annual basis, but in doing so would be primarily guided by the free market price. Furthermore, the actual procurement quota prices paid would tend to deviate from the predetermined 'recommended' annual price. There were two reasons for this. First, as a result of the introduction of regional responsibility (otherwise known as the Governor's Rice-bag Responsibility system), regional governments could use local revenue to subsidise the procurement quota price. Second, quota prices were allowed to vary seasonally, following the same pattern as the free market price (Song, 2000). Furthermore, in some regions, usually those that were self-sufficient in grain, the local SGMAs adopted a more liberal attitude with regard to the compulsory fulfilment of procurement quotas when the gap between quota price and the free market price was small. These reforms seem likely to improve the degree of integration of procurement quota trade with other forms of grain trade.

However, there were sharp price rises in 1994 which were attributed to the recent policy reform and falling levels of grain production. These price rises caused some of the provincial authorities and, to some extent, the central government, to enact retrenchment policies (Rozelle *et al.*, 1997). Retrenchment was a temporary phenomenon that had two main elements. First, the rationed sales system was restored, grain coupons were re-issued and the rationed sales price was fixed at a level much lower than the free market price. Second, for a period of some months in 1994 and early 1995, procurement quota prices were maintained at levels much below the free market price while the government took measures to ensure that quotas were filled. These measures included halting the movement of grain between some regions. Following this period of retrenchment, which ended when free market grain prices began to level off, there was a return to the policies implemented by the further reforms of 1992–1994.

It is important to remember that the relative importance of quota purchases has continually decreased since quota levels were fixed at 500 million tonnes in 1985. Negotiated purchases as a proportion of total government grain purchases (this includes both quota and negotiated purchases) increased from 25 per cent in 1985 to 50 per cent in 1994 and 57.5 per cent in 1996. More recent figures are not available. Demand for food grain has increased quickly since the late 1980s due to the expansion of urban areas, which has accompanied industrial growth. Much of the increase for food grain has been met through free market trade. Further details on the full series of market reforms and their implications for resource utilisation and production can be found in Zhang and Carter (1997), Weersink and Rozelle (1997) and Rozelle *et al.* (2000).

Methodology for testing market efficiency of Chinese grain markets in the presence of non-stationary prices

A conventional definition of market efficiency is given in Fama (1970) and stipulates that prices in an efficient market must always fully reflect available information. In the analysis carried out here we employ a more restrictive definition of market efficiency than that given in Campbell *et al.* (1997), in which the information set includes only the history of prices themselves. However, where more than one price exists in the market for a given commodity, then the same information should be reflected in each price. In the case where there are two prices for the same homogeneous commodity (in the same location and without differences in quality), then market efficiency requires that both prices should reflect available information and, in essence, each price should be an 'unbiased estimator' of the other price. Thus, early tests of the efficient market hypothesis (EMH) were essentially a test of the unbiasedness hypothesis and were conducted by regressing one price on the other in the following equation:

$$P_t^i = \alpha + \beta P_t^j + u_t \tag{7.1}$$

and testing the hypothesis (or conditions) that $\alpha = 0$ and $\beta = 1$. In essence, this approach is used to test if the price paid (received) by one group of market participants is an unbiased estimate of the price paid (received) for the same commodity by an alternative group of market participants. In an efficient market, all the information contained in one price for a commodity should be reflected in all other prices for that commodity. However, this approach is susceptible to the problems associated with the probable non-stationarity of the prices in the test equation. Inference based on the parameters of a classical ordinary least squares regression analysis assumes that certain assumptions are met, one of which is that the variables in the regression are stationary. If the prices in equation (7.1) are integrated of order one (i.e. non-stationary) then conventional testing of the hypothesis that $\alpha = 0$ and $\beta = 1$ will not be valid.

Cointegration analysis provides a useful framework for valid likelihood ratio testing of the conditions of the efficient market hypothesis when the prices in the test equation are non-stationary (Lai and Lai, 1991). Cointegration between non-stationary variables implies that a linear combination of the variables exists that is stationary. Valid inference can be made based on the parameters of a cointegrating regression between two variables. If P^i and P^j are integrated of order one and are found to be cointegrated, then there exists an error correction model (ECM) representation (Engle and Granger, 1987):

$$\Delta P_t^i = a_i(P_{t-1}^i - \alpha - \beta P_{t-1}^j) + \sum_{m=1}^{f} c_m \Delta P_{t-m}^i + \sum_{n=1}^{g} d_n \Delta P_{t-n}^i + e_t \tag{7.2}$$

where ΔP is the change in price $(P_t - P_{t-1})$, e_t is the error term and the term in brackets is the error correction term (ECT), which is the lagged residuals from the cointegrating equation (7.1) and reflects deviations from the long run equilibrium for the two prices (P^i and P^j). Therefore, deviations in this period's price vary in relation to past disequilibria. Under this approach, acceptance of the efficient market hypothesis requires that three sets of conditions, tested sequentially, hold. *Cointegration* is the first necessary condition for market efficiency when prices are integrated of order one. The second necessary condition (closely related to the first) for market efficiency requires that $\alpha = 0$ and $\beta = 1$ in the cointegrating vector. This second condition is referred to as the *unbiasedness* condition and satisfies the Law of One Price (Richardson, 1978). This condition tests the theory that, in an efficient market, separate prices for the same commodity should reflect the same information. The unbiasedness condition is frequently rejected in markets where some of the market participants are able to exert control (regulatory or market power) over the market in order to impose margins between prices.

Efficiency also requires a third set of conditions, that relates in part to the speed of adjustment coefficient (SOAC), a_i in equation (7.2). This coefficient represents the rate at which changes in this period's price, ΔP^i, responds to past long-run disequilibria. In our two-price example, a second speed of adjustment coefficient, a_j, representing how deviations in this period's price, ΔP^j, respond to past long-run disequilibria, can be estimated.[5] The third set of conditions, known as the *adjustment efficiency* conditions, require that the absolute values of the SOACs are not equal to zero (a_i, $a_j \neq 0$) and that $c_m = d_n = 0$. This condition tests whether prices adjust quickly (and in both directions) to a new equilibrium position when disequilibria occur.[6] In an efficient market all prices are expected to adjust when disequilibrium occurs.

Various factors contribute to market inefficiency. These include imperfect information, thin markets and the situation where some market participants can control the market because of market power (i.e. monopoly) or legal authority. If any of these factors are present in a market, then some or all of the conditions for market efficiency may be rejected.

Clearly, the *unbiasedness* and *adjustment efficiency* conditions for accepting the EMH can be examined by applying the appropriate parameter restriction (likelihood ratio) tests.[7] The three sets of necessary conditions combine to provide the sufficient conditions for market efficiency. If these conditions hold then the efficient market hypothesis is accepted. The procedure outlined by Johansen (1991) and Johansen and Juselius (1990) is used here, because it offers a method of directly testing both cointegration and the parameter restrictions on the cointegrating relations using likelihood ratio (LR) tests in order to examine the EMH.

The EMH conditions, as set out above, relate to the situation where there are two prices of interest. Reform of the Chinese grain market has established three different producer prices for the same type and quality of grain: quota price (QP), negotiated price (NP), and the free market price (FMP). These three prices for wheat, observed monthly over the period 1987 to 1998, are illustrated in Figure 7.1. Therefore, in Chinese

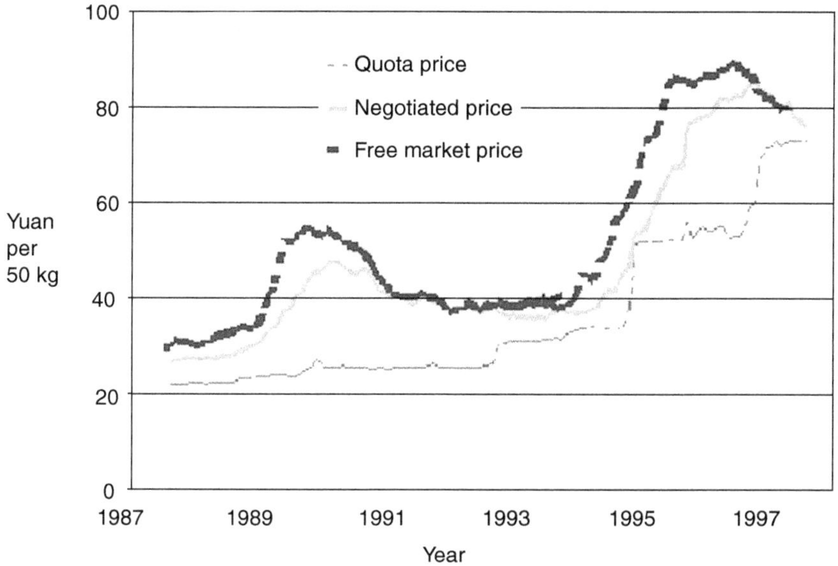

Figure 7.1 Chinese wheat producer prices (1987–1997).

grain markets, there are three prices of interest. In this case the EMH is examined by testing whether the three sets of necessary conditions are met for each – of three possible – price–pair combinations in the wheat, corn, early rice and late rice markets. The EMH is tested in two consecutive periods so that an assessment of whether or not there has been an improvement in grain market efficiency over time can be made. Period one (1987m1–1994m3) follows the early reforms of 1978–1985 and period two (1994m4–1997m10) follows the further reforms implemented between 1992–1994.[8]

Data

The data were sourced from the Ministry of Agriculture (MOA) in Beijing. They are representative monthly grain (wheat, corn, early and late rice) producer prices for quota, negotiated and free market trade collected over the period January 1987 to October 1997. The three prices (FMP, NP and QP) are simple averages of prices collected from 260 selected rural free markets across 28 regions (excluding Tibet). The calculation of weighted average prices was not an option, as reliable data on the levels of trade associated with individual rural markets is not available. However, it is worth noting that the 260 markets from which the data were collected were selected by industry experts on the grounds that these were the most important markets. In collecting the data, the MOA ensured that all three prices related to the same grade and quality (medium) of grain.

Empirical results

An important first step in the analysis is to test the stationarity of the price series for each grain crop. The augmented Dickey–Fuller (ADF) test was used to test the logged form of each price series. The results indicated that, over the entire sample period (January 1987 to October 1997) each of the three prices for the four grains were integrated of order one (see Table 7.1). However, we propose testing the EMH over two sub-periods rather than the entire sample period. The reason for splitting the sample period is

Table 7.1 Unit root test (ADF) of grain price series

Commodity	*Time period*	*Price series*	*Price in levels*	*Price in differences*
Wheat	Jan. 87 to Oct. 97	FMP	−1.36	−4.60
		NP	−0.99	−5.07
		QP	−1.83	−6.57
	Jan. 87 to Mar. 94	FMP	−1.63	−4.83
		NP	−1.91	−3.35
		QP	−1.92	−9.19
	Apr. 94 to Oct. 97	FMP	−2.95	−5.20
		NP	−1.69	−8.21
		QP	−3.10	−6.23
Corn	Jan. 87 to Oct. 97	FMP	−1.26	−3.99
		NP	−1.24	−7.64
		QP	−1.47	−7.38
	Jan. 87 to Mar. 94	FMP	−1.95	−5.78
		NP	−1.57	−3.66
		QP	−1.58	−10.84
	Apr. 94 to Oct. 97	FMP	−2.45	−4.54
		NP	−2.24	−8.41
		QP	−2.99	−6.78
Early Rice	Jan. 87 to Oct. 97	FMP	−1.07	−6.50
		NP	−1.18	−7.42
		QP	−1.67	−6.68
	Jan. 87 to Mar. 94	FMP	−1.35	−4.41
		NP	−1.96	−7.38
		QP	−1.60	−8.04
	Apr. 94 to Oct. 97	FMP	−1.43	−5.51
		NP	−2.17	−6.87
		QP	−2.51	−6.35
Late Rice	Jan. 87 to Oct. 97	FMP	−0.88	−5.82
		NP	−0.82	−8.43
		NP	−0.15	−8.836
	Jan. 87 to Mar. 94	FMP	−1.13	−8.06
		NP	−1.37	−8.75
		QP	−1.97	−8.51
	Apr. 94 to Oct. 97	FMP	−3.18	−8.19
		NP	−1.4	−5.98
		QP	−2.44	−7.52

Note
95% critical value for the augmented Dickey–Fuller statistic = −3.48.

twofold. First, to test the hypothesis that there has been an improvement in market efficiency over time and, second, because it is likely that market efficiency has improved following the further reforms of 1992–1994. The order of integration of the price series in each sub-period was also tested using the ADF test and the results are presented in Table 7.1. The test results support the conclusion that all three producer price series for each grain crop were integrated of the first order in both the entire sample period and the two sub-periods. Given the data series are all non-stationary and integrated of order one, it was appropriate to use cointegration analysis to test the EMH.

Using the Johansen approach (Johansen, 1988, 1991; Johansen and Juselius, 1990) tests for cointegration between each of three possible price pairs within each grain (wheat, corn, early rice and late rice) market were carried out in the two periods of analysis and the results are reported in Table 7.2. The order of the VAR was predetermined by a LR test. In period one (1987 to 1994) the Maximal Eigenvalue and Trace test statistics are significant only in the case of the relationship between FMP and NP (see Table 7.2) within each of the grain markets. Therefore, in this period, cointegration is found between these two prices but not between FMP and QP or NP and QP. This indicates that, in period one, the first condition for market efficiency is met in the non-quota markets for wheat, corn, early rice and late rice, but not in the overall markets for these crops. Therefore, the EMH in the overall markets for these grains is rejected in period one. This result was not unexpected since, during period one, quota purchases were governed by the old central planning system, while non-quota purchases were market orientated.

The results of the tests for cointegration in period two (1994 to 1997) are presented in Table 7.2. In the case of wheat, the results indicate (the Maximal Eigenvalue and Trace test statistics are significant for the three possible bivariate price relationships) that each wheat producer price is cointegrated with each of the other two wheat prices and that, therefore, the first necessary condition for the wheat market efficiency is met in this period. Consequently, when the second period is compared with the first, it is clear that the Chinese wheat market has become more integrated and, by implication, more efficient following the reforms of 1992–1994. In the cases of the corn, early rice and late rice markets, the results in Table 7.2 indicate that FMP is cointegrated with NP and QP, but NP is not cointegrated with QP. Therefore, the first necessary condition for market efficiency is not met for these markets in the second period. However, the number of cointegrating relationships has increased when compared with the first period, which suggests a greater degree of integration in these markets and, by implication, an improvement in market efficiency.

An examination of the long-run bivariate relationships from the cointegrating vectors for both periods presented in Table 7.3 reveals that the second set of conditions for market efficiency, which are referred to here

Table 7.2 Tests for cointegrating vectors between grain producer price pairs

Relationship	*Order of VAR*	*Max. Eigen value* H_0: r = 0 H_1: r = 1	H_0: r <= 1 H_1: r = 2	*Trace test* H_0: r = 0 H_1: r = 1	*Rank*
Period One (1987m1–1994m3):					
Wheat					
FMP vs. NP	1	41.71**	5.64	47.35**	1
FMP vs. QP	1	9.096	0.892	9.988	0
NP vs. QP	1	13.85	0.990	14.84	0
Corn					
FMP vs. NP	1	36.79**	5.06	41.85**	1
FMP vs. QP	1	11.63	1.46	13.10	0
NP vs. QP	1	11.55	1.99	13.54	0
Early Rice					
FMP vs. NP	1	27.81**	1.92	29.73**	1
FMP vs. QP	1	14.51*	1.56	16.07	0
NP vs. QP	2	11.28	2.74	14.03	0
Late Rice					
FMP vs. NP	2	36.96**	3.01	39.97**	1
FMP vs. QP	1	15.23*	1.66	16.89	0
NP vs. QP	1	14.84*	1.97	16.81	0
Period Two (1994m4–1997m10):					
Wheat					
FMP vs. NP	1	29.97**	2.24	32.21**	1
FMP vs. QP	1	32.47**	1.35	33.83**	1
NP vs. QP	1	23.60**	1.05	24.66**	1
Corn					
FMP vs. NP	1	24.44**	6.47	30.91**	1
FMP vs. QP	1	22.33**	0.89	23.22**	1
NP vs. QP	1	13.27	1.43	14.69	0
Early Rice					
FMP vs. NP	1	25.57**	2.74	28.31**	1
FMP vs. QP	1	18.71**	0.57	19.29*	1
NP vs. QP	1	15.39*	0.54	15.93	0
Late Rice					
FMP vs. NP	1	14.49*	8.93*	23.41**	1
FMP vs. QP	1	16.16**	1.53	17.69	1
NP vs. QP	1	14.39*	1.05	15.44	0

Note
** indicates significance at the 95% level, and * indicates significance at the 90% level.

as the unbiasedness conditions ($\alpha = 0$, $\beta = 1$), can be rejected in all cases. Therefore, the strict market efficiency hypothesis is rejected in all four grain markets in both periods of analysis. The rejection of the unbiasedness conditions suggests that there is a difference between the three prices and, indeed, these differences for wheat are clear in Figure 7.1. The difference between FMP and NP can be thought of as similar to the purchasing price differences between large supermarket chains and small retailers. The reason that the negotiated price is lower than the free market price is

Table 7.3 Long run bivariate grain price relationships

Relationship	*Parameters from cointegrating relationship* α	β	*LR test of restrictions:* $\alpha = 0, \beta = 1$
Period One (1987m1–1994m3):			
Wheat			
FMP vs. NP	0.118 (.287)	1.050 (.079)	11.073***
Corn			
FMP vs. NP	0.096 (.205)	−1.064 (.061)	21.586***
Early Rice			
FMP vs. NP	0.199 (.303)	−1.077 (.086)	8.475**
Late Rice			
FMP vs. NP	0.464 (.176)	−0.887 (.048)	13.501***
Period Two (1994m4–1997m10):			
Wheat			
FMP vs. NP	0.920 (.438)	1.227 (.101)	19.194***
FMP vs. QP	14.55 (8.14)	2.445 (1.96)	24.646***
NP vs. QP	−11.134 (6.71)	1.628 (1.61)	17.820***
Corn			
FMP vs. NP	0.372 (0.34)	−1.110 (.082)	16.459***
FMP vs. QP	−12.393 (6.98)	2.083 (1.79)	17.241***
Early Rice			
FMP vs. NP	0.274 (.424)	−1.084 (.098)	14.895**
FMP vs. QP	−10.581 (5.12)	1.519 (1.26)	14.005***
Late Rice			
FMP vs. NP	0.517 (1.36)	−1.133 (.303)	5.158*
FMP vs. QP	−8.581 (4.51)	0.957 (1.08)	11.656***

Note:
*** indicates significance at the 99% level, ** the 95% level and * the 90% level.
The values in parenthesis are standard errors.

probably linked to government (SGMA) bargaining power, which stems from being a (large) willing and easily accessible purchaser in the marketplace. SGMA normally has better information, financing and infrastructure than its competitors and, therefore, farmers can reduce transaction costs by selling to this outlet in preference to the free market. The higher prices that farmers can obtain in the free market have to be set against the extra costs, including the time taken to find suitable non-government buyers in the market. The SGMA receives a premium for these services in the form of a discounted purchase price.

The difference between QP and the other prices is most likely explained by the fact that the SGMAs can use the regulatory power given to them by the government to force farmers to deliver procurement quota grain at lower prices.[9] This is particularly so in the first period when, as the cointegration analysis indicates, there is no co-movement between QP and the other wheat prices. The fact that cointegration is found between QP and the free market prices in the second period for all four grain markets reflects the fact that the government's call for quota prices to follow free market prices was at least partly followed. Clearly, the 'regulatory power' of the SGMAs has declined or altered in nature during this period.

The third set of necessary conditions for market efficiency is that a_i, $a_j \neq 0$ and $c_m = d_n = 0$. If these conditions hold then it suggests that there is adjustment efficiency in the market. Each of the cointegrating VARs estimated over the two periods were of order one and, as such, the condition $c_m = d_n = 0$ cannot be rejected.[10] The condition that the pairs of SOACs should not be equal to 0 (a_i, $a_j \neq 0$) was tested using t-statistics and was accepted for all the cointegrating VARs estimated over the two periods (see Table 7.4). Therefore, the weak exogeneity of any of the prices in the estimated relationships can be rejected. The weak exogeneity of one price (in the price pair relationships) would mean that disequilibrium adjustments are made through the other price, which would indicate inefficiency in market operation and adjustment. Inefficiency of this nature can result from a situation where some of the market participants are able to exert considerable control over the market in order to maintain certain market prices at advantageous levels despite (exogenous) shocks in other prices

Table 7.4 Speed of adjustment coefficients (SOAC)

Relationship	a_i	a_j
Period One (1987m1–1994m3):		
Wheat		
FMP vs. NP	0.1348 (3.661)***	0.1682 (7.055)***
Corn		
FMP vs. NP	0.1092 (1.987)*	0.3071 (6.605)***
Early Rice		
FMP vs. NP	0.1738 (3.388)***	0.2596 (5.593)***
Late Rice		
FMP vs. NP	0.0937 (1.346)	0.3137 (6.085)***
Period Two (1994m4–1997m10):		
Wheat		
FMP vs. NP	0.3326 (5.263)***	0.4275 (6.136)***
FMP vs. QP	−0.0359 (−6.075)***	−0.0431 (−3.782)***
NP vs. QP	−0.0481 (−5.128)***	−0.0547 (−3.838)***
Corn		
FMP vs. NP	0.2392 (2.431)**	0.8805 (5.831)***
FMP vs. QP	−0.0393 (−4.679)***	−0.0586 (−3.052)***
Early Rice		
FMP vs. NP	0.3107 (2.931)***	0.6269 (5.859)***
FMP vs. QP	−0.0511 (−3.650)***	−0.0995 (−3.755)***
Late Rice		
FMP vs. NP	0.1883 (1.832)*	0.3711 (4.162)***
FMP vs. QP	−0.0872 (−3.612)***	−0.0757 (−3.195)***

Note
*** indicates significance at the 99% level, ** the 95% level and * the 90% level.
The values in parenthesis are standard errors.

within the market. The rejection of weak exogeneity in this case suggests that, despite the marketing power that the SGMAs are perceived to have as a result of their large market share in the four grain markets, they do not totally control price levels.[11]

Although all prices in the wheat market do adjust to correct any disequilibrium that occurs, it is clear that the speed of adjustment in the quota purchases market is very slow. This can be seen from the small values of the SOACs in the relationships that include QP (see Table 7.4). A similar pattern can be observed in the corn and rice markets. Although there is significant co-movement between quota prices and some of the grain prices in the non-quota market, there is not a high degree of co-movement. This lack of co-movement probably reflects the lengthy slow moving bureaucratic chain, which is behind quota price movements and exists even if the directive that QP should follow FMP is being followed.

The SOAC values relating to the non-quota market (i.e. those associated with the cointegrating VAR relationships between FMP and NP) are much larger. From Table 7.4 it can be seen that the SOAC values for the non-quota wheat market increase from 0.1348 and 0.1682 in the first period to 0.3326 and 0.4275 in the second period, suggesting that both prices respond more quickly to system disequilibrium.[12] Similar results can be observed for the corn and rice markets. This suggests that non-quota market efficiency (at least in terms of market adjustment to a new equilibrium following a shock to the system) has improved following the further reforms of 1992–1994. In other words, there is faster transmission of unexpected shocks between these two non-quota prices.

Among the four crops, only relatively minor differences in market efficiency levels are observed. This probably reflects the fact that these crops are marketed in similar ways and are subject to similar policies and levels of government intervention.

Discussion and conclusions

The analysis in this chapter tests the efficient market hypothesis in relation to the Chinese grain market. An assessment is made as to whether efficiency in the wheat, corn, early rice and late rice markets has improved after the reforms in early 1990s, as this is one of the objectives of the reforms. For this reason, the analysis was carried out in two separate time periods. The first period follows the initial reforms between 1978 and 1985 and the second period follows the further reforms in 1992–1994.

The full series of reforms created three different markets and, consequently, three different producer prices for each of the four grain crops. The prices used in the analysis related to grains of the same grade and quality. The three prices are quota price, negotiated price and the free market price. In simple terms, market efficiency in the Chinese grain markets requires that the same information should be reflected in all three prices in each of the four grain markets. Furthermore, a long run equilibrium relationship should exist between the prices. In an efficient market, divergences from this long run equilibrium should be swiftly corrected through adjustments in all prices.

As expected, the results of the analysis indicate that the strict efficient market hypothesis can be rejected for all four Chinese grain markets in the two periods of analysis. Few markets around the world meet the strict conditions of the EMH and, to a large extent, the EMH represents an ideal situation against which comparisons can be made. However, with regard to the relative efficiency of the Chinese grain market over the two periods of analysis, there were three significant findings. The first finding was that although quota prices were not cointegrated with free market or negotiated prices in the first period in all four grain markets, they were cointegrated with free market prices in the second period. This indicates that the quota and non-quota markets have become more integrated. Therefore, the Chinese grain market has become more integrated and, by implication, more efficient following the further reforms of 1992–1994. Consequently, a measure of success for these reforms can be claimed. The improvement in grain market efficiency is attributed mainly to the policy of allowing quota price to follow the free market price. Although the operation of this policy was interrupted for a relatively short period by retrenchment, it does not appear that the retrenchment prevented any improvement in market efficiency. However, greater improvements in market efficiency may have occurred if retrenchment had not taken place.

The second finding is that there is improvement in adjustment efficiency within the non-quota markets over the two periods of analysis. The speed at which prices in the non-quota market adjust or correct divergences from the long run equilibrium relationship has increased over the two periods of analysis. Again, this improvement in market efficiency is attributed in part, to the further reforms of 1992–1994. The reforms, which changed the role and functions of the SGMAs and helped to foster competition among these agencies, were particularly important. Outside of the reforms, the huge growth in the volume of non-quota grain trade that occurred over the periods of analysis is undoubtedly another factor contributing to the improved adjustment efficiency in the non-quota grain market.[13] Thin markets, characterised by low trade volumes and few participants, are generally inefficient markets.

The market power of the SGMAs may be a factor explaining the rejection of the EMH in the Chinese grain market. However, in the non-quota sector it is more likely that the most important factor is that farmers' transaction costs are lower when selling grain to the SGMA as opposed to the free market; while, in the quota sector, the regulatory power of the SMGAs is undoubtedly a factor. The rejection of the weak exogeneity of all three prices in the second period of analysis indicates that the SGMAs do not, or are not able to, exert control over the market in order to maintain certain market prices at advantageous levels despite shocks in other prices within the market.[14]

The third finding of the study is that the markets for the four major grain crops operate at similar levels of efficiency. This was attributed to the similarities among these markets, not least the fact that they are subject to the same government policies.

We conclude that the efficiency of the Chinese grain market has improved over time, but as the analysis is based on an average of prices collected across China, it is not possible to say whether the improvement has occurred in all regions or just some regions. However, other authors, such as Rozelle *et al.* (1997), who have addressed the issue of spatial integration and market efficiency have found evidence of improvement. These authors also found that the impact of retrenchment was not as detrimental to efforts to increase liberalisation and commercialisation as some had supposed.

Further reforms, such as bringing to an end the last vestiges of central planning in the grain sector by ending the use of procurement quotas, would further improve grain market efficiency. On the other hand, quota prices now exceed production costs and could be used as a mechanism to provide farmers with guaranteed prices when market prices are low.

Notes

1 Under the rationed grain sales system, urban residents were issued with grain coupons that enabled them to purchase grain from government agencies at fixed prices.

2 SGMA consists of organisations involved in administration and marketing of grains at all government levels, from grain stations at township (formerly commune) level to the Ministry (Bureau) for Grains at the central government level.

3 In 1990, the subsidies to government grain marketing accounted for 6.7 per cent of the budget.

4 The regional SGMAs were already able to trade (negotiated purchases) grain amongst themselves. This trade was permitted from the very introduction of the negotiated purchases scheme.

5 See the following equation:

$$\Delta P_t^i = a_i(P_{t-1}^i - \alpha - \beta P_{t-1}^j) + \sum_{m=1}^{f} c_m \Delta P_{t-m}^i + \sum_{n=1}^{g} d_n \Delta P_{t-n}^i + e_t.$$

6 If cointegration is found between a price pair then both SOACs cannot be equal to zero. However, it is possible for one of these parameters to be equal to zero (not significantly different from zero) and this would indicate that the associated price is weakly exogenous in the two-price relationship.

7 It should be noted that the second and third conditions for market efficiency are very strict in the sense that they describe a perfect market. Most markets, for a variety of reasons, are imperfect. Therefore, in examining market efficiency it is sometimes more meaningful to consider where a particular market is in relation to the ideal of a perfect market and whether or not it is moving towards this ideal situation.

8 As the Chinese grain marketing year ends in March, it was decided that the first period should end in March and the second period should begin in April.

9 The EMH is frequently rejected in markets where some of the market participants are able to exert control (regulatory or market power) over the market in order to affect price margins or price levels (Chang and Griffith, 1998; Larue, 1991).

10 It was not necessary to add any lagged differenced terms to the ECMs in order to ensure the residuals were white noise, which implies that $c_m = d_n = 0$.

11 Sicular (1995) has argued that a large market share does not necessarily translate into control of the market, particularly as the total quantity of grain traded (including quota purchases) only amounts to about 30 per cent of total grain production in China. Most Chinese farmers are still involved in semi-subsistence production; and when free markets are open there is no restriction on entrance, making every farmer a potential trader. Therefore, government control in the grain sector has been far from total.

12 This suggests that disequilibrium is corrected after two or three months, while in the first period the correction process takes six or seven months.

13 Surveys carried out by the Office of Rural Social and Economic Surveys (the policy research office of CCCP and MOA) show that grain traded (this includes free market, negotiated purchases and quota trade) per capita increased from 174kg to 248kg during the last 15 years. Quota levels were fixed over this period so this increase can be attributed to the other types of trade.

14 In the quota market, the short period of retrenchment may be an exception.

Bibliography

Campbell, J.Y., Lo, A.W. and MacKinlay, A.C. (1997) *The Econometrics of Financial Markets* (New Jersey: Princeton University Press).

Chang, H.S. and Griffith, G. (1998). 'Examining long-run relationships between Australian beef prices', *Australian Journal of Agricultural and Resource Economics*, 42, 369–387.

Engle, R.F. and Granger, C.W. (1987) 'Co-integration and error correction: representation, estimation and testing', *Econometrica*, 55, 251–276.

Fama, E. (1970) 'Efficient capital markets: a review of theory and empirical work', *Journal of Finance*, 25, pp. 383–417.

Johansen, S. (1988) 'Statistical analysis of cointegration vectors', *Journal of Economic Dynamics and Control*, 12, 231–254.

Johansen, S. (1991) 'Estimation and hypothesis testing of cointegration vectors in Guassian vector autoregressive models', *Econometrica*, 59, 1551–1580.

Johansen, S. and Juselius, K. (1990) 'Maximum likelihood estimation and inference on cointegration – with application to the demand for money', *Oxford Bulletin of Economics and Statistics*, 52, 169–210.

Lai, K.S. and Lai, M. (1991) 'A cointegration test of market efficiency', *Journal of Futures Market*, 11, 567–575.

Larue, B. (1991) 'Farm input, farm output and retail food prices: a cointegration analysis', *Canadian Journal of Agricultural Economics*, 39, 335–353.

Pesaran, M.H. and Shin, Y. (1996) 'Cointegration and the speed of convergence to equilibrium', *Journal of Econometrics*, 71, 117–143.

Rozelle, A., Park, A., Huang J. and Jin, H. (1997) Liberalisation and rural market integration in China', *American Journal of Agricultural Economics*, 79, 635–642.

Rozelle, A., Park, A., Huang J. and Jin, H. (2000) 'Bureaucrat to entrepreneur: the changing role of the state in China's grain economy', *Economic Development and Cultural Change*, 48, 227–252.

Richardson, D. (1978) 'Some empirical evidence on commodity arbitrage and the law of one price', *Journal of International Economics*, 8, 341–351.

SAIC (State Administration of Industry and Commerce), *Chinese Markets*, Internal Publication.

Sicular, T. (1995) 'Redefining state, plan, and market: China's reforms in agricultural commerce', *China Quarterly*, 1021–1046.

Song, H.Y. (2000) *Development of Agricultural and Rural Economic Policies in China since late 1970s* (Beijing: Chinese Economic Publishing House State Council).

Wang L. and Davis, J. (2000) *China's Grain Economy: The Challenge of Feeding more than One Billion* (UK: Ashgate).

Watson, A. (1997) 'Road to reform for China's grain markets', *Partners in Research for Development*, 10, 24–29.

Weersink, A. and Rozelle, S. (1997) 'Marketing reforms, market development and agricultural production in China', *Agricultural Economics*, 17, 95–114.

Wu, Z. (1995). 'An econometric analysis of supply response for the main grain crops in China, with particular emphasis on the impact of reforms since 1979', Unpublished PhD Thesis, The Queen's University of Belfast.

Zhang, B. and Carter, C.A. (1997) 'Reforms, the weather, and productivity growth in China's grain sector', *American Journal of Agricultural Economics*, 79, 1266–1277.

Zhao, F. (1988) *China Today: Foodgrain* (Beijing: Chinese Social Science Publishing House).

8 Volatility and volatility spillovers in Chinese stock markets

Ping Wang and Aying Liu

Introduction

Over the last decade, Chinese stock exchanges have experienced rapid growth and development. At their inception in 1991, there were only ten listed companies with a total trade value of 1–2 billion yuan. By the end of 2000, the number of listed companies had increased to 1,063 and the total trade value exceeded 4 trillion yuan, or about 50 per cent of the country's GDP. The number of registered investors was over 55 million. Trading was fully computerised and could be conducted on screens from the offices of security dealers.

The Chinese Stock Exchange (CSE) consists of two markets: the Shanghai Stock Exchange (SHSE) and the Shenzhen Stock Exchange (SZSE). SHSE was established on 19 December 1990, and SZSE on 3 July 1991. Most companies listed in SHSE are large state-owned enterprises. Companies listed in SZSE are typically small, joint ventures and export-oriented. Because of these characteristics, SHSE may be sheltered from fluctuations in the world economy but, the SZSE could be more vulnerable to a global slowdown. At present, two types of shares are traded on both markets. One is A shares, which are denominated in RMB and designed for domestic investors; the other is B shares, which are denominated in US dollars and designed for foreign investors.[1] Therefore, there are four major markets representing stock market investment in China.

Despite its rapid growth, however, much less research has been carried out on these markets compared with research on Western mature markets.[2] In recent years, there has been a growing interest in the modelling of time-varying stock return volatility and various aspects have been explored for Western mature markets. As an important and fast growing emerging market in South-east Asia, an interesting topic for research is whether this market's behaviour is similar to that of a developed market. Further, the Chinese stock market is of special interest as it has four major markets running in parallel, with geographically separated trading locations and different shares for different investors. The distinction between A and B shares means that different investors can have different market channels for their investments. The subject thus opens up an opportunity to investigate different price patterns and investors' behaviour.

We construct both univariate and multivariate models. In the univariate model, we explore three aspects of common findings from developed stock markets. In particular, we explore three aspects of common findings from developed stock markets. First, we test whether there exists volatility clustering – large (small) volatility followed by large (small) volatility. Second, we explore a possible relationship between market risk and expected returns – whether the market displays a return and volatility trade-off. Finally, we investigate whether the market exhibits the so-called leverage effect – negative shocks entering the market lead to a larger return volatility than positive shocks of a similar magnitude. These characteristics are important for us to understand how volatility evolves over time and how investors behave. In the multivariate model, we investigate whether there is a volatility spillover effect across the four markets.

The chapter is organised as follows. The next section discusses the data and presents preliminary analysis. The two sections after specify the models from univariate and multivariate settings, respectively. A discussion of the empirical results is then given and the final section concludes.

Data and preliminary analysis

The data used here are the daily closing price indices of four markets. For A shares, we use the Shanghai and Shenzhen Composite Indices and for B shares, the standard Shanghai and Shenzhen indices are used. These indices are value-weighted. The data start from 1 June 1993 to 29 December 2000, so there are 1979 observations in each series. The reason we chose this starting date is to avoid the turbulence period when the stock market was undergoing re-establishment. All the data are from Datastream. Daily returns, R_t, are constructed as the first difference of logarithmic price multiplied by 100:

$$R_t = \ln(P_t/P_{t-1}) \times 100$$

where P_t and P_{t-1} are the closing index value for day t and $t-1$ respectively.[3] Figure 8.1 plots the time series of the four indices and their returns. It shows that, during the sample period, A shares experienced a remarkable growth. On the other hand, B shares stagnated. After December 1996, B shares in both markets became less stable, and the price indices kept on falling from the beginning of 1997. Only after February 1999 did they start to recover, probably reflecting the impact of the Asian financial crisis during that period. Figure 8.1 also suggests that return series display the volatility clustering phenomenon associated with the GARCH process, i.e. large (small) volatility followed by large (small) volatility.

Table 8.1 presents the statistical properties of the four returns. The

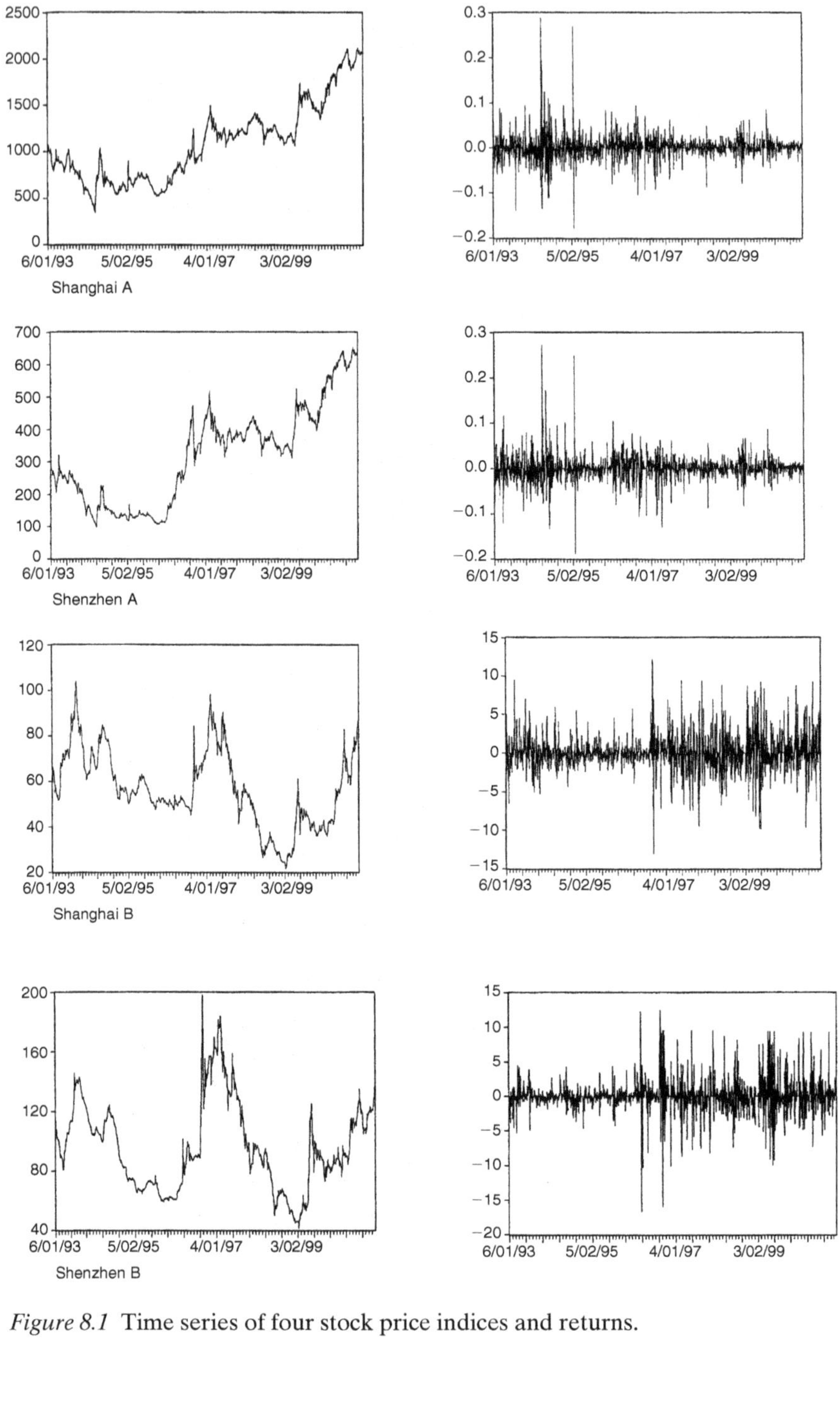

Figure 8.1 Time series of four stock price indices and returns.

Table 8.1 Preliminary analysis of daily returns (%)

	SHCI	*SHBI*	*SZCI*	*SZBI*
Mean	0.041	0.015	0.04	0.01
Maximum	28.86	12.18	27.22	12.45
Minimum	−17.91	−13.06	−18.88	−16.70
Std. Dev.	2.59	2.22	2.55	2.24
Skewness	1.58	0.43	0.88	0.20
Kurtosis	24.69	8.09	16.32	11.67
Jarque–Bera	39,593.56	2,191.28	22,204.75	6,210.00
Q-stats (12)	4.58	1.79	5.79	1.65
Q^2-stats (12)	512.55	760.87	212.59	845.57

Note
Q-stats and Q^2stats are Ljung–Box Q-statistics for the 12th order in the levels and squares of the residuals.

characteristics of the two A shares are quite similar, with the average return being almost the same at around 0.04 per cent. The volatility of Shanghai stock return is slightly higher than the Shenzhen stock return. The standard deviations of daily returns are 2.58 and 2.55 respectively for the SHSE and SZSE. For the B shares, the mean returns are 0.015 per cent and 0.01 per cent for SHSE and SZSE respectively. The volatility of returns in SZSE is slightly higher than that in SHSE.

As far as the distribution of returns over time is concerned, all of the skewness statistics are significant to the right, indicating that the data are not symmetric. Moreover, all returns are characterised by statistically significant kurtosis, suggesting that the underlying data are leptokurtic; that is, all series have a thicker tail and a higher peak than a normal distribution. As a result, the Jarque–Bera test shows that all returns are non-normal.

In Table 8.1, we report the Ljung–Box Q-statistics for the 12th order in the levels and squares of the residuals. It indicates no serial correlation in levels, but the squared residuals are serially correlated, suggesting the existence of volatility clustering as an ARCH process. This preliminary test reveals that, although the first moment presents the white noise in residual series, the second moment exhibits strong autocorrelation in squared residuals, a property that will result in volatility clustering, which justifies using time-varying variance models.

Univariate models

In this section, we explore GARCH effect for individual cases from different perspectives. We set our model as follows. For the mean equation, since our sample period covers the Asian Financial Crisis, we include a crisis dummy variable that takes 1 from 1997:07:01 to 1998:06:30 and 0 at all other times.[4] We also assume that a return generating process follows a simple autoregressive:

$$R_t = a_0 + \sum_{i=1}^{k} a_{t-i} R_{t-i} + \epsilon_t, \quad \epsilon_t | \Omega_{t-1} \sim N(0, h_t)$$

where ϵ_t is an error term, which is serially uncorrelated and distributed as a zero mean and time-varying variance, h_t. After examining the autocorrelation function, we set $k = 0$ for A shares and $k = 3$ for B shares as it is found that, with these lag lengths all return series can yield uncorrelated residuals.

For the conditional variance, one of the most prominent tools for characterising time-varying variances is the AutoRegressive Conditional Heteroscedastic (ARCH) process of Engle (1982) and its various extensions. Specifically, we chose three models as follows.

Model 1 GARCH (p, q)

ARCH models that were introduced by Engle (1982) and generalised as GARCH (Generalised ARCH) by Bollerslev (1986) are specifically designed to model and forecast conditional variances.[5] They take the form,

$$\epsilon_t = h_t^{1/2} u_t$$

$$h_t = \omega_0 + \sum_{i=1}^{q} \alpha_i \epsilon_{t-i}^2 + \sum_{i=1}^{p} \beta_i h_{t-i} \tag{8.1}$$

The conditional variance equation specified in equation (8.1) is a function of three terms: the mean, ω_0; the impact of current news on the conditional variance process, measured as the lag of the squared residual from the mean equation, α_i (the ARCH term); and the persistence of volatility to a shock, β_i (the GARCH term).

In practice, numerous studies have demonstrated that a small lag such as GARCH (1,1) is sufficient to account for time-dependent conditional heteroscedasticity over long sample periods. Therefore, we restrict our attention here to a GARCH (1,1) specification since it has been shown to be a parsimonious representation of conditional variance that can adequately fit many econometric time series (Bollerslev, 1987).

Model 2 GARCH-M

If we introduce the conditional variance into the mean equation, we get the ARCH-in-Mean (ARCH-M) model (Engle et al., 1987), which is the extension to the GARCH model where the conditional mean is an explicit function of the conditional variance. It takes the form

$$R_t = a_0 + \sum_{i=1}^{k} a_i R_{t-i} + \delta_1 h_t^{1/2} + \epsilon_t$$

$$h_t = \omega_0 + \alpha_1 \epsilon_{t-1}^2 + \beta_1 h_{t-1} \tag{8.2}$$

where the coefficient of δ_1 represents the index of relative risk aversion (time-varying risk premium). The ARCH-M model is often used in financial applications where the expected return on an asset is related to the expected asset risk. The estimated coefficient on the expected risk is a measure of the risk–return trade-off.

Model 3 EGARCH

Although the GARCH model can effectively remove the excess kurtosis in returns, the GARCH model cannot cope with the skewness of the distribution of returns. For this reason, a few modifications to the GARCH model have been proposed, explicitly taking skewed distributions into account. One of the alternative non-linear models that can cope with skewness is the Exponential GARCH model or EGARCH. The specification of EGARCH (1,1) can be written as follows:

$$\log(h_t) = \alpha_0 + \beta_1 \log(h_{t-1}) + \alpha_1(|\lambda_{t-1}| - E(|\lambda_{t-1}|)) + \alpha_2 \lambda_{t-1} \tag{8.3}$$

where

$$\lambda_t = \frac{\epsilon_t}{h_t^{1/2}},\ E[|\lambda_t|] = \sqrt{\frac{2}{\pi}}.$$

In equation (8.3), the conditional variance in period t is a function of the last period's variance, h_{t-1}, and a symmetric function of the previous period's standardised innovation, α_1. The asymmetric effect, or so called leverage effect, is captured by the coefficient α_2.

As the above three models are not nested in each other, it is hard to say which one is preferred to the others. Our objective here is to give insight into the mechanism driving the variance process.

Multivariate setting

The issue of volatility spillover effect is explored in this part, where we extend the previous univariate model to multivariate GARCH. It is likely that the conditional variance of the return from one market is related not only to its own past history but also to those of other markets, for example Karolyi (1995), Susmel and Engle (1994) among others. We therefore consider the transmission mechanism of the four Chinese markets.

In a multivariate setting involving N variables, the GARCH model specifies the determination of the conditional variance–covariance matrix, H_t, of the N-dimensional zero mean random variables ϵ_t. If we assume that H_t is measurable with respect to Ω_{t-1}, the information set at the end of the preceding period, then a general form of the multivariate GARCH model can be expressed as

$$\epsilon_t | \Omega_{t-1} \sim N(0, H_t)$$

$$\text{vech}(H_t) = \text{vech}(C) + \sum_{i=1}^{q} A_i \text{vech}(\epsilon_{t-i}\epsilon_{t-i}) + \sum_{i=1}^{p} B_i \text{vech}(H_{t-i}) \tag{8.4}$$

where $\epsilon_t = (\epsilon_{1t}, \ldots, \epsilon_{nt})'$, H_t is an $N \times N$ matrix, C is an $N \times N$ positive definite matrix, A and B are $N(N+1) \times N(N+1)/2$ matrices; and vech is the operator that stacks in a single column the lower triangular portion of a symmetric matrix with $N(N+1)/2$ elements. Hence, for $p = q = 1$, the total number of the parameters in the model is $N^2(N+1)^2/2 \times N(N+1)/2$, which grows with the power of N. Therefore, a number of crucial decisions need to be made at this point, as the model involves far too many parameters to be manageable.[6]

We choose to impose the following constraints. First, we focus on a bivariate model,[7] i.e. a pair of series, and assume the number of lags in the conditional variance process to be no greater than unity, i.e. $p = q = 1$. With these restrictions model (8.4) takes the following form

$$\text{vech}(H_t) = \begin{bmatrix} h_{11,t} \\ h_{12,t} \\ h_{22,t} \end{bmatrix} = \begin{bmatrix} c_{11,t} \\ c_{12,t} \\ c_{22,t} \end{bmatrix} + \begin{bmatrix} a_{11} & a_{12} & a_{13} \\ a_{21} & a_{22} & a_{23} \\ a_{31} & a_{32} & a_{33} \end{bmatrix} \begin{bmatrix} \epsilon^2_{1,t-1} \\ \epsilon_{1,t-1}\,\epsilon_{2,t-1} \\ \epsilon^2_{2,t-1} \end{bmatrix} + \begin{bmatrix} b_{11} & b_{12} & b_{13} \\ b_{21} & b_{22} & b_{23} \\ b_{31} & b_{32} & b_{33} \end{bmatrix} \begin{bmatrix} h_{11,t-1} \\ h_{12,t-1} \\ h_{22,t-1} \end{bmatrix}$$

However, this still leaves 21 parameters to be estimated in the conditional variance process alone, so further restrictions need to be imposed. Following Bollerslev *et al.* (1988), a more parsimonious representation can be obtained by assuming that A and B matrices are diagonal. This simplification implies that a conditional variance depends only on its own lagged squared residuals and lagged values, leaving the effect of volatility transmission between the two variables solely on the covariance term $h_{12,t}$.

A further simplification is to follow the suggestion in Bollerslev (1990) and assume the conditional correlation to be constant, so that all variations over time in the conditional covariances are attributed to changes in each of the corresponding two conditional variances. With these restrictions, the model takes the simplified form

$$\epsilon_t | \Omega_{t-1} \sim N(0, H_t)$$

$$\begin{bmatrix} h_{11,t} \\ h_{22,t} \end{bmatrix} = C + A \begin{bmatrix} h_{11,t-1} \\ h_{22,t-1} \end{bmatrix} + B \begin{bmatrix} \epsilon^2_{1,t-1} \\ \epsilon^2_{2,t-1} \end{bmatrix} \tag{8.5}$$

$$h_{12,t} = \sigma_{12}[h_{11,t} h_{22,t}]^{1/2}$$

where

$$A = \begin{bmatrix} a_{11} & a_{12} \\ a_{21} & a_{22} \end{bmatrix}, B = \begin{bmatrix} b_{11} & b_{12} \\ b_{21} & b_{22} \end{bmatrix}$$

and $\sigma_{12} = \text{Corr}(\epsilon_{1t}, \epsilon_{2t})$ denotes the conditional correlation, which is assumed to be constant. The necessary and sufficient conditions for the model to be defined and for H_t to be positively definite are that all the conditional variances are positive and that the constant matrix of conditional correlations is positively definite. These conditions are easy to impose and verify (Bollerslev, 1990). The parameterisation of this model also offers a parsimonious representation for the test. Note also that this specification allows for stock price influences in the conditional variances through the off-diagonal coefficients in each of A and B matrices.

Given a sample of T observations of the unpredictable return series, both univariate and multivariate models are estimated by the quasi-maximum likelihood described by Bollerslev and Wooldridge (1992). These quasi-maximum likelihood (QML) estimators are robust in the sense that they produce consistent estimates of the parameters of a correctly specified conditional mean, even if the distribution is incorrectly specified.

Results and implications

The results from the univariate setting are reported in Tables 8.2 and 8.3 for A and B shares respectively, with the three models specified above. The estimates from the mean-equations suggest that there is evidence of positive autocorrelation in B-share indices. The crisis dummy variable, indicated by γ, is not significant for the A-shares, but significant for the B-shares in the EGARCH model, and especially for the Shenzhen B-share Index (SZBI). This implies that A-shares are less influenced by the rest of the world than the B-shares. Furthermore, as mentioned previously, Shanghai-listed firms are large and state-owned while those in Shenzhen are small, joint ventures and export-oriented, so compared with the SHSE, the SZSE is more sensitive to the fluctuations in the global economy.

Now let us look at the estimates from the variance equation. In the GARCH model, the coefficients on the lagged squared error α_1 and on the lagged conditional variance β_1 are both significantly different from zero at the 5 per cent level, suggesting that the GARCH phenomenon is strong for these four return series. In addition, the volatility, measured by $(\alpha_1 + \beta_1)$, in all the return series is persistent. It shows that for both A and B shares the degree of persistency in SHSE is greater than that in SZSE.

The GARCH-M model provides us with the tool to investigate the linear relationship between stock return and risk, and the significant influence of volatility on stock return is captured by the coefficient of δ_1.

Table 8.2 Estimates of univariate GARCH for returns from A-shares

	SHCI			*SZCI*		
	GARCH	GARCH-M	EGARCH	GARCH	GARCH-M	EGARCH
a_0	0.0076	−0.0978	−0.0543	0.0482	−0.0362	−0.0182
	(0.066)	(0.175)	(0.059)	(0.063)	(0.206)	(0.059)
γ_{crisis}	0.0732	0.0852	0.0543	−0.0089	−0.0030	−0.0286
	(0.102)	(0.112)	(0.103)	(0.106)	(0.107)	(0.056)
δ_1	–	0.0566	–	–	0.0429	–
		(0.077)			(0.100)	
ω_0	0.3238	0.3229	0.0367**	0.4957**	0.4987**	0.0436**
	(0.244)	(0.267)	(0.018)	(0.219)	(0.223)	(0.029)
α_1	0.1810**	0.1808**	0.1409**	0.1996**	0.4291**	0.1373**
	(0.079)	(0.088)	(0.045)	(0.066)	(0.070)	(0.048)
β_1	0.7860**	0.7863**	0.9883**	0.7389**	0.7379**	0.9842**
	(0.109)	(0.119)	(0.010)	(0.086)	(0.089)	(0.015)
α_2	–	–	0.1232	–	–	0.1368
			(0.131)			(0.160)
Q-stats	14.89	16.84	15.86	17.532	16.116	18.547
Q^2-stats	6.34	6.16	6.12	1.363	1.369	1.345
Log-*L*	−2441.55	−2441.20	−2434.35	−2510.93	−2510.79	−2524.48

Note

Q-stats and Q^2-stats are Ljung–Box *Q*-statistics for the 12th order of the standardised residuals and squares of the standardised residuals. Standard errors are in parentheses.

**significant at above 5% level.

*significant at 10% level.

Table 8.3 Estimates of univariate GARCH for returns from B-shares

	SHBI			*SZBI*		
	GARCH	GARCH-M	EGARCH	GARCH	GARCH-M	EGARCH
a_0	−0.0381	−0.1868**	−0.0934*	−0.0364	−0.2107**	−0.1653**
	(0.037)	(0.084)	(0.051)	(0.036)	(0.075)	(0.035)
a_1	0.1913**	0.1889**	0.1818**	0.1953**	0.1923**	0.1670**
	(0.031)	(0.029)	(0.029)	(0.032)	(0.032)	(0.039)
a_2	0.0175	0.0140	0.0152	0.0024	0.0005	0.0081
	(0.025)	(0.025)	(0.029)	(0.037)	(0.036)	(0.025)
a_3	0.0297	0.0261	0.0230	0.0817**	0.0803**	0.0558**
	(0.024)	(0.024)	(0.027)	(0.031)	(0.027)	(0.018)
γ_{crisis}	−0.0477	−0.0918	−0.3173**	−0.7362	−0.7788	−0.5771**
	(0.264)	(0.230)	(0.168)	(0.494)	(0.520)	(0.252)
δ_1		0.1030**			0.1320**	
		(0.050)			(0.051)	
ω_0	0.1362**	0.1358**	0.0908**	0.3199**	0.3178**	0.2009**
	(0.080)	(0.065)	(0.040)	(0.137)	(0.146)	(0.061)
α_1	0.1816**	0.1833**	0.2939**	0.3754**	0.3792**	0.5094**
	(0.047)	(0.041)	(0.082)	(0.103)	(0.098)	(0.096)
β_1	0.8073**	0.8063**	0.9501**	0.6235**	0.6220**	0.8834**
	(0.053)	(0.046)	(0.026)	(0.071)	(0.058)	(0.040)
α_2			−0.1019			−0.0141
			(0.080)			(0.082)
Q-stats	16.50	17.54	22.56	11.797	14.672	25.76
Q^2-stats	14.21	11.38	45.37	2.167	1.920	20.2
Log-L	−2169.48	−2167.92	−2182.98	−2018.31	−2015.23	−2025.76

Note
Q-stats and Q^2-stats are Ljung–Box Q-statistics for the 12th order of the standardised residuals and squares of the standardised residuals. Standard errors are in parentheses.
**significant at above 5% level.
*significant at 10% level.

Among four markets, we find that this term is significant for two B shares at the 5 per cent level. This implies that investors in B-shares are compensated with higher returns for bearing higher risk. However, the same effect is absent from A-shares. This may imply that investors in B-shares are more sensitive to risk.

As far as the leverage effect is concerned, to our surprise, none of the markets shows significant asymmetry by EGARCH.[8] The result is in contrast with a common finding for developed stock markets that negative shocks entering the market lead to a larger return volatility than positive shocks of a similar magnitude. This result is supported by other studies on the emerging markets, where the asymmetric effect is found to be weak or absent (Shields, 1997). One possible explanation is that, relative to the investors of developed markets, investors of emerging markets have a comparatively lower level of understanding of market operation, leading to some non-rational investment behaviour. However, because B-shares investors are better informed and more sensitive to risk than A-shares investors, the conclusion cannot be simply explained by the non-rational behaviour in China. For B-shares, the absence of a leverage effect may reflect thinly traded stocks in these indices. A-shares investors are mostly individuals, who are more likely to hold shares for short-term speculation than institutional investors. B-shares investors are mostly institutions, who are more likely to hold shares as long-term investment than individual investors.

Moving to the multivariate GARCH, the result is shown in Table 8.4, where the parameters from the mean equation are omitted as there is little difference from those of the univariate model. Hence, only the estimated parameters from the variance part are reported. There are a number of points to be noticed.

1 The constant component of the conditional variance is significant in almost every case. In particular, the significance of the estimates of c_{12} suggests a significant component of volatility shared by the two pairs of series. It shows that SHCI and SZCI have the largest coefficient and SHBI and SZBI have the second largest coefficient, suggesting that these two pairs have the strongest link.
2 As is clear from the table, the diagonal elements of a_{11} and a_{22}, and b_{11} and b_{22} are significant at the 1 per cent level for every case, indicating that they play an important role in the variance processes. In other words, there is a strong univariate GARCH process driving the variances of both pair of series.
3 As indicated in the model specification, the off-diagonal elements of the two matrices measure the volatility spillover effects. Several patterns emerge. For the two different shares exchanged in the same market, for example, SHCI and SHBI, and SZCI and SZBI, the volatility spillover effect is from B-shares to A-shares, but not the other way

round. This is because the estimates of a_{12} and b_{12} are significant and the estimates of a_{21} and b_{21} are insignificant (expect SHCI and SZBI where b_{21} is significant at the 10 per cent level). As A-shares investors are less informed than B-shares investors, it is not surprising that the volatility is transmitted from B to A-shares, but not vice versa.

Table 8.4 Estimation of bivariate GARCH with constant correlation

$$\epsilon_t | \Omega_{t-1} \sim N(0, H_t)$$

$$\begin{bmatrix} h_{11,t} \\ h_{22,t} \end{bmatrix} = C + A \begin{bmatrix} h_{11,t-1} \\ h_{22,t-1} \end{bmatrix} + B \begin{bmatrix} \epsilon^2_{1,t-1} \\ \epsilon^2_{2,t-1} \end{bmatrix}$$

$$h_{12,t} = \sigma_{12}[h_{11,t} h_{22,t}]^{1/2}$$

where

$$A = \begin{bmatrix} a_{11} & a_{12} \\ a_{21} & a_{22} \end{bmatrix}, B = \begin{bmatrix} b_{11} & b_{12} \\ b_{21} & b_{22} \end{bmatrix}$$

Market 1 *Market 2*	*SHCI* *SHBI*	*SZCI* *SZBI*	*SHCI* *SZCI*	*SHBI* *SZBI*	*SHCI* *SZBI*	*SHBI* *SZCI*
C_{11}	1.3044**	0.8867**	0.6718**	0.2098**	0.0890**	0.1408**
	(0.024)	(0.008)	(0.031)	(0.067)	(0.036)	(0.036)
C_{12}	0.3625**	0.3147**	0.8627**	0.5861**	0.3377**	0.3415**
	(0.062)	(0.009)	(0.033)	(0.023)	(0.030)	(0.024)
C_{22}	1.2552	0.8289**	0.0446	0.3764**	0.1916**	0.5534**
	(1.129)	(0.033)	(0.031)	(0.147)	(0.059)	(0.102)
b_{11}	0.4007**	0.1973**	0.2002**	0.1228**	0.0814**	0.1517**
	(0.179)	(0.004)	(0.057)	(0.038)	(0.034)	(0.036)
b_{22}	0.3519**	0.4687**	0.3016**	0.3386**	0.1883**	0.2134**
	(0.060)	(0.036)	(0.122)	(0.069)	(0.057)	(0.062)
b_{12}	0.0419**	0.0209**	0.1044**	0.0526**	0.0112**	0.0018
	(0.007)	(0.002)	(0.036)	(0.022)	(0.007)	(0.002)
b_{21}	0.1664	0.0553*	0.2947**	0.0409	0.0660**	−0.0450
	(0.124)	(0.029)	(0.008)	(0.059)	(0.016)	(0.028)
a_{11}	0.5234**	0.6521**	0.2223**	0.8510**	0.9256**	0.8356**
	(0.020)	(0.002)	(0.011)	(0.062)	(0.033)	(0.033)
a_{22}	0.3717**	0.4135**	0.2516**	0.4587**	0.7929**	0.7554**
	(0.178)	(0.018)	(0.002)	(0.109)	(0.063)	(0.066)
a_{12}	−0.0991**	−0.0208**	0.3871**	−0.0704**	−0.0216**	−0.0053**
	(0.030)	(0.001)	(0.008)	(0.032)	(0.007)	(0.002)
a_{21}	−0.0035	−0.0048	0.5863**	0.1310**	−0.0028**	−0.0330
	(0.010)	(0.003)	(0.006)	(0.082)	(0.001)	(0.008)

Note
**significant at above 5% level.
*significant at 10% level. Standard errors are in parentheses.
Subscript *ij* means the volatility transmission from market *j* to market *i*.

For those pairs with the same shares but exchanged at different markets, such as SHCI and SZCI, and SHBI and SZBI, the transmission is broadly in two ways. That is, the volatility in SHCI (SHBI) is affected by the volatility from SZCI (SZBI), and the reverse is also true. It is shown by the significant off-diagonal elements of matrix A. As the two markets are open at the same time, this bidirectional transmission is not unexpected.

For the pairs with different shares and exchanged at different markets, such as SHCI and SZBI, and SHBI and SZCI, the transmission pattern is slightly different. As far as SHCI and SZBI are concerned, all of the diagonal elements are significant except b_{12}, so the spillover effect is broadly bidirectional. For the pair of SHBI and SZCI, the off-diagonal elements of the *B* matrix are not significant while those of the *A* matrix are significant, suggesting that shocks from one market will not transmit to the other market. On the other hand, as a_{12} and a_{21} are significant, they imply that the volatility originated from one market will induce volatility in the other market. However, the magnitude of this effect is very small.

Conclusions

As an important emerging market in South-east Asia, the Chinese stock market has experienced rapid growth over the last decade. However, compared with the Western developed markets, relatively few studies have been conducted to understand the Chinese market. In this study, we aim to study the market volatility and its spillover effects in two Chinese stock exchanges, using the univariate and multivariate GARCH models. With four stock indices, we found that the GARCH mechanism is at work in all indices. The asymmetric effect, or the leverage effect, is found to be absent in all cases. Our empirical results also show that the return-volatility trade-off effect is strong for the B-shares, but weak for the A-shares.

Regarding the volatility spillover effect, several patterns emerge. If two different types of shares have similar characteristics, the spillover effect is bidirectional, e.g. from SHCI (SHBI) to SZCI (SZBI) and vice versa. In two different types of shares with different characteristics, the spillover effect is only in one direction, e.g. from B to A-shares. The explanation lies in the different natures of B and A-share investors. B-share investors are mostly institutions, but A-share investors are mostly individuals. B-share investors are more experienced, more sensitive to risk and less speculative than the A-share investors.

Notes

1 Since March 2001, B shares have been open to domestic investors but can only be traded either in US dollars in SHSE or in Hong Kong dollars in SZSE.
2 Exceptions are Xu (2000), Lee and Rui (2000), Mookerjee and Yu (1999) and Song *et al.* (1998).

3 Stationarity in the time series is checked by applying the Augmented Dickey–Fuller (ADF) test. The results unanimously fail to reject the null of a unit root in the logarithm of price series, but overwhelmingly reject the null for the first difference of logarithm price series. The results are available upon request.
4 The starting date for the crisis reflects the day when Thailand devalued the Baht. While there is no consensus about the endpoint, the crisis reached a peak in the autumn of 1998, according to Corsetti *et al.* (1999).
5 See Bollerslev *et al.* (1992, 1994) for recent surveys.
6 The difficulty in estimating an unrestricted multivariate model is not simply a matter of degrees of freedom. The problem lies in that, with the available numerical methods, iteration procedures tend either to take an impossibly long time to converge or indeed fail to converge altogether.
7 We also estimated the full multivariate model ($N=4$) with our restricted model and it failed to converge.
8 We also employed the GJR-GARCH model proposed by Glosten *et al.* (1993) and could not find the asymmetric effect for all markets.

Bibliography

Bollerslev, T. (1986) ‘Generalized autoregressive conditional heteroskedasticity,’ *Journal of Econometrics,* 31, 307–327.

Bollerslev, T. (1987) ‘A conditionally heteroskedastic time series model for specificative prices and rates of returns’, *Review of Economics and Statistics*, 69, 542–547.

Bollerslev, T. (1990) ‘Modelling the coherence in short-run nominal exchange rates: a multivariate generalized ARCH approach’, *Review of Economics and Statistics*, 72, 498–505.

Bollerslev, T. and Wooldridge, J.M. (1992) ‘Quasi-maximum likelihood estimation and inference in dynamic models with time varying covariances’, *Econometric Reviews*, 11, 143–172.

Bollerslev, T., Engle, R.F. and Wooldridge, J.M. (1988) ‘A capital asset pricing model with time-varying covariances’, *Journal of Political Economy*, 96, 116–131.

Bollerslev, T., Chou, R.Y. and Kroner, K.F. (1992) ‘ARCH modeling in finance: a review of the theory and empirical evidence’, *Journal of Econometrics*, 52, 5–59.

Bollerslev, T., Engle, R.F. and Nelson, D.B. (1994) ‘ARCH models’, *Handbook of Econometrics*, vol. 4 (North-Holland).

Corsetti, G., Pesenti, P. and Roubini, N. (1999) ‘What caused the Asian currency and financial crisis? Part 1: macroeconomic overview’, *Japan and the World Economy*, 11, 305–373.

Engle, R.F. (1982) ‘Autoregressive conditional heteroskedasticity with estimates of the variance of U.K. inflation’, *Econometrica*, 50, 987–1008.

Engle, R.F., Lilien, D.M. and Robins, R.P. (1987) ‘Estimating time varying risk premia in the term structure: the ARCH-M model’, *Econometrica*, 55, 391–407.

Glosten, L.R., Jagannathan, R. and Runkle, D. (1993) ‘On the relation between the expected value and the volatility of the normal excess return on stocks’, *Journal of Finance*, 48, 1779–1801.

Karolyi, G.A. (1995) ‘A multivariate GARCH model of international transmissions of stock returns and volatility: the case of the United States and Canada’, *Journal of Business & Economic Statistics*, 13, 11–25.

Lee, C.F. and Rui, O.M. (2000) 'Does trading volume contain information to predict stock returns? Evidence from China's stock markets', *Review of Quantitative Finance and Accounting*, 14, 341–360.

Mookerjee, R. and Yu, Q. (1999) 'Seasonality in returns on the Chinese stock markets: the case of Shanghai and Shenzhen', *Global Finance Journal*, 10, 93–105.

Nelson, D.B. (1991) 'Conditional heteroskedasticity in asset returns: a new approach', *Econometrica*, 59, 347–370.

Shields, K.K. (1997) 'Stock return volatility on emerging eastern European markets', *The Manchester School*, Supplement, 66, 118–138.

Song, H., Liu, X. and Romilly, P. (1998) 'Stock returns and volatility: an empirical study of Chinese stock markets', *International Review of Applied Economics*, 12, 129–139.

Susmel, R. and Engle, R.F. (1994) 'Hourly volatility spillovers between international equity markets', *Journal of International Money and Finance*, 13, 3–25.

Xu, C.K. (2000) 'The microstructure of the Chinese stock market', *China Economic Review*, 11, 79–97.

Part III

Openness and social issues

9 The development of the Chinese–EU trade relations

Haico Ebbers and Jianhong Zhang

Introduction

Since the mid-1980s, China's international linkages have grown noticeably. The acceleration of foreign direct investment (FDI) is one feature of this development. Another indicator is the strong increase in external trade relations. Much emphasis has been given to trade and FDI linkages within the Asian region. This is logically due to the fact that, during the 1980s and 1990s, intra-regional development outweighed the development of extra-regional ties. The increase in the Asian intra-trade figure is the result of regional integration, driven by the liberalization of the external sector and the impressive growth figures of the Asian economies. For example, intra-regional trade within East Asia increased from 33 per cent in 1980 to 46 per cent in 1995 (Asian Development Bank, 1999). In addition, intra-regional FDI flows have contributed significantly to the deepening of regional economic interdependencies and the market-driven integration in the region.

During the 1970s and 1980s, trade and FDI relationships between China and the European Union did not receive a lot of attention from European academia. Attention was concentrated on the development of the trade and FDI relations within the Union. Intra-EU trade was high and increasing, mainly due to the static and dynamic effects of the European integration scheme. External trade relations were mainly with other developed countries and, consequently, more than 80 per cent of the Union's trade was conducted between countries with broadly similar income levels (UN Commission for Europe). Capital flows were concentrated even more towards developed economies.

During the 1990s, attention was shifted towards China as a market and trading partner, driven by the gradual liberalization of the external sector and the prospect of China's joining the World Trade Organization. Consequently, more research was done on China's trade relations. In most cases, the research was of a bilateral nature. In this chapter, the emphasis is on the European Union, seen as one economic entity. We shall focus on the Chinese–EU trade relation between 1990 and 1998, a period of increasing regional economic interdependencies in both the EU and Asia.

The aim of the chapter is to provide an analytical structure to analyse trade relations between the two regions. On the one hand, concepts and tools are specified for measuring the level and development of trade relations using concepts such as the trade intensity index and regional diversification of trade flows. On the other hand, theoretical frameworks are used to obtain a picture about the structure of trade, using indicators such as intra-industry trade, terms of trade, the Herfindahl–Hirschman index and the revealed-comparative-advantage index.

The chapter starts by measuring trade relations between China and the EU. This is done through the concept of the trade-intensity index. Research indicates increasing trade relations between the two regions (e.g. Grant, 1995; Strange, 1998). Therefore, the first question we want to answer is whether trade between China and the EU is in line with what would be expected in terms of volume.

The harmonization of trade policy, convergence of economic structure and convergence of growth figures in the EU would suggest that individual countries in the EU might show similar patterns with respect to their trade development with their respective trade partners. Based on this argument, we shall discuss the second question: do individual countries within the EU show similar patterns with respect to their bilateral trade with China? We will again use the trade-intensity indicator as well as other criteria to analyse this question.

In line with the framework of Heckscher–Ohlin, China has relatively abundant resource endowments with respect to natural resources and low-skilled labour, while the EU has relatively abundant resources with respect to technology and capital. Therefore, the third question we want to discuss is whether Chinese exports are mainly concentrated on primary products, and the EU's exports on manufactures. In other words, does China have a comparative advantage in the export of primary products and the EU a comparative advantage in the export of technology-intensive and capital-intensive products? In line with this discussion, we expect Chinese–EU trade to be dominated by inter-industry trade due to the large difference in economic development between the regions (question four). We expect that countries with the largest and most diversified industrial base will have the highest levels of intra-industry trade with China. We also expect that inter-industry trade (IIT) in the manufacturing sector to be higher than in the primary sector due to the exploitation of the possibilities of economies of scale. With the trade structure in line with our expectations related to commodity pattern and intra-industry trade level, we reach our fifth question: are China's terms of trade deteriorating? This expectation is in line with the hypothesis advanced independently by Prebisch (1950) and Singer (1950). In the same vein, we raise our sixth question: has China revealed a comparative advantage (RCA) in the export of primary products to the EU, and is there a visible revealed comparative advantage of EU export of manufactured goods to China?

9 The development of the Chinese–EU trade relations

Haico Ebbers and Jianhong Zhang

Introduction

Since the mid-1980s, China's international linkages have grown noticeably. The acceleration of foreign direct investment (FDI) is one feature of this development. Another indicator is the strong increase in external trade relations. Much emphasis has been given to trade and FDI linkages within the Asian region. This is logically due to the fact that, during the 1980s and 1990s, intra-regional development outweighed the development of extra-regional ties. The increase in the Asian intra-trade figure is the result of regional integration, driven by the liberalization of the external sector and the impressive growth figures of the Asian economies. For example, intra-regional trade within East Asia increased from 33 per cent in 1980 to 46 per cent in 1995 (Asian Development Bank, 1999). In addition, intra-regional FDI flows have contributed significantly to the deepening of regional economic interdependencies and the market-driven integration in the region.

During the 1970s and 1980s, trade and FDI relationships between China and the European Union did not receive a lot of attention from European academia. Attention was concentrated on the development of the trade and FDI relations within the Union. Intra-EU trade was high and increasing, mainly due to the static and dynamic effects of the European integration scheme. External trade relations were mainly with other developed countries and, consequently, more than 80 per cent of the Union's trade was conducted between countries with broadly similar income levels (UN Commission for Europe). Capital flows were concentrated even more towards developed economies.

During the 1990s, attention was shifted towards China as a market and trading partner, driven by the gradual liberalization of the external sector and the prospect of China's joining the World Trade Organization. Consequently, more research was done on China's trade relations. In most cases, the research was of a bilateral nature. In this chapter, the emphasis is on the European Union, seen as one economic entity. We shall focus on the Chinese–EU trade relation between 1990 and 1998, a period of increasing regional economic interdependencies in both the EU and Asia.

The rest of the chapter is organized as follows. In the second section we introduce the concept of trade intensity to measure the trade linkage between China and the EU countries. Complementary to this, we use the geographic composition to illustrate the position of EU countries in Chinese foreign trade. In the third section, we employ criteria such as commodity composition, terms of trade, the intra-industry trade index, and the revealed-comparative-advantage index to analyse the Chinese–EU trade structure. The chapter ends with the conclusion, in which we elaborate on the different questions posed in this introduction.

The statistical data in this chapter originate from the United Nations Statistics Division and are complemented by statistics from the General Administration of Customs of China. The analysis is done on the one-digit and three-digit SITC product groups.

Chinese–EU trade linkage

Measurement

Regional integration is often measured by the development of intra-regional trade as a percentage of total trade. The general idea is that the higher this intra-trade within a region, the more successful the integration scheme is, because of the static and dynamic effects of integration. But this is only a part of the picture. In other publications we made clear that the increase of intra-regional trade is often not the result of regionalism, but only due to the increase in economic power. One should control for the region's growing importance in the world economy (Ebbers, 1997). One way of doing this is through the use of the trade intensity index in line with the analysis of Kojima (1968) and Drysdale and Carnaut (1993). The trade intensity index shows the ratio between the share of a given country's exports (imports) in total imports (exports) of another (member) country and the percentage this country has in total exports (imports) in world trade. This can be calculated on the import side as well as on the export side. See the formulas below.

$$EI = \frac{A_{eB}}{B_i} \bigg/ \frac{A_e}{W_e}$$

EI export intensity,
A_{eB} export from A to B,
B_i total import of B,
A_e total export of A,
W_e total export of the world.

$$II = \frac{A_{iB}}{B_e} \bigg/ \frac{A_i}{W_i}$$

II import intensity,
A_{iB} import from A to B,
B_e total export of B,
A_i total import of A,
W_i total import of the world.

In most tables throughout the chapter, the calculations were run through for the Chinese export and import sides. The intensity indicator reflects the differences in trade shares of partners that cannot be attributed to different economic size. An outcome above one means that the trade flow is more intense than what can be considered as 'normal'. It should be clear that the results have to be normalized with a control group.

To show the problem of intra-trade we have constructed an example. If China's imports from Asian countries make up 50 per cent of total Chinese imports in 1994, while three years later the figure increases to 60 per cent of total imports, one would see an increase of intra-regional trade from the Chinese perspective. Now, assume that owing to high economic growth within the Asian region, the region increases its relative economic power in the world economy. Consequently, its share of world exports has increased, say, from 10 per cent in 1994 to 20 per cent in 1997 (Table 9.1). The increase in intra-trade is influenced by this increase in economic power and, therefore, the rise in intra-trade is not a signal of more intensive trade relations within the region.

The trade intensity analysis is not only a static approach, where a coefficient larger than one indicates greater intra-regional bias. In this case, the bilateral relationship is more important than integration in global trade. The analysis via the intensity indicator is also a dynamic analysis: intra-regional trade expansion in the same proportion as the growth of the region's total markets would result in a constant trade intensity index. A declining trend in the index indicates falling regional trade bias, while an increasing coefficient indicates an increasingly intensive regional trade bias.

Trade intensity between China and its trade partners

To observe the position of the EU among Chinese trading partners, we calculated the trade intensity between China and her main trading partners from 1991 to 1998. The results can be seen in Tables 9.2 and 9.3.

Table 9.1 Trade intensity – an example

Trade development China–Asia	1994	1997
Chinese total imports	80	100
Chinese imports from Asia	40	60
Share of Asia in world trade	10	20
Trade intensity indicator	5	3

Table 9.2 Trade intensity of China 1991–1998

Region		*1991*	*1992*	*1993*	*1994*	*1995*	*1996*	*1997*	*1998*
European Union	Export	0.228	0.220	0.340	0.339	0.337	0.354	0.378	0.397
	Import	0.342	0.320	0.373	0.408	0.400	0.361	0.368	0.355
United States	Export	0.527	0.705	1.165	1.111	1.116	1.165	1.120	1.210
	Import	1.042	0.922	0.828	1.004	1.074	0.996	0.920	0.960
Japan	Export	2.173	2.275	2.707	2.797	2.950	3.174	2.893	3.184
	Import	1.749	1.870	2.312	2.443	2.539	2.738	2.678	2.830
Hong Kong	Export	14.684	13.807	6.599	7.138	6.502	5.949	6.462	6.322
	Import	9.768	7.981	2.801	2.309	1.923	1.673	1.448	1.486
Asia*	Export	3.993	3.618	2.165	2.277	2.162	2.016	2.188	2.200
	Import	2.916	2.737	2.065	1.953	1.915	1.961	1.961	2.100
Africa	Export	0.478	0.545	0.650	0.579	0.684	0.667	0.667	0.920
	Import	0.273	0.227	0.350	0.368	0.526	0.556	0.762	0.535
Middle East	Export	0.550	0.605	0.757	0.727	0.719	0.676	0.657	–
	Import	0.361	0.351	0.444	0.387	0.586	0.733	0.900	–
Western Hemisphere	Export	0.182	0.233	0.370	0.404	0.426	0.400	0.453	0.510
	Import	0.488	0.438	0.353	0.346	0.429	0.490	0.464	0.350

Sources: People's Republic of China, *Customs Statistical Yearbook* 1991–1998.
IMF, *Direction of Trade Statistics Yearbook* 1995, 1999.

Note
*Asia: except Japan.

Table 9.3 Trade intensity between China and European Union countries (China's side)

Country		*1991*	*1992*	*1993*	*1994*	*1995*	*1996*	*1997*	*1998*
Austria	Export	0.059	0.059	0.100	0.097	0.089	0.090	0.095	0.093
	Import	0.479	0.336	0.283	0.316	0.379	0.201	0.169	0.171
Belgium	Export	–	–	0.220	0.223	0.225	0.229	0.266	0.304
	Import	–	–	0.225	0.267	0.242	0.225	0.208	0.193
Finland	Export	0.178	0.199	0.239	0.238	0.218	0.244	0.279	0.306
	Import	0.466	0.488	0.495	0.557	0.610	0.552	0.679	1.161
France	Export	0.159	0.145	0.265	0.221	0.233	0.247	0.266	0.295
	Import	0.397	0.295	0.283	0.303	0.358	0.299	0.435	0.407
Germany	Export	0.304	0.276	0.475	0.441	0.425	0.457	0.508	0.419
	Import	0.415	0.442	0.569	0.612	0.595	0.539	0.533	0.444
Ireland	Export	0.046	0.046	0.114	0.116	0.114	0.092	0.100	0.133
	Import	0.034	0.034	0.034	0.036	0.043	0.035	0.050	0.064
Italy	Export	0.257	0.264	0.365	0.336	0.349	0.317	0.328	0.359
	Import	0.472	0.456	0.583	0.591	0.516	0.497	0.397	0.365
Luxembourg	Export	–	–	0.027	0.038	0.046	0.008	0.069	0.111
	Import	–	–	0.183	0.141	0.248	0.192	0.167	0.227
Netherlands	Export	0.426	0.405	0.535	0.579	0.636	0.703	0.761	0.840
	Import	0.176	0.168	0.185	0.167	0.162	0.179	0.214	0.162
Portugal	Export	0.068	0.068	0.126	0.099	0.114	0.141	0.151	0.163
	Import	0.081	0.058	0.089	0.033	0.067	0.050	0.073	0.043
Spain	Export	0.177	0.150	0.028	0.289	0.298	0.285	0.312	0.344
	Import	0.340	0.240	0.028	0.398	0.319	0.187	0.200	0.173
Denmark	Export	0.236	0.196	0.270	0.266	0.249	0.232	0.258	0.306
	Import	0.149	0.157	0.218	0.246	0.252	0.245	0.299	0.263
Greece	Export	0.156	0.160	0.217	0.223	0.165	0.267	0.275	–
	Import	0.120	0.068	0.132	0.090	0.071	0.236	0.302	–
Sweden	Export	0.174	0.195	0.313	0.345	0.213	0.210	0.250	0.276
	Import	0.338	0.394	0.485	0.497	0.486	0.627	0.609	0.938
UK	Export	0.175	0.189	0.389	0.379	0.369	0.402	0.377	0.444
	Import	0.280	0.248	0.333	0.318	0.316	0.278	0.273	0.279

Sources: People's Republic of China, *Customs Statistical Yearbook* 1991–1998.

Table 9.2 shows trade intensity with specific regions. The calculations were run from the Chinese perspective; 'Chinese export' (first row) and 'Chinese import' (second row). The trade intensity indicators are typically larger than one with respect to Japan, Hong Kong and the rest of Asia, meaning that these regions are more important in the bilateral relationship than in global trade. Trade intensity with the rest of the world is low but increasing. This increase in trade intensity indicates that trade relations with the United States, the European Union and the other regions have expanded more than the growth of the Chinese share in world trade. Therefore, Table 9.2 shows two noticeable features of Chinese–EU trade. One is that the trade linkage between China and the EU is less intense than the linkage between China and rest of the world. The second is that the intensity of the trade linkage between China and the EU is increasing.

The reasons for the low Chinese–EU trade intensity are largely related to distance, regional integration and government policies. Compared with Japanese and other Asian companies, European companies have some disadvantages with respect to geographical and cultural background. Japan and other Asian economies are much nearer to China in physical distance, and the cultures (including consumption preference and commercial habits) are more similar among the Asian countries than with Europe. The cultural similarity, in terms of common values and philosophies, such as an interpersonal orientation, preference toward establishing trust and obligation, and a sense of belonging, facilitate Japanese and other Asian firms enjoying a more cooperative relationship with their Chinese partners than do their western counterparts. One may argue that there is no big difference between the EU and the United States with respect to geographical and cultural distance from China, but Chinese export to the United States is higher than what can be considered 'normal'. Policy is one reason for this. With respect to Chinese–EU trade, Chinese exporters have to face the Common Agricultural Policy with all its trade barriers. With China–United States trade, the reduction of trade barriers (in combination with the most Favored Nation – MFN – clause) played a role in its bilateral development. In addition, the development of a single market in the EU resulted in a greater concentration of trade within the EU due to the abolition of trade barriers, the homogeneity of EU consumers and the demand for differentiated products.

Despite the low intensity of Chinese–EU trade, there is an upward movement. Three factors account for the increase of Chinese–EU trade intensity. First, Chinese economic reform largely facilitated the diversification of the country's foreign trade. Most Chinese products were exported via Hong Kong, and this could be considered as entrepôt trade. The situation has changed since China embarked on trade liberalization. With freedom to choose their trade partners, Chinese companies prefer trading with the EU in a more direct way instead of going through Hong Kong. Second, Chinese industries enhance their competitiveness by using advanced technology and improving the quality of products. Chinese products are increasingly acceptable to EU consumers. Third, in the case of China there is a positive relationship between foreign direct investment inflow and trade flows. Using the panel data of trade intensity and FDI between China and individual EU countries during 1990–1999, we found a significant positive relation between these two variables. Furthermore, the high growth rate and market potential of China attract the attention of EU-based multinational corporations (MNCs), whose activities in China facilitated Chinese–EU trade.

Another interesting feature from Table 9.2 is the fact that the trade intensity of Chinese exports is higher than that of Chinese imports in most cases. As well as economic reasons for the export–import intensity differences, statistical problems can also disturb the picture. It is known that Chinese real imports are much higher than statistics show. This is due to smuggling. Furthermore, it is clear that political factors explain trade flows from both the import and the export side. From the export side, Chinese policies encourage exports through financial instruments, such as taxation refunds. From the import side, trade tariffs and non-tariff barriers keep many products away from the domestic Chinese market. The average tariff was about 35 per cent in 1996. Although the tariffs were reduced gradually, to 15.3 per cent in 2001 (*China Daily*, 1 May 2001), some other formal and informal barriers still work, such as complicated formalities with respect to applying for import licenses. This is what we would call a 'system barrier to imports'.

Trade intensity for the individual EU countries

Table 9.3 gives information about the development of the trade-intensity figures of European countries. It is clear that most of the intensities rose throughout the 1990s, but the level in 1998 was still relatively low, and there was no figure above one. Furthermore, there were large differences. The Netherlands showed a strong increase in trade intensity from the Chinese export perspective, while within the same period the figure with respect to Chinese imports from the Netherlands declined to 0.162. Dutch exporters were not able (or willing) to increase trade intensity with China, while Chinese exporters increased their visibility on the Dutch market. Sweden is also an extreme case. The strong increase in trade intensity from the Chinese import side (from 0.338 in 1991 to 0.938 in 1998) indicates the success of Swedish exporters. The same can be said about Finland. The explanation could be that non-members of the EU were less concentrated on increasing trade relations within the EU and consequently were open to more difficult and distant markets (Sweden and Finland were not members of the EU until 1995). In addition, the product composition partly explains this relatively good export performance of exporters from Sweden and Finland. On a three-digit level, the main product group for both countries is telecommunications equipment (764). It should be stated, however, that the level of bilateral trade between China on the one hand and Sweden and Finland on the other hand is very low and, consequently, a few large transactions will have a large effect on the trade intensity indicator.

The general picture is that Chinese export-trade intensity is rising while, in many EU countries, (Austria, Belgium, Italy, The Netherlands, Portugal, Spain and the UK) the Chinese import-trade intensity index is declining. The difficulty in penetrating the Chinese market is one explanation for this development. Another factor is the concentration on 'easy markets' within Europe.

Geographical composition

In order to offer a complete picture of the trade linkage, it is necessary to give information about the actual trade between China and the European Union. In this way, the trade-intensity indicator can be placed within the correct context. The percentage distribution of exports and imports is given in Table 9.4. Not surprisingly, the Asian region has a significant degree of economic interdependence, which is manifested in its relatively high level of intra-regional trade. The Asian region in 1991 absorbed 71.3 per cent of China's total exports. However, the share declined, and only 50.6 per cent of Chinese exports went to other Asian countries in 1998. It is necessary to emphasize the role of Hong Kong in Chinese international trade relations. As we stated before, much of China's trade passes through Hong Kong. The strong decline of Hong Kong in China's international trade resulted automatically in the strong decline of Asia as a whole, hence the increase of the rest of the world. By subtracting Hong Kong from Asia, the relative position of the Asian countries in Chinese international trade was stable (see Table 9.4). Exports to Japan only increased 13 per cent during the 1990s and one can witness a decline after 1996. Exports to the United States and the European Union increased dramatically. In 1991, only 9 per cent of total Chinese exports went to the United States. In 1998, however, the American market counted for 21 per cent of total exports; an increase of almost 141 per cent in 8 years. In addition, exports to the European Union increased from 10 per cent in 1991 to 15 per cent in 1998. It is interesting to note that Chinese imports from these two regions did not increase in relative terms. In Table 9.4, the column on the right indicates the growth in relative terms of the different regions. Chinese exports increased most dramatically to the United States (141 per cent) and the Western Hemisphere (251 per cent). Import growth was high with respect to the Middle East (108 per cent) and Africa (70 per cent). However, with the exception of the United States, the absolute value of trade to these regions is still at a low level. This development of the relative regional position corresponds with the development of the trade intensity indicator in Table 9.2.

The percentage composition of Chinese trade with individual EU countries is given in Table 9.5. In all cases (with the exception of Finland and

Table 9.4 The geographical composition of China's exports and imports 1991–1998 (%)

Region		*1991*	*1992*	*1993*	*1994*	*1995*	*1996*	*1997*	*1998*	*1991–1998 growth*
EU	Export	9.94	9.39	12.81	12.72	12.79	13.12	13.50	14.85	49.41
	Import	14.57	13.47	14.71	16.09	16.08	14.31	14.09	14.20	−2.59
USA	Export	8.57	10.12	18.49	17.74	16.61	17.67	17.90	20.65	140.82
	Import	12.55	11.04	10.28	12.08	12.26	11.64	11.45	12.04	−4.10
Japan	Export	14.22	13.75	17.20	17.83	19.13	20.44	17.42	16.14	13.44
	Import	15.72	16.98	22.37	22.77	21.96	21.02	20.37	20.16	28.22
Hong Kong	Export	44.73	44.16	24.05	26.75	24.20	21.78	23.96	21.08	−52.88
	Import	27.50	25.49	10.10	8.21	6.51	5.64	4.91	4.75	−82.74
Rest of Asia*	Export	12.37	10.84	12.75	13.55	15.80	15.52	15.64	13.42	8.54
	Import	14.20	16.11	24.60	25.39	27.19	29.46	31.95	32.85	131.37
Africa	Export	1.10	1.20	1.30	1.10	1.30	1.40	1.40	1.84	67.22
	Import	0.60	0.50	0.70	0.70	1.00	1.00	1.60	1.02	69.36
Middle East	Export	2.20	2.30	2.80	2.40	2.30	2.30	2.30	–	4.55
	Import	1.30	1.30	1.60	1.20	1.70	2.20	2.70	–	107.69
Western	Export	0.80	1.00	1.70	1.90	2.00	2.00	2.40	2.81	251.04
Hemisphere	Import	2.10	2.10	1.80	1.80	2.10	2.50	2.60	2.07	−1.60

Sources: People's Republic of China, *Customs Statistical Yearbook* 1991–1998.
MIF, *Direction of Trade Statistics Yearbook* 1995 and 1999.

Note
*Rest of Asia: except Japan and Hong Kong.

Table 9.5 The percentage composition of Chinese trade with individual EU countries

Country		*1991*	*1992*	*1993*	*1994*	*1995*	*1996*	*1997*	*1998*	*1991–1998 growth*
Austria	Export	0.08	0.08	0.13	0.12	0.11	0.11	0.11	0.11	37.45
	Import	0.56	0.40	0.30	0.34	0.43	0.22	0.18	0.20	−65.03
Belgium	Export	0.58	0.64	0.66	0.67	0.69	0.69	0.74	0.89	53.81
	Import	0.65	0.57	0.76	0.90	0.83	0.74	0.64	0.63	−3.76
Finland	Export	0.11	0.11	0.11	0.13	0.12	0.13	0.15	0.17	61.93
	Import	0.31	0.31	0.31	0.39	0.47	0.40	0.48	0.90	192.19
France	Export	1.02	0.90	1.41	1.18	1.24	1.26	1.27	1.54	50.53
	Import	2.46	1.86	1.58	1.68	2.00	1.61	2.28	2.29	−7.26
Germany	Export	3.28	2.88	4.33	3.93	3.81	3.87	4.02	3.53	7.78
	Import	4.78	4.98	5.81	6.17	6.09	5.28	4.93	4.41	−7.79
Ireland	Export	0.03	0.03	0.06	0.07	0.07	0.06	0.07	0.11	303.20
	Import	0.02	0.03	0.03	0.03	0.04	0.03	0.05	0.08	221.45
Italy	Export	1.30	1.29	1.42	1.31	1.39	1.22	1.22	1.40	8.07
	Import	2.29	2.17	2.63	2.65	2.36	2.34	1.72	1.63	−28.90
Luxembourg	Export	0.00	0.00	0.01	0.01	0.01	0.00	0.01	0.02	4720.57
	Import	0.01	0.01	0.03	0.02	0.04	0.03	0.02	0.03	161.56
Netherlands	Export	1.48	1.41	1.75	1.87	2.17	2.34	2.41	2.81	89.80
	Import	0.67	0.63	0.69	0.61	0.62	0.66	0.75	0.59	−11.57
Portugal	Export	0.05	0.05	0.08	0.06	0.07	0.09	0.09	0.11	124.46
	Import	0.04	0.03	0.04	0.01	0.03	0.02	0.03	0.02	−48.83
Spain	Export	0.46	0.39	0.06	0.62	0.66	0.64	0.68	0.83	82.04
	Import	0.58	0.44	0.05	0.78	0.69	0.37	0.39	0.34	−41.46
Denmark	Export	0.21	0.18	0.22	0.21	0.21	0.19	0.20	0.25	17.51
	Import	0.15	0.17	0.22	0.24	0.24	0.23	0.26	0.23	48.07
Greece	Export	0.09	0.10	0.13	0.11	0.08	0.14	0.14	0.21	125.18
	Import	0.03	0.02	0.03	0.02	0.00	0.04	0.05	0.01	−52.12
Sweden	Export	0.24	0.25	0.35	0.41	0.27	0.26	0.29	0.34	41.88
	Import	0.53	0.59	0.65	0.72	0.76	0.99	0.91	1.46	173.73
UK	Export	1.01	1.09	2.10	1.99	1.88	2.12	2.09	2.52	148.69
	Import	1.48	1.26	1.60	1.53	1.49	1.35	1.39	1.39	−5.69

Sources: People's Republic of China, *Customs Statistical Yearbook* 1991–1998.

Sweden) Chinese exports to the EU countries increased more than Chinese imports from these countries. The main EU destinations for Chinese exports are Germany, the UK, France, Italy and the Netherlands. In 1991, these five countries absorbed 80 per cent of Chinese exports to the EU. In 1998, the percentage of these countries in the total EU market for China's exports had declined only marginally to 79 per cent. Chinese imports from the EU were also very concentrated: 70 per cent and 79 per cent, respectively, in 1991 and 1998.

In the previous sections, the emphasis has been on the intensity of trade linkages. The conclusion from Tables 9.2 and 9.3 is that bilateral trade flow between China and the European Union is less than would be expected in terms of the economic weight of the two sides. However, this does not say that the trade flow is not of any importance for China. In 1998, almost 15 per cent of Chinese exports went to the European Union and more than 14 per cent of Chinese imports originated from the EU. From the EU perspective, trade with China is still low. According to the statistics from China's side, the share of Chinese products in total EU imports is 1.3 per cent, while China is the destination of only 0.9 per cent of total EU export (1998). Trade intensity analysis made clear that there was some increase in bilateral trade between China and the EU during the 1990s, but that a further increase on economic terms is to be expected in the coming years. This analysis has so far made clear that there are differences within the European Union. Germany, France, Finland and Sweden increased their trade intensity with China from the export side as well as from the import side. The Netherlands, Italy and the United Kingdom were not able to increase their exports to China in line with their shares in total world exports.

Chinese–EU trade structure

Commodity composition

The commodity composition of Table 9.6 indicates strong concentration on manufacturing (SITC 5–8). In 1998, 68.8 per cent of total Chinese imports from the EU were within group 7, and 67.2 per cent of total Chinese exports to the EU were within groups 7–8.

This concentration on manufactured products is not in line with our assumption. Furthermore, the share of manufactured goods in total import trade with the EU was higher than that of the Chinese import trade with the world. In 1998, the share of products within SITC groups 7 and 8 in total imports from the EU was 94.3 per cent, compared with 83.6 per cent in total imports from the world. The shares in total exports for these categories were 91.7 per cent to the EU and 80.0 per cent to the world. Traditional trade theory may perhaps explain why the share of manufactured goods imported from the EU is higher than from the rest of the world. For

Table 9.6 Percentage composition of Chinese trade with the EU and the world

		1993 (%)		*1998 (%)*	
		Import	*Export*	*Import*	*Export*
China to EU	Primary goods	4.2	13.4	5.7	8.3
	0 Food and live animals	0.6	6.2	1.0	3.6
	1 Beverages and tobacco	0.3	0.5	0.5	0.2
	2 Crude materials (inedible)	2.3	5.2	3.3	3.0
	3 Fuels, lubricants, etc	0.5	1.1	0.2	1.5
	4 Animal and vegetable oils, fats, wax	0.5	0.4	0.7	0.1
	Manufactured goods	95.8	86.6	94.3	91.7
	5 Chemicals and related products	8.6	8.2	9.3	8.3
	6 Manufactured goods	16.8	15.8	11.3	16.1
	7 Machines and transport equipment	66.9	18.3	68.8	33.1
	8 Miscellaneous manufactured product	3.2	44.3	4.6	34.1
	9 Goods not classified by kind	0.2	0.0	0.2	0.0
China to world	Primary goods	13.7	18.2	16.4	20.0
	0 Food and live animals	2.1	9.2	2.7	5.2
	1 Beverages and tobacco	0.2	1.0	0.1	0.5
	2 Crude materials (inedible)	5.2	3.3	7.6	1.7
	3 Fuels, lubricants, etc	5.6	4.5	4.8	2.6
	4 Animal and vegetable oils, fats, wax	0.5	0.2	1.1	10.0
	Manufactured goods	86.3	82.2	83.6	80.0
	5 Chemicals and related products	9.4	5.1	14.4	5.1
	6 Manufactured goods	27.4	17.9	22.1	15.5
	7 Machines and transport equipment	42.9	16.7	40.5	24.8
	8 Miscellaneous manufactured product	6.0	42.1	6.0	34.6
	9 Goods not classified by kind	0.7	0.4	0.5	0.0

Source: United Nations Statistics Division, Commodity Trade Statistics Section.

exports, however, it is hard to explain if we use the data only at the one-digit level. However, when we break down the goods into the six-digit level, we find the answer. The manufactured goods exported to the EU are dominated by labor-intensive products.

Within the European Union there are countries for which the concentration on a narrow range of products is even more pronounced than can be seen in Table 9.6. As stated before, telecommunications equipment (SITC 764) is an important item in Chinese imports from Finland and Sweden, with percentages of 37.6 per cent and 68.4 per cent respectively. More than 50 per cent of Chinese imports from Greece, for example, consist of manufactured fertilizers (SITC 562). It is to be expected that China's comparative advantage can be seen in the product groups 5–8. We shall elaborate on this when we discuss this later.

Terms of trade

The terms of trade is a criterion for measuring the change of export prices against the change of import prices. There are different measurements for this criterion. This study employs the net terms of trade, proposed by Taussig (1927), which is the ratio of export price index to import price index, denoted as TOT. The formula is:

$$TOT = \left(\frac{\sum_{i=1}^{n} q_{eit} P_{eit}}{\sum_{i=1}^{n} q_{eit} P_{ei0}} \right) \Big/ \left(\frac{\sum_{i=1}^{s} q_{mit} P_{mit}}{\sum_{i=1}^{s} q_{meit} P_{mi0}} \right) \times 100$$

q_{eit} the export volume of *i* goods in year *t*,
p_{eit} the export price of *i* goods in year *t*,
p_{ei0} the export price of *i* goods in the base year,
q_{mit} the import volume of *i* goods in year *t*,
p_{mit} the import price of *i* goods in year *t*,
p_{mi0} the import volume of *i* goods in the base year.

$TOT > 100$ implies that a given amount of exports buys more imports than in the base year, which means that the terms of trade has improved;
$TOT < 100$ implies that a given amount of exports buys less imports than in the base year, which means that the terms of trade has deteriorated;
$TOT = 100$ means that the terms of trade is unchanged.

Using UNFD (United Nations Foreign Department) data, which refer to the 3-digit level of SITC, we chose 1993 as the base year to calculate Chinese commodity terms of trade. On this base, China's terms of trade in 1998 was 109, and the terms of trade of China to the EU was 115. From this we can draw the cautious conclusion that the improvement in China's terms of trade with respect to the EU was greater than in China's terms of trade with the world. To explain this phenomenon, we argue that the composition of commodity trade plays an important role in the change of the terms of trade.

According to the statistics, the prices of 35 per cent of China's export products (at the three-digit level) declined from 1993 to 1998. Among the products whose prices declined, 66.7 per cent were primary products. With regard to China's imports, prices of 45 per cent of products dropped during the same period. Among the import products of which prices dropped, 61 per cent were primary products. These statistics imply that the more primary products there were in a basket of goods, the more likely the weighted price index would have dropped over this period.

The high concentration in manufactured products, stated in Table 9.6, partly explains the improvement of China's terms of trade. Table 9.6 shows at least two points. First, the share of manufactures in total exports from China to the EU is much higher than that of China to the world: the former is 91.7 per cent, and the latter is 79.98 per cent. Second, the share of manufactures in exports from China to the EU increased from 86.61 per cent in 1993 to 91.69 per cent in 1998. In contrast, the share of manufactures in exports from China to the world slightly decreased in the same period, from 82.16 per cent to 79.98 per cent. This evidence can partly explain why the improvement in terms of trade of China with the EU is more significant than that of China with the world.

The commodity diversification

The previous section offered a general picture of commodity composition, but that was done at the one-digit level. Using such broad categories does not make much sense because commodity diversification cannot be seen on a one-digit level. To make an in-depth analysis of commodity diversification, we use the Herfindahl–Hirschman index (HH index). The HH index is commonly used as a measure of market structure. In this chapter, however, we use it to measure the concentration of Chinese trade with respect to the EU countries (Daems and Douma, 1989). The calculations are run through the three-digit SITC product groups, for China's imports and exports separately. The index can be calculated from either the export side or the import side by using the following formula:

$$\text{HH index} = \sqrt{\Sigma\sigma^2}$$

where σ stands for the share of exports (imports) of a specific product in total exports (imports).

The index is one if trade consists of just one product, while an index close to zero means almost perfect commodity diversification. The calculations in Table 9.7 give the following conclusions.

Table 9.7 Herfindahl–Hirschman index of Chinese exports and imports

	Import	*Export*
EU	0.199	0.153
Austria	0.239	0.191
Belgium–Luxembourg	0.233	0.163
Denmark	0.210	0.227
Finland	0.389	0.197
France	0.333	0.167
Germany	0.178	0.148
Greece	0.555	0.266
Ireland	0.285	0.236
Italy	0.263	0.142
Netherlands	0.165	0.283
Portugal	0.276	0.175
Spain	0.198	0.144
Sweden	0.686	0.200
UK	0.196	0.163
Rest of the world	0.134	0.133
World	0.129	0.133

Source: United Nations Statistics Division, Commodity Trade Statistics Section.

- Chinese exports to the EU are less concentrated than Chinese imports from the EU. This relatively high import HH index from the Chinese perspective is partly due to the low share of Chinese imports in total EU exports (1.3 per cent) and the relatively high share of EU imports in total Chinese exports. Moreover, the EU is a large economic entity.
- Chinese imports are concentrated in a relatively narrow range of products: imports from Greece are concentrated in SITC group 562, while imports from Sweden (SITC 764) and Finland (SITC 764) are also dominated by one product group. This results in a high import HH index with these three countries. The high concentration in a narrow range of product groups makes clear that small countries in economic terms can specialize in specific product groups and, simultaneously, within these product groups they must differentiate due to the absence of a large domestic market. Especially when trade values are low, this concentration on some products can influence the HH index dramatically.
- Countries with relative large shares in China–EU trade, such as Germany, Italy and the UK, have, with only a few exceptions, a relatively low HH-index. The countries with the lowest shares in China–EU trade, mostly, have a relatively high HH-index with respect to Chinese exports.
- The HH-index between China and the rest of the world is lower than that of China with the EU. This can be explained by the fact that the rest of the world contains more countries and, as a result, a more diversified product range is possible.

Intra-industry trade of China

In this section, we discuss the Chinese–EU trade relation within the context of intra-industry trade. Intra-industry trade (IIT) means simultaneously exporting and importing products belonging to the same SITC product group. In earlier work, we put an emphasis on the fact that the development of intra-industry trade is essential to forecast the stability of a trading block (Ebbers, 1997). The higher the proportion of trade involving intra-industry trade, the fewer adjustment costs will be induced by asymmetrical shocks. It is clear that the likelihood of these asymmetrical shocks is higher, the more the countries within an integration scheme have different economic structures. With respect to Chinese–EU trade, one would expect low intra-industry trade due to differences in economic structure; hence, intensive adjustment problems may occur between the two regions. Besides the adjustment problem within integration schemes, intra-industry trade can be used as a measure of comparative advantage. We shall elaborate on this relationship in the following section.

It is clear that IIT is influenced by the level of aggregation. The more aggregated data are used the higher is the intra-industry trade and, obviously, a very detailed classification might lead to an extremely low IIT. In our analysis of Chinese–EU intra-industry trade, we used the three-digit product group classification. Table 9.8 shows China's intra-industry trade with the European Union for 1998. We also calculated some indices for 1993. In addition, the IIT ratio with the world has been computed to normalize the results. Measuring IIT between China and individual EU

Table 9.8 China's intra-industry trade ratio with the EU and the world in 1993 and 1998

	1993	*1998*
EU	18.2	30.1
Austria	–	17.4
Belgium–Luxembourg	15.8	43.3
Denmark	11.9	16.7
Finland	–	25.5
France	16.5	20.0
Germany	16.1	23.7
Greece	11.9	21.7
Ireland	5.6	48.4
Italy	19.7	26.5
Netherlands	21.0	43.4
Portugal	3.6	28.9
Spain	13.0	41.6
Sweden	–	31.1
UK	9.7	39.8
World	37.5	46.3

Source: United Nations Statistics Division, Commodity Trade Statistics Section.

countries was done via the adjusted Grubel–Lloyd index (1), in which imbalance bias was tackled. The IIT of commodity groups was calculated via the weighted average Grubel–Lloyd index (2) (Grubel and Lloyd, 1975).

$$IIT = \frac{\Sigma(Xi + Mi) - \Sigma\,|\,Xi - Mi\,|}{\Sigma(Xi + Mi) - |\,\Sigma Xi - \Sigma Mi\,|} \times 100 \tag{1}$$

$$IIT = \frac{\Sigma(Xi + Mi) - \Sigma\,|\,Xi - Mi\,|}{\Sigma(Xi + Mi)} \times 100 \tag{2}$$

where *Xi* and *Mi* stand, respectively, for the values of exports and imports of *i* product group.

For IIT with the EU as a whole and IIT with the world, one can witness an increasing trend between 1993 and 1998. This is to be expected because mutual trade liberalization would spur exploitation of gains from intra-industry specialization in differentiated products. In general, the IIT between China and the European Union can be considered as low. Partly this can be explained by the large difference in economic development between the EU members on the one hand and China on the other hand and by the large cultural, geographical and social discrepancies between the two regions. Furthermore, the economic structure and the level of national income may explain the low IIT from the Chinese perspective; the relatively low level of income per capita, and the importance of natural resources in the country's economic structure lead Chinese trade to be dominated by inter-industry trade.

Table 9.9 indicates IIT ratios between China and the EU and between China and the world by commodity group. We can observe a pattern, which is common for most empirical work on intra-industry trade – the

Table 9.9 Intra-industry trade ratio between China–EU and China–world by commodity

	China–EU		*China–world*
	1993	*1998*	*1998*
0 Food and live animals	10.7	19.3	27.0
1 Beverages and tobacco	24.3	38.0	31.0
2 Crude materials (inedible)	11.5	30.4	17.1
3 Fuels, lubricants, etc	4.7	16.4	43.9
4 Animal and vegetable oils, fats, wax	67.4	6.9	33.1
5 Chemicals and related products	53.2	49.7	39.1
6 Manufactured goods	16.6	33.2	52.8
7 Machines and transport equipment	14.1	26.0	56.3
8 Miscellaneous manufactured product	7.1	10.4	17.4
9 Goods not classified by kind	12.8	2.5	1.5

Source: United Nations Statistics Division, Commodity Trade Statistics Section.

level of IIT is higher in sectors 5–8 than in sectors 0–4 (Globerman and Dean, 1990; Torstensson, 1996; Hu and Ma, 1999). However, the rate of growth in IIT between China and the EU appears to have been higher in sectors 0–4; and IIT of sectors 1–2 reached a high level by 1998. In contrast, the IIT of sectors 6–8, which accounts for over 80 per cent of the trade flow between China and the EU, was far behind the corresponding index for trade with the world. This is not in line with what would be expected. But again, the importance of south-east Asia in Chinese trade can explain this feature. The complementarity between international trade and foreign direct investments results in high levels of IIT.

One would expect that the similarities in the industrial structure of the EU countries (most clearly marked in the case of northern and southern EU countries considered separately) would result in similar patterns of IIT. This is clearly not the case. Denmark (17) and the Netherlands (43) are considered as being very close in terms of economic structure, but are at almost the two extremes with respect to IIT. Some country-specific characteristics and the level of economic relations may be used to explain these differences. For example, a large difference between the Netherlands and Denmark is that FDI inflow to China from the Netherlands is much higher than that from Denmark. In 1998, FDI inflow was US$718.8 million from the Netherlands, but only US$62 million from Denmark (MOFTEC, 1999). Mostly this FDI was to increase the parent–subsidiary relationship, which may increase intra-industry trade between host country and home country. In the case of China, vertical intra-industry trade is probably enhanced by FDI (Hu and Ma, 1999).

Revealed comparative advantage

The actual trade structure can, under specific assumptions, give information regarding comparative advantage. This is the essence of the concept of revealed comparative advantage (RCA) propounded by Balassa (1961). Mostly, an emphasis is placed on manufactured products due to the fact that a large number of primary products are subject to subsidies, quotas and special arrangements, so that the actual trade pattern can hardly reflect comparative advantage. The revealed comparative advantage index (RCA index) is calculated as the ratio of the share of a given commodity group in exports of country A to country B to the share of the same group in total imports of country B from third countries. The formula is:

$$RCA\ index = \frac{X_{iAB}/X_{AB}}{M_{iB}/M_B}$$

X_{iAB} export value of *i* group from A to B,
X_{AB} total export value from A to B,
M_{iB} total import value of *i* group of B,
M_B total import value of B.

If the index is higher than one, the country or region is said to have a comparative advantage in that specific product group compared with other countries.

The RCA index on China's side is calculated as the ratio of the share of a given commodity group in Chinese exports to the EU to the share of the same group in total EU imports from the world. The RCA index on the EU side is calculated as the ratio of the share of a given commodity group in EU exports to China to the share of the same group in China's total imports from the world.

Table 9.10 indicates only two sectors in China as having a revealed comparative advantage in exports: manufactured goods (SITC 6) and miscellaneous manufactured articles (SITC 8). This is consistent with the observation we made from Table 9.6 that the product groups 'manufactured goods', 'machines and transport equipment' and 'miscellaneous manufactured articles' were the most important products in Chinese exports. In addition, the EU revealed the comparative advantage of their exports to China consists of two product groups, namely 'beverages and tobacco' (SITC 1) and 'machines and transport equipment' (SITC 7). Again, Table 9.6 makes clear that 'machines and transport equipment' was the most important product group in Chinese imports from the EU. Table 9.9 shows a relatively low level of IIT in the product group 'miscellaneous manufactured articles' with respect to the EU (10.4 per cent) and the world (17.4 per cent). This means that trade relations in SITC 8 are characterized by a high level of inter-industry trade, and consequently the RCA index is high.

Table 9.10 is the average of the calculations, which were run from the three-digit product classification. The low incidence of industries having a revealed comparative advantage is, in our view, a positive characteristic. A low number of sectors having a high revealed comparative advantage is a

Table 9.10 Revealed comparative advantage index, 1998

	RCA index China side	*RCA index EU side*
0 Food and live animals	0.43	0.36
1 Beverages and tobacco	0.20	4.12
2 Crude materials (inedible)	0.73	0.44
3 Fuels, lubricants, etc	0.23	0.04
4 Animal and vegetable oils, fats, wax	0.15	0.65
5 Chemicals and related products	0.76	0.65
6 Manufactured goods	1.02	0.51
7 Machines and transport equipment	0.91	1.70
8 Miscellaneous manufactured product	2.53	0.76
9 Goods not classified by kind	0.00	0.45

Source: United Nations Statistics Division, Commodity Trade Statistics Section.

sign of a relatively developed trade pattern, in which intra-industry trade is an important characteristic.

Conclusions

We have set out to examine the Chinese–EU trade relations by using a comprehensive analytical framework. The first question was whether trade between China and the European Union is in line with what would be expected in terms of volume. The answer to this question appears to be negative. Calculating the 'trade intensity indicator' and the linkage to the geographical distribution makes clear that bilateral trade is less than what would be expected from the economic weight of the partners. Saying this, however, does not mean that trade with the European Union from the Chinese perspective is unimportant. Almost 15 per cent of China's total trade is conducted with the European Union. Furthermore, the low level of trade intensity indicates a high potential for expanding bilateral trade flows. The analysis in terms of the trade intensity between China and particular EU countries indicates differences within the European Union with respect to Chinese trade.

Our answer to the second question – whether individual EU countries show similar patterns with respect to their bilateral trade with China – is negative. During the 1990s, the Netherlands, Italy and the UK were not able to increase their exports to China in line with their shares of world exports; Germany, France, Finland and Sweden, however, increased their bilateral trade with China to a greater extent than their shares in world exports.

The third part of the chapter is about the product composition of China's trade with the EU. The analysis of the indicators related to product composition, such as the Herfindahl–Hirschman index and the intra-industry trade index (IIT) for individual EU countries, again resulted in a negative answer to our second question. The Herfindahl–Hirschman index indicates an extremely high concentration in imports from Greece, Sweden, Finland and France. As might be expected, the countries with the largest share in China–EU trade are also the countries having a relatively low Herfindahl–Hirschman index. Large differences related to IIT can be seen within the European Union. On the one hand there is Ireland with IIT of 0.48, while, on the other hand, there is Denmark with a low IIT of 0.17.

We use the commodity composition to answer the third question: whether China exports mainly primary products to the EU and the EU largely exports manufactured goods to China. The use of a control group indicates a commodity composition with a strong concentration of manufacturing in both exports and imports from the Chinese side. The declining trend of concentration in manufacturing generally conflicts strongly with the Chinese–EU trade flow. Between 1993 and 1998, the manufacturing sector increased its relative weight in total bilateral trade.

Another way of analysing the product composition is through IIT. We calculated the Chinese intra-industry trade ratio with the European Union via the weighted Grubel–Lloyd index. Our fourth question, as to whether the EU–China trade is mainly of an inter-industry trade nature, is answered partly in the affirmative. However, the relationship between the diversification of economies and intra-industry trade with China requires further investigation. With respect to product groups, some high indices were found in the SITC product groups 1, 2 and 5. This is not in line with our expectation; which was that the IIT in the manufacturing sector would be higher than in the primary sector.

On a three-digit analysis, we calculated China's commodity terms of trade with 1993 as the base year. The terms of trade for China with the world in 1998 was 109 while its terms of trade with the EU was calculated as 115. From this we can draw the cautious conclusion that the improvement in China's terms of trade to the EU was more significant than that of its terms of trade with the world. Behind this phenomenon, the commodity composition of trade plays an important role.

Finally, we calculated and analysed the revealed comparative advantage (RCA) Index of Balassa in its application to China and the EU. We indicated that only two sectors have a revealed comparative advantage in China's exports: manufactured goods and miscellaneous manufactured articles. Furthermore, the EU's revealed comparative advantage in its exports to China appears in two product groups, namely beverages and tobacco, and machines and transport equipment. The low incidence of industries having a comparative advantage is, in our view, a positive characteristic. A low number of sectors having high revealed comparative advantage is a sign of a relatively developed trade pattern, in which intra-industry trade is an important characteristic.

Bibliography

Asian Development Bank (1999) *Asian Economic Outlook*, 1999 (Manila: Asian Development Bank).

Aturupane, C., Djankov, S. and Hoekman, B. (1999) 'Horizontal and vertical intra-industry trade between eastern Europe', *Weltwirtschaftliches Archiv*, 135(1), 62–81.

Balassa, B. (1961) *The Theory of Economic Integration* (London: George Allen & Unwin).

Daems, H. and Douma, S. (1989) *Competitive Strategy and Company Strategy* (Deventer: Kluwer).

Drysdale, P. and Carnaut, R. (1993) 'The Pacific; application of a general theory of economic integration', In F. Bergsten and M. Noland (eds), *Pacific Dynamism and the International Economic System* pp. 183–223 (Washington, DC: Institute for International Economics).

Ebbers, H.A. (1997) *Economic and Monetary Integration: Options for Countries in Central and Eastern Europe* (Delft: Eburon).

Globerman, S. and Dean, J.W. (1990) Recent Trends in Intra-industry Trade and Their Implications for Future Trade Liberalization, *Weltwirtschaftliches Archiv*, 126, 25–49.

Grant, R.L. (ed.) (1995) *The European Union and China: a European Strategy for the Twenty-First Century* (London: Royal Institute of International Affairs, Asia Pacific Programme; distributed by Brookings Institution, Washington, DC).

Grimwade, N. (1998) *International Trade: New Patterns of Trade, Production and Investment* (London: Routledge).

Grubel, H.G. and Lloyd, P.J. (1975) *Intra Industry Trade: the Theory and Measurement of International Trade in Differentiated Products* (London: Macmillan).

Hu, X. and Ma, Y. (1999) 'International intra-industry trade of China', *Weltwirtschaftliches Archiv*, 135(1), 82–101.

Kojima, K. (ed.) (1968) *Pacific Trade and Development*, Paper No 9 (The Japan Economics Research Center).

MOFTEC (1999) *Foreign Trade and Economy Year Book of China 1999* (Beijing: Ministry of Foreign Trade and Economy Cooperation).

Prebisch, R. (1950) *The Economic Development of Latin America and Its Principal Problems* (New York: United Nations).

Singer, H. (1950) 'The distribution of gains between investing and borrowing countries', *American Economic Review*, 40, 473–485.

Strange, R. (1998) *Trade and Investment in China: the European Experience* (London: Routledge).

Taussig, F.W. (1927) *International Trade* (New York: MacMillan).

Torstensson, J. (1996) 'Determinants of intra-industry trade: a sensitivity analysis', *Oxford Bulletin of Economics and Statistics*, 58, 507–524.

10 Comparative productivity of foreign and local firms in Chinese industry

Xiaming Liu

Introduction

From late 1978, when China adopted the economic reform and open-door policy, to the end of 1999, China approved over 340,000 foreign-invested enterprises (FIEs) and, by the end of that period, pledged and actual foreign direct investment (FDI) reached US$613.7 billion and US$307.8 billion respectively (Wei and Liu, 2001). FIEs have played an increasing role in economic development. For instance, in 1995, FIEs employed 6.1 per cent of total employees but produced 14.8 per cent of total value added in Chinese industry (*The Data of the Third National Industrial Census of the People's Republic of China in 1995*, hereafter the *Third Industrial Census*).

While there have been a few comparative studies of productivity and efficiency for local firms (recent examples include Dong and Putterman, 1997; Bai *et al.*, 1997; Zheng *et al.*, 1998) and studies of efficiency of foreign-invested firms in China (e.g. Cheng and Wu, 2001), little research on the relative performance of local and foreign firms in Chinese industry has been carried out. This may be partly due to the lack of reliable data. One exception is Sun (1998, chapter 5) who provides detailed comparisons of the production characteristics and efficiency of FIEs and state-owned enterprises (SOEs) using the data from the *Third Industrial Census* – State Statistical Bureau (1997). However, in Sun's study, such factors as capital intensity and scale economies, which are identified in the literature as important for economic efficiency, are not incorporated into any production functions employed. Furthermore, human capital or labour quality is ignored.

Instead of comparing FIEs with local firms as a whole, the current study compares labour productivity in FIEs, SOEs and other local-owned enterprises (OLOEs). The inclusion of OLOEs in the comparison will produce more useful information because this group of firms behave differently not only from FIEs but also from SOEs. We first test for any differences in labour productivity among the three groups of firms. We then examine how capital intensity, labour quality and scale economies affect the economic performance of these groups. We also examine the question of whether FIEs contribute to a higher income level in Chinese industry. Other specific advantages, which contribute to higher efficiency in FIEs, are also discussed. The rest of the chapter is organised as follows. In the following section, the relevant literature is reviewed. The section after presents empirical models and describes the data. Our estimation results and the corresponding discussions are then provided. The final section offers concluding remarks and discusses policy implications.

Literature review

Received theory explains the existence and growth of FDI. For instance, the monopolistic advantages approach of Hymer (1960, published in 1976) and Kindleberger (1969) regard a multinational enterprise (MNE) as a creature of market imperfections that lead a firm to possess specific advantages over local firms in the host country. Vernon (1977) emphasises the level of technological sophistication in the industry as an important cause of FDI. The transactions cost approach of Casson (1982), Rugman (1981) and Hennart (1982, 1991) argues that MNEs emerge when it is more beneficial to internalise the use of such intermediate goods as technology than externalise them through the market. The eclectic paradigm of Dunning (1981, 1988, 1991) stipulates that FDI is determined by three sets of factors, namely ownership (firm-specific) advantage, internalisation advantage and location (country-specific) advantage.

Clearly, the dominant theme in received theory is that multinationals are firms that have developed specific assets that are best exploited by overseas production (Davies and Lyons, 1991). Although the fact that MNEs possess unique income-generating assets relative to indigenous firms might suggest that they could be both more productive and profitable, there is no *a priori* presumption that they should be so. Dunning (1993, Chapter 15) provides five reasons why one cannot predict the relative productivity of MNEs. The first is related to the investment environment in the host country. As Hymer (1976) among others suggests, foreign firms may be faced with certain competitive disadvantages vis-à-vis local firms in penetrating the latter's markets.

The second factor has something to do with the purposes of FDI. Dunning (1988, pp. 33–34) lists five types of FDI: resource based, market based, rationalised specialisation of products or processes, trade and distribution, and miscellaneous. Not all types of FDI will automatically lead to higher efficiency relative to local firms in the host country. For instance, the specific purpose of the first type of FDI is to ensure stability of supplies at the right price, control markets or obtain technology. This implies that local firms can have easier access to local markets and/or possess more advanced technology than MNEs. On the other hand, the efficiency may be of secondary concern to MNEs that wish to safeguard their supplies of raw materials or intermediate products or acquire superior technologies or capabilities to advance their global strategic goals. Thus, it is often not necessary for MNEs to earn higher average rates of return than local firms.

Third, although MNEs may be more efficient as suppliers of intermediate products, they are not necessarily better at adding value to these products than domestic firms. Like any international firms, MNEs may also fail. Fourth, MNEs may use their ownership advantages to exploit a monopolistic position rather than to improve efficiency. For instance, an increase in productivity or profitability may accrue entirely to the investing company by means of transfer pricing, and will not be reflected in the performance of subsidiaries. Finally, MNEs may be satisfied by earning profits from an FDI project that are equal to its opportunity costs.

The relative performance of MNEs depends on the configurations of ownership, location and internalisation (OLI) advantages with which they are faced and their responses to these configurations. Thus, the nature of relative efficiency is essentially an empirical question. By reviewing the following selected recent comparative efficiency studies, we are able to identify the main determinants of relative performance, compare different approaches to the topic and contrast the results from developed and developing countries.

For developed countries, both cross-country and within-country comparisons seem to be popular. Relatively recent cross-country studies include Prais *et al.* (1981), Davies and Caves (1987), Broadberry and Crafts (1990), van Ark (1990a, 1990b, 1992), and Carr (1992). In these studies, matched or paired comparisons are made between foreign and local firms or industries in different countries. The determinants of productivity efficiency identified include plant and production scale, technical training, capital supply and utilisation, labour relations, market structure, research outlays, and international competitive pressures. As can be seen below, many of these determinants coincide with those in the following within-country comparative studies.

In the case of developed countries, relative efficiency of foreign firms in the US, UK and Canada are often examined. Based on a sample of 108 firms operating in the US, Kim and Lyn (1990) carry out a univariate analysis of the differences in group means of a number of measures for monopoly power, profitability, fixed asset intensity, firm size, and others, and find that foreign-owned firms as a whole are less profitable than randomly selected American-owned firms. They also find that Japanese firms are more R&D and advertising intensive, but Western European firms are more profitable, than other foreign firms. Thus, foreign firms may have different motivations for investing in the US. However, Kim and Lyn (1989) provide no systematic investigation of the determinants of profitability or productivity.

Applying a two-tier decomposition analysis, Davies and Lyons (1991) examine the extent to which the aggregate productivity advantage of foreign-owned enterprises is due to a 'better' industrial distribution (the structural effect), and how much it reflects a widespread tendency for foreign-owned enterprises to be more productive than their domestic counterparts within each industry (the ownership effect). It appears that the role of ownership explains a substantial part of low productivity in UK-owned firms. The ownership effect might be due to differentials in technology, labour skills, capital input, vertical integration or monopoly power in the product market.

Using a very large sample, Globerman *et al.* (1994) compare the comparative economic performance of Japanese, US and European-owned establishments in Canada. They first test whether home country differences exist in value-added per worker after correcting for sectoral differences. They then examine whether the home country (nationality) differences in productivity can be attributed to differences in capital intensity, scale, and human resource management practice. They conclude that foreign-owned firms have significantly higher labour productivity than Canadian-owned establishments. But the differences disappear when such factors as capital intensity and scale are controlled for.

The above studies indicate that foreign firms are not necessarily more productive than local firms in developed countries. This confirms that we cannot offer clear-cut prediction as to whether foreign firms are more efficient than local firms in host developed countries where OLI configurations are similar. Any meaningful study should be made on a case-by-case basis.

In the case of host developing countries, the situation can be somewhat different. Differences in OLI configurations between developed countries are much smaller than between developed and developing countries. MNEs from developed countries are normally assumed to have far more specific advantages than local firms. They have much newer or cheaper technology, cheaper credit or better management. Thus, MNEs may be more likely to enjoy relatively higher productivity in developing countries than in developed countries. As indicated in the extensive literature surveys by Lall (1978), Caves (1982) and Dunning (1993), most studies show positive – but sometimes non-significant – differences in profitability and productivity between MNEs and local firms.

Relatively recent within-country comparisons of multinational and local firms in developing countries include Newfarmer and Marsh (1981), Asheghian (1982), Willmore (1986), Blomstrom (1988), Sterner (1990), and Sun (1998). Using the data on 150 Brazilian and transnational firms operating in Brazil's electrical industry, Newfarmer and Marsh (1981) compare the behaviour of foreign and domestic firms in four areas: association with particular types of market structure, technology, trade conduct and profitability, and find that Brazilian firms are slightly more profitable than MNEs. Newfarmer and Marsh argue that this is because Brazilian firms are more sensitive to local environmental conditions, including relative prices of factors, and consequently use more efficient techniques. They find that the market power of MNEs and Brazilian firms plays a decisive, positive role in determining overall profitability. Labour productivity is not compared in their study.

Another within-country comparison for Brazil was carried out by Willmore (1986), in which 282 pairs of foreign-owned and private Brazilian firms are matched by sales and by four-digit manufacturing industry. The statistical analyses indicate that foreign firms in Brazil typically enjoy higher levels of labour productivity than local firms of a similar size operating in the same industry. Willmore suggests several factors for higher efficiency in foreign firms: (1) employees with greater skills and training, (2) more machinery and equipment per worker, (3) greater technical efficiency, or (4) some combination of the three possibilities. However, since these factors and labour productivity are compared individually, it is not clear which of these factors is (are) significantly associated with labour productivity.

It is obvious that the results from the Brazilian study of Willmore are not comparable with those of Newfarmer and Marsh since they use different indexes of efficiency, cover different industries, and adopt different methods.

Applying the Wilcoxon tests, Asheghian (1982) compares the relative efficiency of 11 matched Iranian firms (IFs) and Iranian–American joint ventures (IAJVs) and finds that IAJVs enjoy higher capital, labour and total factor productivity. Without any careful discussion, the higher labour productivity is attributed to either the higher wages and non-wage benefits paid to the labour by IAJVs or the better supervision, training, and research of IAJVs. Similarly, the higher total factor productivity is related to either the efficiency of the superior management process or advanced technology as compared with IFs. Thus, the assumed relationship between productivity and factors such as research and training is not justified.

Similar to Brazil, Mexico is a developing country for which several comparative efficiency studies have been carried out. For instance, based on data from 215 four-digit industries, Blomstrom (1988) compares labour productivity functions for domestically owned and foreign-owned firms. After controlling for differences in capital intensity, labour quality, scale and concentration, foreign affiliates are found to be significantly more productive than their Mexican counterparts in Mexican manufacturing industry. This indicates that multinational corporations have other advantages that are specific to that type of ownership. However, the limitations of the data prevent an investigation of these advantages.

Sterner (1990) uses a frontier production function to estimate the relative technical efficiency of 24 cooperatives, ordinary domestic and foreign firms in the Mexican cement industry, but does not find multinationals to be more efficient or cooperatives to be less efficient than non-cooperative domestic firms.

As for China, Sun (1998) compares various efficiency indicators of FIEs and domestic-owned firms, and then uses various production functions to estimate the relationship between total output and total labour and capital inputs. It is found that FIEs have higher capital intensity, use capital-intensive production methods (higher fixed capital scale), and have a higher capital and labour productivity than local Chinese firms. As mentioned earlier, since capital intensity and scale are not incorporated into regressions, the impact of these factors on labour productivity is still unclear.

Although it is difficult to establish a meaningful comparison among different studies, the above host-developing-country cases do show that MNEs are generally more efficient than local firms.

Methodology and data

MNEs behave differently from local firms because of the different OLI configurations with which the different groups of firms are faced. Although it is useful to compare various configurations individually, it will be more fruitful to identify why, if at all, MNEs and local firms have different productivity. As indicated by the literature, capital intensity, labour quality and firm size are among the important determinants. If we control for these factors, then differences in productivity are eventually associated with other specific advantages, such as superior technology, marketing and managerial skills. This approach is consistent with Globerman *et al.* (1994).

Following this methodology, we first examine whether there are significant differences in productivity among FIEs, SOEs and OLOEs. This can be easily done by the following regression:

$$VAL_i = \alpha_j + \beta_j Dfor + \delta_j Doth + \epsilon_j \tag{10.1}$$

where VAL is value-added per worker, a proxy for labour productivity; α is a constant that represents the average effect of SOEs in an industry, $Dfor$ is a dummy variable equal to one if firms are FIEs and zero otherwise, and $Doth$ is a dummy variable equal to one if firms are OLOEs and zero otherwise. j = 1, 2, 3,. . . 6 for equations (10.1–10.6).

Using Equation (10.2), we then relate capital intensity (KL), labour quality (LQ) and firm size (FS) to labour productivity in order to examine the extent to which the differences in labour productivity can be explained by these variables. By so doing, the effects of these variables can be separated from those of other variables which are specific to the type of ownership.

$$VAL_i = \alpha_j + KL_i + LQ_i + FS_i + \beta_j Dfor + \delta_j Doth + \epsilon_j \tag{10.2}$$

We then examine whether there are significant differences in the individual determinants of labour productivity across different types of ownership by establishing the following equations:

$$KL_i = \alpha_j + \beta_j Dfor + \delta_j Doth + \epsilon_j \tag{10.3}$$

$$LQ_i = \alpha_j + \beta_j Dfor + \delta_j Doth + \epsilon_j \tag{10.4}$$

$$FS_i = \alpha_j + \beta_j Dfor + \delta_j Doth + \epsilon_j \tag{10.5}$$

Finally, we compare wage rates (*WG*) across different groups of firms to establish the relationship between labour productivity and wage rates by

$$WG_i = \alpha_j + \beta_j Dfor + \delta_j Doth + \epsilon_j \tag{10.6}$$

The data used in this research are from *the Third Industrial Census*, published by the State Statistical Bureau (1997). This is an industrial survey on a cross-section of 191 branches of Chinese industry. The *Third Industrial Census* shows the existence of a variety of ownership: state-owned, collectively owned, domestic joint ventures, joint corporations, individually owned, private operated, and 'foreign, Hong Kong, Macao and Taiwan invested' firms. Although, at the time, the *Third Industrial Census* was the most comprehensive one ever published by the Chinese authorities, information is provided at relatively aggregate levels. For instance, statistics are provided for foreign, Hong Kong, Macao and Taiwan invested firms as a whole, and it is not possible to separate these four groups from each other. In addition, although there are aggregate statistics for 191 industrial branches, and some detailed data for SOEs and, to a less extent, for foreign, Hong Kong, Macao and Taiwan invested firms in these branches, much fewer data are available for individual groups of non-state-owned local firms. Because of the data limitation, we can compare only three groups of firms: SOEs for all state-owned enterprises, OLOEs for all other locally owned enterprises, and FIEs for all foreign, Hong Kong, Macao and Taiwan invested enterprises. These three groups of firms represent three major different types of ownership, and are expected to behave very differently.

In contrast to Globerman *et al.* (1994), where the cost of fuel and electricity per production employee is used to measure capital intensity (*KL*), we use the ratio of the net value of fixed assets to the number of employees. In addition, we do not use the proportion of the workforce involved in production or the ratio of male employees to total employees to measure human-resource-management practice. Instead, we introduce labour quality (*LQ*). Because of the lack of data on employees' on-the-job training, we use the proportion of university/college graduates to the total work force as a proxy for labour quality. For the purpose of comparison, we use three alternative measures for firm size (*FS*): sales, fixed assets, or the number of employees, each being divided by the number of firms in each ownership group.

In such a cross-sectional study as ours where small-, medium- and large-sized firms/industrial branches are sampled together, heteroscedasticity is generally expected. In the presence of heteroscedasticity, the ordinary-least-square estimators, although unbiased, are inefficient. We first carry out White's heteroscedasticity tests. If there is heteroscedasticity, White's heteroscedasticity-corrected standard errors and the corresponding *t* statistics are provided.

Empirical results

The regression results of equations (10.1)–(10.6) are presented in Table 10.1. As indicated by the White tests, all but column (5) indicate the existence of heteroscedasticity. Thus, except for column (5), the *t* statistics given are the White's heteroscedasticity-corrected ones.

From column (1) labour productivity in FIEs is significantly higher than in both OLOEs and SOEs. This finding is consistent with many studies on developing countries. While value added per employee in OLOEs is higher than in SOEs, the difference is not significant. After a general picture of the relative efficiency for the three groups of firms is presented in column (1), some important determinants are identified and further compared in the remaining columns.

Turning to column (2), when such factors as capital intensity, labour quality and firm size are controlled for, FIEs are still significantly more productive than both SOEs and OLOEs. This suggests that FIEs have other specific advantages than higher capital intensity and labour quality, which make them more efficient than local firms in Chinese industry. What are the 'other specific advantages' possessed by FIEs? Received theory indicates that FDI is a package of advanced technology, managerial and marketing skills as well as financial capital. The level of embodied technology may be captured in our model because capital intensity is sometimes assumed to be positively associated with technology level (see for example, Kokko, 1994). However, like many other studies, the current model is not able to incorporate non-embodied technology.

Although we are unable formally to incorporate the managerial/marketing skill variables because of the lack of data, it is evident that enterprise management skills in local Chinese firms are far lower than in FIEs. In the pre-reform period, local Chinese firms, particularly SOEs, were under direct control by state plans, and the main responsibility of enterprise management was to fulfil the government's production tasks. As the central part of economic reform, the Chinese government has introduced several market-oriented measures to improve management of SOEs, including contract-management responsibility, asset-management responsibility, leasing and the share system (for details see, Zheng *et al.*, 1998). However, enterprise reforms still need to be deepened, since the inflexible operating mechanism inherited from the central planning system is still a major problem in SOEs (Jiang, 1999). On the other hand, because their

Table 10.1 Regression results

Dependent variable	*VAL*				KL	LQ	*FSSale*	*WG*
	(1)	*(2)*	*(3)*	*(4)*	*(5)*	*(6)*	*(7)*	*(8)*
Constant	1.4910	0.0085	0.0099	0.0110	0.0313	0.0802	0.9300	5.0661
	(11.28)*	(0.20)	(0.23)	(0.25)	(4.83)*	(25.05)*	(3.50)*	(44.01)*
Dfor	0.2976	0.1671	0.1663	0.1646	0.0669	0.0179	−0.6118	1.8767
	(7.86)*	(6.72)*	(6.60)*	(6.50)*	(7.26)*	(2.60)*	(−1.62)	(11.50)*
Doth	0.0220	0.0851	0.0839	0.0826	−0.0119	−0.0406	−0.8397	−0.6400
	(1.36)	(3.42)*	(3.35)*	(3.27)*	(−1.29)	(−9.28)*	(−2.23)*	(−3.92)*
KL		1.7784	1.7754	1.7845				
		(4.72)*	(4.68)*	(4.72)*				
LQ		1.0066	1.0100	1.0126				
		(1.92)*	(1.92)*	(1.92)*				
FSSale		0.0044						
		(1.09)						
FSAsset			0.0042					
			(1.13)					
FSEmployee				0.0065				
				(1.16)				
R^2	0.1651	0.4608	0.4593	0.4586	0.1302	0.1449	0.0093	0.3111
White tests	(8.29)*	(162)*	(121)*	(122)*	(4.10)	(9.63)*	(2.34)	(33.13)*

Notes

Estimated coefficients are shown together with *t*-statistics in parentheses. Except for those in column (6), all *t*-statistics are obtained from White's heteroscedasticity-corrected regressions.

* denote significance (two-tailed)

The number of observations is 556 for all cases.

foreign parent companies are normally from mature market economies, the management system in FIEs is far more flexible and can respond efficiently to changing market conditions. Superior management skills are an important part of the 'other specific advantages' possessed by FIEs.

From columns (1) and (2), it is interesting to note that labour productivity is significantly higher in OLOEs than in SOEs after we control for capital intensity, labour productivity, and firm size. Since the market-size variable is not statistically significant, the comparison of these two columns suggests that it is the superiority in capital intensity and/or labour quality in SOEs that prevents the labour productivity in SOEs from significantly lagging behind the labour productivity in OLOEs.

From columns (2), (3) and (4), we can compare the results obtained by estimating equation (10.2) using three different measures of firm size. In any of these columns, the coefficient on the firm size variable is insignificant, although it has the expected positive sign. It appears that scale economies do not play any role in raising labour productivity at all. However, when examining the observations of the three measures for firm size for SOEs and OLOEs, we observe very few variations. This indicates that any change in sales revenue, fixed assets or the number of employees is accompanied by a change of similar scale in the number of firms. Separate regressions using equation (10.2) for the SOE and OLOE sectors indicate that nether SOEs nor OLOEs enjoy economies of scale. On the other hand, the separate regression for FIEs does suggests that scale economies are exploited in this particular group of firms (detailed results not reported).

One important reason for SOEs and OLOEs not to exploit economies of scale is the prolonged irrational repetition of construction (Jiang, 1999). The central and local governments have traditionally had their own development plans. However, these plans have often not been well coordinated because the central and local government often have different objectives to pursue. In addition, many OLOEs are not subject to state control. This has led to repeated construction of relatively small-sized plants in many traditional industrial branches. In these branches, there have been similar growth rates for fixed assets, employees, and sales revenues as well as for firms.

Columns (5), (6) and (7) present the estimation results of equations (10.3), (10.4) and (10.5). Since only one particular determinant of labour productivity is related to the types of ownership in each regression, the relative role of each determinant in explaining productivity differences across different groups of firms can be identified. From column (5), FIEs have significantly higher capital intensity than SOEs and OLOEs. It follows that FIEs enjoy a higher level of embodied technology than local firms. Since capital intensity has a significant impact on labour productivity as indicated by the regression results of equation (10.2), the relatively higher level of embodied technology contributes to higher labour productivity in FIEs.

Also from column (5), capital intensity in SOEs is higher than that in OLOEs, but the difference is not statistically significant. Thus, the level of embodied technology in SOEs is apparently not significantly higher than in OLOEs. However, this result does not seem to be consistent with the observed fact that the technologies used by OLOEs are often regarded as backward compared with SOEs (see, for instance, Zheng *et al.*, 1998). As a matter of fact, capital intensity may not be a good proxy for technology levels in the case of SOEs. As estimated by UNIDO (1992), 80 per cent of SOEs were 15–20 per cent overstaffed. Thus, the capital intensity, measured by the ratio of fixed capital to the number of employees, was lower than it otherwise would be.

The significant differences in labour quality across the three different groups of firms are identified in column (6). While FIEs enjoy the highest labour quality, OLOEs have the lowest. This indicates that the highest labour quality leads to the highest labour product in FIEs. The results in this column also suggest that the higher labour quality is an important reason for SOEs not to lag significantly behind OLOEs in productivity performance, as indicated by column (1).

One unanswered question emerges from the above statistical comparison of SOEs and OLOEs: if labour quality were not significantly higher in state-owned enterprises than in other local-owned firms, what factors would explain what would then presumably be the significantly lower labour productivity in state-owned enterprises? One likely reason may be the difference in management systems and operating mechanisms between the two different groups of firms. Although enterprise reforms aim to establish a modern corporation system with clear property rights for SOEs and to give them more autonomy to operate according to market conditions, these difficult tasks can only be fulfilled gradually. On the other hand, OLOEs are more market-oriented and have much higher incentive to improve economic efficiency. In addition, as explained above, overstaffing in SOEs is also a reason for lower labour productivity in SOEs.

The regression results of equation (10.5) are presented in column (7). All three different measures of firm size are tried and very similar results are produced. Thus, we only report the result from the ratio of sales revenue to firm number. It is rightly expected that the average firm size of SOEs is significantly larger than OLOEs since collectively owned firms, domestic joint ventures, joint corporations, individually owned firms, or private operated firms are generally small-sized in China. However, as indicated earlier, the firm-size variable has no significant impact on labour productivity in SOEs and OLOEs. As a result, the relatively larger size of SOEs does not contribute to their efficiency advantage over OLOEs. Column (7) also indicates that the average firm size of FIEs is smaller than that of SOEs, although the difference is not significant.

While the influences of ownership on individual determinants are examined in columns (5), (6) and (7), the results of wage-rate comparisons are presented in column (8). It is found that FIEs pay the highest wage rates, followed by SOEs and OLOEs. The finding that the wage rates are higher in FIEs than in local firms is consistent with many other studies, including Willmore (1986) and Globerman *et al.* (1994). Thus, the employees in FIEs benefit from productivity advantages in the form of higher wage rates. Put another way, FIEs contribute to a higher income level in Chinese industry.

Two reasons are identified in the literature for the higher payment by foreign compared with local firms: stronger countervailing bargaining power in the form of a more highly unionised workforce, and the 'premium' wage rates to discourage shirking among workers (Eaton and White, 1983; Oi, 1990). In the case of China, the first reason is not applicable since the workforce in FIEs is often less unionised than in SOEs. FIEs in China pay higher salaries in order to attract more qualified employees. The higher labour quality in FIES than in local firms is an indicator of this strategy.

As indicated in columns (1), (2) and (8), although the labour productivity in SOEs is not as high as, or is probably lower than, that in OLOEs, SOEs pay significantly higher wage rates than OLOEs. In a similar strategy to that adopted by FIEs, SOEs try to improve their human capital by offering better earnings to well qualified personnel. The relatively higher labour quality in SOEs may partly result from the relatively higher payments. This, in turn, prevents SOEs from falling significantly behind OLOEs in labour productivity.

Conclusions

This empirical study compares the relative productivity of FIEs, SOEs and OLOEs in Chinese industry. It shows that FIEs have significantly higher value-added per worker than both SOEs and OLOEs. This can be attributed to the higher level of embodied technology, higher labour quality and other advantages specific to FIEs. The other advantages can be managerial skills and superior technologies not embodied in fixed assets. The availability of data does not allow us to confirm the impact of the other advantages. Economies of scale are exploited in FIEs, but not in local firms because of the irrational repetition of construction in the domestic sector of many traditional industrial branches.

OLOEs are not significantly more productive than state-owned enterprises unless capital intensity and labour quality are both controlled for. The findings indicate the importance of technology and labour quality in enabling SOEs to catch up with OLOEs in labour productivity. If labour quality in SOEs were not significantly higher than in OLOEs, labour productivity would be significantly higher in OLOEs because OLOEs are much more market-oriented and have much higher incentives to improve economic efficiency.

Of course, caution should be used when we discuss the efficiency implications of higher labour productivity. As Dunning (1993) notes, a higher productivity or profitability in foreign firms may not necessarily mean superior technical efficiency. For instance, manipulation of transfer prices of intra-firm transactions might be used by an MNE to lower or raise profits in one or other of its subsidiaries; host government tax and other policies may discriminate in favour of foreign subsidiaries. Although little research has been carried out on transfer pricing practice in FIEs in China, it is clear that FIEs have been favourably treated by the Chinese government in terms of fiscal and financial policies. Furthermore, Bai *et al.* (1997) argue that, if firms like some SOEs are not profit maximisers, then higher productivity may be consistent with lower economic efficiency.

Because of the data limitations, this study is conducted based on cross-section regressions at the industrial-branch level. Ideally, a panel-data approach at the firm level would provide much richer information.

Despite the limitation, this study offers several important policy implications for those who are interested in productivity improvements in Chinese industry. First, FDI should be further encouraged. The superiority of FIEs in factors of production and the resulting higher labour productivity help enhance the economic performance of Chinese industry as a whole. In addition, higher wage rates paid by FIEs to their employees help raise income levels.

Second, domestic investment in physical and human capital needs to be further encouraged. Accumulation and upgrading of physical capital is an important way to expand technological capabilities. Education and on-the-job training are essential for superb productivity performance, not only for local enterprises but also for FIEs. In addition, the availability of human capital is a prerequisite for attracting FDI. The higher level of labour quality in FIEs in China suggests the importance of human capital supplies.

Finally, economic reforms need to be deepened. Structural adjustment in Chinese industry is justified in order to increase allocation efficiency. Furthermore, the potentially lower productivity in SOEs suggests the need for further market-oriented enterprise reforms. A modern corporation system with clear property rights and responsibilities will enhance the SOEs' incentive to improve efficiency.

References

van Ark, B. (1990a) 'Comparative levels of labour productivity in Dutch and British manufacturing', *National Institute Economic Review*, 131.

van Ark, B. (1990b) 'Manufacturing productivity levels in France and the United Kingdom', *National Institute Economic Review*, 133.

van Ark, B. (1992) 'Comparative productivity in British and American manufacturing', *National Institute Economic Review*, 133, 63–73.

Asheghian, P. (1982) 'Comparative efficiencies of foreign firms and local firms in Iran', *Journal of International Business Studies*, Winter 1982, 113–120.

Bai, C.E., Li, D.D. and Wang, Y.J. (1997) 'Enterprise productivity and efficiency: when is up really down?', *Journal of Comparative Economics*, 24, 265–280.

Blomstrom, M. (1988) 'Labour productivity differences between foreign and domestic firms in Mexico', *World Development*, 16(11), 1295–1298.

Broadberry, S.N. and Crafts, N.F.R. (1990) 'Explaining Anglo-American productivity differences in the mid-twentieth century', *Oxford Bulletin of Economics and Statistics*, 52(4), 375–402.

Carr, C. (1992) 'Productivity and skills in vehicle component manufacturers in Britain, Germany, the USA and Japan', *National Institute Economic Review*, 79–87.

Casson, M. (1982) 'The theory of foreign direct investment'. In J. Black and J.D. Dunning (eds), *International Capital Movements* (London: Macmillan).

Caves, R.E. (1982) *Multinational Enterprise and Economic Analysis* (Cambridge: Cambridge University Press).

Cheng, L.K. and Wu, C. (2001) 'Determinants of the performance of foreign invested enterprises in China', *Journal of Comparative Economics*, 29(2), 347–365.

Davies, S. and Caves, R.E. (1987) *Britain's Productivity Gap* (Cambridge: Cambridge University Press).

Davies, S. and Lyons, B.R. (1991) 'Characterising relative performance: the productivity advantage of foreign owned firms in the UK', *Oxford Economic Paper*, 43, 584–595.

Dong, X.Y. and Putterman, L. (1997) 'Productivity and organisation in China's rural industries: a stochastic analysis', *Journal of Comparative Economics*, 24, 181–201.

Dunning, J.H. (1981) *International Production and the Multinational Enterprise* (London: Allen and Unwin).

Dunning, J.H. (1988) *Explaining International Production* (London: Harper Collins).

Dunning, J.H. (1991) 'The eclectic paradigm of international production: a personal perspective'. In C. Pitelis and R. Sugden (eds), *The Nature of the Transnational Firm* (London: Routledge).

Dunning, J.H. (1993) *Multinational Enterprise and Global Economy* (Wokingham, UK: Addison-Wesley).

Eaton, B.C. and White, W. (1983) 'Agent compensation and the limits of bonding', *Economic Inquiry*, 20, 330–343.

Globerman, S., Ries, J.C. and Vertinsky, I. (1994) 'The economic performance of foreign affiliates in Canada', *Canadian Journal of Economics*, XXVII(1), 143–155.

Hennart, J. (1982) *A Theory of Multinational Enterprise* (Michigan: University of Michigan Press).

Hennart, J. (1991) 'The transaction cost theory of the multinational enterprise'. In C. Pitelis and R. Sugden (eds), *The Nature of the Transnational Firm* (London: Routledge).

Hymer, S.H. (1976) *The International Operations of National Firms, A Study of Direct Foreign Investment* (Cambridge: MIT Press).

Jiang, Z. (1999) 'Strengthening confidence, deepening reform, opening up a new prospect for the development of state-owned enterprises', *People's Daily, Overseas Edition*, 13 August.

Kim, W.S. (1990) 'FDI theories and the performance of foreign multinationals operating in the U.S.', *Journal of International Business Studies*, First Quarter, 41–54.

Kindleberger, C.P. (1969) *American Business Abroad: Six Lectures on Direct Investment* (New Haven: Yale University Press).

Kokko, A. (1994) 'Technology, market characteristics, and spillovers', *Journal of Development Economics*, 43, 279–293.

Lall, S. (1978) 'Transnationals, domestic enterprises and industrial structure in host LDCs: a survey', *Oxford Economic Papers*, 30(2), 217–248.

Newfarmer, R.S. and Marsh, L.C. (1981) 'Foreign ownership, market structure and industrial performance', *Journal of Development Economics*, 8, 47–75.

Oi, W. (1990) 'Employment relations in dual labour markets', *Journal of Labour Economics*, 8, S124–S149.

Prais, S.J., Daly, A. Jones, D.T. and Wagner, K. (1981) *Productivity and Industrial Structure: a Statistical Study of Manufacturing Industry in Britain, Germany and the United States* (Cambridge: Cambridge University Press).

Rugman, A.M. (1981) *Inside the Multinationals: the Economics of Internal Markets* (London: Croom Helm).

State Statistical Bureau (1997) *The Data of the Third National Industrial Census of the People's Republic of China in 1995* (Beijing: China Statistical Publishing House).

Sterner, T. (1990) 'Ownership, technology, and efficiency: an empirical study of co-operatives, multinationals, and domestic enterprises in the Mexican cement industry', *Journal of Comparative Economics*, 14, 286–300.

Sun, H. (1998) *Foreign Investment and Economic Development in China: 1979–1996* (UK: Ashgate).

UNIDO (United Nations Industrial Development Organisation) (1992) *China: Towards Sustainable Industrial Growth* (Oxford, UK, and Cambridge, MA: Blackwell).

Vernon, R. (1977) *Storm over the Multinationals* (Cambridge, MA: Harvard University Press).

Wei, Y. and Liu, X. (2001) *Foreign Direct Investment in China: Determinants and Impact* (Cheltenham, UK: Edward Elgar).

Willmore, L.N. (1986) 'The comparative performance of foreign and domestic firms in Brazil', *World Development*, 14(4), 489–502.

Zheng, J.H., Liu, X.X. and Bigsten, A. (1998) 'Ownership structure and determinants of technical efficiency: an application of data envelopment analysis to Chinese enterprises (1986–1990)', *Journal of Comparative Economics*, 26, 465–484.

11 Total factor productivity in Chinese industries

Does foreign direct investment matter?

Xiaohui Liu and Chengang Wang

Introduction

With the rapid expansion of multinationals and foreign direct investment (FDI) in the global economy, the effect of FDI on the host economy, particularly on technological progress, has been of great interest to both academics and governments, and remains a contentious issue. Empirical tests of the effect of FDI on technology transfer have generated mixed results. Some studies have found that FDI has a positive effect on productivity (Caves, 1974; Kokko, 1994; Oulton, 1998; Blomstrom and Sjoholm, 1999; Xu, 2000), while others have reported that there is an inverse relationship between FDI and industrial productivity in host countries (Haddad and Harrison, 1993; Aitken and Harrison, 1999).

The phenomenal economic growth in China has been accompanied by a rapid increase in the inflows of FDI; for example, annual inflows of FDI increased from US$1.91 billion in 1983 to US$41.23 billion in 1999 (MOFTEC, 2000), and China has now become the largest recipient of FDI in the developing world (World Bank, 1998). A few studies, for example, Sun *et al.* (1999) and Liu (2000), have been conducted on the relationship between FDI and labour productivity, and have attempted to find whether there are spillover effects or technology transfer from FDI to domestic sectors in China. The results from the studies have shed light on the issue and generated policy implications.

These studies, however, assume implicitly that two-way links do not exist between FDI and labour productivity in a sector, and that productivity is indifferent in the investment decisions of multinational enterprises (MNEs) without full justification of its applicability. Comparatively little empirical research has been conducted on the relationship between FDI and total factor productivity (TFP) in Chinese industries. Labour productivity is a partial productivity in which only one factor, labour, is considered. It is difficult to distinguish whether labour productivity is high in a sector because of a high degree of technological efficiency or because of a large stock of physical capital, given that labour productivity fails to capture all of the influences on productivity. TFP evaluates technological progress, and constitutes a measure of the efficiency with which all the factors of production are employed.

It is widely believed that technological progress is facilitated through inward FDI; thus it is important to examine the relationship between TFP and FDI in a sector. The evidence of the existence of spillovers from FDI would provide one potential justification for the use of fiscal incentives to attract inward FDI and would generate important policy implications for development strategy in developing countries. Therefore, the aim of this research is twofold. First, we test explicitly whether there is endogeneity between FDI and total factor productivity in order to apply an appropriate estimation method. Second, we examine empirically whether FDI presence in a sector leads to a high level of TFP.

The chapter is organised as follows. The second section briefly reviews the relationship between FDI and productivity. In the section after, the model and data are presented. The next section analyses the empirical results, and the final section concludes.

Literature review

As far as the effect of FDI is concerned, three approaches provide theoretical explanations: industrial organisation theories, international trade theories and endogenous growth theories. The industrial organisation approach attempts to examine the indirect effect or externality of FDI on host countries. It investigates explicitly the role of FDI in technology transfer and the diffusion of knowledge, as well as the impact of FDI on market structure and competition in host countries (Hymer, 1976; Buckley and Casson, 1976; Dunning, 1993; Caves, 1996).

It is argued that firms must possess specific advantages in order to overcome the difficulties of doing business abroad. The firms investing in foreign countries therefore represent distinctive kinds of enterprises and have distinctive characteristics that may differ from firms in host countries. The effect of MNEs' entry on a host economy is beyond that of a simple import of capital into the country. FDI is not merely a source of capital, it is also a conduit for technology transfer and human skills augmentation in host countries. There are two main reasons for this. First, when MNEs invest in host countries, they bring with them advanced technology that constitutes their specific advantage and provides them with the power to compete successfully with local firms who have superior information on local markets, consumer preferences and local business practices. Second, the entry of MNEs breaks the existing equilibrium, and eliminates the monopolistic power of local firms. These are forced to be more efficient in using existing technology and resources, or they have to introduce new technologies in order to protect and maintain their market share or, through direct contact with MNEs, local firms observe and imitate the way foreigners operate and can therefore become more productive. As a result, the effect of competition, demonstration and learning-by-doing on local industry may lead to an increase in productivity (Blomstrom and Kokko, 1996).

In international trade theories, the main focus is to examine why FDI occurs and how firms choose between exporting, FDI and licensing as an entry mode (Ethier, 1986; Horstmann and Markusen, 1992; Brainard, 1993). The feature of FDI is defined as knowledge-capital, which has a joint-input or 'public goods' property (Markusen, 2000). This implies that spillovers or externality of FDI can occur in host countries. However, how FDI or multinationals affect the pace and pattern of technological progress has not been discussed explicitly. One exception is that Markusen and Venables (1999) have formally shown how it is possible for FDI to act as a catalyst, leading to the development of local industry through linkage effects.

The endogenous-growth model considers FDI as an important source of human capital augmentation, technology change and spillovers of ideas across countries (Grossman and Helpman, 1995), and therefore FDI is expected to have a positive effect on growth. However, the spillovers from FDI do not arise automatically. In the model of Wang and Blomstrom (1992), technology transfer channelled through FDI is considered as an endogenised equilibrium phenomenon that results from strategic interaction between foreign firms and local firms. The magnitude of spillovers depends on the extent to which local firms respond positively to the technology gap and invest in 'learning activities'. Rodriguez-Clare (1996) extends this idea to explore cases where MNEs affect the host country through the generation of backwards and forwards linkages. Multinationals are beneficial to the host country when they generate linkage effects beyond those generated by the local firms displaced, given that the technology gap between home and host countries is not excessively large. Other models formally show that the scope of technology transfer from FDI also depends to a large extent on host country characteristics and the policy environment in which MNEs operate (Ethier and Markusen, 1996).

Empirical studies investigating spillovers or technology transfer from MNEs' affiliates to indigenous firms either estimate the production function for domestic firms in which the variable of TFP could be calculated, or use labour productivity as a dependent variable. The foreign share or foreign ownership share in an industry is used as an explanatory variable to test whether there is a positive association between FDI presence and productivity in a sector. The results from the studies are mixed. Caves (1974) conducted econometric tests for productivity spillovers using cross-sectional Australian manufacturing data for 1966, and he found that the presence of foreign firms had a positive effect on labour productivity in the host country. Similar single-country studies by Glober (1979) for Canada, by Blomstrom and Perssow (1983), and Kokko (1994) for Mexico confirm Caves' findings. More recent studies regarding both developed and developing countries have found sound evidence for a positive link between foreign ownership and productivity in host countries' industries (e.g. Blomstrom and Sjoholm, 1999; Liu, 2000; Xu, 2000). However, Haddad and Harrison (1993), and Aitken and Harrison (1999) found that FDI, or foreign ownership, had no significant effects on productivity in the case of Morocco and Venezuela. Based on the previous studies, the present research focuses on whether there is evidence that FDI facilitates technology progress in Chinese industries.

Models and data

In this section, first we specify the following production function of sector *i* in order to obtain the variable TFP; then the determinants of the TFP are tested.

$$Y_i = AK_i^{\alpha}L_i^{\beta} \tag{11.1}$$

where *Y* denotes the gross output value of a sector, *K* and *L* are capital and labour inputs, respectively, and *A* equals an indicator that picks up changes in technology and represents technological progress, defined as TFP. α and β represent the elasticity of the factors of production in the equation.

There are some differing views about whether human capital should be included in the Cobb-Douglas production function. Some studies suggest that human capital does contribute substantially to output (Mankiw *et al.*, 1992). Others report that human capital is insignificant in explaining output, and propose that human capital does not enter the production function as an input; rather there may exist direct links between human capital and TFP through which human capital affects growth (Islam, 1995; Benhabib and Spiegel, 1994). In the current study, We adopt the latter approach.

Rewriting equation (11.1) in natural logarithms generates the following:

$$\ln Y = \ln A + \alpha \ln K + \beta \ln L + \ln H \tag{11.2}$$

Estimating equation (11.2), we can calculate the level of TFP in industrial sectors.

Following Coe and Helpman (1995), and Miller and Upadhyay (2000), R&D and FDI are viewed as important sources for increasing TFP. Human capital intensity, representing the ability to absorb the advanced technology of host countries, particularly in developing countries, is also included. Economies of scale in a sector also affect TFP in that production efficiency can be increased, and it is justified to consider this variable as one of the determinants of TFP. Therefore, TFP is endogenised as a function of the average R&D, foreign presence, human capital intensity and economies of scale. All the variables are expected to have a positive sign and contribute to an increase in TFP. In particular, we are interested in the variable of a foreign presence in a sector, which represents the externality and spillovers of FDI. TFP in sector *i* can be expressed as

$$TFP_i = f(AR\&D_i, RFDI_i, HI_i, FS_i) \tag{11.3}$$

Equation (11.3) states that TFP is affected by the average level of R&D (*AR&D*), foreign presence (*RFDI*), human capital intensity (*HI*) and firm size (*FS*).

From equation (3), a log-linear functional form is adopted to reduce the possibility or severity of heteroscedasticity and directly obtain TFP elasticity with respect to explanatory variables. The model is of the form:

$$\ln TFP_i = a_1 + a_2 \ln AR\&D_i + a_3 \ln RFDI_i + a_4 \ln HI_i + a_5 \ln FS_i + \epsilon_\iota \tag{11.4}$$

where ϵ represents the error term.

From a theoretical point of view, the relationship between FDI and TFP in a sector is not clearly asserted; FDI is expected to have a positive effect on TFP. On the other hand, the level of TFP in a sector may also be one of the important factors in influencing a MNE's investment decisions. If there exists a two-way relationship between FDI and TFP, the estimation of a single equation for TFP using the OLS method will lead to spurious results. In order to determine whether an alternative estimation method should be used, the endogeneity between RFDI and TFP is tested by applying Hausman's test in equations (11.4) and (11.5).

$$\ln RFDI_i = \beta_0 + \beta_1 \ln EX_i + \beta_2 \ln DS_i + \beta_3 \ln TFP_i + \beta_4 \ln SI_i + \beta_5 \ln PDV_i + \nu_i \tag{11.5}$$

Equation (11.5) expresses the notion that FDI in a sector is affected by the level of exports (*EX*), the level of domestic sales (*DS*), the level of TFP, skill intensity (SI) and policy towards FDI (*PDV*) (Liu, 2000). A brief justification for including these explanatory variables in equation (11.5) is given below. The level of exports, viewed as an indicator of a country or industry's degree of openness, is an important factor in determining the foreign presence in a sector. Domestic sales as a proxy of market size are expected to have a positive association with FDI. Skill intensity, measuring the quality and skills of the labour force, is also expected to have an impact on industry level FDI. The policy towards FDI plays an important role in determining the sectoral distribution of FDI.

The equations are likely to be simultaneously determined if the residual of the reduced form of one equation has a significant impact on the dependent variable. The following procedure has been applied to detect the endogeneity between RFDI and TFP

First, we estimate the following equation:

$$\ln RFDI_i = \phi_0 + \phi_1 \ln DS_i + \phi_2 \ln FS_i + \phi_3 \ln SI_i + \phi_4 \ln HI_i + \phi_5 \ln AR\&D_i + \phi_6 \ln EX_i + \phi_7 \ln PDV_i + \eta_i \quad (11.6)$$

and obtain the residual named as u. Second, equation (11.4) is estimated by including u as one of the explanatory variables. If the coefficient of u, denoted as λ, is statistically different from zero, then RFDI is endogenous and, as a result, the OLS estimate will be inconsistent. Instead, a two-stage least squares (TSLS) method should be used. If λ is not statistically significant, then it is justified to employ the OLS method to estimate equation (11.4).

One common problem encountered in cross-sectional studies is heteroscedasticity because, if it exists, the OLS estimators are inefficient. White's heteroscedasticity tests are carried out to tackle this problem, and the estimation procedure is then applied accordingly.

Data

The data used in this research are drawn from 'The Data of the Third National Industrial Census of the People's Republic of China (Third Census)'. The industrial survey was conducted by the China State Statistic Bureau (SSB) in 1995, and the data were published in 1997. In the Third Census, the industry level data are classified into 191 sub-sectors according to the industry classification system adopted by the SSB. The data start with coal mining and processing (with 19 sub-sectors in mining), followed by food processing (with 165 manufacturing sub-sectors), and end with seven sub-sectors in public utilities such as electricity, gas and water supply. This is the most up-to-date and detailed data on Chinese industrial sectors currently available. Owing to some missing data in a few sectors, the sample used for estimations consisted of 189 of the 191 sub-sectors. The data reveal that the largest foreign presence is in certain industries such as electronic communication equipment, textiles, non-metal mining products and electrical machinery and apparatus, which represents a combination of high technological and labour intensive sectors (Table 11.1). From the data source, the following measurement variables are chosen.

Dependent variable

RFDI: the ratio of FDI to total capital in a sector, which stands for the foreign presence in a sector.

Table 11.1 Top ten industries with accumulated FDI by 1995

Rank	*Sectors*	*Accumulated FDI by 1995 (billion of RMB yuan)*	*%*
1	Electronic & communication equipment manufacturing	30.29	9.77
2	Textile	25.09	8.1
3	Non-metal mining products	22.35	7.22
4	Electrical machinery & apparatus	18.43	5.95
5	Electricity, power, water supply	17.37	5.61
6	Transportation equipment	16.31	5.27
7	Chemical materials & products	15.81	5.11
8	Metal products	15.56	5.03
9	Dress & other clothing products	15.39	4.91
10	Rubber products	13.53	4.37

Source: The Data of the Third National Industrial Census of the People's Republic of China 1995.

Independent variables

AR&D: average R&D expenditure per employee, which represents the level of domestic R&D.

DS: the domestic sales value of a sector, which represents the market size.

EX: the ratio of exports to gross output value of a sector.

FS: firm size, the ratio of sales value to the total number of firms in a sector, which is used as a proxy for economies of scale. In the absence of data at the level of individual firms, it is difficult to measure economies of scale, as the various proxies proposed require more disaggregated data. For example, Wenders (1971) has employed a cost–advantage ratio of production which is measured as the ratio of value added per employee of the largest plants to the value added per employee in the remaining small plants. Unfortunately, such data are not available in the census.

HI: human capital intensity, the ratio of workers with a secondary school certificate to total employees in a sector.

K: book value of fixed assets, which is used as a proxy of the stock of physical capital by following Blomstrom and Sjoholm (1999).

L: the total number of employees in a sector.

PDV: policy dummy variable, based on the categories for encouraging foreign direct investment across sectors, published in 1996 (MOFTEC, 1996).

SI (skill intensity): the ratio of total wage to total employees, which is used to proxy the level of skilled labour in a sector.

Y: gross output value of a sector.

Empirical results

The endogeneity test shows that λ is statistically insignificant even at the 10 per cent level, suggesting that there is no evidence for the two-way link between TFP and foreign presence in a sector; therefore, it is appropriate to apply the OLS method to estimate the TFP equation. White's heteroscedasticity test generates a highly significant result $(nR^2) = 33.76$, indicating the presence of heteroscedasticity (probability = 0.001). Thus, the t statistics from equations (11.2) and (11.4) are corrected using White's heteroscedasticity estimators.

The results from the production function (equation (11.2)) reported in Table 11.2, indicate that both physical capital and labour force are statistically significant at the 1 per cent level. The contribution of physical capital to the level of output is highest with the value of 0.529 to the elasticity of output, and the magnitude of the coefficient of labour force is 0.428. The results suggest that both physical capital and labour force are important factors in determining the level of output in industrial sectors.

The results from the TFP equation summarised in Table 11.3 show that there are three main factors that enhance TFP in Chinese industries: FDI presence, the average R&D and firm size in a sector. The ratio of FDI to total capital has a significantly positive effect at the 1 per cent level. More FDI associates with higher TFP in a sector, implying that there is a positive relationship between technological progress and FDI since the rate of technological progress is the prime determinant of rates of TFP growth in the long run (Cameron *et al.*, 1999). This finding corroborates the result from a survey in which FDI or foreign-invested firms are found to play a more important role in technology transfer than other factors – notably, licensing in China (Wang and Zhou, 1999). Based on a questionnaire survey in the machine-tool industry and the electronics industry, it reveals that the technology gap between developed countries and China in the

Table 11.2 Results from the production function (Dependent variable: $\ln Y$)

Independent variables	*Coefficient (t-statistics)*
$\ln K$	0.529 (8.078)***
$\ln L$	0.428 (5.449)***
C	1.383 (18.724)***
Adjusted R^2	0.924
Observations	189

Note
*, ** and *** represent the significant level of 10%, 5% and 1%, respectively.

Table 11.3 Top ten sectors with TFP in 1995

Sectors	*TFP*
Computer manufacturing	12.78
Communications equipment	11.18
Cruel oil processing	10.84
Toy equipment	10.57
Automobile manufacturing	10.31
Cigarette manufacturing	10.07
Daily electronic apparatus	9.94
Electronic components	9.86
Grain & feed processing	9.03
Radar manufacturing	8.79

Source: Calculated based on the Third Industrial Census.

machine tool industry is still large after more than 20 years of technology transfer through licensing, since the firms have generally been unable to acquire the latest product technology. In contrast, the electronics industry mainly uses joint ventures and wholly foreign-owned companies as means of acquiring technology. As a result, the industry has become a leading global player in consumer electronic goods, indicating that FDI is one of the most effective channels through which technology transfer takes place.

The coefficient of average R&D is positive and statistically significant at the 5 per cent level. This result is similar to cross-country studies in which domestic and foreign R&D is found to be a most important source of TFP (Bayoumi *et al.*, 1999).

The effect of human-capital intensity on TFP is inconsistent with theoretical predictions, given that a statistically insignificant result has been obtained. This finding is similar to other studies, which have found that this variable is insignificant in explaining TFP (Miller and Upadhyay, 2000). One possible reason is that the rigidity of personnel management systems in stated-owned firms prevents well-educated employees from contributing fully to the firm's performance. In addition, because of the lack of an effective reward system, skilled workers may be tempted to engage in rent-seeking activities. As a result, human capital has not reached its potential in production, suggesting innovative human resource practices and incentive mechanisms need to be established in order to maximise the utility of human capital in Chinese industries.

Pissarides (1997) argues that human capital is less productive where it does not have access to advanced technology, implying that an interaction may exist between human capital and advanced technology and innovation. We adopt this approach to take the interaction between human-capital intensity and the level of R&D into account. The product of human-capital intensity and the level of R&D, representing the interaction between these two variables, is used as an explanatory variable in the regression, and the results are improved (column 3 of Table 11.4). The

Table 11.4 Results from TFP equation: dependent variable ln*TFP*

Independent variables	*ln* TFP *coefficient* *(*t-*statistics)*	*ln* TFP *coefficient* *(*t-*statistics)*
ln*RFDI*	0.16 (8.36)***	0.16 (8.10)***
ln*FS*	0.08 (4.45)***	0.06 (4.28)***
ln*AR&D*	0.03 (2.22)**	0.06 (3.77)***
ln*HI*	0.11 (0.61)	
ln*HI* ln*AR&D*		0.03 (2.21)**
Adjusted R^2	0.40	0.41
Observations	189	189

coefficient on the interaction term is positive and statistically significant at the 5 per cent level, suggesting that human capital is found to affect TFP through interaction with R&D, rather than in isolation. The interaction between these two variables also indicates that higher spending on innovation, such as R&D expenditure, enables human capital to be more efficient and hence enhance TFP in a sector.

The firm-size variable also has the expected positive sign, and is statistically significant at the 1 per cent level. That is, other things being constant, a 1 per cent increase in FS would raise TFP by 0.08 per cent. The positive relationship between FS and TFP supports the hypothesis that the existence of scale economies leads to an increase in TFP. The larger the firm size, the more efficient it is, and the higher the total factor productivity in a sector.

Conclusions

This chapter empirically studies the effect of FDI on TFP for a cross-sectional sample of Chinese industrial sectors. TFP is estimated from a production function involving physical capital and labour forces. The possible determinants of TFP are sought, with a special focus on FDI.

The results from the production function suggest that physical capital and the labour force are the main determinants of industrial production, implying that both capital and labour inputs are important to the output level in industrial sectors.

It is also found that foreign presence, average domestic R&D and firm size are the most important factors enhancing TFP in Chinese industries. We view the positive effect of FDI on TFP as evidence that indicates that

FDI inflow is not merely a source of capital, it is also a conduit for technology transfer. The effect of FDI on Chinese industries is beyond that of a simple import of capital into the country, as found in the case study of the machine tool and electronics industry (Wang and Zhou, 1999). Human-capital intensity is found to benefit TFP only when the interaction between this variable and R&D in a sector is taken into account, implying that the higher the level of R&D, the more productive human capital becomes.

The findings offer a number of implications for policymakers. First, Chinese industries should continue to attract high quality, technologically intensive FDI and provide incentives for MNEs to upgrade production at their sites in China. Second, the government should build on an economic environment conducive for MNEs to introduce advanced technology into Chinese industries and conduct R&D activities. It is imperative for China to enhance TFP through spillovers from FDI as technological progress is the driving force sustaining economic growth in the long run. Third, China's accession to the WTO will create great opportunities that further encourage inward FDI if foreign investors can be granted WTO's principle of national treatment and a fully transparent system for regulating FDI can be established as well as effective reinforcement of intellectual property rights.

Acknowledgements

An earlier version of this chapter was presented at the 28th Annual Conference of the Academy of International Business, Manchester, April 2001. The authors would like to thank the participants of the conference for their helpful comments. The usual disclaimer applies.

References

Aitken, B. and Harrison, A. (1999) 'Do domestic firms benefit from foreign direct investment? Evidence from Venezuela', *American Economic Review*, 89, 605–618.

Barro, R.J. and Lee, J.W. (1993) 'International comparisons of educational attainment', *Journal of Monetary Economics*, 32, 361–394.

Bayoumi, T., Coe, D.T. and Helpman, E. (1999) 'R&D spillovers and global growth', *Journal of International Economics*, 47, 399–428.

Benhabib, J. and Spiegel, M. (1994) 'The role of human capital in economic development: evidence from Aggregate cross-country data', *Journal of Monetary Economics*, 34, 143–173.

Blomstrom, M. and Perssow, H. (1983) 'Foreign direct investment and spillover efficiency in an underdeveloped economy: evidence from the Mexican manufacturing industry', *World Development*, 11, 493–501.

Blomstrom, M. and Kokko, A. (1996) 'Multinational corporations and spillovers', CEPR Discussion Paper, No. 1365.

Blomstrom, M. and Sjoholm, F. (1999) 'Technology transfer and spillovers: Does local participation with multinationals matter?' *European Economic Review*, 43, 915–923.

Borensztein, E., Gregoiro, J. and Lee, J. (1998) 'How does foreign direct investment affect economic growth', *Journal of International Economics*, 45, 115–135.

Brainard, L.S. (1993) 'A simple theory of multinational corporations and trade with a trade-off between proximity and concentration', NBER Working Paper, No. 4269.

Buckley, P.J. and Casson, M. (1976) *The Future of the Multinational Enterprise* (London: Macmillan).

Cameron, G., Proudman, J. and Redding, S. (1999) 'Openness and its association with productivity growth in UK manufacturing industry', Bank of England Working Paper Series, No. 104.

Caves, R.E. (1974) 'Multinational firms, competition and productivity in host-country markets', *Economica*, 41, 176–193.

Caves, R.E. (1996) *Multinational Enterprise and Economic Analysis*, 2nd edn (Cambridge: Cambridge University Press).

China State Statistics Bureau (1997) *The Data of the Third National Industrial Census of the People's Republic of China in 1995* (Beijing: Chinese State Statistic Press).

Coe, D.T. and Helpman, E. (1995) 'International R&D spillovers', *European Economic Review*, 39, 859–887.

Dunning, J.H. (1993) *Multinational Enterprises and the Global Economy* (Reading: Addison-Wesley).

Ethier, W.J. (1986) 'The multinational firms', *Quarterly Journal of Economics*, 102, 805–833.

Ethier, W.J. and Markusen, J.R. (1996) 'Multinational firms, technology diffusion and trade', *Journal of International Economics*, 41, 1–28.

Globerman, S. (1979) 'Foreign direct investment and 'spillover' efficiency benefits in Canadian manufacturing industries', *Canadian Journal of Economics*, 12, 42–56.

Grossman, G. and Helpman, E. (1995) *Innovation and Growth in the Global Economy* (Cambridge, MA: MIT Press).

Haddad, M. and Harrison, A. (1993) 'Are there positive spillovers from direct foreign investment? evidence from panel data for Morocco', *Journal of Development Economics*, 42, 51–74.

Helpman, E. and Krugman, P.R. (1985) *Market Structure and Foreign Trade* (Cambridge and London: MIT Press).

Horstmann, I.J. and Markusen, J.R. (1992) 'Endogenous market structures in international trade', *Journal of International Economics*, 32, 109–129.

Hymer, S.H. (1976) *The International Operations of National Firms, a Study of Direct Foreign Investment* (Cambridge: MIT Press).

Islam, N. (1995) 'Growth empirics: a panel data approach', *Quarterly Journal of Economics,* 110, 1127–1170.

Kokko, A. (1994) 'Technology, market characteristics, and spillovers', *Journal of Development Economics*, 43, 279–293.

Liu, X.M. (2000) 'Comparative productivity of foreign and local firms in Chinese industry', *27th UK Chapter AIB Conference Proceedings*, vol. 2, 115–136.

Liu, X.H. (2000) 'Determinants of the sectoral distribution of China's inward foreign direct investment', *27th UK Chapter AIB Conference Proceedings*, vol. 2, 137–159.

Mankiw, G., Romer, D. and Weil, D. (1992) 'A contribution to the empirics of endogenous growth', *Quarterly Journal of Economics*, 108, 739–773.

Markusen, J.R. (2000) 'Foreign direct investment and trade', Centre for International Economic Studies, Policy Discussion Papers No. 0019. University of Adelaide, Australia.

Markusen, J.R. and Venables, A.J. (1997) 'The theory of endowment, intra-industry, and multinational trade', NBER Working Paper, No. 5529.

Markusen, J.R. and Venables, A.J. (1999) 'Foreign direct investment as a catalyst for industrial development', *European Economic Review*, 43, 335–356.

Miller, S. and Upadhyay, M. (2000) 'The effect of openness, trade orientation, and human capital on total labour factor productivity', *Journal of Development Economics*, 63, 399–423.

MOFTEC (2000) web-site: http://www.moftec.gov.cn/moftec/official/html/statistics_data.

MOFTEC. (196) *Regulations towards Foreign Direct Investment* (Beijing: Social Science Press).

Oulton, N. (1998) 'Investment, capital and foreign ownership in UK manufacturing', National Institute of Economic and Social Research (NIESR) Discussion Paper, No. 141.

Pissarides, C. (1997) 'Learning by trading and the returns to human capital in developing countries, *The World Bank Economic Review*, 11, 17–32.

Rodriguez-Clare, A. (1996) 'Multinationals linkages and economic development', *American Economic Review*, 36, 852–873.

Sun, H., Hone, P. and Doucouliagos, H. (1999) 'Economic openness and technical efficiency in China: a case of Chinese manufacturing industries', *Economics of Transition*, 7, 615–631.

Wang, J.Y. and Blomstrom, M. (1992) 'Foreign direct investment and technology transfer', *European Economic Review*, 36, 137–155.

Wang, X.M. and Zhou, X. (1999). 'A new strategy of technology transfer to China', *International Journal of Operations & Production Management*, 19, 527–537.

Wenders, J.T. (1971) 'Collusion and entry', *Journal of Political Economy*, 79, 1258–1277.

World Bank (1998) *Global Development Finance* (Washington, DC: World Bank).

Xu, B. (2000) 'Multinational enterprises, technology diffusion, and host country productivity growth', *Journal of Development Economics*, 62, 477–493.

12 Openness and economic performance in China

Shujie Yao and Zongyi Zhang

Introduction

Rapid economic growth in China over the last two decades has drawn serious attention all over the world. China's success has been due to Deng Xiaoping's open-door policy, which followed closely the development path of the Asian NIEs.[1] Before economic reforms, the apparent lack of modern capitalism under Mao's leadership, particularly during the Cultural Revolution, was a main constraint on economic performance.

Rapid economic growth in the late 1970s and early 1980s was explained by the successful reforms in agriculture (Yao, 2000). From the late 1980s, China entered a period of large-scale rural industrialisation (Rozelle, 1994) and active reform of the urban industrial sector. The change of state policy on international trade played an important role in creating an external environment conducive to sustainable domestic economic growth. This constitutes the so-called openness in this chapter. China's trade policy changed from a strategy of import-substitution and self-reliance, before economic reforms, to one of export promotion after the reforms (Groves *et al.*, 1994; Hay *et al.*, 1994). The export-promotion policy was pursued with a number of radical reforms, including liberalisation of the foreign-exchange market, encouragement on foreign direct investment (FDI), and industrial restructuring to utilise China's comparative advantages in international trade.

The gradual reform of the foreign-exchange market was a prerequisite for the new trade policy. Without bringing the official exchange rate towards the free market equilibrium level, China would not have been able to promote international trade and to attract foreign capital so successfully. Unlike the NIEs, the Chinese currency (Renminbi, RMB) was unconvertible and persistently overvalued for decades, up to the late 1980s (Chou and Shih, 1998; and Lardy, 1995).[2] Currency overvaluation inhibited international trade and foreign investments. After 1979, the RMB was gradually devalued. By 1994, it was made convertible in current account transaction for international settlement. The dual exchange system introduced in 1979 was replaced by a single exchange system from January 1994.[3]

In the literature, there are numerous studies examining the linkage between openness and economic performance in Asia. Most studies find that FDI and international trade contribute positively to economic growth (Pomfret, 1997; Harrold, 1995; Lardy, 1995, for China; Sengupta and Espana, 1994, for South Korea; Yue, 1999, for South-east Asia; Dowling, 1997, for the Asian high performing economies; and Greenaway, 1998, for the developing countries in general). FDI involves a significant component of technological transfers and spillover, as inferred from the new theory of endogenous growth (Romer, 1986). Export-orientation forces producers to respond to international competition. In the NIEs, the outward looking strategy has been associated with relatively free labour and capital markets (Balassa, 1988). Following the NIEs, China started to exploit its comparative advantage by focusing on labour-intensive manufacturing for exports. The experience of China and the NIEs was in marked contrast to the inward orientation of development in most Latin American countries, which have been marked by considerable distortions in labour and capital markets, debts, budget deficits and economic stagnation (Brohman, 1996).

There are three theoretical explanations of the effects of openness on economic growth: the industrial organisation theory, international trade theory and endogenous growth theory. The industrial organisation theory explains the direct effect and externality of openness on economic growth. It investigates the role of FDI and international trade in technology transfer, knowledge diffusion and the effect of these on market structure and competition (Hymer, 1976; Dunning, 1993; Caves, 1996). The international trade theory examines why FDI and international trade take place and how firms choose between exporting, FDI and licensing as an entry mode (Ethier and Markusen, 1996; Brainard, 1993). The endogenous growth theory considers openness as an important source of human capital augmentation, technological change and spillovers of ideas across countries (Grossman and Helpman, 1995).

Empirically, many recent econometric analyses have focused on understanding the causality between the dependent and independent variables. For example, does FDI cause GDP to grow, or vice versa? Most empirical results support the argument that FDI (or trade) can promote output growth. In the Chinese case, since foreign-exchange policy is a precondition for the rapid growth in FDI and exports, it can be inferred that the exchange-rate mechanism must also have played an important role in economic performance. To prove this, we establish an econometric model system to examine how the real exchange rate, FDI and exports interact and how they contribute to economic growth in the Chinese regions using provincial level data for the period 1978–1998. To avoid spurious regression results, we use a panel unit root test on all the variables involved, and panel cointegration test on the specified models using the techniques developed by Pedroni (1999). We then use the dynamic panel data approach with instruments to overcome the problems of endogeneity, heteroscedasticity and non-stationarity in the regression models using the techniques developed by Arellano and Bond (1998).

The rest of this chapter is organised as follows. The second section assesses the economic performance and openness of China and the NIEs in comparison with the rest of the world in the last two to three decades. The following section presents some empirical analyses on the linkage between openness and economic growth. Next are discussed the Asian economic crisis and how China and the Asian NIEs coped with the crisis. Conclusions are given in the final section.

Economic performance and openness: a brief review

Since economic reforms started in 1978, China's economic growth has been almost unmatched by any other economy in the world. Its gross domestic product (GDP) has more than quadrupled in 20 years (1978–1998). Real per capita disposable income has more than tripled in the cities and almost quadrupled in the countryside (Yao, 2000). From 1994, China has become a major host of foreign direct investment (FDI) (Nolan and Wang, 2000). The latest figures show that China became the world's ninth largest trading (and exporting) economy in 1999, moving from the 23rd in 1978 (*People's Daily*, 2000a). Due to the Asian economic crisis, China's exports plummeted in late 1998 and early 1999, but they recovered strongly from mid-1999. Overall, total exports in 1999 reached a record high of \$194.9 billion, up 6.1 per cent from 1998; imports were \$165.7 billion, up 18.2 per cent. In the first three months of 2000, China's total imports and exports were \$60.3 billion, up 47.1 per cent from the previous year (*People's Daily*, 2000a).

Like that of the Asian NIEs, China's economic success is due to a high rate of savings, export push, and investments in physical and human capital. High saving rates may reflect the traditional culture of the Chinese and the East Asian people rather than being a result of government policy. This traditional culture has been extremely helpful for capital accumulation and education in the developing economies. All the NIEs had a savings/GDP ratio of more than 30 per cent. In Singapore and China, the savings rate is as high as 40–50 per cent, which compares favourably with a 22 per cent world average and 17 per cent in the low-income economies (World Bank, 1999). In some sub-Saharan African countries, the savings rate is negligible. Needless to say, saving is a prerequisite for domestic investment, which in turn is an important factor for positive economic growth. In 1965–1997, most NIEs and China maintained an average annual growth rate of 7.7 per cent to 10.9 per cent in physical investments, compared with 3.9 per cent in the low-income economies and the 3.2 per cent world average.

The endogenous-growth theory suggests that investment in human capital is as important as physical investment. Accumulation of human capital is reflected in a number of areas, particularly in health and education. Improvement of people's health has led to a significant increase in life expectancy and a large reduction in child and infant mortality. In China and the NIEs, life expectancy is significantly higher, and child mortality lower, than in the low-income economies (World Bank, 1999). In education, the campaign to popularise primary and secondary school education has been highly successful. By 1997, almost all Chinese children were able to receive primary education and over 70 per cent (rising from 46 per cent in 1980) of the relevant-aged children were able to receive secondary education. In the low-income economies, in the same year, the gross enrolment rate in secondary schools was only 43 per cent (World Bank, 1999). The popularisation of primary and secondary education in China and the NIEs led to a significant reduction in adult illiteracy. Young-population illiteracy was almost eliminated in Korea and Singapore by the late 1990s. It was reduced to 1–3 per cent of the relevant-age population in China and other NIEs. This is in contrast to 32 per cent in low-income economies.

Another common feature of China and the NIEs is their integration with the global economy. This is reflected in their export-push development strategy and the absorption of foreign capital. Hong Kong and Singapore are the most open economies measured by the trade/GDP ratio. The volume of trade is two to three times that of purchasing power parity (PPP) GDP. The trade/GDP ratios are also high in other NIEs, ranging from 16.9 per cent in Thailand to 90 per cent in Malaysia. These ratios are significantly higher than the average ratio of the low-income economies (Table 12.1).

In terms of international trade, China is still far less open than the NIEs. In 1997, for example, the trade/PPP-GDP ratio was only 8.5 per cent. However, the figures in Table 12.1 may understate China's openness in two respects. First, because China is a large country, it is difficult or impossible to achieve the same level of trade/GDP ratio as that of the small city economies of Hong Kong and Singapore. Second, the GDP figures are calculated in PPP terms. If they were calculated in nominal terms, the trade/GDP ratio in 1997 would be 31 per cent for China, rising from 8.81 per cent in 1977 (Pomfret, 1997).

Another indication of openness is the absorption of foreign capital. In 1978, there was little FDI in China. Since 1995, China has been a major recipient of FDI in the world. The most rapid growth in FDI was registered in the late 1980s and 1990s. The FDI/PPP-GDP ratio rose sixfold from 0.2 per cent to 1.2 per cent over 1987–1997. Total FDI inflows rose almost 13-fold from \$3.5 billion in 1990 to \$44.2 billion by 1997 (Table 12.1). In 1998, China accounted for 28 per cent of the total FDI flowing into the developing countries (Table 12.2). China's absorption of foreign capital followed the recent development path of Malaysia, Korea and Singapore. In general, the NIEs and China have been much more open to

Table 12.1 Integration with the world economy

	Trade in goods (% of PPP GDP)		*FDI inflows (% of PPP GDP)*		*FDI inflows current prices ($billion)*	
	1987	*1997*	*1987*	*1997*	*1990*	*1997*
China, P.R.	6.8	8.5	0.2	1.2	3.5	44.2
Hong Kong	125.0	250.4	...	...	...	...
Indonesia	11.1	13.7	0.1	0.7	1.1	4.7
Japan	20.8	25.0	1.2	1.0	1.8	3.2
Korea	36.6	44.9	0.5	1.2	0.8	2.8
Malaysia	49.4	90.0	0.7	2.9	2.3	5.1
Singapore	200.7	290.7	10.0	14.3	5.6	8.6
Thailand	16.9	29.7	0.4	1.0	2.4	3.8
Low income	7.0	8.4	0.1	0.3	1.1	10.6
Middle income	10.3	18.6	0.3	1.4	22.6	150.0
High income	27.4	38.7	2.2	3.1	167.0	233.9
World	20.6	29.6	1.5	2.4	192.7	394.5

Sources: World Bank (1999, pp. 324–326) (Trade & FDI).

Table 12.2 Top ten recipients of FDI in the developing world (1998)

	FDI ($billion)	*As % of total*
All LDCs	160.0	100.0
China	44.8	28.0
Brazil	25.6	16.0
Mexico	10.7	6.7
Argentina	5.9	3.7
Poland	5.9	3.7
Malaysia	5.3	3.3
Chile	5.3	3.3
Thailand	5.1	3.2
Venezuela	4.0	2.5
Russia Fed	3.2	2.0
Rest of world	44.2	27.6

Sources: World Bank (1999) *World Development Indicators* p. 323 (Washington, DC: World Bank).

FDI than most of the low-income and middle-income economies over the last three decades.

How does openness affect growth?

Growth and openness: an international perspective

One relevant study on the NIEs is by Sengupta and Espana (1994). They use time-series data to estimate an augmented Cobb–Douglas production function including export as an explanatory variable for GDP growth. In their sample, there are two NIEs (Korea and Taiwan), three mature industrialised countries (Japan, Germany and Belgium) and one developing economy (the Philippines). The regression results show that, in all cases except Japan, exports had a positive and significant effect on GDP growth. An earlier study by Caves (1974) finds that openness (measured by FDI) had a positive effect on labour productivity in Australia's manufacturing industries. Similar single-country studies by Globerman (1979) for Canada and Kokko (1994) for Mexico confirm Caves' finding. Cross-countries studies by Blomstrom and Sjoholm (1999) and Liu *et al.* (1997) also find strong evidence for a positive link between FDI and productivity in host countries.

Figure 12.1 shows further evidence on the positive relationship between GDP and export growth. Over the period 1990–1995, China achieved the fastest growth in GDP and exports among the APEC (Asian Pacific Economic Corporation) members. The NIEs are among the best performers. The mapping of cross-country growth shows a clear and positive relationship between GDP and exports.

Some recent studies on FDI focus on how it is determined but not on

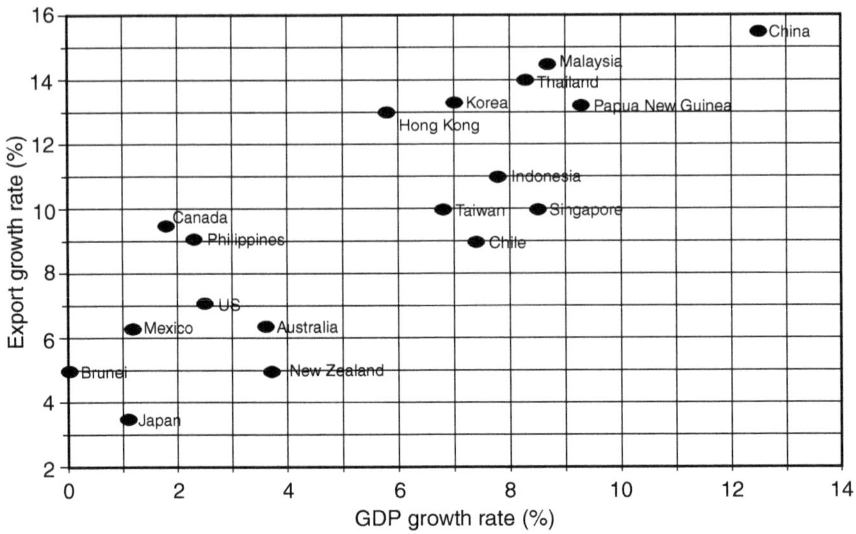

Figure 12.1 GDP and export growth in APEC economies (1990–1995).
Source: Pan (1998, Figure 4.9).

how it is linked to economic growth. Liu *et al.* (1997) show that FDI is determined by GDP growth, international trade, and other variables. Some more descriptive studies (e.g. Chen *et al.*, 1995; and Lardy, 1995) suggest that FDI has an important role in China's economic performance. However, there have been no studies that quantify the triangular relationship between FDI, exports and economic growth. However, in a cross-country study, Pan (1998) finds a positive relationship between the ratios of trade/GDP and FDI/GDP among the APEC economies (Figure 12.2). Three of the NIEs (Singapore, Hong Kong and Malaysia) had the highest FDI stock/GDP and trade/GDP ratios.

Growth and openness: evidence from the Chinese regions

Before economic reforms, import-substitution and rigid price control were two major features of China's development strategy. For example, there was little FDI as late as 1982, four years after the inception of economic reforms in 1978. The total amount of FDI was only \$0.64 billion in 1983, but increased gradually thereafter, reaching \$4.37 billion by 1991. After Deng's famous tour to South China in 1992, there was a sudden surge of FDI. The total inflow jumped to \$11.3 billion in that year, rising to \$27.5 billion in 1993, \$33.8 billion in 1994 and \$44.8 billion in 1998 (Table 12.3).

It is obvious that the history of FDI is much shorter in China than in the NIEs. In addition, FDI is highly concentrated in a number of provinces

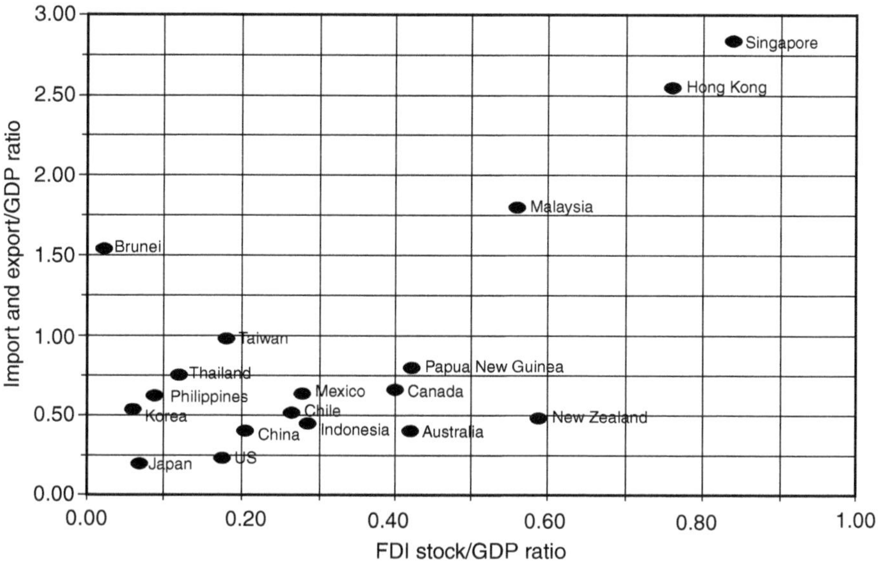

Figure 12.2 Trade/GDP and FDI/GDP ratios in 1995 in the APEC economies.

Source: Pan (1998, Figure 4.10).

Table 12.3 China's inward FDI, exports and structure, 1980–1999

Year	*Actual FDI ($billion)*	*Total exports ($billion)*	*Export by foreign invested firms as % of total*	*Manufactured exports as % of total*
1980	0.2	18.2	0.0	49.7
1985	2.0	27.4	1.1	49.4
1986	2.2	30.9	1.6	63.6
1987	2.6	39.4	3.0	66.5
1988	3.7	47.5	5.2	69.7
1989	3.8	52.5	8.3	71.3
1990	3.8	62.1	12.5	74.4
1991	4.7	71.8	16.8	77.5
1992	11.3	85.0	20.4	79.9
1993	27.5	91.8	27.5	81.8
1994	33.8	121.0	28.7	83.7
1995	37.7	148.8	31.7	85.6
1996	41.7	151.1	n.a.	85.5
1997	44.2	182.7	n.a.	86.9
1998	44.8	183.7	n.a.	n.a.
1999	n.a.	194.9	n.a.	n.a.

Sources: Lardy (1995, Tables 1, 6 and 7) and Pomfret (1997, Tables 2 and 3) for data up to 1995. Data for 1996 and 1997 are derived from NBS (1997–1999). Data for 1998–1999 are from *People's Daily* (2000a).

along the eastern coast (Guangdong, Shanghai, Tianjin, Fujian, Shangdong, Jiangsu, Zhejiang, Hainan, Liaoning and Hebei). In 1995, for example, the eastern region accounted for over 88 per cent of total FDI, with Guangdong alone accounting for 27 per cent. One important reason for the skewed distribution of FDI across regions is the early reforms that focused on opening up four special economic zones in Guangdong and Fujian in 1980, 14 coastal cities in 1984, Hainan Island in 1988 and Shanghai Pudong Development Zone in 1989. Of course, there are fundamental reasons why the coastal cities were selected as open zones. Compared with the inland areas, the coastal regions had a more productive agricultural and industrial basis, a more efficient transportation system, better environmental and human resources and, above all, easier access to China's largest investors, especially Hong Kong.[4]

China's strategy to open its market for foreign investors coincided with, and was reinforced by, its effort to promote exports. Right from the inception of economic reform, China emphasised that foreign-invested firms (foreign-owned companies, equity joint ventures, and cooperative ventures) must produce a large proportion of their output for export. As a result, many foreign-invested firms were concentrated in the export-processing and manufacturing areas in the special economic zones, the open cities and Hainan Island. This investment strategy produced some spectacular results. First, total exports increased dramatically from only \$18.2 billion in 1980 to \$194.9 billion by 1999. Second, the share of manufactures in total exports rose from 49.9 per cent in 1980 to 86.9 per cent by 1997. This rapid expansion of exports and significant change in the export mix resembled the export performance of Korea and Taiwan in the 1960s and 1970s, and of the second-tier NIEs in the 1980s and early 1990s. Third, foreign-invested firms played an important role in China's export drive. Their exports were negligible in the first half of the 1980s, but increased to \$46.9 billion, or 31.7 per cent of total exports, by 1995 (Table 12.3).

Although China's success in attracting FDI and promoting exports can be explained by many factors, it is important to note that gradual reform in the foreign exchange market played a critical role. Without devaluing the RMB, it would have been impossible to make the Chinese market attractive for foreign investors whose transactions involve frequent exchanges of foreign currencies and the RMB. In the early 1980s, when the official exchange rate was substantially lower than the black market rate, foreign investors had little incentive to invest in China.[5]

In the late 1980s, the government established a few official swap markets to facilitate the reallocation of foreign exchange and to maintain a dual exchange-rate mechanism. The swap market was an official channel allowing investors to change foreign currencies into RMB at a higher rate than the official exchange rate. It was the first important step of the government to provide incentives to attract FDI and promote exports. As foreign-exchange reserves increased rapidly in the early 1990s, the dual rate system was abolished in January 1994, and so were the swap markets. By then, the RMB had been gradually devalued towards its market-equilibrium level (Chou and Shih, 1998). The official exchange rate was devalued from 1.68 yuan per dollar in 1978 to 8.321 yuan in 1995, or by almost 400 per cent. In real terms, when adjusted by the US and Chinese consumer price indexes, the real exchange rate rose by over 200 per cent in the same period (Table 12.4).

China's systematic reforms in the foreign-exchange market, its efforts to promote exports and to attract FDI all have the same objective – that is, creating a better environment for economic growth. If we consider economic growth as the core of the model, then output is determined by physical inputs (physical capital and labour), the internal production environment (human capital, transportation, institutions, and the like), and the external environment (FDI, export and foreign exchange mechanism). This economic-growth model can be illustrated in Figure 12.3.

Output (GDP) is basically determined by two physical inputs: labour and capital. However, the efficiency of input usage, or economic performance, is further determined by two sets of factors: external and internal. The external factors are related to openness, including FDI, export, and the foreign-exchange mechanism. The internal factors include human

Table 12.4 Nominal (official) and real exchange rates of RMB/US$

Year	*Nominal exchange rate*	*Real exchange rates*
1978	1.680	1.740
1979	1.550	1.750
1980	1.500	1.820
1981	1.705	2.220
1982	1.893	2.570
1983	1.976	2.730
1984	2.327	3.260
1985	2.937	3.920
1986	3.453	4.430
1987	3.722	4.610
1988	3.722	4.050
1989	3.766	3.650
1990	4.784	4.780
1991	5.323	5.390
1992	5.515	5.460
1993	5.762	5.190
1994	8.619	6.540
1995	8.321	5.660
1995/1978	4.953	3.253

Sources: NBS (1996), for the official exchange rates and China's CPI. US Department of Commence (1980–1996), for the US CPI.

Notes

$RE_t = OE_t\ (CPI_{US}/CPI_{China})$, *RE* and *OE* respectively denote real and official exchange rates, *CPI* is consumer price index using 1990 as the base year.

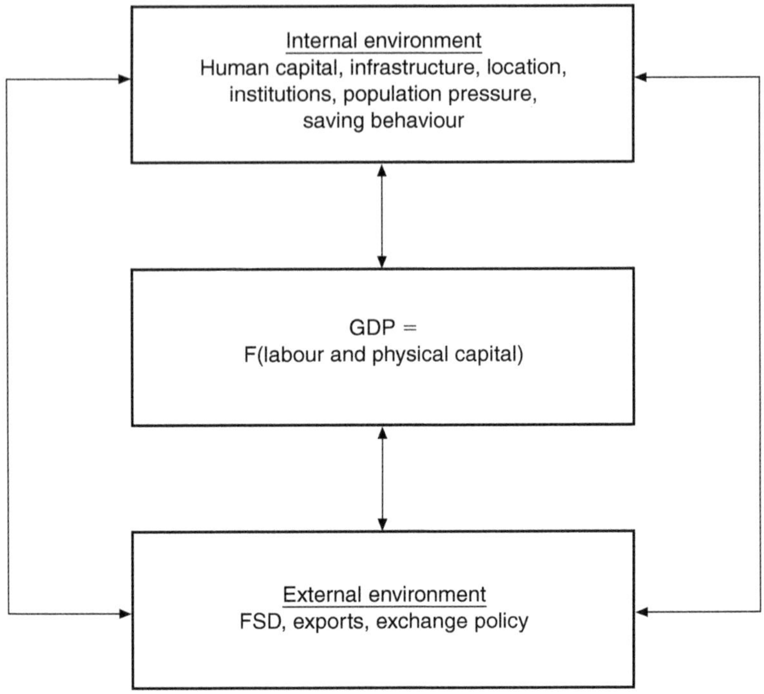

Figure 12.3 Economic growth and the production environment.

capital, infrastructure, location, and institutions (e.g. government policy, legal regulations, etc). Economic performance varies significantly across countries due to the variations in both internal and external factors. Some recent cross-country studies reveal that human capital, saving and population growth are the three main variables responsible for inter-country growth differences (Islam, 1995; Sala-i-Martin, 1996).

However, few studies have considered all the internal and external factors in a cross-country, or cross-region analysis. This may be due to some difficult technical problems, such as multicollinearity and simultaneity, that cannot be reconciled in a single regression model. To overcome these problems, instead of estimating one single equation, we have three regression models at the same time.

We use a panel unit root test for all the variables involved and find that they are all non-stationary but integrated of degree one, or I(1). This means that the models can be formulated in level terms if cointegration exists. The panel cointegration test confirms that all three models are cointegrated.

To avoid spurious regressions, however, the models are estimated in a dynamic-system with appropriate instruments in the DPD (dynamic panel data estimation) proposed by Arellano and Bond (1998). The DPD estimators have a number of advantages over the OLS estimators. They overcome the problem of non-stationarity if the variables are non-stationary. The models are estimated in first differences for the non-stationary variables. They also overcome the problem of endogeneity if the right-hand-side variables are endogenous. The endogeneity problem is overcome through using appropriate instruments for the endogenous variables. In addition, the diagnostic tests show whether the models are subject to serial correlation. If there is series correlation, the lagged terms of variables will be added to the models for estimation.

Since the model definitions and explanations of the methodology are complicated, they are presented in the appendix. The following presents the main estimated results and interpretations.

The data period is from 1978–1998. The data give a large number of observations for the models and cover the period of the Asian economic crisis. The empirical results are presented in Table 12.5. GDP is defined as a function of capital stock, employment, human capital, real exchange rate, FDI, export and transportation. Other variables include a dummy variable representing the eastern economic area (East), a dummy variable representing the unusual economic boom in 1992–1995 after Deng's famous tour to South China, and a time trend.

The results suggest that, apart from capital and labour, both internal and external factors have a significant impact on GDP. Among the external factors, the effects of exports and the real exchange rate are much stronger than that of FDI. The output elasticity of exports is over 0.11, of the real exchange rate 0.10, and of FDI less than 0.01. Among the internal factors, human capital is more important than transportation and location. The output elasticity of human capital is 0.051. The location effect (East) is insignificant. This may be due to the fact that regional productivity differences have been largely explained by the variations in other external and internal factors. The estimated coefficient on the time trend indicates that Hicks-neutral technological progress was 1.1 per cent per annum. It reflects a location-invariant macro productivity shock over the data period.

Exports are modelled as a function of GDP, real exchange rate, location and the lagged dependent variable. The dummy variable for the period 1992–1995 is also included. All the explanatory variables are significant at the usual 5 per cent level. Referring to the regression results on GDP, it is clear that exports and GDP are inter-dependent. The long-run elasticity of exports with respect to GDP is 0.903, suggesting that a 10 per cent rise in GDP will lead to an 9.03 per cent rise in exports, holding other conditions unchanged.[6] The real exchange rate is another important factor affecting exports. In other words, without reform in the exchange market, China's exports would have been severely disadvantaged.[7] Although the location factor is not significant in the GDP equation, it is significantly associated with exports. This indicates that the eastern area is

Table 12.5 Regression results based on panel data of 30 Chinese provinces in 1978–1998

GDP			*Export*			*FDI*		
X	*β*	t-*values*	*X*	*β*	t-*values*	*X*	*β*	t-*values*
Constant	−17.50	−1.75	Constant	−0.781	−3.11	Constant	−3.044	−4.05
Labour	0.408	12.10	GDP	0.187	4.83	GDP	0.165	2.31
Capital	0.470	8.75	Exchange	0.141	1.95	Wages	0.114	0.96
Human	0.051	2.36	East	0.281	3.15	Exchange	0.626	2.73
Exchange	0.102	6.76	D92–95	0.216	3.45	Transport	0.151	1.66
FDI	0.006	1.69	Export (−1)	0.793	13.19	Human	0.041	0.51
Export	0.111	10.29				East	0.370	3.57
Transport	0.039	1.78				D92–95	0.629	4.96
East	0.030	0.49				FDI (−1)	0.798	16.83
D92–95	0.019	2.61						
Time	0.011	2.01						
Test-statistics			Test-statistics			Test-statistics		
R^2		0.961	R^2		0.941	R^2		0.911
Wald		$p = 0.000$	Wald		$p = 0.000$	Wald		$p = 0.000$
Sargan		$p = 0.881$	Sargan		N.A.	Sargan		N.A.
M1	−1.56	$p = 0.118$	M1	−1.295	$p = 0.184$	M1	−0.898	0.333
M2	−0.864	$p = 0.388$	M2	0.718	$p = 0.463$	M2	−0.819	0.484

Notes
All the variables are in natural logarithms. Values are measured in 1990 constant prices. Detail explanations on data, model specification, estimation techniques, test-statistics are provided in the appendix.

Data sources: NBS (1996).

far more export-oriented than the inland provinces, even after all the other factors are controlled for.

FDI is defined as a function of GDP, effective wages (nominal wages adjusted by productivity), real exchange rate, transportation, human capital, location and the lagged dependent variable. The dummy variable for 1992–1995 is also included. Like exports, FDI is mainly determined by GDP, with a long-run elasticity of 0.817. The real exchange rate also plays an important role in FDI. The location factor is significant, indicating that the eastern area is much more successful in attracting FDI than the rest of the country. The effects of human capital and wages on FDI are positive but not significant, implying that wage differentials across provinces were not a significant concern of foreign investors in the data period. In reality, wage differences may just reflect the variation in labour quality.

The quantitative relationship between GDP and the three factors of openness can be summarised and illustrated in Figure 12.4. In the model, the real exchange rate is treated as an exogenous variable. The results suggest that it had a significant and sizeable effect on the three endogenous variables: FDI, exports and GDP. It is clear that the gradual devaluation of the RMB towards its real equilibrium exchange rate with the US dollar over the data period has been one of the most important factors responsible for China's success in attracting FDI, promoting exports and, above all, stimulating economic growth.

FDI and exports have a simultaneous relationship with GDP. FDI inflows and exports stimulate GDP growth, which, in turn, provides a solid basis for attracting more FDI and export push. Such an interaction among these three economic variables formed a virtual circle of openness, growth, more openness and more growth.

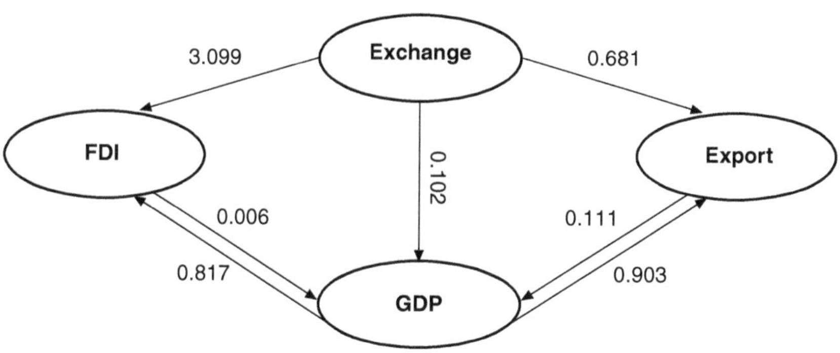

Figure 12.4 Linkage between openness and output in the Chinese regions, 1980–1995.

Source: Table 12.5.

Notes: The values are long-run elasticities. Arrows indicate the direction of impact.

Asian economic crisis and recovery

Only four years after the World Bank published the book *The East Asian Miracle* (World Bank, 1993), all the high performing economies in East Asia, in late 1997 and 1998, were plunged into a deep financial and economic crisis. The crisis was first triggered by the collapse of the Thai baht and stock market. The contagion soon spread into Malaysia, Indonesia and Korea. All these countries were so severely affected that the International Monetary Fund (IMF) was asked to pump in huge sums of money to rescue the economies.[8]

The Asian crisis brought down world GDP growth from 4.8 per cent in 1997 to just 1.9 per cent in 1998. Japan was already in recession before the crisis, but the crisis hit Japan particularly hard, with its recession contributing to 0.5 percentage points of the decline in world GDP in 1998. Since Japan was the power engine in East Asia, its own recession accelerated the decline of the NIEs. The worst hit economies were Thailand, Indonesia, Malaysia and Korea. In 1998, output fell by 13 per cent in Indonesia, 8 per cent in Thailand, 6.7 per cent in Malaysia and 6.0 per cent in Korea. Even Hong Kong and Singapore were forced into negative growth in 1998. Only Taiwan and China managed to maintain positive growth, but at a much lower rate than before the crisis (Table 12.6). The scale of crisis was unprecedented in these economies during their recent development history.

In early 1998, the crisis seemed to spread into the already fragile Russian and other eastern European economies. A worldwide economic depression looked imminent as the US and western European stock markets suffered severe losses in mid 1998. In the third quarter of 1998, there was strong speculation that China might have to devalue the RMB to maintain a competitive edge against the NIEs. It also looked as if the potential collapse of the RMB and the Chinese economy would serve as a final blow to trigger a global crisis. Suddenly, China's ability and willingness not to devalue its currency became the centre of world attention. In late 1998, Mr Zhu Rongji, China's premier, promised that China would not devalue the RMB. In early 1999, the central government also ordered the central bank, the People's Bank of China, to issue 100 billion yuan of investment bonds to boost its domestic economy in the face of a depressed external market. For the first time in over 20 years, China experienced significant negative growth in exports in late 1998 and early 1999. However, China's effort not to devalue the RMB and its ability to achieve a GDP growth of 7.8 per cent in 1998 played a significant role in easing the crisis in Asia.

During the economic crisis, many economic analysts thought that the Asian miracle might have been over, and the 'bubble' might have burst. Paul Krugman shares the view that Asia's crisis was due to corruption and crony capital (Krugman, 1998). He argues that the failure of the financial

Table 12.6 GDP growth of the NIEs in the economic crisis of 1997–1999 by quarter

	China	*Hong Kong*	*Indonesia*	*Korea*	*Malaysia*	*Singapore*	*Taiwan*	*Thailand*
1997Q1	9.4	6.1	6.6	5.4	8.2	3.8	6.8	−0.4
1997Q2	9.6	6.4	6.6	6.3	8.4	7.8	6.3	−0.4
1997Q3	8.1	5.7	6.6	6.3	7.4	10.1	6.9	−0.4
1997Q4	8.2	2.7	6.6	3.9	6.9	5.6	5.9	−0.4
1998Q1	7.2	−2.8	−6.2	−3.8	−1.8	5.6	5.9	−8.0
1998Q2	6.8	−5.2	−16.5	−6.6	−6.8	−1.5	5.2	−8.0
1998Q3	7.6	−7.1	−17.4	−6.8	−8.6	−0.7	4.7	−8.0
1998Q4	9.6	−5.7	−13.9	−5.3	−8.6	−0.8	3.7	−8.0
1999Q1	8.3	−3.4	−10.3	4.6	−1.3	1.2	4.3	0.1
1999Q2	7.1	0.7	1.8	9.8	4.1	6.7	6.5	3.5
1999Q3	7.0	4.5	0.5	12.3	8.1	6.7	5.1	3.5
1999Q4	6.8	8.7	5.8	12.3	10.6	7.1	6.8	7.7

Sources: *The Economist* (1997–1999, various issues), Economic Indicators.

Notes
Average of latest 3 months compared with average of previous 3 months. The rates for Thailand in 1997 and 1998, for Indonesia in 1997 are annual rates.

system in East Asia was due to excessive investments in risky and low-return (or unprofitable) projects. It was therefore logical to infer that the bubble must burst once bad debts and financial losses had accumulated to a point that even the government could not bear them. Krugman's explanation is valid in the sense that the Asian economies have some fundamental problems in financial institutions and in the governments' soft-attitudes towards large state enterprises and banks. His hypothesis, however, may not be sufficient to explain the sudden occurrence of a deep crisis. Radelet and Sachs (1998) suggest that there were other important factors responsible for the sudden collapse of Thailand, Malaysia, Indonesia and Korea. In our view, two of their explanations are still valid today: (1) panicked reversals in capital flows, and (2) the lack of a legal and regulatory framework to support a liberalised and wide-open financial system in the world market.

Panicked reversals in capital flows were caused by the so-called herd behaviour of domestic depositors and foreign investors: if one decides to withdraw money in anticipation of a crisis, others will follow. The worst hit economies – Thailand, Indonesia, Malaysia and Korea – had the highest short-term debt-to-reserve ratios, which rendered them the most vulnerable to attacks by investors rushing to draw out money in panic. Panicked outflows of capital may be due to the premature opening of domestic financial markets to foreign investors. In Thailand, Indonesia, Malaysia and Korea, new banks and finance companies were allowed to operate without supervision and adequate capitalisation. This financial environment was partly responsible for the capital withdrawals, panic and deep economic contraction that followed. In contrast, Hong Kong, Singapore and Taiwan had much more mature financial markets with far better monitoring and supervision mechanisms than Indonesia, Thailand, Malaysia and Korea. This explains why the former suffered far less during the crisis than the latter.

As with the worst-hit economies, China's financial system had similar problems of corruption, crony capital, huge non-performing loans and losses by the state-owned enterprises and banks. However, China was able to escape a similar crisis. In retrospect, it was not because China had better economic fundamentals than the crisis economies, but because it had a more pragmatic approach to financial market reforms. The Chinese government understood well that it could not entirely open up its financial market for foreign investors given the poor state of its financial institutions and the unpredictable volatility of stock markets. Foreigners were restricted to investing in B shares in the Shanghai and Shenzhen stock exchanges. The RMB was gradually devalued but it was kept unconvertible in capital account transactions even after a unified exchange rate was introduced in 1994. Moreover, foreign banks and other financial institutions are not allowed to open branches in China without going through a tedious administrative procedure. China's gradual reform and openness in the financial market resembled its gradual reform approach in the real sectors of the economy.

In the middle of the Asian crisis, some observers suggested that Asia's development was somehow a bubble, rather than a miracle, and that when the bubble burst, the remarkable achievements of these economies in the past decades would be completely wiped out by the crisis. This view is obviously mistaken. In the past decades, there have been enormous gains in income levels, health and education. It is precisely the development strategies of export-push, FDI attraction and massive investments in physical and human capital that make these economies strong enough to withstand such an unanticipated shock without totally collapsing.

No one was able to predict a deep crisis in Asia before it happened. Equally surprisingly, no one was able to predict a quick recovery. Many observers suggested that it might take many years for the crisis economies to move from negative to positive growth. The latest statistics, however, show that none of the crisis economies suffered more than six consecutive quarters of negative growth. Figure 12.5 shows that the quarterly GDP growth rates of the worst hit economies – Indonesia, Thailand, Malaysia and Korea – exhibit a clear V-shape pattern, which is not dissimilar to that experienced by Mexico and Argentina in their crisis years of 1994–1996 (Figure 12.6).

In most economies, GDP growth slowed down from the first quarter to the last quarter in 1997. It then plunged into real contraction throughout 1998 (except in China and Taiwan, and Singapore in the first quarter), but recovered into positive territory from the first quarter of 1999 in Thailand and Korea, and from the second quarter of 1999 in all the other crisis

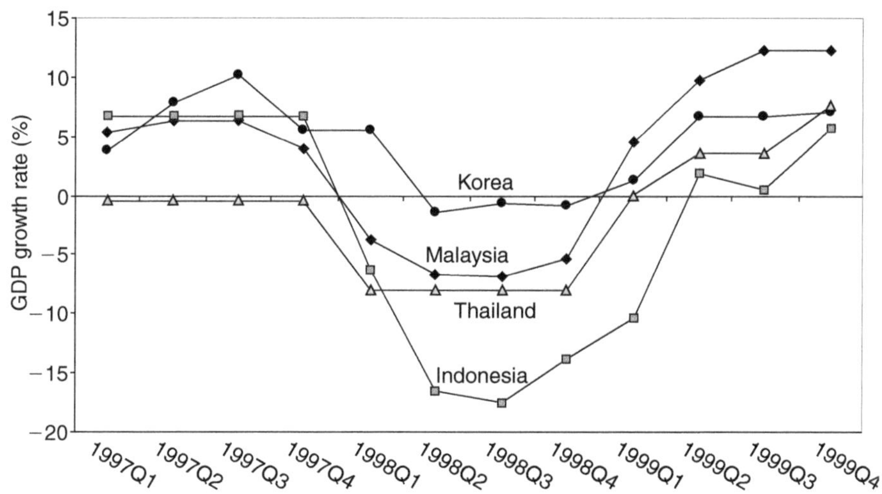

Figure 12.5 GDP growth rates of crisis economies in Asia, 1997–1999.

Source: Table 12.6.

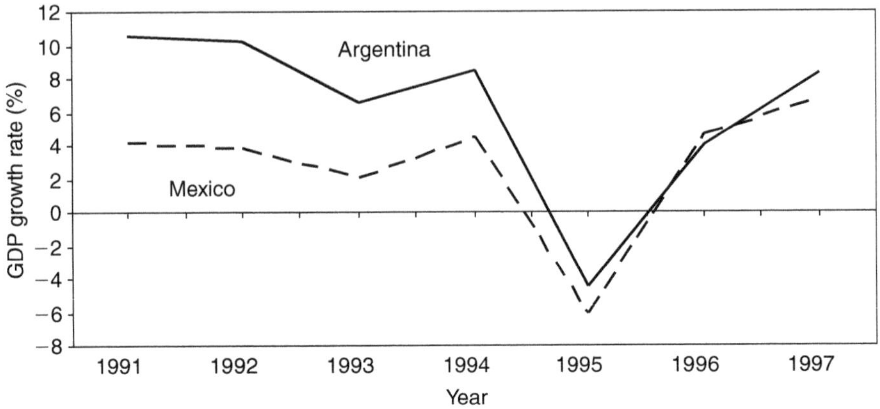

Figure 12.6 Real GDP growth rates, Argentina and Mexico, 1991–1997.
Source: Redelet and Sachs (1998, Figure 1).

economies. By the end of 1999 and early 2000, the recovery trend appeared unstoppable. In the last quarter of 1999, GDP grew 12.3 per cent in Korea, 10.6 per cent in Malaysia, 6.8 per cent in Thailand and 5.8 per cent in Indonesia (Table 12.6). Singapore, Taiwan and China also achieved significant GDP growth.

After the Asian crisis, China still pursued its policy of openness. From the second part of 1999, both exports and imports increased rapidly. By the end of 2000, China became the ninth largest trading nation in the world (*People's Daily*, 2000a). In addition, China continued to be the largest recipient of FDI in the developing world. Continuing openness also helped China to achieve remarkable growth in GDP. The annual growth rate of GDP was 8.3 per cent over the period 1996 to 2000 (*People's Daily*, 2000b). In 2000, total GDP surpassed the landmark of one trillion US dollars, reaching 8.9 trillion yuan. Per capita GDP of the richest province, Shanghai City, surpassed 4,000 US dollars, reaching 34,560 yuan (*People's Daily*, 2001).

Conclusions

Openness of the Chinese economy came about in a gradual fashion. The initial step was the devaluation of the RMB. The second step was the introduction of FDI. These two steps set a solid foundation for rapid export growth, which, in turn, enabled the economy to absorb more FDI and maintain a stable and fair (undistorted, or less distorted) foreign-exchange market. Export-push, FDI, and a stable exchange market are three important elements of openness, which created a favourable external environment for rapid and sustainable economic growth.

Although China has been successful in terms of economic growth, it has a number of important weaknesses, including the inefficiency and loss-making of state-owned industries, the debt-ridden financial institutions, corruption and crony capital, uneven regional development, environmental degradation, and rising income inequality. These problems may greatly undermine its ability to maintain high economic growth and to avoid any deep economic recession, but the experiences and lessons learned from the 1997–1998 economic crisis in Asia are useful for its future economic development. One such lesson is that the timing and scale of financial reforms need to be carefully designed. China is about to join the World Trade Organisation (WTO). Joining the WTO means that the economy has to be far more open than it is today. The real challenges will come from the most vulnerable sectors of the economy: banking, insurance, capital and technology-intensive manufacturing and agriculture. If China has to open all these sectors to international competition, there is the danger that it may not be able to cope with the cyclical shocks that are typical of international capitalism. Some sectors may be so unprofitable that a large number of firms have to be closed down, with thousands of people losing their jobs. The stock markets and the financial sectors may have to withstand huge short-term capital flight and international speculation, as was the case in the NIEs during the recent crisis.

However, China has to be prepared for such challenges. The main conclusion drawn from this paper is that openness can promote economic growth, but it needs to be emphasised that it can also incur some unforeseen risks. Hence, economic success has depended, and will continue to depend, on the ability of the country to use openness to stimulate growth and manage the risks associated with this openness. As far as the Chinese economy is concerned, it has been successful in this regard over the last two decades of economic reforms.

At the time of the Asian economic crisis, people were pessimistic about the Asian development model and were concerned with China's ability to sustain its rapid economic growth. Two years after the crisis, all the economic indicators in China and the Asian NIEs show that these economies have been successful in coping with the crisis. The growth of the Chinese economy slowed down in the crisis years. Imports, exports and FDI declined for six quarters. However, China did not experience any crisis. Its economy performed remarkably well during and after the crisis period. This implies that China's open policy, which includes liberalised international trade and capital mobility, was successful in the past, and will continue to help China achieve sustainable growth in the future.

Appendix

This appendix provides the details on data, methods of regression and interpretation of results for Table 12.5 in the main text.

Model specifications

The GDP equation

The equation for GDP is a Cobb–Douglas production function, which includes the basic inputs of labour and capital, the internal environmental factors (human capital, location, and transportation), and the external environmental factors (export, FDI, and real exchange rate). The final form of the estimated equation is expressed in equation (12.A1).

$$\ln(\text{GDP})_{it} = \alpha_0 + \alpha_1\ln(\text{labour})_{it} + \alpha_2\ln(\text{capital})_{it} + \alpha_3\ln(\text{human capital})_{it} + \alpha_4\ln(\text{exchange})_t + \alpha_5\ln(\text{FDI})_{it} + \alpha_6\ln(\text{export})_{it} + \alpha_7\ln(\text{transport})_{it} + \alpha_8(\text{east}) + \alpha_9\text{D9295} + \alpha_{10}(\text{time}) + e_{it} \quad (12.\text{A1})$$

The subscript (*it*) denotes provinces ($i = 1, 2, \ldots, 30$) and year ($t = 1978, 1979, \ldots, 1998$). The error term ($e_{it}$) is assumed to be a stochastic white noise. All the variables are calculated in 1990 constant prices. Price indices are province specific. All the data required are available from the official statistics (NBS, 1996; NBS, 1997–1999) except physical capital stock, which is derived from a special procedure to be discussed below.

It is difficult to define a variable that represents human capital. In most empirical studies, it is approximated by the secondary-school enrolment rate of the relevant-aged population (Islam, 1995). In this study, however, we find that the secondary enrolment rate does not perform well in our model. We suspect that the main difference in education between provinces and over time is the number of students enrolled in higher education (Fleisher and Chen, 1997, use university graduates/population and a proxy for human capital). As a result, we use the ratio of the number of students enrolled in higher education over the number of students enrolled in secondary education to represent the changes in human capital. This ratio reflects the propensity of secondary school students to be enrolled in higher education. The rapid development in higher education reflects the rapid economic growth in China over the data period. In addition, the variation in higher education also represents the variation in the economic activities among the provinces.

The values of exports and FDI are provided in US dollars in the official statistics. Since they are measured in US dollars, most economic analysts do not bother to deflate the values in current prices into values in constant prices (e.g. Liu *et al.*, 1997). We feel that it is important to conduct an appropriate deflation. One relevant deflator is the US consumer price index. Therefore, we deflate the values of exports and FDI in current prices, US dollars, by the US consumer price index based in 1990. We then convert the deflated values into equivalent values in RMB by multiplying the value by the official exchange rate in 1990 ($1 = RMB 4.784). In regression analysis, it is not important to convert the values in US dollars into values in RMB because all the values will be logged. However, since all the other variables in the model are measured in RMB, it is useful to change these two valuables into RMB as well.

The exchange rate is the real exchange rate as calculated in the main text. This variable is time-variant but location-invariant as all the provinces faced the same foreign exchange rate. Ideally, when we calculate the real exchange rate we should use the exchange rates and the price indexes of China's main trading partners. However, since RMB follows the US dollar very closely (although RMB is not pegged to the dollar), we only use the dollar exchange rate and the US price index to calculate the real exchange rate.

Transportation is measured as the equivalent mileages of railways, highways and waterways per 1,000 square kilometres. The highway is the dominant means of transportation in terms of mileages. The ratios of the lengths of railways, highways and waterways are 1.00/16.84/1.90 at the national level. The simplest way to measure transportation is to add the total lengths of these three different means of transportation (e.g. Liu *et al.*, 1997, Fleisher and Chen, 1997) However, the transportation capacity of one mile of railway is different from that of one mile of highway or waterway. As a result, it is necessary to convert railways and waterways into equivalent highways. The conversion ratios are derived from the volumes of transport per mile by each of the three means of transportation. At national average, the conversion ratios are 4.27/1.00/1.06. In other words, we multiplied railways by 4.27 and waterways by 1.06 to convert them into the equivalent length of highways. This method of conversion may not be perfect as the relative capacity of different transportation means may not be the same in different provinces. However, any possible conversion errors should be small because highways account for a predominant proportion of the total transportation volume. One possible way to correct the conversion errors is to instrument the length of transportation. This is done through the DPD (dynamic panel data) estimation as discussed below.

Finally, capital stock has to be calculated using the flows of capital investments according to equation (A12.2).

$$K_{it+1} = (1-\delta)K_{it} + \frac{I_{it+1}}{p_i^K} \tag{12.A2}$$

where K is physical capital stock, I investment, p^K the price index for investment, the subscripts are for province (i) and time (t), and δ a depreciation rate of capital stock. To work out the time series of capital stock, we need to know its initial level and the average depreciation rate of capital. Both of these two values are unknown; so it requires some reasonable assumptions before capital stocks are derived. The first assumption is that the initial capital stock in each province is equal to twice the level of initial GDP; that is, the capital stock in 1978 is equal to twice the GDP in that year for each province. This assumption implies that the capital share was 50 per cent in 1978. This share is similar to the capital elasticity of output. Given that the Chinese economy was not quite capital-intensive, a capital elasticity of 0.5 is not unreasonable. The second assumption is that the average depreciation rate of capital stock is 7.5 per cent. This rate is arbitrary but it implies that the average life of capital equipment is 13.3 years. Finally, since the price index of capital stock is not available, the GDP deflator is used to deflate investments.

The export equation

Export level is determined by GDP and the real exchange rate. There may be some other factors that can affect exports (e.g. foreign demand) but these factors can be represented by a lagged dependent variable. The inclusion of a lagged dependent variable can also resolve the serial correlation problem that exists in the model without the lagged term (see below for more explanation). The location dummy for the eastern region and a dummy for the boom years in 1992–95 are also included in the regression. The final specification is given in equation (12.A3).

$$\ln(\text{export})_{it} = \beta_0 + \beta_1 \ln(\text{GDP})_{it} + \beta_2 \ln(\text{exchange})_{it} + \beta_3(\text{east}) + \beta_4 \text{D9295} + \beta_5 \ln(\text{export})_{it-1} + e_{it} \qquad (12.\text{A3})$$

All these variables and the required data have been given above for equation (12.A1).

The FDI equation

The basic explanatory variables for FDI are GDP, effective wages, real exchange rate, transportation and human capital. The two dummies for the eastern region and the period 1992–1995 are also included. The lagged dependent variable is added to resolve the problem of serial correlation and to account for the effects of some other variables that may be omitted from the model. The final specification is given in equation (12.A4).

$$\ln(\text{FDI})_{it} = \theta_0 + \theta_1 \ln(\text{GDP})_{it} + \theta_2 \ln(\text{wages})_{it} + \theta_3 \ln(\text{exchange})_{it} + \theta_4 \ln(\text{transport})_{it} + \theta_5 \ln(\text{human capital})_{it} + \theta_6(\text{east}) + \theta_4 \text{D9295} + \theta_8 \ln(\text{FDI})_{it-1} + e_{it} \qquad (12.\text{A4})$$

The data and explanations for FDI, GDP, exchange, transportation, human capital and the two dummy variables are exactly the same as those given for equation (12.A1). The wages variable is the effective wage rate, which is the ratio of real wages divided by real GDP per employee in the respective year and province. Real wages are wages in current prices divided by the consumer price index for each province.

All the explanatory variables except the wages variables are expected to have a positive effect on FDI. The effect of the wages variable on FDI may not be decisive. On the one hand, wages reflect the cost of production and should have a negative effect on FDI. On the other hand, wages may reflect the quality of labour and should have a positive effect on FDI. This is why real wages have to be divided by labour productivity (we call this ratio effective wages). The net effect of the wages variable will depend on the interaction of its negative effect as a cost of production and its positive effect as a measurement of labour quality.

Unit root test for the variables and cointegration test for the model

The models in equation (12.A1) may produce spurious results if they were estimated with OLS as the variables may not be stationary. To test whether the variables are stationary, we use the panel unit root test techniques and programmes developed by Pedroni (1999).

Pedroni provides four standardised and normally distributed statistics for left-tailed tests. This means that we need a negative value less than −1.96 to reject the null hypothesis of a unit root for a single variable. The results for all the variables involved in the models are presented in Table 12.A1.

All the variables except human capita are found to be non-stationary. The first differences of all the variables are stationary (the results are not reported here to save space). This means that they are all I(1). Hence, it is possible to construct the model in level terms although the models have to

Table 12.A1 Panel unit root tests for individual variables (30 provinces and 21 years)

	Levin-Lin ρ	*Levin-Lin* $t-\rho$	*Levin-Lin* *ADF*	*IPS* *ADF*
Capital assets	5.33	7.86	5.11	7.28
Human capital	−2.36	−4.93	−0.67	−0.13
Effective wages	0.67	2.31	1.54	0.71
Employment	2.17	1.38	3.39	3.72
Exports	2.36	3.41	3.84	4.46
FDI	0.61	1.52	1.39	−1.37
GDP	4.00	5.23	6.41	8.62
Transportation	3.48	5.04	5.62	6.49
Wages	3.25	4.21	4.12	5.54
Exchange rate	1.82	2.13	2.28	3.09

Notes

Human capital = enrolment rate of higher education students as a proportion of secondary school graduates. The critical value is −1.96 to reject the null hypothesis of a unit root at the 5% significance level as all the statistics are left-tailed tests.

Table 12.A2 Cointegration tests in heterogeneous panels with multiple regressors

	Equation (12.A1) for GDP	*Equation (12.A4) for FDI*	*Equation (12.A3) for export*
Panel-*pp*	0.44	−6.78	−5.35
Panel-ADF	−1.28	−4.80	−6.39
Group-ρ	−5.03	−3.18	−1.98
Group-*pp*	0.61	−7.20	−5.39
Group-ADF	−3.32	−12.31	−8.25

Notes
The critical value is −1.96 to reject the null hypothesis of no cointegration at the 5% significance level as all the statistics are left-tailed tests.

be tested as to whether there is cointegration among the dependent and explanatory variables. We conduct a cointegration test for all three models in the first section of the Appendix in heterogeneous panels with multiple regressors. The test results are given in Table 12.A2. There is clear evidence of cointegration in the FDI and export equations as all the statistics have large negative values. Hence, the null hypothesis of no cointegration is strongly rejected. For the GDP equation, three test statistics are not clear but two statistics (group-ρ and group-ADF) show strong evidence of cointegration.

Estimation

Although there is evidence of cointegration in all the three models, there are some econometric problems if they are estimated using the OLS technique. First, the three equations are unlikely to be independent of each other, and ideally they should be estimated in a simultaneous system. However, they cannot be run in a simultaneous system because there are not enough observations (and degrees of freedom) to generate reliable and robust results. As a compromise, they are run in a seemingly unrelated system. Second, equation (12.A1) has a simultaneity problem in OLS as some of the explanatory variables (exports, capital stock, labour and human capital) are unlikely to be exogenous. To solve this problem, we use GMM estimators in DPD to run the regression in a dynamic system (see Arellano and Bond, 1998, for more explanation). More precisely, capital and exports are treated as endogenous variables, whose levels dated $(t-2, t-3)$ are used as instruments for the difference equations and differences dated $(t-1)$ are used for the levels equation. We cannot treat any other right-hand side variables in the same way due to data restriction. As a result, labour, human capital, the real exchange rate and transportation are treated as exogenous variables, but, to overcome the problem of multicollinearity, they are all instrumented. Third, the export and FDI equations exhibit a serial correlation problem. To solve the problem, it is necessary to add a lagged dependent variable to the models. Finally, it is necessary to stress that all the variables are non-stationary in levels but stationary in first differences, i.e. they are I(1) variables. The problem of non-stationarity may render OLS regression results spurious. However, with the GMM estimators in DPD, all the I(1) variables are changed into first differences in the estimations to deal with the problem of non-stationarity. The M1 and M2 tests (see below) show that the regressions provide the long-run cointegration relationships among the variables defined in the models.

Results and interpretations

The M1 and M2 are N(0,1) distributed tests for first and second order serial correlation (see Arellano and Bond, 1998). In the GDP equation, there is no serial correlation without adding the lagged dependent variables. In the export and FDI equations, serial correlation is removed after adding the lagged dependent variables. Sargan is the *p*-value from a test of the validity of the instruments. The test result cannot reject the validity of instruments in the GDP equation. The Wald test gives the *p*-value for joint significance.

The results are derived from the one-step estimates with robust test statistics. The goodness-of-fit (R^2) indicates that more than 90 per cent of the variation in the dependent variable is explained by the explanatory variables in all regressions. In the GDP equation, the *t*-statistics show that the estimated coefficients of labour, physical capital, human capital, the real exchange rate, exports, the dummy variable for the period 1992–1995 and the time trend are significant at or below the usual 5 per cent level. The estimated coefficients of FDI and transportation are significant only at the 10 per cent level. In the export equation, all the estimated coefficients are significant at the 5 per cent level. In the FDI equation, the estimated coefficients of GDP, the real exchange rate, the two dummy variables and the lagged dependent variable are significant at or below the 5 per cent level. The estimated coefficients of human capital and wages have the expected sign but they are not significant.

Notes

1 In this chapter, NIEs include the four tiger economies, Taiwan, South Korea, Hong Kong and Singapore (first-tier NIEs) and Malaysia, Thailand and Indonesia (second-tier NIEs).
2 Chou and Shih estimated that the RMB was overvalued by 57 per cent in 1978. Overvaluation was brought down to 33 per cent in 1983 and only 5 per cent in 1984 due to successive devaluation (Chou and Shih, 1998, Table 2).
3 The evolution of foreign exchange liberalisation is referred to in Chou and Shih (1998) and Pomfret (1997).
4 Hong Kong and Macao accounted for 54.31 per cent of China's accumulative

FDI in 1984–1995, Japan 8.2 per cent, Taiwan 7.82 per cent, USA 8.0 per cent, Singapore 3.81 per cent, Korea 2.85 per cent and UK 2.34 per cent (NBS, various issue, 1984–1998).

5 Ding (1998) has a detailed study on the foreign exchange black market and exchange flight in China in this period.

6 The equations for Export and FDI are defined as partial adjustment models. The estimated coefficients are short-run elasticities. The long-run elasticities are the short-run elasticities divided by 1 minus the estimated coefficient on the lagged dependent variable. For example, the short-run elasticity of export with respect to GDP is 0.187. The estimated coefficient on the lagged dependent variable is 0.793 so that the long-run elasticity of export with respect to GDP is $0.187/(1-0.793)=0.903$.

7 A relevant study by Brada *et al.* (1993) also shows that devaluation (change in the real exchange rate) had a positive effect on the balance of trade in China.

8 The IMF signed emergency lending agreements with Thailand in August 1997 ($17 billion), with Indonesia in November 1997 ($35 billion), and with Korea in December 1997 ($57 billion). The actual amounts of disbursement were, however, much smaller. The IMF also attached a number of conditions for the loans. Such conditions, including a drastic restructuring of the financial systems in the middle of a deep crisis, are blamed for aggravating, rather than easing the crisis (Radelet and Sachs, 1998).

Bibliography

Arellano, M. and Bond, R.S. (1998) 'Dynamic panel data estimation using DPD98 for Gauss', mimeo, Institute for Fiscal Studies, London.

Balassa, B. (1988) 'The interaction of factor and product market distortions in developing countries', *World Development*, 11(2).

Blomstrom, M. and Sjoholm, F. (1999) 'Technology transfer and spillovers: does local participation with multinationals matter?', *European Economic Review*, 43(4–6), 915–923.

Brada, J., Kutan, A.M. and Zhou, S. (1993) 'China's exchange rate and the balance of trade', *Economics of Planning*, 26, 229–242.

Brainard, L.S. (1993) 'A simple theory of multinational corporations and trade with a trade-off between proximity and concentration', *NBER Working Paper*, No. 4269.

Brohman, J. (1996) 'Postwar development in the Asian NICs: does the neoliberal model fit reality?', *Economic Geography*, 72(2), 107–130.

Caves, R.E. (1974) 'Multinational firms, competition and productivity in host-country markets', *Economica*, 41, 176–193.

Caves, R.E. (1996) *Multinational Enterprise and Economic Analysis*, 2nd edn. (Cambridge: Cambridge University Press).

Chen, C., Chang, L. and Zhang, Y. (1995) 'The role of foreign direct investment in China's post-1978 economic development', *World Development*, 23(4), 691–703.

Chou, W.L. and Shih, Y.C. (1998) 'The equilibrium exchange rate of the Chinese Renminbi', *Journal of Comparative Economics*, 26, 165–174.

Ding, J. (1998) 'China's foreign exchange black market and exchange flight: analysis of exchange rate policy', *The Developing Economies*, 36(1), 24–44.

Dowling, P. (1997) 'Asia's economic miracle: a historical perspective', *Australian Economic Review*, 30(1), 113–123.

Dunning, J.H. (1993) *Multinational Enterprises and the Global Economy* (Reading: Addison-Wesley).

Ethier, W.J. and Markusen, J.R. (1996) 'Multinational firms, technology diffusion and trade', *Journal of International Economics*, 41(1–2), 1–28.

Fleisher, B.M. and Chen, J. (1997) 'The coast-noncoast income gap, productivity, and regional economic policy in China', *Journal of Comparative Economics*, 25, 220–236.

Globerman, S. (1979) 'Foreign direct investment and "spillover" efficiency benefits in Canadian manufacturing industries', *Canadian Journal of Economics*, 12, 42–56.

Greenaway, D. (1998) 'Does trade liberalisation promote economic development?' *Scottish Journal of Political Economy*, 45(5), 491–511.

Grossman, G. and Helpman, E. (1995) *Innovation and Growth in the Global Economy* (Cambridge, MA: MIT Press).

Groves, T., Hong, Y., McMillan, J. and Naughton, B. (1994) 'Autonomy and incentives in Chinese state enterprises', *Quarterly Journal of Economics*, 109, 1, 183–209.

Harrold, P. (1995) 'China: foreign trade reform: now for the hard part', *Oxford Review of Economic Policy*, 11(4), 133–146.

Hay, D., Morris, D., Liu, G. and Yao, S. (1994) *Economic Reform and State-Owned Enterprises in China 1979–89* (Oxford: Clarendon Press).

Hymer, S.H. (1976) *The International Operations of National Firms, A Study of Direct Foreign Investment* (Cambridge, MA: MIT Press).

Islam, N. (1995) 'Growth empirics: a panel data approach', *Quarterly Journal of Economics* 110, 1127–1170.

Kokko, A. (1994) 'Technology, market characteristics, and spillovers', *Journal of Development Economics*, 43, 279–293.

Krugman, P. (1998) 'Bubble, boom, crash: theoretical notes on Asia's crisis', MIT, mimeo.

Lardy, N.R. (1995) 'The role of foreign direct investment in China's economic transformation', *China Quarterly* 1065–1082.

Liu, X. (2000) 'Comparative productivity of foreign and local firms in Chinese industry', *27th UK Chapter AIB Conference Proceedings*, 2, 115–136.

Liu, X., Song, H., Wei, Y. and Romilly, P. (1997) 'Country characteristics and foreign direct investment in China: a panel data analysis', *Weltwirtschaftliches Archiv*, 133(2), 311–329.

Nolan, P. and Wang, X. (2000) 'Reorganising amid turbulence: China's large-scale industry'. In S. Cook, S. Yao, and J. Zhuang (eds), *The Chinese Economy under Transition* (Basingstoke, UK: Macmillan).

Pan, S. (1998) 'Asia Pacific economic cooperation and regionalism in the world of globalisation and regionalisation', unpublished PhD dissertation, University of Sheffield, UK.

Pedroni, P. (1999) 'Critical values for cointegration test in heterogeneous panels with multiple regressors', *Oxford Bulletin of Economics and Statistics*, 61, Special Issue, November, 653–670.

People's Daily (2000a) 14 March, p. 1 (China becomes the ninth largest exporting nation in the world).

People's Daily (2000b) 'China's GDP surpasses the landmark of one trillion US dollars', 31 December 2000, p. 1.

People's Daily (2001) 'Shanghai's per capita GDP surpasses 4000 US dollars', 3 January 2001, p. 1.
Pomfret, R. (1997) 'Growth and transition: why has China's performance been so different?' *Journal of Comparative Economics*, 25, 422–440.
Radelet, S. and Sachs, D.J. (1998) 'The east Asian financial crisis: diagnosis, remedies, prospects', *Brooking Papers on Economic Activity*, 1, 1–90.
Rozelle, S. (1994) 'Rural industrialisation and increasing inequality: emerging patterns in China's reforming economy', *Journal of Comparative Economics*, 19, 362–391.
Romer, P. (1986) 'Increasing returns and long-run growth', *Journal of Political Economy*, 94(4), 1002–1037.
Sala-l-Martin, X.X. (1996) 'The classical approach to convergence analysis', *Economic Journal*, 106(July), 1019–1036.
Sengupta, J.K. and Espana, J.R. (1994) 'Exports and economic growth in Asian NICs: an econometric analysis for Korea', *Applied Economics*, 26, 342–357.
National Bureau of Statistics (NBS) 1996) *China Regional Economy: a Profile of 17 Years of Reform and Open-up* (Beijing: China Statistical Press).
National Bureau of Statistics (NBS) 1997–99), *Statistical Yearbook of China* (*various issues*) (Beijing: China Statistical Press).
US Department of Commerce, Economics and Statistics Administration, and Bureau of Census, *Statistical Abstract of the United States*, 1980–1996.
World Bank (1993) *The east Asian miracle* (Washington, DC: World Bank).
World Bank (1999) *World Development Indicators* (Washington, DC: World Bank).
Yao, S. (2000) 'Economic development and poverty reduction in China over 20 years of reforms', *Economic Development and Cultural Chang*, spring issue, 48(3), 447–474.
Yue, C.S. (1999) 'Trade, foreign direct investment and economic development of Southeast Asia', *The Pacific Review*, 12(2), 249–270.

13 Financing long-term care

A challenge to China's social welfare reform

Jane Zhang, Simon Gao and Shanyou Guo

Introduction

The issue of population ageing is currently high on the policy agenda in China, as it is elsewhere. Population ageing is the most significant demographic trend with far-reaching ramifications for the economy and social stability. It has earned the nickname 'the demographic time bomb'. In China, it is estimated by the World Bank that, by 2030, around 22 per cent of China's population of 1.2 billion will be over 60 years old (World Bank, 1997). In response to the prediction, the Chinese government needs to develop policies aimed at reducing the long-term financial consequences of this 'greying' of the population and at providing adequate pensions and resources for long-term care (LTC) to these elderly whenever they need it. The Chinese family-planning policy of 'one couple with one child (two plus one)' has driven the dilemma to a high level because China's current social policy is based on the assumption that a family is always available and willing to provide LTC for the elderly. Both the current demographic and household changes – and the economic and social reforms – in China have challenged this assumption.

The People's Republic of China has achieved significant improvement in health for its population since 1949. During the past 20 years, there has been a spectacular increase in life expectancy in China, brought about by a fall in the infant mortality rate. For example, in 1993, the country reduced infant mortality from 250 to 22 deaths per 1,000 live births and increased the average life expectancy from 35 to 69 years (*Chinese Yearbook of Health*, 1994). In 1998, China's life expectancy reached 71 (*Asiaweek*, 21 May 1999, p. 64).

Associated with the increase of life expectancy, there is also evidence that China's population is ageing. In 1949, there were 541.67 million people living on the mainland. The lack of controls and appropriate education on the subject of population, together with the improvement of people's living standards, led to a rapid increase in China's population, which had reached 806.71 million by 1969. Facing the serious problem of overpopulation, China has implemented family planning to control the population growth since the 1970s. The basic demands of family planning are late marriage and late childbirth – having fewer but healthier babies – specifically, one child for one couple.[1] As a result of this policy, the distribution of the population in China has recently shifted rapidly in both the number and proportion of the population aged 65 and over. This subgroup has grown faster than the rest of the population in the last two decades and expects to continue to grow at a more rapid rate into the twenty-first century. For example, in 1985, 5.3 per cent of the population was over the age of 65 in China and the population over the age of 65 was 55.57 million. In 1997, the percentage had risen to 7 per cent and the population over the age of 65 was 87.476 million (Liu, 1986; *China Statistical Yearbook*, 1998). The percentage of people over retirement age is forecast to rise to 21.9 per cent in 2030, according to the World Bank (1997).[2] Table 13.1 shows a projection of China's population and population ageing in the twenty-first century.

Academic researchers have devoted a considerable amount of attention to the ageing of the population across the world over the past 20 years, focusing in particular on the costs of health and LTC for the elderly (e.g. LTC is frequently characterised as a 'problem'). The discussions in the literature were often dominated by the issue of affordability and whether current levels of provision would be sustainable economically, socially and politically (e.g. Assous, 2001; Chen, 2001; Bernard and Phillips, 2000; Fine and Chalmers, 2000; Glendinning *et al.*, 1997; Richards and Coote, 1996; Baldwin, 1995; Clark, 1995; Hughes, 1995; Evers, 1994; Laing, 1993; Glendinning, 1992; Arber and Ginn, 1990). Most of those studies are predominantly concerned with LTC experience and circumstances from developed countries. The literature has recognised that population ageing has important and profound economic effects, including a significant impact on savings, and there has been a shortage of funds to finance LTC in many of these developed countries (e.g. James, 1997; World Bank, 1994). The situation in developing nations is much worse. Although China will be one of the most rapidly ageing societies in the next 30 years, relatively little is known about the current status of LTC and LTC financial provision.

Table 13.1 Population and population ageing in China

Year	*2000*	*2030*	*2050*	*2100*
The number of population* (100 million)	13	15.8	14	13.5
Proportion of population over age 60[t]	10	22	26	30
Demographic dependency rate[a,t]	18	43	53	63
Average age of population[t]	31	38	40	42

Note
*Authors' estimate, based on the government reports released on 8 May, 2000.
t Based on Friedman *et al.* (1996, p. 37).
a Population over age 60/population aged 20–59.

Whilst China is currently undertaking social-welfare reform, research has yet to provide theoretical underpinnings for the formulation of policy on sustainable social and economic growth. This study attempts to examine the need for LTC as a major social and economic problem facing the Chinese government in the twenty-first century, and it analyses various options of financing long-term care in China. Among those options, LTC social insurance has been specifically examined, focusing on its advantages and applicability to China. It suggests that LTC social insurance, with contributions from individuals (through a tax on savings income), employers (through a business tax) and the state (by reallocating state social-welfare funds) should be adopted by the Chinese government.

The remainder of this chapter is organised as follows. The next section is concerned with the need for LTC in China and the challenges facing the Chinese authorities. The section after discusses financial options for LTC including provident funds, employer liability, social assistance and LTC insurance. The fourth section specifically considers LTC social assurance and its applicability in China. Conclusions are given in the final chapter.

Long-term care and challenges to China

The US Department of Health and Human Services (1981) defined LTC as representing:

> a range of services that address the health, social and personal care needs of individuals who, for one reason or another have never developed or have lost some capacity for self care. Services may be continuous or intermittent, but it is generally presumed that they will be delivered for the 'long-term', that is indefinitely to individuals who have demonstrated need, usually measured by some index of functional incapacity.

In theory, the need for LTC is usually associated with the degree of dependency (functional incapacity). However, dependency is a subjective notion whose definition and scope are based on criteria that vary from one individual to the next (Blondeau and Dubois, 1997, p. 49). For example, dependency can be described as a chronic risk in the sense that a person remains autonomous up to a certain age and thereafter requires the help of another person for the performance of many daily activities. A person ceases to be autonomous when the person ceases to be able to perform these everyday acts alone: for example, taking a bath; getting dressed and undressed; washing, combing their hair, shaving; standing up, lying down, sitting down, moving about; going to the toilet; eating and drinking. A number of countries have set up laws to specify the level of dependency. In Germany, the dependence law divides essential activities into four separate categories: personal hygiene (washing, combing the hair, shaving,

Table 13.2 The percentage of handicapped persons increases with age

Age	*Percentage of handicapped persons (all degrees)*
70	7
80	10
90	40
95	65

Source: Blondeau and Dubois (1997, p. 49).

going to the toilet), feeding (eating and drinking), movement (getting up, lying down, getting dressed and undressed, walking, climbing the stairs, going out), housework (shopping, cleaning, doing the washing). Each category is assessed in terms of dependency and the level of care provision is accordingly determined by the level of dependency. The degree of dependency generally increases with age as shown in Table 13.2. Although the percentage varies across countries, dependency provision has become unavoidable for the majority of people in old age.

The Council of Europe estimates that the dependent account, on average, for from 12 to 18 per cent of the population over 65 years old. At present, across the EU, there are more than four people of working age on average to support each person aged 65 or over. By 2030 the average support ratio will have declined to scarcely over two. Most European countries run aid schemes for the elderly which are, as a rule, tied in with other services provided under pension or handicap-allowance schemes, or through social assistance systems, or again as exceptions to services that were not originally designed to benefit the dependent elderly (Blondeau and Dubois, 1997, p. 52). The cost of LTC is expected to increase in the future as a result of the increasing elderly population across the world. Clearly, care for the dependent requires substantial financial resources from both society and individuals, even when care is provided within families.[3]

As a developing country, China is unquestionably facing mounting national problems in financing and delivering adequate social welfare programmes (in particular, retirement pensions and LTC) to its population, which is simultaneously both growing larger and getting older. At present, less than 30 per cent of the total 1.2 billion Chinese population are covered by rural means-tested pension programmes, which are predominantly administrated and financed at the village level; or by rural pension programmes organised by village enterprises in wealthier rural areas; or by the government-run urban labour-insurance system. Families have provided more than three-quarters of all LTC for the elderly in China. This has been part of Chinese tradition, influenced by Confucianism and Taoism. Elderly people normally prefer to be cared for at their own homes by their own family relatives, and family members have a moral and statutory responsibility for looking after their elderly parents.

However, this tradition has been challenged since China's economic reform towards a market economy in the early 1980s. Changing socio-economic patterns in China have had significant impacts on families' ability to care – both in kind and through financial support. As a result of the economic reform, the pattern of work in China, particularly in urban areas, is becoming less stable – contract work, periods of unemployment, layoffs and early retirement are all on the increase while job security and continuity are on the wane. The change of work patterns and reduction in job security have put severe pressure on the family and its ability to provide care for the elderly. Women in their middle years, who have traditionally provided much of the care at home, may have changing aspirations, a need to secure their own economic positions and are in the labour market. The current huge layoffs as a result of state-enterprise reforms might appear to increase the provision workers for family care. However, the financial burden caused by reduced income resulting from layoffs may also force those laid-off to search for other employment opportunities or to take part in skill-retraining and education, which may reduce the supply of family carers.

In the next 30 years, there is likely to be a growing 'care gap' in China between the needs of elderly people and the supply of carers from their families. This is because: (1) the decline in fertility and the 'one couple with one child' policy in China mean that the generation who are going to be in their 70s in the near future will have fewer children than any previous generation. As a result, there will be less family carers available. (2) Many Chinese people will not have families to support them in the future because they are single or because their child is far away from them as a result of work, migration or marriage.[4] (3) Family breakdown and the change of marriage patterns are likely to have an impact on the future availability of carers. Recent trends show increasing age at first marriage and birth of first child, decreasing marriage rates, increasing divorce and remarriage rates, and a big increase in cohabiting couples.[5] (4) The increased involvement of married women in the labour market and self-employment – in 1996 over 80 per cent of married women aged 25–35 and 90 per cent of those aged 35–54 were economically active (*China Statistical Yearbook*, 1997) – will reduce their commitment to home care. (5) The rising cost of living makes it difficult for families to support the elderly. The need to pay towards further and higher education for the only child and towards personal pensions puts increasing demands on family budgets and may well have a significant effect on the capacity of families to have the time, energy and resources to provide the care. In urban areas, smaller apartments make it harder for adult children to share accommodation with their parents. In the countryside, where most Chinese live, adult children are expected to take care of their parents. However, as more rural young people seek their fortunes in the cities, this traditional care system could weaken. Community care, which is available only in the urban areas, does not take people from rural areas and the countryside (Chen, 1996).

Apparently, Chinese people are confronted with two coexistent and sometimes incompatible facts. On the one hand, there is the moral and natural desire of the family to minister generously to the needs and comfort of old age; on the other hand, the burden of maintaining the aged may become so great as to result in a lowering of the standard of living of the family. The majority of elderly people do not have resources to pay for their own care in later life, particularly if they need intensive personal health and social care (Chen, 1996).[6] However, the government lacks resources to respond (Silverman, 1995). The problem is currently demanding the attention of a wide range of institutions from the government, enterprises and individuals. It is expected that the government will have a key role to play in addressing the issue and managing the problem. However, the question remains as to how the government will be able to tackle this difficult problem.

Financing long-term care

Financing LTC will become an important social and economic issue facing every country in the world. It is well argued that the methods used to finance LTC services have considerable impacts on the use of care services by the elderly and their level of health and well-being, as well as on the growth and development of the care sector itself (Chen, 2001). In addition, the methods used to finance LTC services influence the distribution of income between the sick and the well, the old and the young, the general public (who are supposed to be taxpayers) and the recipients of care. Moreover, the provision of LTC is associated with the financial resources of individuals and the economic development of a particular country. Therefore, the means of financing LTC may have contrasting effects on the behaviour of society and households. As Harding *et al.* (1996) argue, a framework of values and principles is needed to inform the debate about funding options. Glennerster (1996) suggests four basic objectives that need to be considered in seeking to develop a secure system of financing LTC, including: (1) people reaching retirement should be secure in the knowledge that they do not face catastrophic costs or stressful burdens on their families; (2) the care they receive should be an agreed and integrated pattern of services and family support, and not dominated by a set of perverse institutional and financial incentives; (3) claims on public and private budgets should be sustainable; and (4) individual savings should be encouraged, not deterred (Glennerster, 1996, p. 19).

Of particular concern to LTC financing is the relationship between the elderly and the working population. In the next 25 years, the elderly dependency ratio (population aged 60 and above divided by population aged 15–59) will increase significantly in China. This increased dependency means that a declining share of the adult population will be available as contributors for financing the needs of an increasingly elderly population.

This has implications for the viability of all financing techniques for fulfilling long-term contingency needs. Elderly protection now absorbs a significant share of overall social security expenditures in China (ILO, 1993). This suggests that frequent assessments of demographic trends are essential to guide periodic adjustments in resource allocation and benefits for social welfare to ensure long-term financial stability and intergenerational equity in financing the needs of the elderly – both pensions and LTC.

There has been a considerable debate about the economic and social advantages of the cradle-to-grave protection system and the user-pays mechanism. Part of the problem in the debate lies in the difficulty of identifying the cost of LTC, how it may change and under what circumstances people need LTC. It is argued that what people actually need depends on their living conditions, social and family relationships, their financial circumstances, cultural backgrounds, their own preferences and aspirations as well as their physical or mental conditions. In an industrialised society, two main arguments are commonly advanced for the introduction of user-pays principles and practices in areas such as health and aged care. The first concerns the general advantages and benefits entailed in the operation of market mechanisms. The second arises from the need to raise revenue, either to pay for provisions directly, or to raise revenue for other purposes (Fine and Chalmers, 2000, pp. 11–12). Self (1993) argues that the introduction of user-pays principles serves two objectives. First, it slims the state and introduces market forces in a variety of ways, such as deregulation and through monetary and fiscal policy. Second, it introduces market concepts and incentives into the operations of government itself (Self, 1993, p. 59).

The four basic methods available to finance LTC – namely, provident funds, employer liability, social assistance and insurance – have their advantages and limitations in terms of specific features, scope and uses. Compulsory national provident funds usually provide for gratuity or pensions on retirement, or in case of invalidity or death prior to retirement. Compulsory national provident funds have the advantage that they force individual and family savings and place the responsibility for financial preparation for old age care with individuals themselves. They can thus avoid the necessity either of an increasingly higher rate of contributions under a social-insurance method of financing or of long periods of contributions into fully-funded schemes during which no benefits are paid. The provident fund has the further advantage of being withdrawable in part or in full for financing housing, business initiatives or other needs of members. It also provides governments with access to substantial resources for development. The disadvantage of a provident fund is that there is no pooling of risks as under social insurance, and the usual lump-sum payments from provident fund accumulations do not guarantee a periodic payment throughout the length of LTC. Although China is one of the highest-saving nations in the world, economic uncertainty, along with rising living costs and increasing education and medical care expenses, is likely to exhaust the vast amount of savings of individuals before many reach their retirement age. The current inequality in income and savings between the rich and the poor makes the provident funds scheme difficult to operate, as it may exclude the urban poor and many rural residents (about 20 to 60 per cent of the total population) who do not have regular income and savings.

Employer-liability schemes are relatively simple and a faster method of introducing benefits for LTC to their retired employees. However, employers may find it costly and to their disadvantage in a competitive business world, particularly because of the differing incidence of the liability for financing LTC across business sectors internally and internationally. In addition, cash benefits under employer-liability schemes are frequently inadequate to cover care costs. Very often, employer liability is difficult to substantiate and consequently benefits fail to materialise. This option will be difficult to apply in China, because state-owned enterprises have already been burdened with a number of social responsibilities, including housing for their employees, schools (at present, there are over 18,000 schools with 600,000 teachers and staff), factory hospitals and clinics (over 110,000) which, it is argued, should not be shouldered by enterprises (Hu, 1996; World Bank Country Study, 1997; and Zhu, 1999). These enterprises are no longer capable of sustaining their business survival if more burdens are added. At the moment, most of the enterprises are loss-making and thus it is impossible for them to cover the liability of financing the LTC of their retired employees. In addition, the employer-liability approach appears to be difficult to operate in China, as the majority of its population live in the countryside and have never had a formal employment contract.

China has operated various levels of social assistance to the elderly since the establishment of the People's Republic. The provision of such assistance was mainly through employers' contributions from special funds, trade unions and governmental welfare departments. There was no formal system for the assistance; it was based on individual cases. The coverage of such assistance is quite limited. Obviously, limited public revenue poses problems for any substantial expansion of publicly financed schemes of social assistance. For a country with a population of over 1.2 billion it will be extremely difficult (if not impossible) to establish and operate a social assistance scheme – whether it is universal or means-tested. China is a developing country with a constraint on resources; therefore, social assistance for LTC can only be sought as an auxiliary option.

With regard to LTC, not everyone will require such care, but when people do it can be very expensive. In fact, the need for LTC is a risk that may carry with it substantial, even catastrophic, financial consequences to an individual or his or her family, but it actually occurs only to a relatively small and predictable proportion of persons in a population at any one time (Chen, 2001, p. 657). In a sense, this is the perfect 'insurable' event, in which the risks ought to be shared across a large group, an observation leading to advocacy of LTC insurance. Nevertheless, the private sector across the world has been slow to develop such insurance, despite a well-demonstrated need. Social insurance, which can extend to cover most contingencies, enables a sharing of risks and resources among state, individuals and employers, and is widely used throughout the world. It remains an option, although not a substitute for all other options. The next section is specifically concerned with this option.

Long-term care insurance and its applicability to China

The basic requirement of insurance is the ability to spread the risk and costs across a large pool of persons or entities so that no one person has a more significant burden than another (Silver, 1999). Chen (2001) and Fine and Chalmers (2000) argue that insurance, for governments as for individuals, represents the most attractive and viable way in which potential service users can be enabled to pay for their care. Over time, insurance contributions have the virtue that they also provide a simple savings mechanism, with individuals making contributions in measured amounts at a time in their lives when it spreads risk amongst a larger pool of potential beneficiaries, reducing the amount that each individual may be required to put aside.

For LTC insurance, two types of insurance operate in various countries: private insurance and social/national insurance. Private LTC insurance has been developed in the US and recently in the UK, paralleling other social assistance schemes. In the US, however, 'it has not yet become a significant form of financing long-term care' (Friedland, 1997). In the UK, the Royal Commission on LTC in a recent report suggests that private LTC insurance policies are unlikely to become universally affordable; people are reluctant to take out private LTC insurance, and the market does not want to offer policies to all (Royal Commission, 1999). Less than 1 per cent of households in the UK where the head is aged 55 or over has a LTC policy (ABI, 2000, p. 56).

Fine and Chalmers (2000) observe that private LTC insurance has proved neither popular nor successful in both countries. This is because private insurers are cautious about marketing products where the liabilities will not be known for many years. Private insurance requires insurers to operate conservatively so they are certain to have the resources to pay benefits in the future. This conservative policy, combined with the costs of marketing and selling largely to individuals – with the resultant marketing and advertising costs – may make the price too high for many individuals. Furthermore, private insurers often offer coverage only to individuals in good health at the time of enrolment. In addition to people with current disability, individuals with hypertension, arthritis, any history of heart disease, diabetes or recent hospitalisations may be screened out. As yet, there is little evidence that such factors are actually good indicators of later need for LTC, but nonetheless individuals with such medical histories are unlikely to be able to purchase individual LTC insurance policies. Thus, there will always be gaps left by private insurance provision.

In contrast, social insurance represents an important funding mechanism for LTC in a number of countries, including the Netherlands, Germany, Israel and, more recently, Japan. Table 13.3 provides a simple comparison of LTC insurance between private and social provisions. LTC insurance represents a form of user payment that spreads the costs of contributions among a large pool of potential beneficiaries over a period of many years (Fine and Chalmers, 2000, p. 25). Social insurance is a defined-benefit system, leaving contributions to be determined as required (Lyer, 1993). The pooling of risks and resources (i.e. redistribution) within any given generation is implicit in a fully-funded model for social insurance. The principle can extend to include an element of intergeneration redistribution. This permits a choice of funding methods within a wide range. There are many variations in methods within this range for financing LTC social insurance, but any funding method will necessarily lead to the accumulation of reserves, which could be invested to produce income to supplement contributions. This needs to be accompanied by an ongoing process of evaluation to ensure sustainability by balancing incoming and outgoing funds. With a rise in the elderly dependency ratio, the rates of contributions may have to be substantially adjusted upwards to meet

Table 13.3 A comparison of LTC private and social insurance

Private LTC insurance	*Social/national LTC insurance*
USA – Dependency insurance 1970s	The Netherlands – Algemene Wet Bijzondere Ziektekosten 1967 (the Exceptional Medical Expenses Act)
UK – in the 1990s	Germany – The Law on Dependency in the Elderly 1994
	Israel – The Community Long Term Care Insurance Law 1988
	Japan – The Long Term Care Insurance Bill, effective from 2000
Common features	Common features
(1) Selected targets (insured and coverage).	(1) The emphasis is given on care in the home.
(2) High premium.	(2) Clearly defined, limited to the entitlements.
	(3) Cash allowances payment, rather than providing services.
	(4) A minimum amount is guaranteed, while insufficient to meet real needs, does leave room for complementary cover.
	(5) Contribution range: 0.2% to 5% of gross salary.

increased payment requirements placed upon the fund to ensure its stability. Normally, social insurance schemes need to be 'actuarially valued' at intervals of three to five years in order to introduce adjustments to contribution rates (Lyer, 1993). Another way of dealing with the problem is to postpone the age of retirement in order to reduce demand on the pension system, thus resulting in more contributions to LTC insurance. It is argued (for example, by Chen, 2001) that LTC social insurance is the most persuasive approach available, because it combines the force of government and the private providers, offering affordable costs to individuals, enterprises and the government. However, the government's role is normally as organiser, regulator and guarantor of the provision of basic cover, but not necessarily as the provider of services.

In Chen's (2001) view, a good funding method in the US needs to be found by (a) more widespread use of the insurance principle for both private- and public-sector programmes, and (b) linking several sources of funds in each sector that already exist so as to increase the efficiency with which these resources may be used. Chen (2001, p. 656), therefore, proposes a 'three-legged stool' funding model, consisting of social insurance, private insurance, and personal savings. We argue that, presently, China does not have a sound basis for developing LTC private insurance. This is because, on the one hand, the capital market in China is still unsophisticated and financial operators have little experience in long-term finance and insurance management. Even though China has newly joined the WTO, Chinese insurers still have a long way to go in building up the capability of developing LTC insurance products and gaining marketing experience. On the other hand, many families in China cannot afford to purchase such private LTC coverage. Financial resources and asset value (e.g. property) are low and these families would effectively be lowering their standards of living for many years to purchase benefits that may not protect them over time. Therefore, a public component must be at least part of the solution if China wants to expand the availability of LTC private insurance services for low and moderate-income individuals. At a minimum, considerable expansions of social insurance, contributed by the government, would be necessary to fill the gaps left by a private insurance provision.

Taking into account the current development of the Chinese economy and social-welfare system, we argue that China should adopt social-insurance schemes by imposing compulsory contributions from employers, individuals and the state. Table 13.4 shows suggested LTC social-insurance contribution proportions and funding sources.

With regard to personal contributions, we argue that the individual contributions through wage deductions, as operated in most western societies, will be difficult to apply in China because (1) in many cases wages are paid in cash and goods; and (2) the vast majority of the population in the rural areas do not have regular wages and many of them cannot afford to pay

Table 13.4 Suggested LTC social insurance contribution and source

Contributors	*Proportion**	*Means of souring*
Individuals	1/3	A special LTC tax on savings income
Employers	1/3	From rising business tax
State/government	1/3	Shared by social security and welfare funds and state pension funds

*The proportion of contributions can be adjusted, based on the economic development and the change of population structure in the future.

the contributions. Therefore, we suggest levying LTC tax on savings income as an alternative to deduction from wages. This will guarantee contributions from individuals and households. This is because, since the 1970s, China has achieved a significant growth of national savings and the savings rate is ranked among the highest in the world. These savings accounted for more than 35 per cent of the country's gross national product and reached a total of RMB 5.91 trillion (US$712 billion) by 1999 (*China Daily*, 1999). A special tax levied on savings income retains the advantages of both means-tested and pay-as-you-earn (save) pensions, and it will not impose an additional burden on those people who cannot afford. It may be argued that taxes on savings would adversely affect saving behaviour and discourage people from savings and investment. However, a report on consumer confidence, released on 22 October 1999 by the National Bureau of Statistics, shows that 60 per cent of the consumers surveyed indicated that the interest tax would not affect their tendency to save (CBIN, 1999). For most households, depositing money in a bank is not just to earn interest. The money is typically set aside for children's education and marriage, housing and rainy days. Therefore, this source of contribution, based on a tax on savings income, is expected to be sustainable. Unquestionably, an LTC tax on savings income would also create other operational problems. For example, there would be a need to clarify the scope of taxation and consider whether other non-traditional savings income (e.g. from investments, bonds, mutual funds, or insurance policies) should be taxed. There would also be a need to determine whether savings income should be levied at a flat or at a progressive rate. Obviously, a progressive tax would serve much better than a flat rate tax to narrow the contribution-burden gap between the rich and the poor because those with more savings income would be taxed at a higher rate. However, a progressive tax requires a comprehensive collection and supervision system, which China has not yet established. Therefore, a flat rate is to be recommended at the initial stage of the practice.

An employer's contribution of one third could expect to be guaranteed from levying employers, while the government also contributes one third, possibly by reallocating some social welfare funds and investing part of the pension fund accumulated. From our point of view, if the equity and cost-containment aspects of LTC have to be improved, a new balance of responsibility in LTC has to be developed between the state, enterprises, individuals and LTC users in China, and a basic LTC provision should be extended to the whole population irrespective of where they live, where they work and their status. The provision of a common legislative and administrative framework for extending basic LTC benefits to the whole population, and yet allowing variations and differences along geographical and employment lines is a major challenge for health-care and social welfare reforms, even beyond the next 50 years. Of course, it is difficult to draw a line to determine what is 'basic' and what is not. As a result, it is worthwhile having further policy debate and academic research.

LTC insurance can possibly be linked with health-care insurance and established as an integrated health insurance system providing protection for the health and LTC of the population. In this aspect, the government can play two important roles to improve the equity in both health care and LTC. First, instead of allowing the well-off cities and rural areas to experiment continually with health-insurance innovations, which are characterised by the variation of the extent of coverage and scope and different financing, management and reimbursement mechanisms, the state should seriously consider the option of providing a basic legislation infrastructure in setting up health and LTC insurance on a country-wide basis. The target groups should not only include civil servants, workers, and self-employed persons but also their dependants. The state should recognise that citizens' access to basic health and LTC is their basic right. Currently, different health insurance schemes are administered under different departments or bureaux. Therefore, an extension of basic health insurance to the whole population has to go along with a restructuring and simplifying of the administrative mechanism in running health-insurance schemes.

Second, there is an urgent need for the authorities to redefine the role of the state in health care, particularly in rural health care within the context of a market economy, as deprived people and poor areas, particularly in rural China, usually find themselves unable to afford even a modest health-insurance package. In view of this, different levels of government – central, provincial and local – have the responsibility for redistributing financial resources from well-off areas to poorer areas and to enable the latter to establish a health and LTC insurance scheme. The suggested imposition of a tax on savings income appears to be an effective means of achieving this redistribution.

In social insurance, however, the high level of mandatory contributions may cause many individuals and employers to seek ways and means of reducing what they pay to the system. These avoidance strategies may result in the continued importance of the grey zone of the economy. Introducing and sequencing LTC insurance in China will demand significant time resources and political determination against vested interests. LTC insurance and pension funds are a significant part of a market economy and take considerable time to develop. Their close dependence on financial stability and on the emergence of institutions that bolster capital–market efficiency account for the need for considered crafting of such reforms (EBRD, 1997, p. 87). In addition, special attention needs to be given to those living in the countryside who do not have regular income. Financial viability is critically important for financing LTC schemes in any form. The long-term sustainability of the accumulated reserves of social-insurance schemes is a major concern throughout the world. Sound policies relating to investments of accumulated revenues are of critical importance to viability.

Conclusions

Owing to the increased life expectancy and the family planning policy of 'one couple having only one child', China is facing severe pressure from an ageing population, and this is expected to lead to a slow down of the country's economic development in the twenty-first century. Unless the government can tackle this problem soon, the problem will risk tipping the country into a social crisis and dragging economic growth down for many years to come.

In the face of growing pressures from its ageing population, China is grappling with social-welfare and security reform. The state pension and social-security system has run into financial difficulties and has come to pose a large financial burden on state-owned enterprises. The question facing policymakers is how to reform the social-security system in the context of the current enterprise reformation, and how to finance the increasing demand on resources for pensions and care of aged dependants. There is a growing recognition that better approaches are needed for financing LTC in the current period of demographic transition towards an ageing society.

This chapter has discussed the need for LTC as a major social and economic problem facing the Chinese government in the twenty-first century, and has analysed various options for financing LTC. Among those options, LTC insurance has been specifically examined, with a focus on its advantages and applicability to China. In our view, LTC social insurance, contributed by individuals through levying an LTC tax on savings income, on enterprises through business tax, and on the state through the reallocation of social welfare funds, is a relatively practicable option available to China for pooling resources to finance LTC for the elderly in the new century. It combines the force of government, individuals and enterprises. The issues brought up in this chapter are of potential interest both to China's policymakers in social welfare reform and to actors in the private sector who are interested in the provision of long-term care. It is also likely that there will be an increasing debate in the future on a number of issues related to LTC in China. LTC and solutions to providing it are multidimensional. It is a problem that is growing, rather than dissipating. In China, the socialist cradle-to-grave protection is no longer available to people. An alternative protection system needs to be established that is expected to provide sufficient resources to cover the living costs of the elderly and the costs of LTC if they need it. Truly, this is a great challenge for the Chinese authorities as they reform their social-welfare system in the next decade.

Notes

1 In rural areas, a couple who are short of labour force or have other difficulties may have a second baby, but must wait several years after the birth of the first child. In areas inhabited by minority peoples, a couple may have more children. But the new rules released by the Government on 7 May 2000 require the minorities to implement family planning as well.

2 The World Bank reports that 140 years elapsed in France before the proportion of the population over age 60 doubled to 18 per cent in 1976. But because of its one-child policy and improved health care, China will take just 34 years. By 2030, the World Bank reckons 21.9 per cent of China's population will be over 60 – a higher percentage than any country in the world, other than Sweden by the start of that decade.

3 In the US, for example, families involved in the care of the elderly spend about $2 billion per month of their own money to provide care (Silver, 1999). In the UK, the current spending on LTC is estimated at £12 billion per annum, which is around 1.5 per cent of GDP. The cost is expected to increase to £45 billion by 2051, according to the estimates by the Personal Social Services Research Unit at the University of Kent.

4 The current gender imbalance in China, caused by selective abortion, excess mortality and missing girls, implies that many men will have to accept bachelorhood forever. By 2020, the surplus of Chinese males in their 20s will exceed the entire female population of Taiwan, according to the OECD (OECD Observer, 1999).

5 According to a survey by the Institute of Social Science of China in 1997, there is a trend for women to get married later (26–35) compared with ten years ago (22–28 years). The divorce rate in China has been increased significantly since the open door policy and economic reform in 1978. In some areas the divorce rate reached 20 per cent.

6 There is going to be little change in this in the next 30 years since the majority of the elderly, particularly those over the age of 70, will be women who had much lower incomes than men in their working life.

References

ABI (Association of British Insurers) (2000) *Insurance – Facts, Figures and Trends* (London: November).

Arber, S. and Ginn, J. (1990) 'The meaning of informal care: gender and the contribution of elderly people', *Ageing and Society*, 10, 429–454.

Assous, L. (2001) 'Long-term health and social care for the elderly: an international perspective', *The Geneva Papers on Risk and Insurance*, 26(4), 667–683.

Baldwin, S. (1995) 'Love and money: the financial consequences of caring for an older relative'. In I. Allen and E. Perkins (eds), *The Future of Family Care for Older People* (London: HMSO).

Bernard, M. and Phillips, J. (2000) 'The challenge of ageing in tomorrow's Britain', *Ageing and Society*, 20, 33–54.
Blondeau, J. and Dubois, D. (1997) 'Financing old-age dependency in Europe: towards overall management of old-age', *The Geneva Papers on Risk and Insurance*, 22(2), 46–59.
CBIN (China Business Information Network) (1999) 'Interest rate expected to have little impact on consumption', 25 October.
Chen, S. (1996) *Social Policy of the Economic State and Community Care in Chinese Culture* (Aldershot: Avebury).
Chen, Y.-P. (2001) 'Funding long-term care in the United States: the role of private insurance', *The Geneva Papers on Risk and Insurance*, 26(4), 656–666.
China Daily (1999) 'Tax on savings interest helps economic growth', September.
China Statistical Yearbook (1997, 1998) (Beijing: China Statistical Publishing House).
Chinese Yearbook of Health (1994) in Chinese (Beijing: Health Publishing Houses).
Clark, L. (1995) 'Family care and changing family structure: bad news for the elderly?' In I. Allen and E. Perkins (eds), *The Future of Family Care* (London: HMSO).
EBRD (European Bank for Reconstruction and Development) (1997) *Transition Report 1996. Infrastructure and Savings* (London: EBRD).
Evers, A. (1994) 'Payments for care: a small but significant part of a wider debate'. In A. Evers, M. Pijl and C. Ungerson (eds), *Payments for Care; a Comparative Overview* (Vienna: European Centre; Aldershot: Avebury).
Fine, M. and Chalmers, J. (2000) '"User pays" and other approaches to the funding of long-term care for older people in Australia', *Ageing and Society*, 20, 5–32.
Friedland, R.B. (1997) 'Financing long-term care'. In D.M. Fox and C. Raphael (eds), *Home-Based Care for a New Century* (Malden, MA: Milbank Memorial Fund and Blackwell).
Friedman, B., James, E, Kane, C. and Queisser, M. (1996) *How Cane China Provide Income Security for Its Rapidly Aging Population?* Policy Research Working Paper 1674 (Washington, DC: The World Bank).
Glendinning, C. (1992) *The Costs of Informal Care: Looking Inside the Household* (London: HMSO).
Glendinning, C., Schunk, M. and McLaughlin, E. (1997) 'Paying for long-term domiciliary care: a comparative perspective', *Ageing and Society*, 17, 123–140.
Glennerster, H. (1996) *Caring for the Very Old: Public and Private Solutions*. Discussion Paper WSP/126, Suntory, and Toyota International Centres for Economic and Related Disciplines (London: London School of Economics and Political Science).
Harding, T., Meredith, B. and Wistow, G. (1996) 'Options for long term care: economic, social and ethical choices'. In T. Harding, B. Meredith and G. Wistow (eds), *Options For Long Term Care* (London: HMSO).
Hu, X.Y. (1996) 'Reducing state-owned enterprises' social burdens and establishing a social insurance system'. In H.G. Broadman (ed.), *Policy Options for Reform of Chinese State-Owned Enterprises,* World Bank Discussion Paper, No. 335, 125–148.
Hughes, B. (1995) *Older People and Community Care* (Buckingham: Open University Press).

International Labour Office (ILO) (1992) *The Cost of Social Security: Thirteenth International Inquiry, 1984–1986* (Geneva: ILO).

International Labour Office (ILO) (1993) *Report to the Government of the People's Republic of China on Social Security Reform* (Geneva: ILO).

James, E. (1997) *New Systems for Old Age Security – Theory, Practice and Empirical Evidence.* World Bank Policy Research Working Papers, No. 1766.

Laing, W. (1993) *Financing Long-Term Care: the Crucial Debate* (London: Age Concern).

Liu, W.T. (1986) *China Social Statistics 1986* (People's Republic of China: China Statistical Publishing House).

Lyer, S.N. (1993) *Pension Reform in Developing Countries*, Social Security Department, International Labour Office, May.

OECD Observer (1999) 'China, a demographic time bomb', *The OECS Observer*, Summer, 217/218: 31–32.

Richards, E. and Coote, A. (1996) *Paying for Long Term Care* (London: Institute for Public Policy Research).

Royal Commission on Long Term Care (1999) *With Respect to Old Age: Long Term Care – Rights and Responsibilities*, Cm419201 (London: The Stationery Office).

Self, P. (1993) *Government by the Market? The Politics of Public Choice* (London: Macmillan).

Silver, I. (1999) 'Long-term care: alternative solutions,' *Compensation and Benefits Review*, 31(6), 55–58.

Silverman, G. (1995) 'Promises, promises', *Far Eastern Economic Review*, 2 March p. 54.

United States Department of Health and Human Services (1981) *A Government Report on Long-term Care* (Washington, DC: US Department of Health and Human Services).

World Bank (1994) *Averting the Old Age Crisis: Policies to Protect the Old and Promote Growth* (Washington, DC: World Bank and Oxford University Press).

World Bank Country Study (1997) *China's Management of Enterprise Assets: the State as Shareholder* (Washington, DC: World Bank).

World Bank (1997) *China 2020* (Washington, DC: World Bank).

Zhu, T. (1999) 'China's corporatisation drive: an evaluation and policy implications,' *Contemporary Economic Policy*, 17(4), 530–539.

14 Micro-intervention for poverty reduction

The case of Guizhou, China

Ajit S. Bhalla and Shufang Qiu

Introduction

In most developing countries, anti-poverty policies and programmes are designed to alleviate poverty by targeting assistance through credit or jobs to the poor who may not otherwise benefit from normal programmes. There are three main views concerning anti-poverty policies and programmes. First, rapid economic growth is the best means of poverty reduction, although some public intervention may be necessary to make sure that the fruits of growth are widely shared. Second, measures may need to be designed to alleviate poverty directly. Third, even if direct measures are introduced, the damaging effects of poverty in terms of poor health, nutrition and education may not be addressed. Therefore, special action may be necessary to overcome the adverse *indirect* effects of poverty (Lipton, 1998). During China's reform period (1978–to date) economic growth rates were very impressive and, at least until 1995, poverty was considerably reduced. However, despite a decline in the proportion of the population below the poverty line, a substantial number of people, especially in rural areas, have remained absolutely poor.

In this chapter, we present a case study of Guizhou, one of the poorest provinces in south-west China. The choice of Guizhou is guided by several considerations: the existence of acute absolute poverty, a substantial minority population and limited Western literature on the province. Guizhou, located in the south west, is one of the poorest provinces of China. Guizhou accounted for 5.3 per cent of China's rural poor in 1988 and 7.6 per cent in 1996. Between 1988 and 1995, the incidence of poverty based on the headcount ratio, rose from 58 per cent to nearly 62 per cent. The poverty gap ratio declined only slightly, from 21 per cent to 19 per cent (Khan and Riskin, 2001).

Three main micro interventions for poverty reduction are discussed and assessed, namely, the food-for-work programme (FFW), the micro-credit programme and the labour mobility programme.[1] As the poverty situation in Guizhou remains acute, it is important to analyse the impact of various government measures adopted to reduce poverty.

Micro-interventions for poverty reduction in Guizhou

In this section we analyse the impact of anti-poverty policies and programmes. Table 14.1 shows the per capita poverty alleviation fund (PAF) in 1990 and 1997 for the poor counties in Guizhou. More detailed official statistics not presented here show that, since 1993, subsidized credit allocation has been growing much more rapidly than the other two funds of poverty alleviation. The FFW funding has flattened out, which suggests that the grant element in total poverty alleviation (RAF) funds has

Table 14.1 Guizhou: rural per capita accumulated PAF (1990–1997, yuan)

	1990		*1997*
Xifeng	270.35	Jianhe	429.04
Panxian	225.91	Taijiang	459.92
Liuzhi special zone	214.40	Liping	188.03
Shuicheng	352.84	Rongjiang	358.12
Zheng'an	203.32	Congjiang	404.65
Wuchuan	405.67	Leishan	524.86
Fenggang	272.81	Majiang	284.93
Xishui	132.24	Danzai	569.08
Shiqian	268.24	Libo	424.31
Yinjiang	299.76	Dushan	256.20
Dejiang	388.49	Pingtang	262.71
Yanhe	268.34	Luodian	903.05
Suntao	149.09	Changshun	522.86
Xingren	246.33	*Sandu*	395.47
Pu'an	416.57	Xiuwen	39.06
Qinglong	340.62	Zhongshan District	215.25
Zhenfeng	402.04	*Daozheng*	96.44
Wangmo	461.99	Chishui	15.69
Ceting	515.44	Tongchuan City	141.07
Anlun	210.82	Jiangkuo	61.23
Dafang	165.67	*Yuping*	89.29
Zhijin	146.86	Sinan	24.30
Nayong	200.78	Wanshan special zone	144.82
Weining	137.61	Bijie city	49.54
Hezhang	235.54	Qianxi	60.79
Puding	204.75	Anshun city	20.00
Guanling	339.62	Pingba	26.88
Zhengning	472.77	Kaili	201.04
Ziyun	378.47	Zhenyuan	137.86
Huangping	454.52	Jingping	57.23
Shibing	270.96	Fuquan	
Shanshui	220.67	Guiding	
Chenggu	285.57	Lunli	
Tianzhu	191.95	Huishui	47.33

Source: Based on data supplied by the Poverty Alleviation Office, Guizhou Province, Guiyang.

Note
Minority counties are in italics.

become less important. A shift in priority is based on the assumption that grants create disincentives. Although the percentage shares of subsidized loans, FFW fund and budgetary grants did not change much between 1990 and 1997, in absolute terms the annual total PAF increased dramatically for Guizhou's 48 poor counties, from 181.7 million yuan to 1314 yuan, or an increase of over 632 per cent.

Table 14.2 ranks poor counties in ascending order of rural per capita net income. We choose the poorest of the poor counties, which are all minority counties, designated poor by the central government, and the five

Table 14.2 Guizhou: ranking of poor counties by rural net per capita income (1990 and 1997) (yuan in current prices)

1990				*1997*			
Danzai	146	Dushan	285	Leishan	866	Jingping	1156
Qinglong	167	Shiqian	286	Qinglong	877	Xingren	1157
Dejiang	173	Bijie city	294	Wangmo	893	Wanshan	1161
Yanhe	175	Majiang	306	Rongjiang	935	Zhengning	1162
Pu'an	175	Anshun	316	Yanhe	945	Liuzhi	1164
Ceting	179	Liping	317	Jianhe	947	Puding	1165
Yinjiang	183	Wuchuan	328	Congjiang	955	Majiang	1167
Zhenfeng	186	Sinan	329	Daozheng	961	Panxian	1171
Leishan	192	Rongjiang	331	Ceting	978	Jiangkuo	1173
Shuicheng	206	Zhongshan	332	Nayong	983	Wuchuan	1181
Xifeng	208	Cishui	333	Huangping	994	Chenggu	1184
Wangmo	210	Tianzhu	336	Danzai	1023	Xishui	1187
Panxian	214	Anlun	338	Zhenyuan	1041	Shibing	1204
Weining	214	Shanshui	339	Liping	1042	Libo	1206
Jianhe	214	Libo	340	Suntao	1045	Shanshui	1224
Taijiang	215	Jingping	354	Hezhang	1046	Zhongshan	1265
Puding	218	Xishui	361	Yinjiang	1071	Dejiang	1268
Dafang	219	Chenggu	375	Shuicheng	1072	Lunli	1286
Ziyun	226	Guiding	391	Zhenfeng	1082	Guiding	1301
Zhijin	231	Yuping	397	Sinan	1083	Anlun	1311
Huangping	234	Daozheng	398	Sandu	1087	Kaili	1315
Luodian	235	Wanshan	404	Weining	1091	Fuquan	1328
Suntao	240	Lunli	404	Changshun	1095	Xifeng	1353
Hezhang	240	Zheng'an	414	Zheng'an	1098	Bijie city	1364
Guanling	251	Fenggang	429	Pu'an	1101	Dushan	1370
Zhengning	252	Shibing	440	Taijiang	1101	Pingba	1408
Congjiang	253	Jiangkuo	442	Dafang	1102	Qianxi	1416
Changshun	260	Zhenyuan	443	Luodian	1110	Tongchuan	1427
Sandu	267	Pingba	449	Ziyun	1113	Yuping	1455
Liuzhi	268	Xiuwen	451	Shiqian	1118	Huishui	1460
Xingren	268	Huishui	478	Guanling	1126	Anshun	1498
Nayong	274	Fuquan	482	Tianzhu	1128	Cishui	1510
Qianxi	282	Tongchuan	507	Pingtang	1131	Fenggang	1599
Pingtang	283	Kaili	554	Zhijin	1143	Xiuwen	1610

Source: Based on data supplied by the Poverty Alleviation Office, Guizhou Province, Guiyang.

least poor, among which one is centrally-designated poor and others are provincially-designated poor. In 1997, the poorest of the poor counties received much higher funding than the less poor counties. Per capita funding for the poorest five for FFW and subsidized credit is generally higher than that for the five least poor among the poor counties. The only exception is Fenggang county, which is centrally-designated poor and thus receives much higher allocation than the other provincially-funded poor counties in that group.

The destination of PAF by economic activity shows a relative neglect of manufacturing in the early 1990s when the overall PAF amount was low. With a gradual increase in PAF, allocation to the sector picked up significantly, exceeding that for agriculture in 1994–1995. This may be due to an emphasis on town and village enterprises (TVEs). However, since then, funding of agricultural activities under PAF far exceeds that for manufacturing.

One of the problems faced by the Guizhou anti-poverty programme is the relatively large size of the poor population, which makes attainment of targets difficult. Guizhou has the largest proportion of extremely poor people living in limestone areas with serious soil erosion and a poor ecological system. The tenth Five-Year Plan (2001–2005) aims at the provision of two-thirds of Guizhou's population with minimum living standards and the elimination of poverty among the remaining three million poor. The new anti-poverty component of the Plan also aims at the stabilization of production conditions to ensure sustainable development and to prevent poor people (brought above the poverty line) from falling back into poverty. The government has advanced the target date of nine years of compulsory schooling from 2010 to 2005.[2]

Table 14.3 links the performance of selected poor counties to the PAF grant/loans during 1990–1997 for which we have data. Several features of the table are worth noting. First, the top performers (measured by growth in rural net per capita income during 1990–1997) receive larger per capita (cumulative) PAF (almost twice as much if one compares the top performers with the bottom performers) than the weakest performers. Their population growth during the period was generally lower than that of the weakest performers. Second, minority counties are found in both the top performers and weak performers. This suggests that these counties are not necessarily the poorest; neither do they necessarily lag behind the non-minority counties. The top performers may be better off because of a more diversified production structure, reflected in the existence of TVEs.

It is rather odd that the weak performers in terms of real rural per capita income receive lower per capita PAF. This apparent anomaly may be explained by the fact that subsidized loans are granted on the basis of collateral, which the less-poor counties are more likely to provide than the poorest counties. Often, the latter have no collateral and are thus barred from obtaining subsidized credit (see below).

Table 14.3 Per capita funding of poor counties in Guizhou (1997)

County	*Per capita funding for food-for-work (yuan)*	*Per capita funding for subsidized loans (yuan)*	*Per capita budgetary grant (yuan)*	*Minority population in county (% of total population)*	*Rural per capita net income (yuan)*
Poorest counties					
Leishan*	20.13	61.00	10.64	87.25	866
Qinglong*	21.10	60.13	25.16	51.05	877
Wangmo*	2.81	116.19	18.43	79.08	893
Rongjiang*	5.78	51.88	23.71	72.91	935
Yanhe*	14.73	38.52	5.62	53.52	945
Least poor among poor					
Huishui	3.82	5.18	4.08	58.21	1,460
Anshun city	–	10.69	2.01	17.33	1,498
Chishui	3.52	0.00	0.37	1.40	1,510
Fenggang*	13.51	32.50	17.57	3.68	1,599
Xiuwen	1.65	3.12	1.08	7.08	1,610

Source: Based on data supplied by the Poverty Alleviation Office of Guizhou Province, Guiyang.

Note
*Centrally designated poor; others are provincially designated poor.

The real rural per capita income of all the weakest performers declined between 1990 and 1997, which means that their poverty situation actually worsened despite the PAF. On the basis of the above information, one cannot conclude that the best performers necessarily owe their better performance to higher PAF allocations. There may be two other factors at work; namely, the superior initial conditions of these counties when PAF was introduced, and differences in rural population growth during the period. However, rather surprisingly, rural population growth rates are generally higher among the top performers than among the weak performers, which suggests that the population factor is not important (even though there are wide variations in rural population growth among the 48 poor counties, see Table 14.4).

Having given a brief general picture of poverty reduction in Guizhou, we now turn to the particular anti-poverty interventions: food-for-work programme (*Yigong-daizhen*), micro-credit programme, and rural labour mobility programme.

Food-for-work programme (*Yigong-daizhen*)

This is a public works programme that replaced the earlier poverty relief measures under which work or job creation was not a condition for securing relief.[3] The programme, which started in 1984, differed from the regular capital construction projects in several respects. Until 1996, the

Table 14.4 Performance of selected poor counties to poverty alleviation funding (1990–1997)

County	*Growth of real rural per capita income (%)*	*Rural population growth (%)*	*Change in rural population share in total population 1997–1990*	*Minority population share (%)*	*Per capita cumulative poverty alleviation fund (yuan)*
	(1990–1997)	*(1990–1997)*		*(1990)*	*(1990–1997)*
Top performers					
Deijing*	430.4	14.2	1.5	61.3	362.2
Danzai*	398.1	13.3	0.8	83.7	526.9
Xifeng*	347.9	15.2	2.8	49.3	239.5
Pu'an*	326.5	21.0	2.2	24.8	385.4
Yinjiang*	282.7	13.3	1.7	69.1	280.1
Weakest performers					
Jiangkuo**	−37.2	14.7	1.8	49.3	53.0
Zheng'an*	−37.4	15.5	1.4	4.5	190.8
Daozheng**	−61.1	9.8	0.24	57.3	173
Kaili**	−65.2	9.6	−5.1	62.2	133.9
Zhenyuan**	−67.6	11.5	2.0	37.5	123.4

Source: Based on data supplied by the Poverty Alleviation Office of Guizhou Province, Guiyang.

Note
*Centrally designated poor counties. **Provincially designated poor counties.

Central Government provided partly in-kind investment (which has since been discontinued) and partly financial investment for the food-for-work programmes. The Central Government payments in kind (generally surplus of food and goods) were paid to workers in the form of wages. The local governments are expected to allocate matching funds for investment in the schemes. Initially, the local public works projects consisted mainly of building and construction, besides drinking water supply. More recently, projects have been diversified to include farming, water conservation, health care facilities, education and so on.

In Guizhou, the total central government expenditure for the programme amounted to 3.6 billion yuan between 1984 and 2000. The provincial government provided an additional funding of 1.6 billion yuan, which includes contributions by prefectures and counties. Table 14.5 compares PAF funding in Guizhou, Sichuan and Yunnan, and shows that the importance of FFW declined while that of subsidized credit increased in all three south-west provinces. However, in 1995, the FFW share in Guizhou was much larger.

These PAFs were spent on the following types of economic activities: road building, land improvement, irrigation, drinking water supply for

Table 14.5 PAF for Guizhou, Sichuan and Yunnan (1995–1997) (million yuan and percentages)

	Guizhou		*Sichuan*		*Yunnan*	
	1995	*1997*	*1996*	*1997*	*1995*	*1997*
Food for work	313.4	265.0	262.4	286.1	292.7	312.3
	(41.7)	(19.7)	(29.9)	(18.3)	(28.2)	(14.2)
Subsidized loans	360.0	850.0	462.3	972.3	465.6	1032
	(47.9)	(63.3)	(52.8)	(62.3)	(44.9)	(47)
Fiscal grant	78.0	228.0	139.7	280.5	181	516.7
	(10.4)	(17.0)	(15.9)	(18)	(17.5)	(23.5)

Source: World Bank (2000) for Sichuan and Yunnan. Data for Guizhou was supplied by the Poverty Alleviation Bureau.

Note
Figures in brackets are percentage shares of the total.

rural people and animals, forestation, generation of hydropower, installation of new telephone lines and resettlement of poor people to new areas. The building of roads and other infrastructure is one of the major components of the FFW programme under which the government supplies equipment and materials, whereas the local people supply free labour, especially if they benefit directly. Free labour contribution amounts to 20 days per year (reduced to 15 days per year in 1995) under a law promulgated in the 1950s. Any additional labour input is rewarded by a wage payment in cash, which varies from county to county and project to project, depending on the local labour supply situation, opportunity cost of labour or the level of rural farm incomes.[4] Workers have to pay a penalty if they fail to contribute free physical labour (Zhu and Jiang, 1996). Some Chinese scholars believe workers are unlikely to offer labour in the absence of compulsion, presumably because of alternative income-earning opportunities, the cost involved in moving and sheer laziness. No wage payments are made when workers benefit from the infrastructure. Instead, 1 yuan a day is paid as compensation for foregone production. Infrastructure, which does not benefit the farmers directly, is built by contractors through a bidding procedure. In Zhenning county in the western part of Guizhou, contractors hired labour by paying an average wage of 12–15 yuan a day, which is well above the average rural farm income of 5–6 yuan a day (information collected during field visit in April 2001).

Zhu and Jiang (1996) argue that the focus of the food-for-work programme on poverty alleviation was diluted by the lowering of programme wages paid to farmers. The provincial and county governments, supposed to provide matching funds, have been using central government funds for other purposes, leading to the lowering of wages and raising of compulsory workdays. Thus, the conditions of the poor may have actually become worse! Zhu and Jiang, (1996, p. 130) note that 'at most, projects' earnings compose one-sixth of disposable income for rural households'. The Chinese situation seems similar to that of the Indian JRY programme where many workers interviewed during an evaluation noted that the programme wage was too low (Neelakantan, 1994).[5]

The level of the wage paid under the food-for-work programmes is of critical importance for various reasons. First, if the wage is set too high (above the minimum wage, for example), it will attract the non-poor and thus defeat the purpose of reaching the poor. On the basis of the National Sample Survey (NSS) data for 1987–1988, Gaiha (2000) concludes that the Indian rural public works programme could have benefited the poor more if the wage rate relative to the agricultural wage was lower. Second, high wage rates will also imply that only a limited amount of employment could be created for a given level of investment. In other words, the cost of the programme will be higher than if the wage was kept low. A process of self-selection or targeting can be ensured if the wage is set low, or at least no higher than the prevailing market wage. In general, low wage rates will improve self-targeting and attract only the poor (Ravallion, 1991a, 1991b). However, if the wage rate is kept too low, it may not attract rural workers, especially if they have alternative income-earning opportunities and a cost is involved in their participation in the food-for-work programme.

In many developing countries, political and legal considerations prevent the programme wage from being fixed below the minimum wage. In China, there is no minimum wage. In the absence of landless labour (which is substantial in India and other developing countries) wage employment in rural areas is also rare. Therefore, neither the minimum wage nor rural wage can be used as a yardstick to assess the level of the programme wage offered under food-for-work programmes. It may be more appropriate to use the level of rural per capita income to determine whether the programme wage is high or low. To some extent, the level of the programme wage will be determined by whether the opportunity cost of labour is high or low and whether the cost of participation in public works is positive and significant. In poor rural areas, the opportunity cost of labour is likely to be low or close to zero, especially during the slack agricultural season when the rural public works are implemented. However, during the busy agricultural season it may not be all that low and rural labour may have to be attracted only by paying a higher programme wage. The opportunity cost of labour may also be positive, at least in certain areas, since rural to urban migration is now much easier and is actually encouraged (see below). By moving to urban areas, the rural migrants can earn much more than they would by working on food-for-work programmes.

The Chinese food-for-work programme does not directly target the poorest segments of the population. However, if a low wage was a requirement for self-targeting, it is likely that, at a low wage, only the very poor (who cannot afford to stay idle for long) will come forward. Furthermore,

China's anti-poverty strategy does seem to go for some targeting of the poor. As Lipton and Ravallion (1995, p. 2617) note, it 'relies heavily on regional targeting'. This implies that, in areas with high concentration of the poor, regional targeting will benefit the poor, although some leakage to the non-poor may occur. It is useful to make a distinction between targeting by location or region and targeting by poverty groups. Direct targeting of the poor is likely to achieve better results if poverty reduction is the main programme objective. However, one can argue that, in a region/locality where everyone is absolutely poor, as is the case in Guizhou, direct targeting may not be necessary.

The organizational and institutional arrangements of the public works projects determine the nature of targeting. Projects target the village communities instead of rural individuals or households. Beneficiaries are chosen by the Chinese government on the basis of the selection of project sites and the specific investment orientation of various projects. The village communities chosen as targets have generally tended to enjoy 'favourable socio-economic conditions' (Zhu and Jiang, 1996, p. 188). The poorest villages and the poorest people may not necessarily benefit since the village communities are responsible for the mobilization of labour for the projects (see Zhu and Jiang, 1996). This is also true of the Indian JRY programme, which is administered by the local village *panchayats* (councils). However, unlike the Chinese programme, the JRY is directly targeted towards women and the poor low-caste groups (scheduled castes and tribes) (Gaiha, 2000).

From subsidized loans to the micro-credit programme

Since the mid-1980s the most important funding source for poverty alleviation in China has been subsidized credit provided to the poor areas. Initially (until 1984) the central government provided funds for credit to the rural poor out of the state budget. Subsequently, additional funds for credit were channelled through such financial institutions as rural credit cooperatives and the Agricultural Development Bank of China, established in 1994. It is reported that between 1984 and 1993, the combined resources for poverty alleviation out of the state budget and the banking system amounted to over 38 billion yuan, out of which bank credits accounted for 74 per cent (Wu, 1994). Since 1995, much of the credit for rural projects has been channelled through the Agricultural Development Bank and various branches of the Agriculture Bank (the branches of the Agricultural Development Bank are limited to the provincial capital cities). However, in 1997, the management of rural credit again reverted to the Agricultural Bank: it was felt that the Agricultural Development Bank was rather relaxed about lending and loan repayment as it was not a commercial bank.

The Agricultural Bank sets credit limits for each county, which passes on this information to townships and villages within its jurisdiction, which in turn select poor households for loan applications. The names of the selected households are reported to the Poverty Alleviation Development Office (PADO). There is a clear conflict between the Agricultural Bank and PADO. While PADO favours the poor, the Bank favours the non-poor who have greater capacity to pay back loans.

Interest is charged for the use of loans for poverty alleviation but the difference between the prevailing market rate and the rate for specialized loans is subsidized by the central government. The nominal interest rates for such loans (generally for 1–3 years) are at least 20 per cent lower than the normal official rates. Demand for rural credit in China remains very high because of the low or negative real interest rate.[6]

Generally speaking, the amount of loans a county can obtain depends on several factors: (i) the size of the population below the poverty line; (ii) the location of the county; whether it is located in an area of strategic industrial importance (a poor county in such an area will be preferred for loan allocation); (iii) the ethnicity of the county; whether it is a minority autonomous county, and (iv) the previous record of loan repayment; a good repayment record entitles a county to more loans (Wang and Zhu, 1997).

Obviously, the Chinese poverty-alleviation loan programme has contributed positively to the economic development and poverty reduction of poor areas. However, the mechanism of loan grants and their allocation has caused many concerns among domestic and international scholars and government officials. One of the main criticisms is that subsidized loans are targeted to poor areas, not poor people. Often, the local authorities and officials are the main beneficiaries. Zhu (1997) notes that the poor do not enjoy access to rural credit although the programme was started to 'provide credits to assist the poor'. This is due to the way in which the loans are granted and used. The process of loan approval is quite subjective; it depends on the ability and preference of the leaders of the poverty alleviation offices. Furthermore, since the Agricultural Bank is responsible for the repayment of loans, the return from the subsidy on the interest rate is less important than the principal itself. Finally, the Bank often uses delaying tactics in order to maximize profits. Very often it uses the subsidized loan funds for normal commercial lending. The really poor people do not have the ability or connections to set up a project and the rural credit market is less developed in China than in other developing countries particularly South Asia. The banks are reluctant to lend to the poor, especially in remote areas for fear of non-payment (or inadequate collateral). A survey under the World Bank Poverty Reduction Project in south-west China showed that 32 per cent of the households did not receive any loan, and that lower priority was given to poor households in the Guangxi and Guizhou project areas during 1998–1999. A comparison of the loan grants and households by income levels shows that over 30 per cent of the loans went to households with an income above 1,000 yuan and only 23 per cent to those with income below 500 yuan (see *Poverty Monitoring Report 1999* – Leading Group Office of Poverty Alleviation and Development, 1999, p. 47).

A centrally-administered loan scheme follows a top-down approach, under which loans are allocated in a hierarchical manner from the centre to the provinces and from there to the poor counties. The objectives of central, provincial and county governments are often different and in conflict. Collateral is not easily available to the poor farmers as, until recently, land leases were not transferable (see Hoff *et al.,* 1995). The rural credit cooperatives are still reluctant to accept land as collateral; they prefer financial deposits as a guarantee. Thus, poor farmers are often denied access to formal credit. They have to rely on friends and relatives (who do not require either collateral or guarantees) for informal credit for both consumption and investment purposes. It should be noted that in China, for ideological reasons, lending for profit continues to be viewed as something bad (Zhu *et al.*, 1997, p. 127). Thus, subsidized loan funds often fall into the hands of the non-poor.

The experiences of Guizhou versus Guangxi and Yunnan

Table 14.6 compares information for Guizhou, Guangxi and Yunnan on lending by banks and credit cooperatives. Bank lending is much less important than lending by friends and relatives, which is generally for both consumption and investment purposes. This may partly reflect the difficulties encountered by the poor in providing collateral to obtain a bank loan.

Loans made to poor households are used for various purposes: agricultural development (for example, crop planting, animal husbandry, crop tree management and terracing), rural infrastructure and education and health. However, the bulk of the loans are used for improvements in agriculture (see Table 14.7).

During 1996 and 1997, loan repayment rates were the lowest in Guizhou (the poorest province) and quite high in Guangxi and Yunnan. The repayment rate in Guangxi and Yunnan, varies between 49 to 69 per cent, which compares favourably with the average recovery rate of 57 per cent or less for the special subsidized loans by the Agriculture Bank since 1991 (see Zhu, 1997, p. 14). Several reasons explain the delays in loan repayments: political interference by the local governments, which prevents banks from selecting bankable projects; a significant welfare component of the credit programmes; and poor accounting systems, short periods of loan repayment and long periods for returns to accrue on capital investment. Generally, the loan repayment rate is higher in the informal credit market than in the formal credit market. Under the former, symmetric information between borrowers and lenders, peer pressures and ethical norms (including fear of social unrest) keeps the monitoring of loans and their repayment more orderly and at lower cost.

Table 14.6 Bank loans versus borrowing from friends and relatives (per household, 1995–1997)

	1995	*1996*	*1997*
Guizhou			
Loans from banks and credit cooperatives (yuan)	28.0	10.6	30.3
Borrowing from friends and relatives (yuan)	41.6	104.0	62.4
Repayment of bank loan (yuan)	–	2.7	2.9
Rate of repayment (%)	–	25.5	9.5
Guangxi			
Loans from banks and credit cooperatives (yuan)	31.8	20.9	33.4
Borrowing from friends and relatives (yuan)	91.8	151.0	81.4
Repayment of bank loan (yuan)	–	14.5	16.3
Rate of repayment (%)	–	69.3	48.8
Yunnan			
Loans from banks and credit cooperatives (yuan)	36.3	30.1	32.7
Borrowing from friends and relatives (yuan)	54.7	63.3	56.4
Repayment of bank loan (yuan)	–	19.0	20.8
Rate of repayment (%)	–	63.1	63.6
Average			
Loans from banks and cooperatives (yuan)	31.9	20.1	32.2
Borrowing from friends and relatives (yuan)	64.0	109.7	67.6
Repayment of bank loan (yuan)	–	13.4	13.2
Rate of repayment (%)	–	66.6	41.0

Source: *Poverty Monitoring Report 1997.*

Table 14.7 Loans/subsidies to survey households by economic activity (1997) (in 000s yuan)

	Guangxi	*Guizhou*	*Yunnan*	*Total*
Agricultural development	162.8	139.3	49.1	351.2
Crop planting	63.2	34.8	13.2	111.2
Animal husbandry	74.8	86.8	21.8	183.4
Crop tree management	24.8	9.3	14.0	48.1
Terracing	0	8.4	0	84.0
Infrastructure	10.7	1.2	1.8	13.7
Education	2.3	0.8	1.6	4.8
Health	1.9	0.02	0.2	2.1
Total	177.8	141.3	52.7	371.8

Source: *Poverty Monitoring Report 1997*, p. 158.

Micro-credit

The above problems led the Chinese Government in 1997 to adopt a micro-credit programme along the lines of the Grameen Bank (GB) in Bangladesh under which funds are channelled directly to households (see Table 14.8 for distinguishing features of the Chinese old subsidized loan

Table 14.8 Chinese subsidized loan programme and the micro-credit programme

The subsidized loan programme	*The micro-credit programme*
Targeting of project area	Targeting of group of poor households
Rate of repayment	Higher rate of repayment*
Need for collateral	Absence of collateral
Mainly domestic sources of funding	Domestic and international financing
Centralized structure and administration	Decentralized structure and administration

Note

*The Chinese micro-credit programme was introduced as an experiment only recently. Therefore, it is difficult to determine at this stage whether the loan repayment rate is actually higher. On the basis of household survey data of six counties in different provinces in 1997, Park and Ren (2001) show that loan repayment is very high, especially among the non-governmental programmes.

programme and the new micro-credit programme). By 1998 this programme is reported to have reached 200 poor counties, accounting for investment of about 800 million yuan (World Bank, 2000). This micro-credit programme is regarded as one of the most important components of public intervention for poverty alleviation by both donors and developing countries (Lipton, 1998; Zhao and Dong, 1999).

The Grameen Bank is characterized by some unique features. First, unlike most banks, the GB does not require any collateral in the form of land or other assets. Peer pressure, social sanctions and guarantees are used as substitutes for collateral. Much against initial expectations, loan repayment rates have been remarkably high thanks to group pressure, social sanctions and grass-roots organization of the loan programme. A high repayment rate of loans may also be partly due to the insistence of the Bank to encourage borrowers to save. Participation of the potential beneficiaries and the local cooperative nature of lending is an important reason for the success of the Bank. Lipton (1998, p. 44) notes that 'mutual monitoring by small groups or borrowers, as in Grameen, was the central tenet of cooperative credit before it became politicized'. The Indian experience with credit programmes shows that local popular selection of borrowers by the village councils, for example, works much better than their selection/identification by the state bureaucracy (Lipton, 1998, p. 49). Loans are targeted to the very poor who own less than 0.5 acres of land. This limit is not relevant in Guizhou as there are no landless in China. The bank has adopted a cooperative or group-based lending scheme, which requires a minimum group of five villagers, not relatives or from the same household (to avoid bias) to obtain a loan. Although each member of the group receives an individual loan, the group is collectively responsible for total credit, which provides 'peer monitoring' and mutual insurance against default. Group lending is known to have been successful in reaching the poor target groups.

In December 1997, a survey was done of six nationally-designated poor counties in different provinces to determine the impact of micro-credit (based on the Grameen model) on poverty reduction (see Park and Ren, 2001). The programmes covered were of three types: an NGO programme, a mixed (government and NGO) programme, and a government-funded programme. The survey results show that (a) loan repayments are particularly high under NGO programmes, but low under government programmes; repayment improves if the borrowers are female with more and better-quality land; (b) financial self-sufficiency is achieved even with low interest rates thanks to access to donor funds and low operating costs; and (c) the government programmes do not target the poor, and are thus similar to the earlier loan subsidization programme. Park and Ren (2001, p. 59) conclude: 'there is considerable evidence that only some of the poor will benefit from greater credit access, so that there is a real danger that the recent surge in donor funding of micro-finance programs may overlook more pressing needs facing many of the poor'.

In Guizhou, under the Grameen-type micro-credit scheme, loans of up to 2,000 yuan repayable in 1–2 years are granted when a minimum of five households together offer a guarantee of repayment. Between 1998 and 2000, 1.8 billion yuan were provided by the Agricultural Bank. In 1998, the interest rate charged was 2.8 per cent, but since 1999 a unified interest rate of 3 per cent has been charged for all types of loans, against a commercial rate of 5.2 per cent. Like the Grameen loans, there is no collateral, although a clause in the loan agreement states that non-repayment when a household has the capacity to repay can lead to seizure of property. The loan repayment rate is lower than that in neighbouring Guangxi province, where repayment is at more frequent intervals. As Guizhou is quite poor, loan repayment is required at the end of one year. The lower repayment is explained by two main factors: transport difficulties, especially in remote mountainous areas, and the relative inefficiency of the Agricultural Bank in collecting repayments.

In Zhejin county (Guizhou), between 1998 and 2000, 3.20 million yuan were spent on micro-credit, which covered 32 townships and towns and 32 villages, 3,338 poor households, and 14,000 poor people. Loans were granted for agriculture and animal husbandry. The criteria for loan grants include annual household net income of 600 yuan and less than 325 kg of grain output. In this county, 70 per cent of the poor are from ethnic minorities and only 50 per cent of these receive micro-credit, which suggests that the ethnic minorities are not granted any preference. As loans are targeted to the poor, and the bulk of the ethnic minorities are poor, it is assumed that ethnic minorities would benefit (interviews with county staff in April 2001). Micro-credit cannot be granted under the following situations.

i If financial support is received from the welfare and civil affairs office.
ii If an earlier loan has not been repaid.
iii If the household fails to comply with family planning rules.

Loans cannot be used to repay old loans, or to pay agricultural tax or to pay any penalty. Neither can loans be used for any purpose other than that proposed under the agreement. Local county agents and representatives of the Agricultural Bank undertake periodic monitoring to ensure that the loan is properly utilized. Households are also trained in self-monitoring.

The labour mobility programme

Government intervention in labour mobility can be classified into three categories: the population migration programme, induced labour mobility through public projects, and the employment promotion programme. We briefly discuss these below before discussing the programme in Guizhou.

The population migration programme

In some areas, natural conditions are so adverse that there is no hope of eliminating poverty through economic development. Therefore, the central and local authorities and some international institutions provide financial grants to organize the movement of people away from their homes to new and better areas. For example, from 1993 onwards, 180,000 people migrated from the mountain areas in the north of Guangdong province. The local authority provided a special grant of 5,000 yuan to each migrating household (see Zhou, 1997). It is estimated that, in Guizhou, about 500,000 people need to be resettled in areas with better income-earning opportunities. The provincial government plans to resettle one-third of this population by 2005 and another one-third by 2010.

The induced labour mobility programme

In recent years, the government has substantially increased its investment in such infrastructure as building roads, dams and bridges, as part of its fiscal policy to stimulate the sluggish economy and to reduce the income gap between coastal and inland provinces. These projects create large labour demand and induce voluntary (as against organized) migration from the poor areas to fill job vacancies.

The employment promotion programmes

The government provides grants to set up employment agencies to bridge the gap between demand for labour and its supply. This programme (funded partly by the World Bank) helps to transfer labour from the poor counties and areas with low labour demand to the high labour-demand areas, either within the same province or other provinces, particularly in the coastal areas. The origin of this public intervention is guided by the notion that economic and social development involves an inter-sectoral shift of labour from agriculture to manufacturing and services. Within the Lewis–Fei–Ranis framework of labour surplus models, rural labour surpluses spontaneously move out of agriculture and into higher income-earning opportunities in non-agricultural activities in the rural and urban areas. Labour demand has increased within rural areas through agricultural modernization (the use of advanced biological and mechanical technologies, changes in cropping and cultivation patterns), and the development of village and township enterprises. Yet many of the poor counties have substantial labour surpluses that cannot be absorbed in non-farm activities within those areas. Therefore, the labour mobility programme is intended to smooth the transfer of surplus labour from poor areas to more rapidly growing areas and regions.

Although there is sizeable unemployment in cities, many job vacancies exist because of a mismatch between available jobs and people's expectations. The urban unemployed are not willing to accept some of the job opportunities owing to low payment, adverse working conditions and low social prestige. Many of these vacancies are filled with the workers from rural areas.

It is generally believed that the poorer the people the lower is their mobility. This is partly due to the cost of moving and partly to the fear of the unknown. In south-west China most of the very poor people (especially minorities) live in remote mountainous areas. They are attached to their homes and their religious, cultural and linguistic environments. This is particularly true of the older people. On the other hand, young people migrate more easily. There seems no clear evidence on migration patterns by gender; both men and women migrate. However, male members of households are more likely to move in search of jobs than female members, who generally stay back to do farming and rear children.

The experience of Guizhou

In 1996, the Chinese State Statistical Bureau (SSB) conducted a detailed survey of rural migrants (within the framework of the World Bank-funded poverty reduction programme) in a selected number of villages of Guizhou, Guangxi and Yunnan. The survey shows that employers and local government agencies play a very limited role in placing migrants who find jobs by themselves or through the informal network of friends and relatives. The bulk of migrants are engaged in manufacturing and construction activities. A survey (undertaken by the Development Research Centre – DRC) of 168 migrants returning home showed that the proportion migrants engaged in construction was 20 per cent, whereas 9 per cent were absorbed in loading and unloading, and 5 per cent in casual work. With the exception of Guizhou, farming is not an important occupation for migrants. Most of the migrants spend 10–12 months away from home, with the exception of Yunnan, where the majority of migrants are away for a shorter period. Very short-term migrants form only a small proportion in all three provinces. Rapidly growing coastal provinces suffering from labour shortages are the most attractive destination for the majority of rural migrants. The net per capita annual income of migrants is much higher than the average rural net per capita income. Many migrants earn more than 5,000 yuan per annum. Remittances per capita are the highest for Guangxi followed by Guizhou and Yunnan (see Table 14.9). In Guizhou, income from migrants is equivalent to the entire tax revenue of the government from the tobacco industry. Between 1987 and 2000, there were 13 million migrants from Guizhou who remitted 21 billion yuan. Remittances can be an important equalizing factor in rural–urban income disparities. Of the total number of migrants from Guizhou, about 0.5 to 0.8 million represent rural to urban migration within the province. Migration is induced by both push and pull factors. The push factor is the large rural surplus labour, estimated at nearly 8 million, or 55 per cent of the total rural labour force. The TVEs can absorb no more than about 1.6 to 2 million, which means that nearly 6 million people need to migrate to other provinces every year. On a field visit to Guiyang (Guizhou) in April 2001, we discussed the labour mobility programme with the Development Research Centre (DRC) of the Provincial Government. We were told that there were 2 million migrants from Guizhou to other provinces such as Guangdong, Fujian, Jiangsu and Zhejiang. These four provinces account for over 70 per cent of the migrants. Although the bulk of the migrants at present go to Guangdong, more and more migrants are beginning to go to Zhejiang. With rapid development, the Guangdong economy requires more highly skilled labour for industry, which is not available in Guizhou. On the other hand, in Zhejiang, there continues to be demand for low-skilled workers in industry and services.

The experience of Ludian county in labour mobility has been particularly successful. In 1996, this county had 290,000 inhabitants, of which 10,000 were migrants. The remittances of these migrants amounted to 120 million yuan, which is three times the county's budgetary revenue.

It is not very easy for migrants to find jobs in large-scale factory manufacturing, because of the migrants' low skills and education. Many of the migrants are from minority nationalities whose education is even lower. About 11 per cent of rural migrants have primary education, 27 per cent secondary education, and only 2 per cent have high school education. Because of low education, the average earnings of rural migrants are low: between 3,000 yuan and 10,000 yuan per annum, or 400–500 yuan per month.

Large-scale migration from Guizhou has not adversely affected agriculture or food production. The survey cited above shows that the available land continues to be cultivated by the remaining family members and relatives. A new phenomenon of leasing of land to friends and relatives on payment of wages is emerging in Guizhou as a result of rural-to-urban migration. A portion of output is made as payment for leasing of land.

Table 14.9 Characteristics of rural migrants in selected villages in south-west China (%)

	Guangxi		*Guizhou*		*Yunnan*	
	1997	*1999*	*1997*	*1999*	*1997*	*1999*
Means of finding a job						
Relatives/friends	42	37	34	40.3	33	38.3
Oneself	52	60	61	56.5	62	59.6
Employer	1.1	1.2	4.9	–	4.2	–
Local government agency	3.4	0.8	–	3.2	–	2.1
Economic activity						
Farming	3.9	2.8	17.4	3.2	2.1	–
Industry	49.4	56	36.6	24.2	33.3	23.4
Construction	21.9	23.4	17.1	33.9	39.6	53.2
Services	13.5	10.5	19.5	17.7	22.9	21.3
Duration away from home						
1–3 months	9.3	–	6.4	–	6.3	–
4–6 months	15.2	–	11.2	–	35.4	–
7–9 months	14	–	4.9	–	31.3	–
10–12 months	68	–	41.5	–	16.7	–
Migrants' destination						
Other counties within province	12.4	19	4.9	9.7	66.7	46.8
Other inland provinces	24.2	7.7	7.3	8.1	8.3	19.1
Other coastal provinces	36	54.4	75.6	54.8	–	6.4
Income (yuan/year/head)	4,016	–	3,429	–	2,861	–
Percentage of migrants earning:						
500–1,000 yuan	16.3	–	24.4	–	10.4	–
1,000–3,000 yuan	13.5	–	12.2	–	14.6	–
3,000–5,000 yuan	32.6	–	26.8	–	47.9	–
more than 5,000 yuan	28.1	–	26.8	–	8.3	–
Per capita annual living expenditure (yuan)	2,217	1,893.1	1,794	1,849.8	1,923	2,134
Remittances per capita (yuan)	1,119	1,482.6	897	1,734.1	557	896.3

Source: *Poverty Monitoring Report 1997, 1999.*

Apart from a substantial amount of remittances, one of the other benefits noted by the DRC staff was the saving of foodgrains, to the tune of 2.6 million tons, due to the departure of migrants. Formerly, Guizhou used to be a food-deficit province, which had to import foodgrains from other provinces. Now it is food self-sufficient even though it does import some crops which it does not grow itself. Guizhou has insufficient land for crop production, only about 0.8 mu per capita.

The negative aspects of returning migrants to their villages from time to time, especially during New Year, are exaggerated. While it creates temporary transportation bottlenecks, it creates additional demand for goods, tourism and other services.

One cannot argue against the movement of people from low productivity areas to high-productivity areas. After all, this is the whole purpose of economic development. But rural-to-urban migration is by no means an unmixed blessing. The social costs of dislocation of rural people need to be taken into account in designing and implementing the labour mobility programme for poverty alleviation. Illiterate and semi-literate migrants, women and older people are particularly vulnerable to poor working conditions and low incomes and employment security in urban areas. Migrants often work in very bad and unhygienic conditions in coal mines and on construction sites at wages below the legal minimum. Many of the jobs are of a contract or casual nature involving risk and insecurity.

Urban unemployment in urban areas has been increasing lately with the increasing retrenchment of workers from state-owned enterprises. This means that rural migrants (particularly the minorities) will have to compete with these redundant state workers, who are better trained, to the extent that they look for the same sorts of jobs. To some extent, segmented labour markets will prevent or mitigate against such competition. Furthermore, the educational and training profiles of rural migrants will keep them in non-competitive markets. However, increasing unemployment pressures can break down the walls between the two types of labour markets.

Thus, appropriate policies and action programmes (in addition to simply ensuring labour mobility) are needed in order to minimize the social costs of migration. Measures required may include: better labour market information about jobs by strengthening Labour Bureaus' employment service systems, training schemes for rural migrants, and a monitoring system to ensure safety and good living conditions (including housing). The provincial and local governments have an important role to play in introducing new and innovative institutional arrangements for the placement of migrants, improvement of job information networks, provision of housing, and channelling of migrants' remittances into productive investments in rural areas.

Conclusions

In this chapter, we have discussed three main anti-poverty programmes, namely the food-for-work programme, micro-credit and labour mobility, with special reference to Guizhou. Further, we have described three types of labour mobility interventions: population migration, induced labour mobility (through public projects) and employment promotion through the establishment of employment agencies. Using county-level data for Guizhou, per capita funding for food-for-work (FFW) and subsidized loans is compared between the poorest and least poor among the poor counties. A comparison between the minority counties (with ethnic minorities forming more than 50 per cent of the population) and non-minority counties suggests that the former are not necessarily the poorest. Linking the performance of the selected poor counties to the poverty alleviation funding (PAF) during 1990–1997 shows that those with rapid growth in rural per capita net income receive larger per capita cumulative PAF than those with slow growth in rural per capita income.

A comparison of the subsidized loan programme with the more recent micro-credit programme suggests that the loan repayment rate is generally higher under the latter. In 1996 and 1997, the loan repayment rate in Guizhou was much lower compared with Guangxi and Yunnan, due partly to transport shortages in remote mountainous areas. A good deal of emphasis is placed on labour mobility programmes for reducing poverty. One of the significant benefits of this programme is the substantial amount of remittances, which for Guizhou equalled the entire government tax revenue from the tobacco industry.

Since 1996, the poverty reduction programme in Guizhou (following the national policy shift) has targeted the poorest households instead of concentrating on the poor regions. Targeting the poor reinforces the importance of subsidized credit and micro-credit, which has not been very effective judging by the low loan repayment rate. It is estimated that about one-third of the loans are not recovered. This can be seen by the lack of any correlation between subsidized loans and rural per capita income. In comparison, the food-for-work funds, which are much smaller, and some other development funds tend to be more beneficial for the poor than the subsidized loan scheme. These funds are used for improving agricultural infrastructure and land productivity, with possible significant long-term effects on the incomes of the poor households in rural areas.

Notes

1 China's poverty reduction policy can be analysed in terms of three distinct periods. During the first period, covering 1979 to 1985, government efforts were concerned mainly with providing (financially and in kind) the so-called 'money-food-cotton support' to the backward and remote areas. For example, during the 31 years since the establishment of the Tibet autonomous region, while output

increased only fourfold (annual rate of growth of 5.4 per cent), the central budgetary grant increased 65 times (at an annual rate of growth of 14.9 per cent) (see Xu, 1997). The second period, covering 1986 to 1995, refers to the Poor Area Development Programme and the 8–7 Poverty Reduction Plan. The Poverty Reduction Plan (1994–2000) aimed at achieving the following targets by the year 2000: net per capita income for the majority of the households in designated poverty counties to exceed 500 yuan at 1990 prices; assistance to poor household to create conditions to solve the food problem; provision of adequate drinking water for people and livestock; and strengthening of the infrastructure facilities linking most poor townships to highway systems, power grids and telecommunications networks in order to connect them to commodity and other rural product markets. The 8–7 Plan was supposed to have been completed by the end of 2000. As its targets have not been fully achieved the Plan has been extended. The new phase of the Plan is not yet official but there are indications that efforts will be concentrated on ensuring that those who are now above the poverty line do not fall back into destitution. The third period, from 1996 to date, involved a State Council directive to shift the emphasis from area development to targeting of the poorest households.

2 By the end of 2000, only 35 per cent of the school-age population received nine years of schooling, compared with 85 per cent for China as a whole (information provided by the Provincial Planning Commission during a meeting in April 2001).

3 Work requirement (workfare) as distinct from social welfare has become increasingly popular, not only in developing countries but also in developed ones (see Besley and Coate, 1992). This requirement is designed partly to provide incentives to recipients of poverty relief, and partly to impart skills to improve their future employability. Several authors (notably Murray, 1984) suggest that welfare programmes, which do not insist on work requirements, have discouraged welfare recipients from acquiring the human capital necessary for poverty reduction. In the developed countries, poverty alleviation programmes were known in the nineteenth century. Under the English system, the Poor Law of 1834 is a good example. Under this system, poverty relief was provided on the basis of residence in a workhouse. Workfare was also common in France where poverty relief was granted in 'charity workshops' (see Besley and Coate, 1992).

4 There are wide variations in wage payments on the Chinese food-for-work programmes. The State Planning Commission notes 1 to 3 yuan per workday under the first food-for-work programme. Zhu and Jiang (1996) note that the programme wage varied between 3 to 6 yuan in 1991 in the counties surveyed, namely, Ningxia, Sichuan and Shandong. These variations seem to be a reflection of the local labour supply situation and the opportunity cost of rural labour.

5 Cross-country comparisons of the level of programme wage show wide variations: in Chile, the programme wage was set at 70 per cent of the minimum wage, whereas in India under the *Jawahar Rozgar Yojana* (employment generation scheme) the wage was set at the level of the minimum wage, which was well above the market wage in many regions of the country (Subbarao, 1997).

6 It is reported that during the second half of 1993, the official annual rate of interest for capital construction projects was 12.4 per cent, whereas it was about 3 per cent for rural credit for poverty alleviation (Zhu *et al.*, 1997, p. 29). Since the inflation rate during the same period was about 15 per cent, interest on rural credit implied a significant element of subsidy.

References

Besley, T. and Coate, S. (1992) 'Workfare vs. welfare: incentives arguments for work requirements in poverty reduction programs', *American Economic Review*, 82(1), 249–261.

Gaiha, R. (2000) 'Do anti-poverty programmes reach the rural poor in India?', *Oxford Development Studies*, 28(1).

Hoff, K., Braverman, A. and Stiglitz, J.E. (eds) (1995) *The Economics of Rural Organization* (Oxford: Oxford University Press).

Khan, A.R. and Riskin, C. (2001) *Inequality and Poverty in China in the Age of Globalization* (New York: Oxford University Press).

Leading Group Office of Poverty Alleviation and Development (1995 to 1999) *Poverty Monitoring Report* (for the World Bank Poverty Alleviation Project Area in south-west China) (Beijing: Economic Science Publishing House).

Lipton, M. (1998) *Successes in Anti-Poverty* (Geneva: ILO).

Lipton, M. and Ravallion, M. (1995) 'Poverty and policy'. In J. Behrman and T.N. Srinivasan (eds), *Handbook of Development Economics*, vol. 3 (Amsterdam: North-Holland).

Murray, C. (1984) *Losing Ground: American Social Policy 1950–1980* (New York: Basic Books).

Neelakantan, M. (1994) 'Jawahar Rozgar Yojana: an assessment through current evaluation', *Economic and Political Weekly*, 3 December.

Park, A. and Ren, C. (2001) 'Microfinance with Chinese characteristics', *World Development*, 29(1), 39–62.

Ravallion, M. (1991a) 'Employment guarantee schemes: are they a good idea?', *Indian Economic Journal*, 39(2), October–December.

Ravallion, M. (1991b) 'Reaching the rural poor through public employment: arguments, evidence and lessons from South Asia', *World Bank Research Observer*, 6(2), 153–175.

Subbarao, K. (1997) 'Public works and anti-poverty program: an overview of cross-country experience', *American Journal of Agricultural Economics*, May.

UNDP (1997) *China Human Development Report* (Beijing: United Nations Development Programme China).

Wang, S. (1997) 'Institutional innovation is needed for increasing efficiency in the use of poverty alleviation funds'. In J. Zhao (ed.), *The Theory and Practice of Poverty Alleviation in China* (Kunming: Yunnan Scientific Publishing House).

Wang, S. and Zhu, X. (1997) 'Distribution and management of loans for poverty alleviation and poor area development, special reference to Zhijin County (Guizhou)'. In J. Zhao (ed.), *The Theory and Practice of Poverty Alleviation in China* (Kunming: Yunnan Scientific Publishing House).

World Bank (2000) *China: Overcoming Rural Poverty* (East Asia and Pacific Region, World Bank), Report no. 21105–CHA, 18 October.

Wu, G. (1994) 'Research report on credit policies for poverty alleviation', paper presented at the International Workshop on the Anti-Poverty Strategies of China, Beijing, 4–7 December.

Xu, X. (1997) 'Review of the poverty alleviation policy of the Chinese government: the subsidized loans'. In J. Zhao (ed.), *The Theory and Practice of Poverty Alleviation in China* (Kunming: Yunnan Science and Technology Publishing House).

Zhao, Y. and Dong D. (1999) *An Action Research Focus on the Extremely Poor Population*, Yunnan Social Forestry Project Study Series no. 3 (funded by the Ford Foundation) (Kunming: Yunnan Science and Technology Press).

Zhou, S. (1997) 'Development through migration, experience of the mountain areas in the northern Guangdong province'. In J. Zhao (ed.), *The Theory and Practice of Poverty Alleviation in China* (Kunming: Yunnan Scientific Publishing House).

Zhu, L. (1997) '*Poverty Alleviation During the Transition in Rural China*', UNU/WIDER Research in Progress (RIP), April (Helsinki: WIDER).

Zhu, L. and Jiang, Z. (1996) *Public Works and Poverty Alleviation in Rural China* (New York: Nova Science Publishers, Inc.).

Zhu, L., Jiang, Z. and von Braun, J. (1997) *Credit Systems for the Rural Poor in China* (New York: Nova Science Publishers, Inc.).

Index

For Product Safety Concerns and Information please contact our EU representative GPSR@taylorandfrancis.com
Taylor & Francis Verlag GmbH, Kaufingerstraße 24, 80331 München, Germany

www.ingramcontent.com/pod-product-compliance
Ingram Content Group UK Ltd.
Pitfield, Milton Keynes, MK11 3LW, UK
UKHW020018200926
475702UK00014B/1945
* 9 7 8 1 1 3 8 3 7 1 1 2 5 *